Kitchen Princess

7

Natsumi Ando

Story by Miyuki Kobayashi

Translated by Satsuki Yamashita

Adapted by Nunzio DeFilippis and Christina Weir

Lettered by North Market Street Graphics

Ballantine Books · New York

Kitchen Princess volume 7 is a work of fiction. Names, characters, places, and incidents are the products of the author's imagination or are used fictitiously. Any resemblance to actual events, locales, or persons, living or dead, is entirely coincidental.

A Del Rey Manga/Kodansha Trade Paperback Original

Published in the United States by Del Rey Books, an imprint of The Random House Publishing Group, a division of Random House, Inc., New York.

Publication rights arranged through Kodansha Ltd.

First published in Japan in 2007 by Kodansha Ltd., Tokyo.

ISBN 978-0-345-50405-0

Printed in the United States of America

www.delreymanga.com

9 8 7 6 5 4 3

Translator: Satsuki Yamashita
Adaptors: Nunzio DeFilippis and Christina Weir
Lettering: North Market Street Graphics
Original cover design by Akiko Omo

Contents

I always challenge myself to
make the recipes in every volume.
Now I know how to make a fabulous
rare cheesecake!

—Natsumi Ando

Honorifics Explained

Throughout the Del Rey Manga books, you will find Japanese honorifics left intact in the translations. For those not familiar with how the Japanese use honorifics and, more important, how they differ from American honorifics, we present this brief overview.

Politeness has always been a critical facet of Japanese culture. Ever since the feudal era, when Japan was a highly stratified society, use of honorifics—which can be defined as polite speech that indicates relationship or status—has played an essential role in the Japanese language. When addressing someone in Japanese, an honorific usually takes the form of a suffix attached to one's name (example: "Asuna-san"), is used as a title at the end of one's name, or appears in place of the name itself (example: "Negi-sensei," or simply "Sensei!").

Honorifics can be expressions of respect or endearment. In the context of manga and anime, honorifics give insight into the nature of the relationship between characters. Many English translations leave out these important honorifics and therefore distort the feel of the original Japanese. Because Japanese honorifics contain nuances that English honorifics lack, it is our policy at Del Rey not to translate them. Here, instead, is a guide to some of the honorifics you may encounter in Del Rey Manga.

-san: This is the most common honorific and is equivalent to Mr., Miss, Ms., or Mrs. It is the all-purpose honorific and can be used in any situation where politeness is required.

-sama: This is one level higher than "-san" and is used to confer great respect.

-dono: This comes from the word "tono," which means "lord." It is an even higher level than "-sama" and confers utmost respect.

-kun: This suffix is used at the end of boys' names to express familiarity or endearment. It is also sometimes used by men among friends, or when addressing someone younger or of a lower station.

-chan: This is used to express endearment, mostly toward girls. It is also used for little boys, pets, and even among lovers. It gives a sense of childish cuteness.

Bozu: This is an informal way to refer to a boy, similar to the English terms "kid" and "squirt."

**Sempai/
Senpai:** This title suggests that the addressee is one's senior in a group or organization. It is most often used in a school setting, where underclassmen refer to their upperclassmen as "sempai." It can also be used in the workplace, such as when a newer employee addresses an employee who has seniority in the company.

Kohai: This is the opposite of "sempai" and is used toward underclassmen in school or newcomers in the workplace. It connotes that the addressee is of a lower station.

Sensei: Literally meaning "one who has come before," this title is used for teachers, doctors, or masters of any profession or art.

-[blank]: This is usually forgotten in these lists, but it is perhaps the most significant difference between Japanese and English. The lack of honorific means that the speaker has permission to address the person in a very intimate way. Usually, only family, spouses, or very close friends have this kind of permission. Known as *yobisute*, it can be gratifying when someone who has earned the intimacy starts to call one by one's name without an honorific. But when that intimacy hasn't been earned, it can be very insulting.

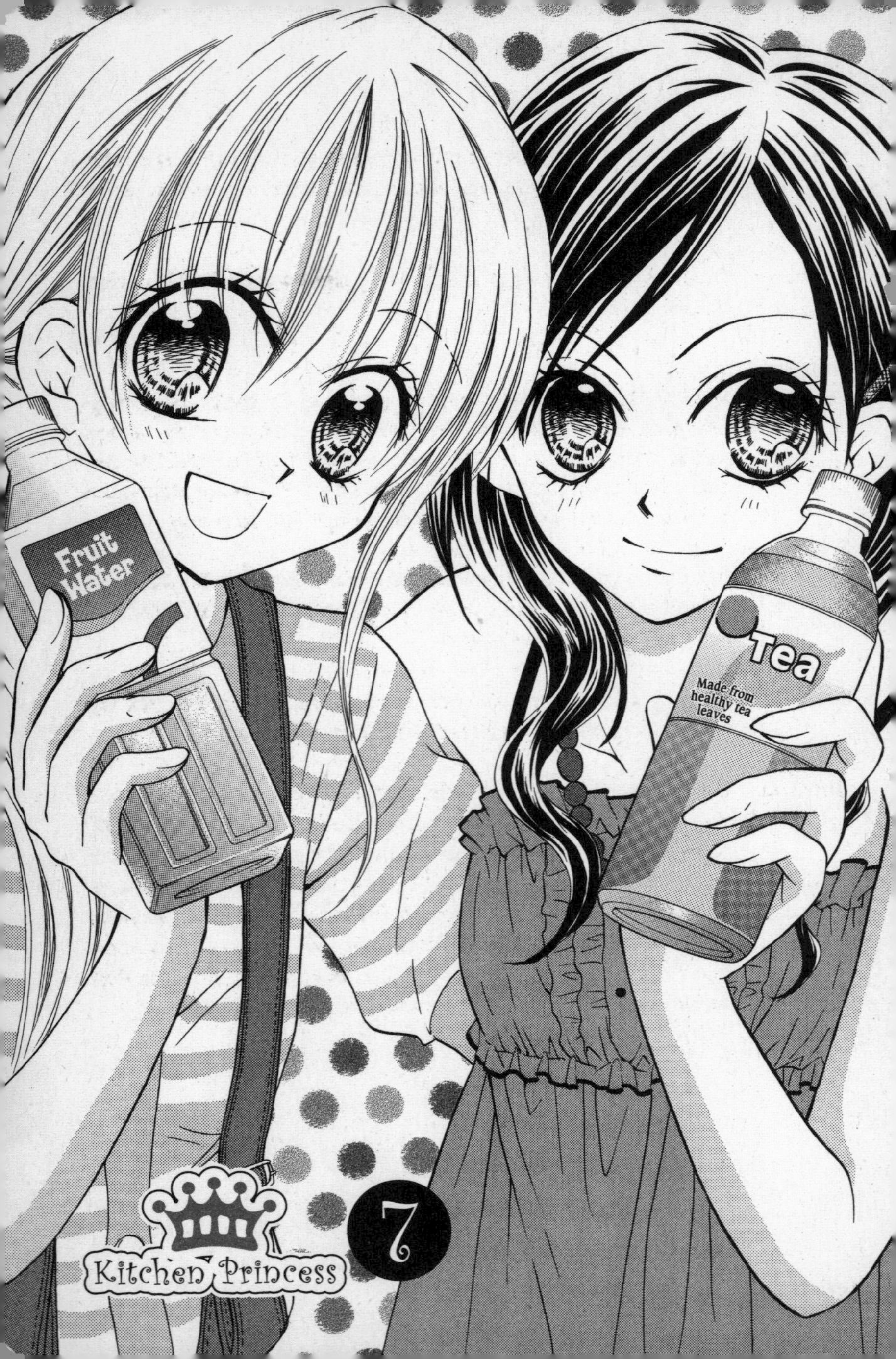

Fruit Water
Tea
Made from healthy tea leaves
Kitchen Princess
7

Kitchen Princess

Table of Contents

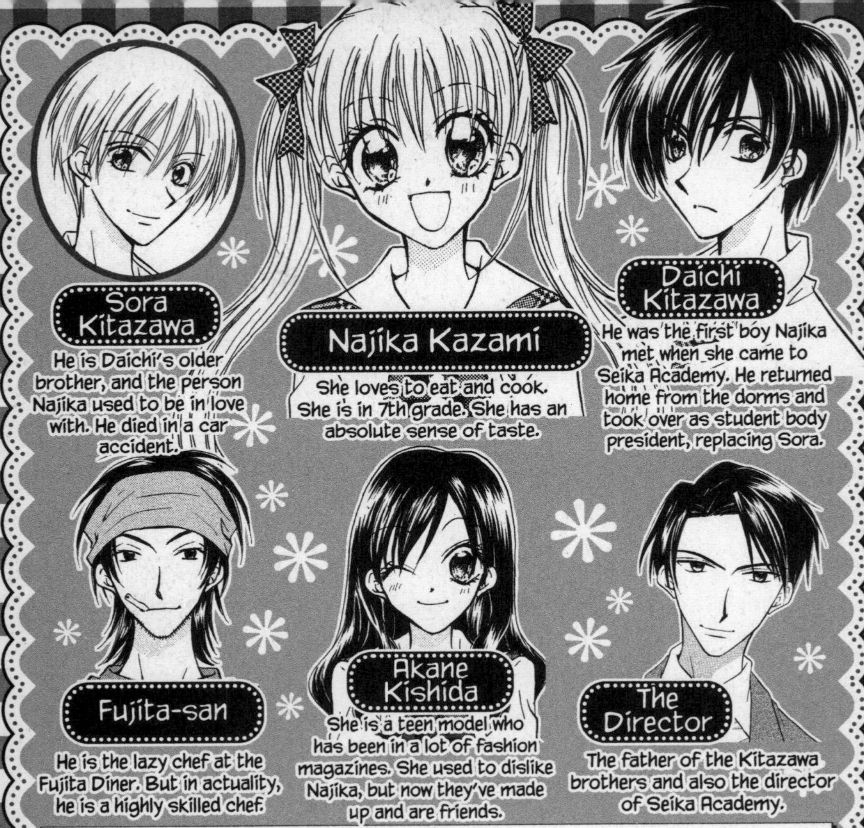
Sora Kitazawa
He is Daichi's older brother, and the person Najika used to be in love with. He died in a car accident.
Najika Kazami
She loves to eat and cook. She is in 7th grade. She has an absolute sense of taste.
Daichi Kitazawa
He was the first boy Najika met when she came to Seika Academy. He returned home from the dorms and took over as student body president, replacing Sora.
Fujita-san
He is the lazy chef at the Fujita Diner. But in actuality, he is a highly skilled chef.
Akane Kishida
She is a teen model who has been in a lot of fashion magazines. She used to dislike Najika, but now they've made up and are friends.
The Director
The father of the Kitazawa brothers and also the director of Seika Academy.

The Story So Far...

Kitchen Princess

Najika lost her parents when she was young and grew up in Lavender House, an orphanage in Hokkaido. She joined Seika Academy in Tokyo to find her Flan Prince, a boy who saved her from drowning when she was young. There she met Sora, Daichi, and Akane. Najika entered the National Confectionary Competition and went to the final round. But during the competition, Sora got into an accident and died. The shock caused Najika to lose her sense of taste... and she also lost the competition. Najika was kicked out of the Academy, but was allowed to stay, thanks to Daichi, though in the regular class. One day, a boy named Seiya Mizuno appeared at the Fujita Diner. And he looks just like Sora!

Ever since he started studying, Daichi's eyes are getting worse. But it's not so bad that it affects his daily life.

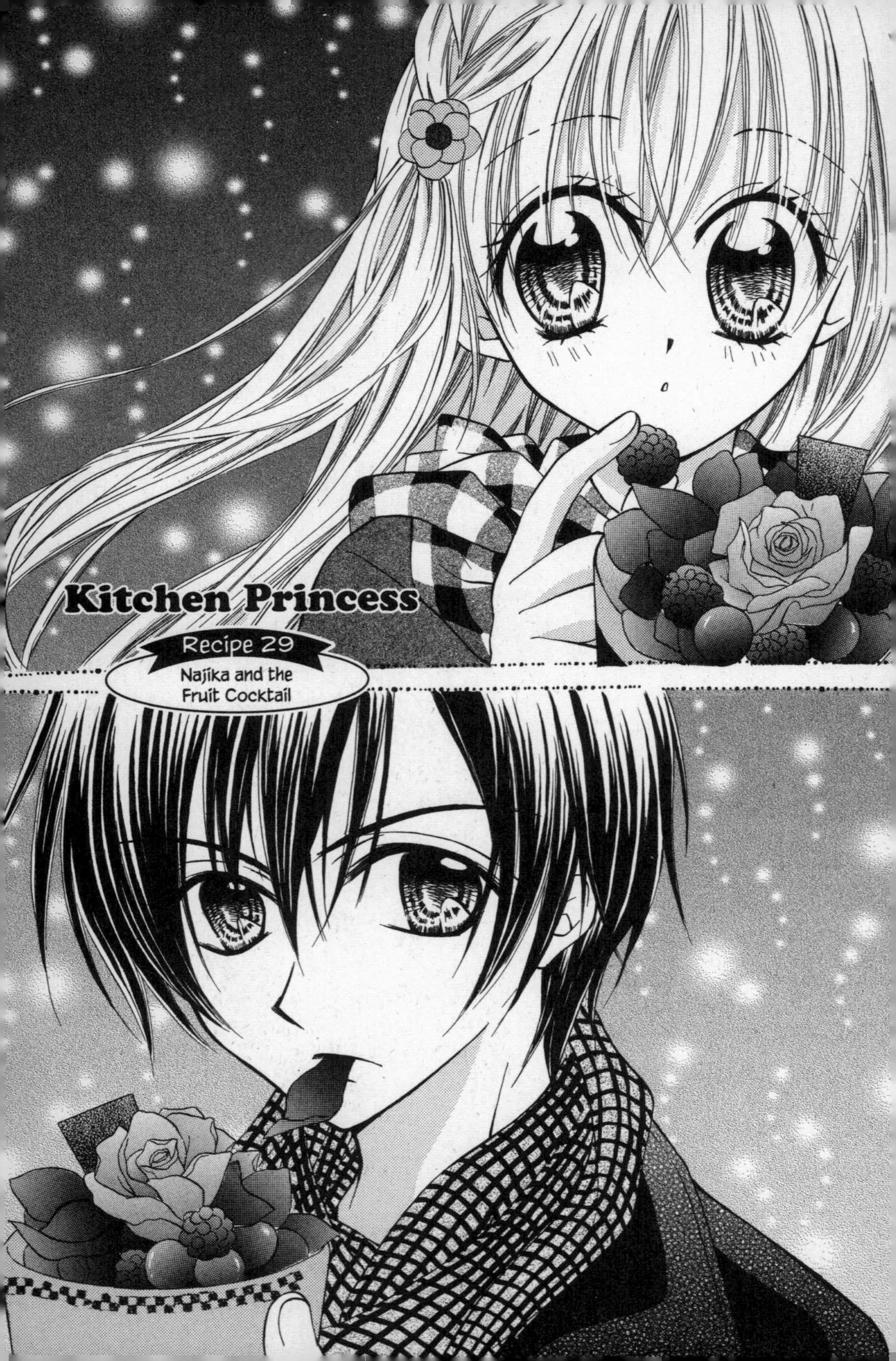
Kitchen Princess
Recipe 29
Najika and the Fruit Cocktail

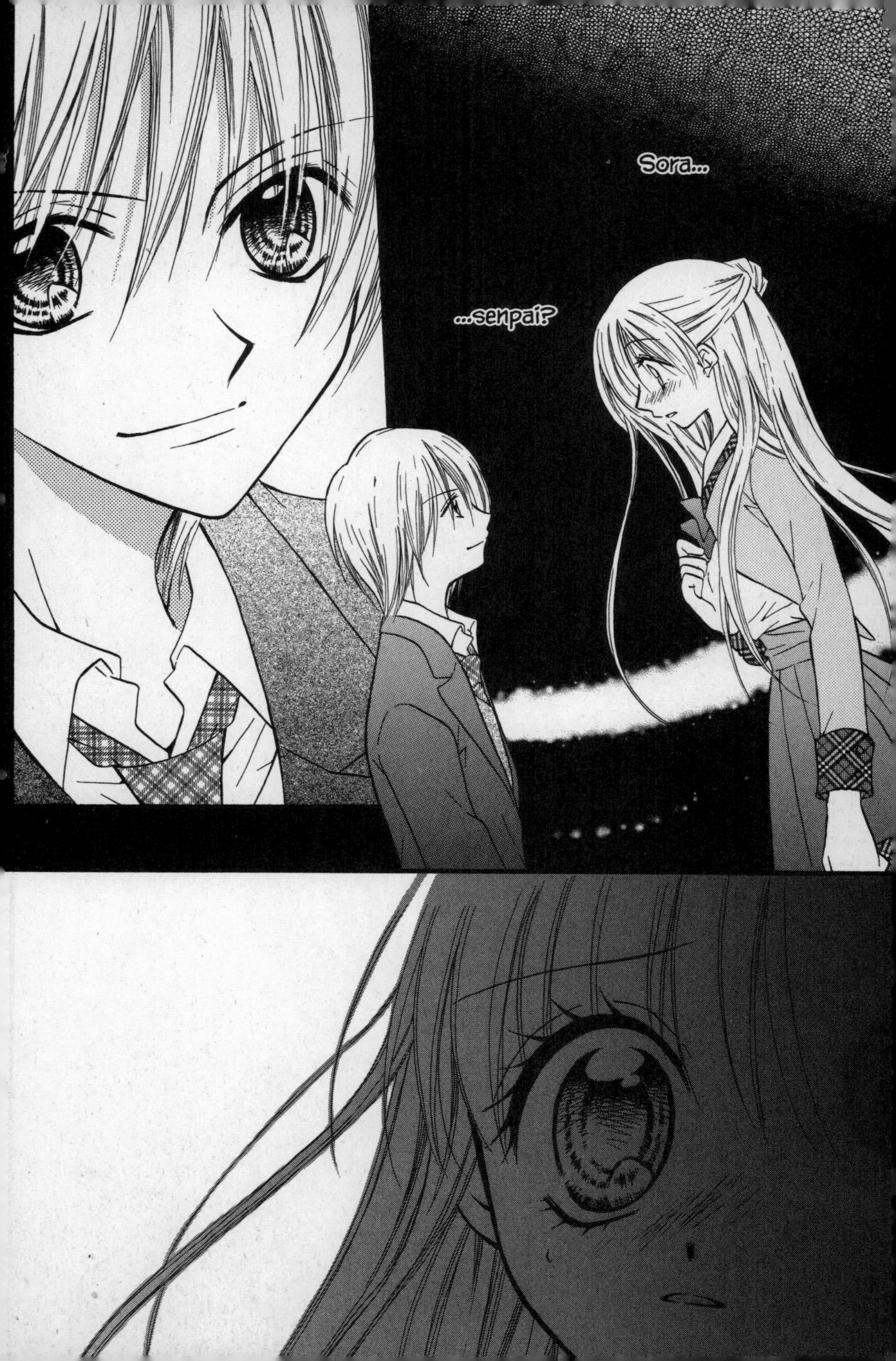
Sora...
...senpai?

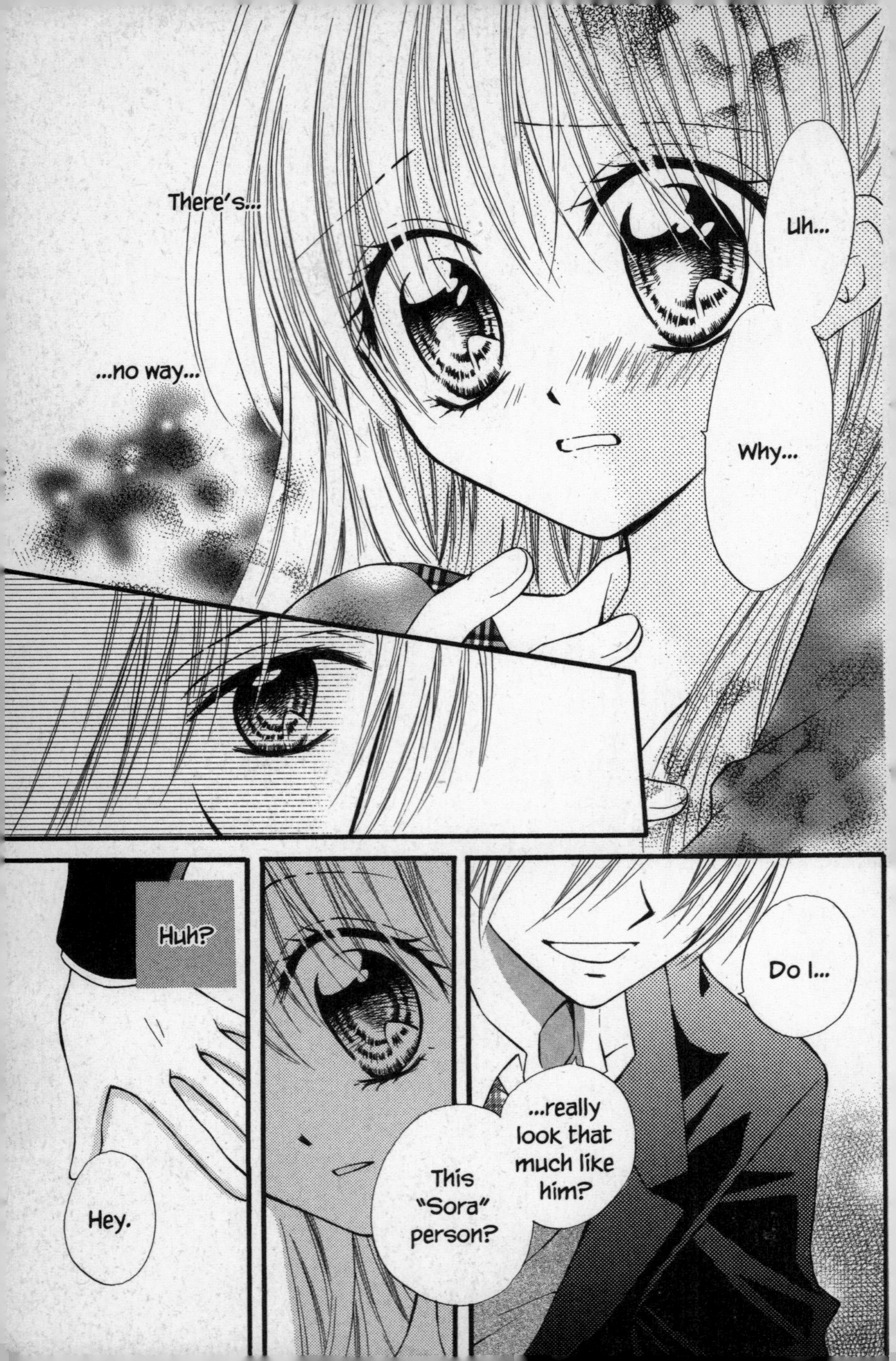
Uh...
Why...
There's...
...no way...
Do I...
...really look that much like him?
This "Sora" person?
Huh?
Hey.

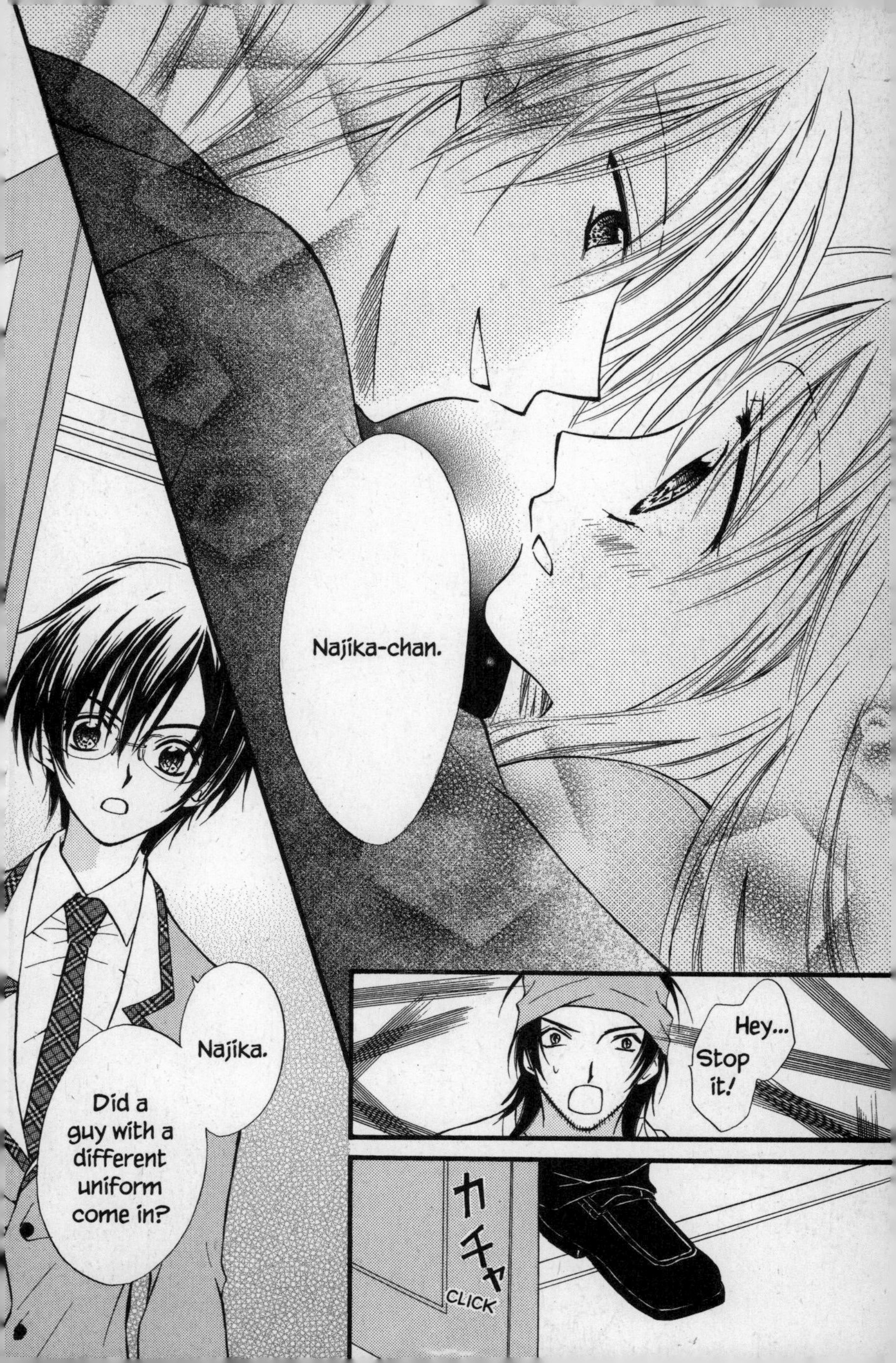

Najika-chan.
Hey... Stop it!
カチャ
CLICK
Najika.
Did a guy with a different uniform come in?

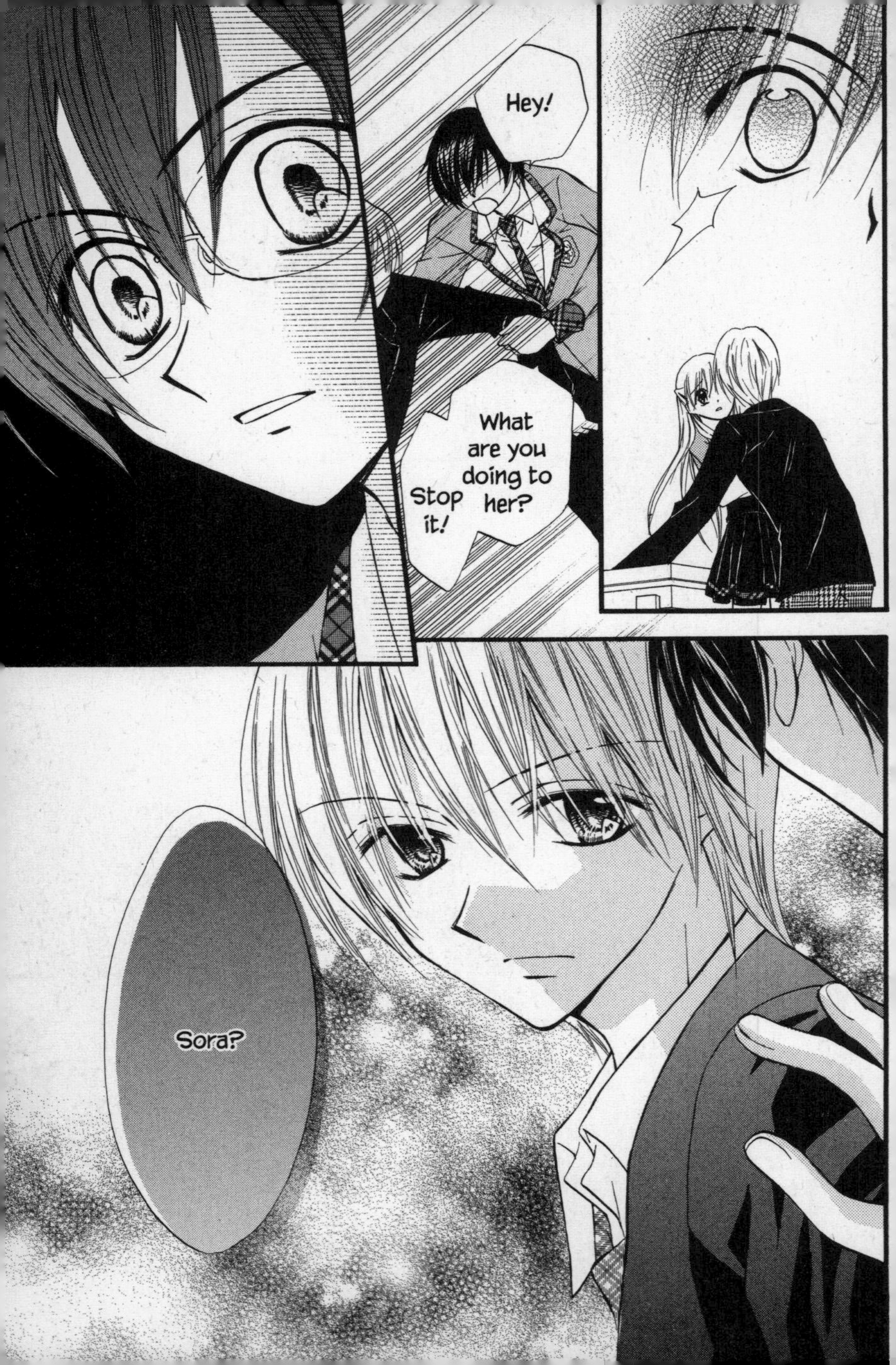
Hey!
What are you doing to her?
Stop it!
Sora?

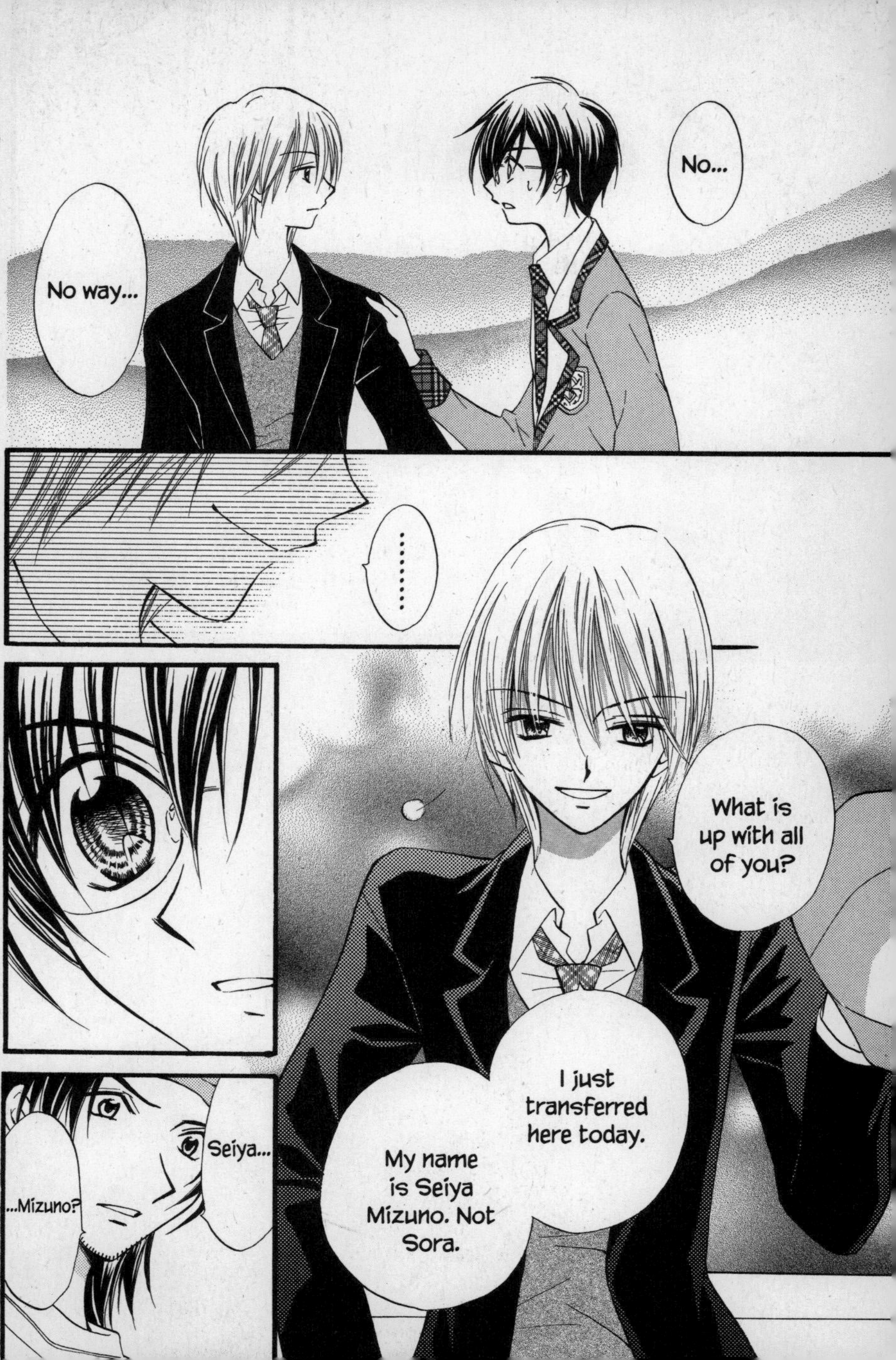
No...
No way...
......
What is up with all of you?
I just transferred here today.
My name is Seiya Mizuno. Not Sora.
Seiya...
...Mizuno?

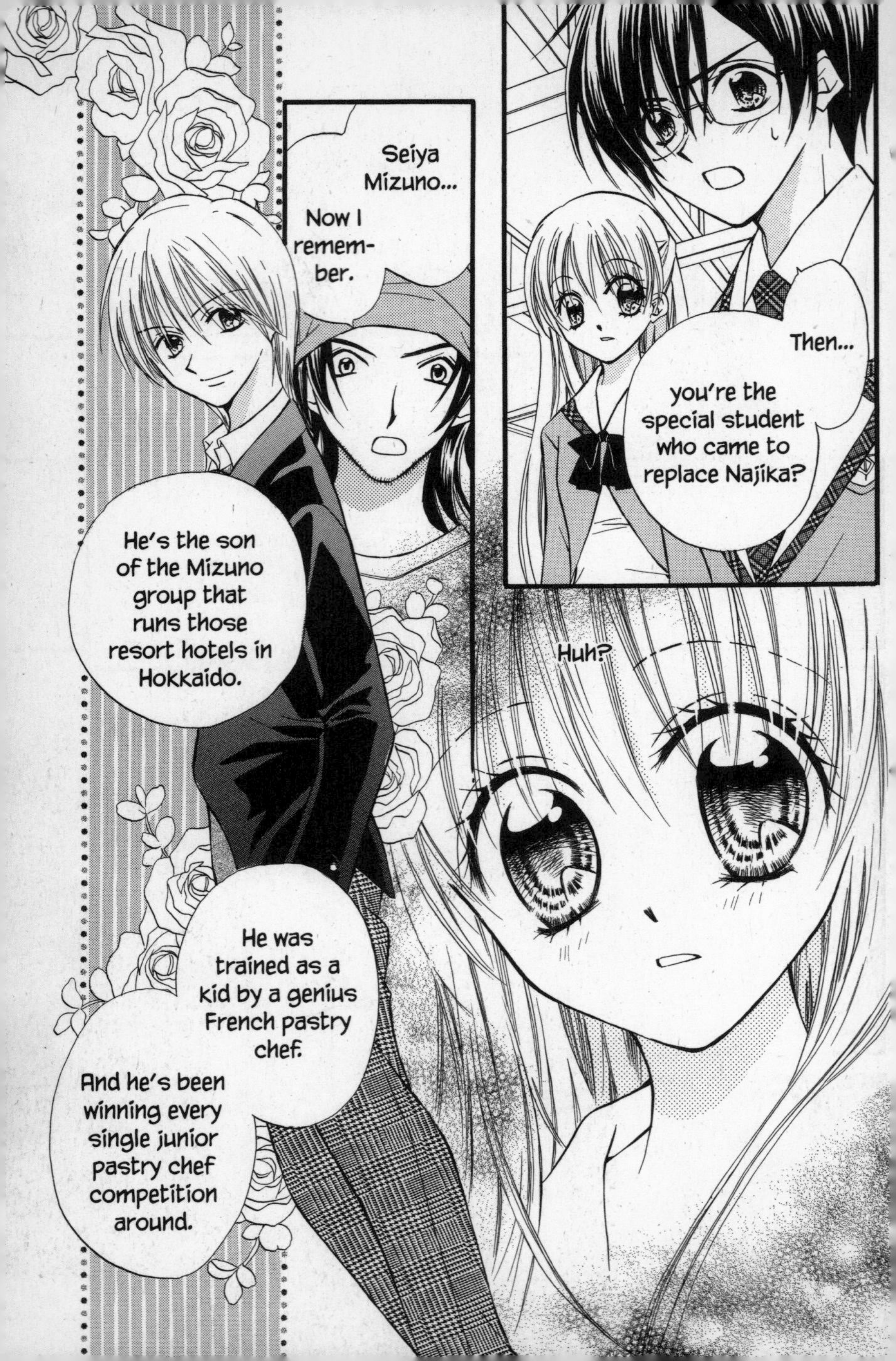
Then...
you're the special student who came to replace Najika?
Seiya Mizuno...
Now I remember.
He's the son of the Mizuno group that runs those resort hotels in Hokkaido.
Huh?
He was trained as a kid by a genius French pastry chef.
And he's been winning every single junior pastry chef competition around.

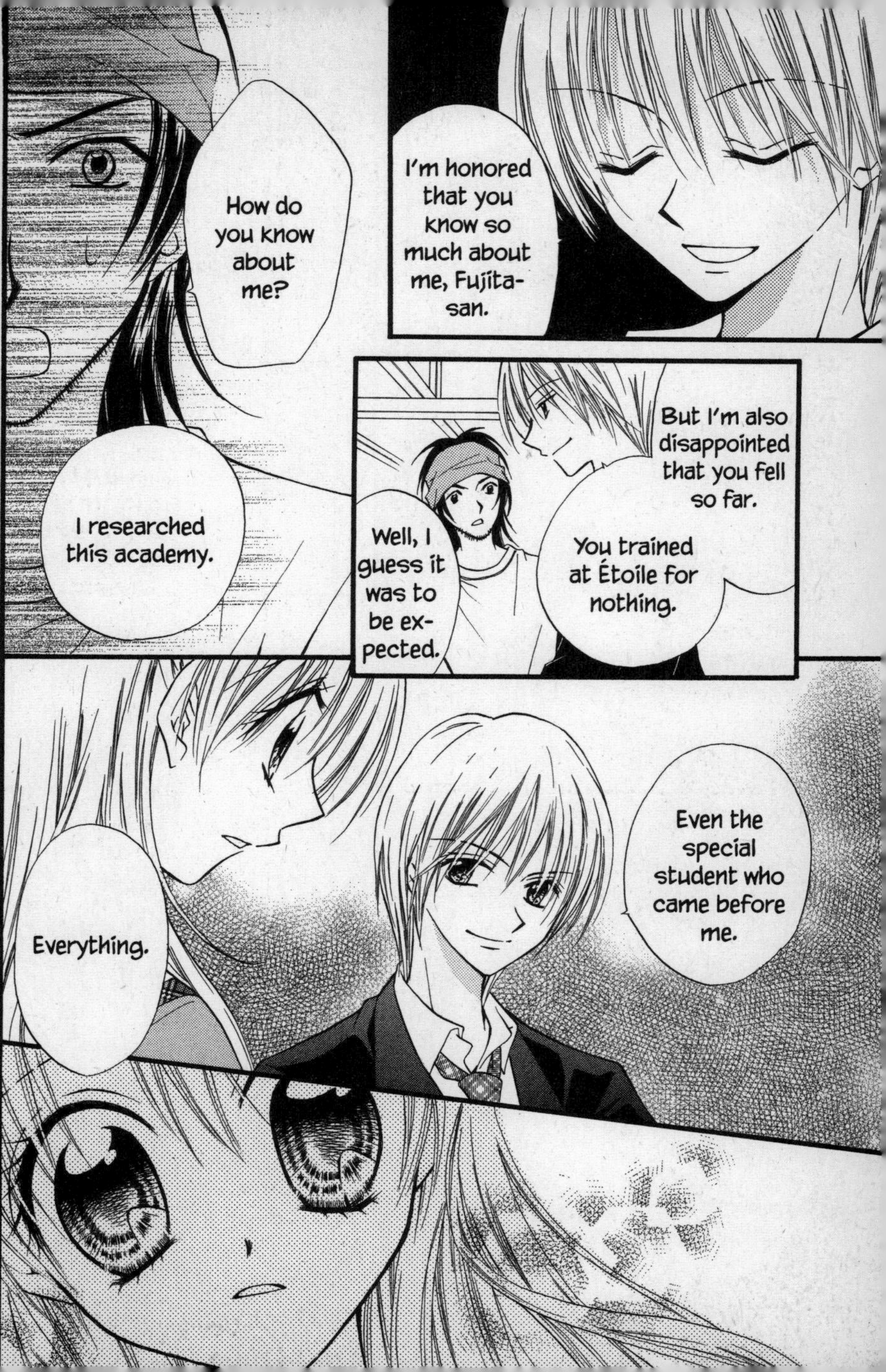
I'm honored that you know so much about me, Fujita-san.
But I'm also disappointed that you fell so far.
You trained at Étoile for nothing.
Well, I guess it was to be expected.
How do you know about me?
I researched this academy.
Even the special student who came before me.
Everything.

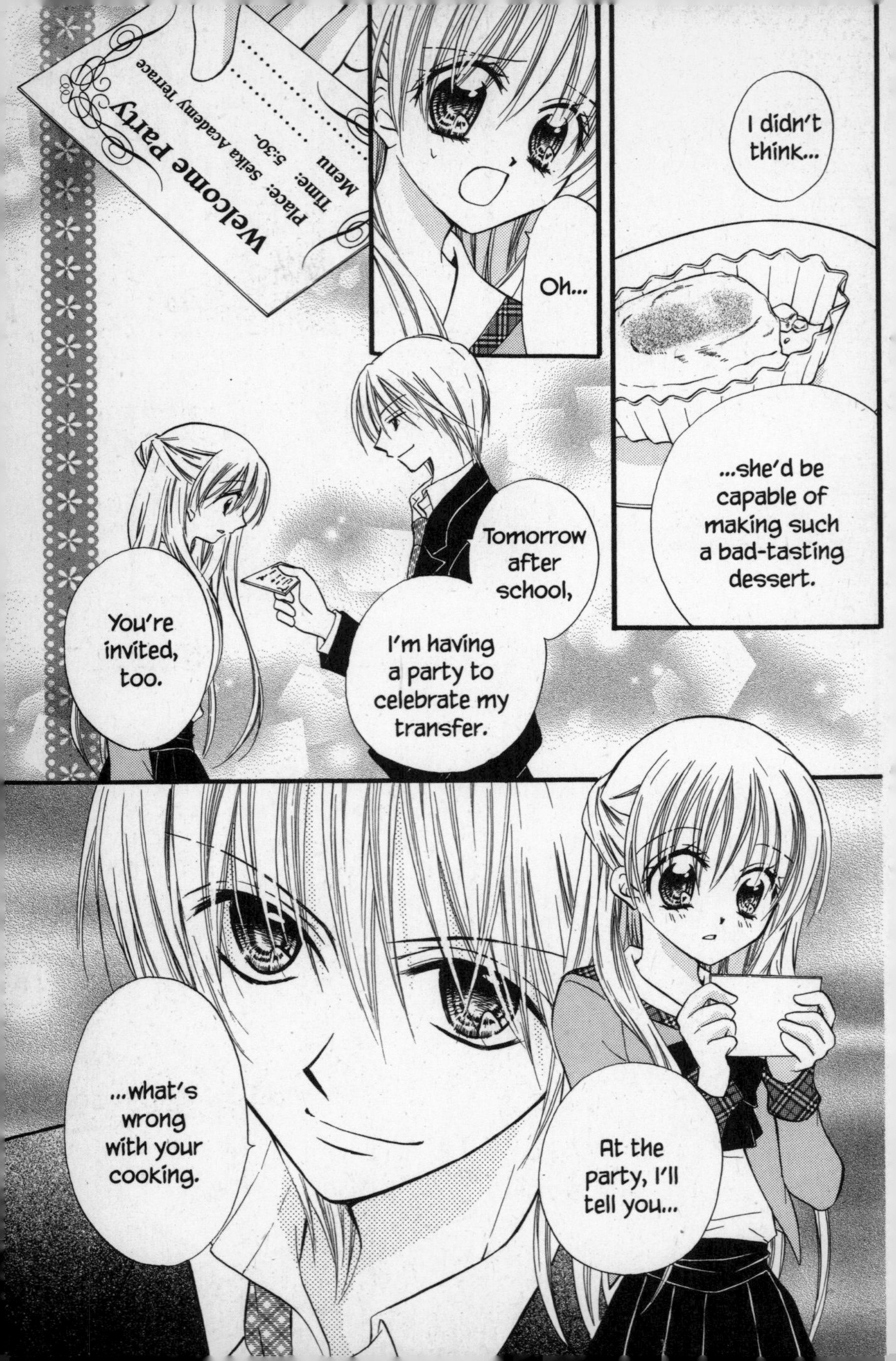
I didn't think...
...she'd be capable of making such a bad-tasting dessert.
Oh...
Welcome Party
Place: Seika Academy Terrace
Time: 5:30~
Menu
Tomorrow after school,
I'm having a party to celebrate my transfer.
You're invited, too.
At the party, I'll tell you...
...what's wrong with your cooking.

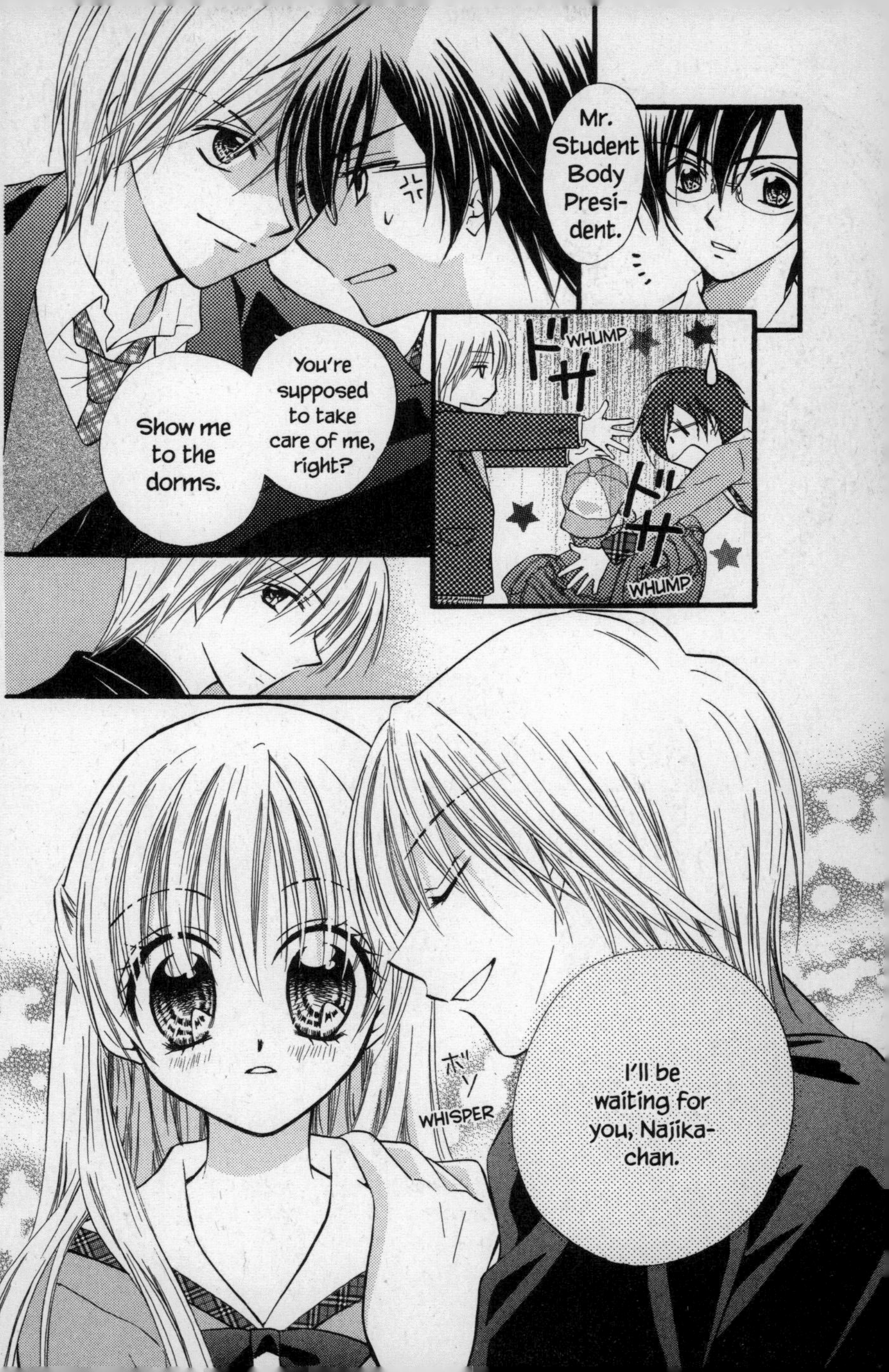
Mr. Student Body Presi-dent.
You're supposed to take care of me, right?
Show me to the dorms.
ドサ
WHUMP
ドサ
WHUMP
I'll be waiting for you, Najika-chan.
ボソ
WHISPER

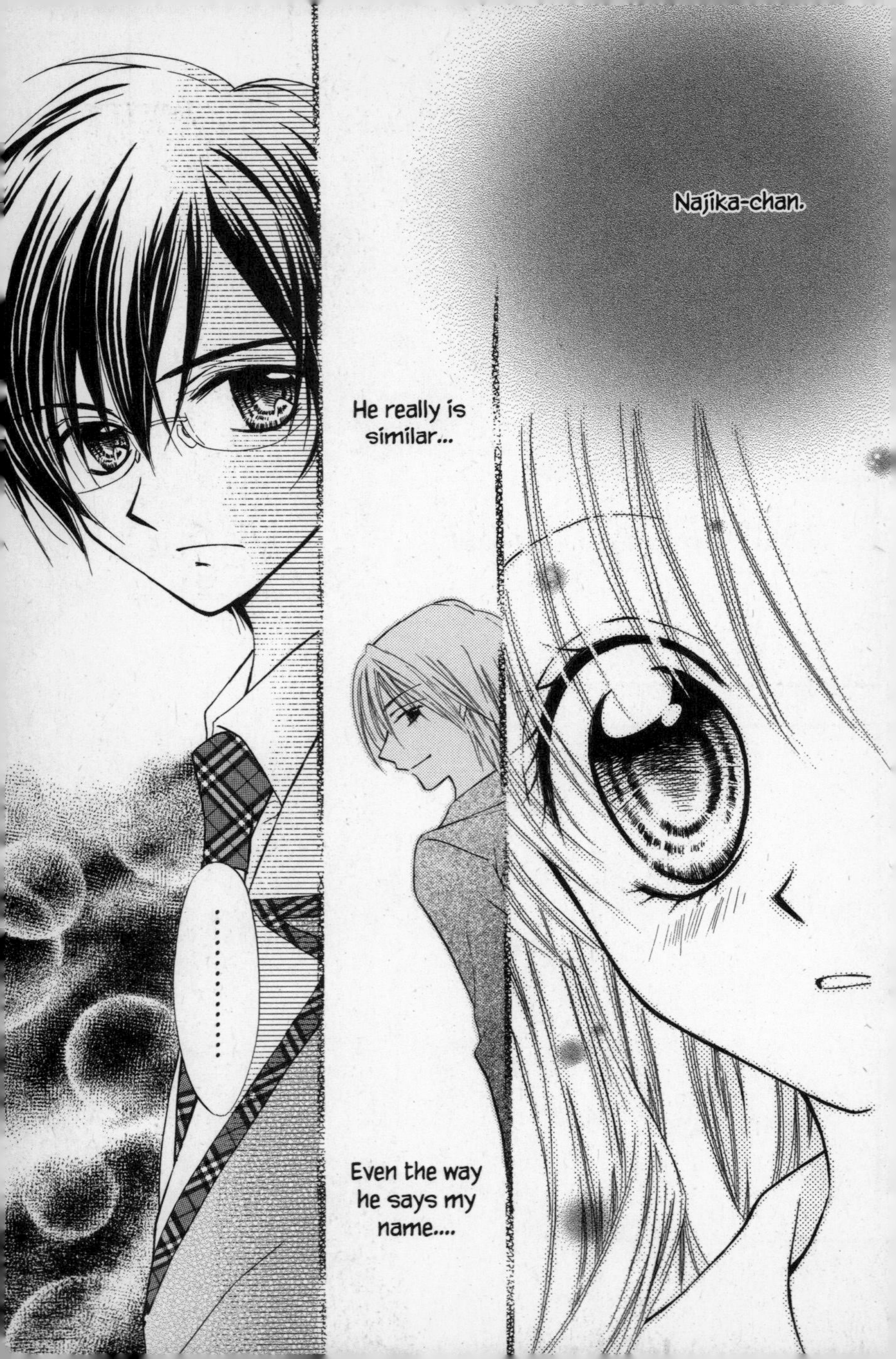
Najika-chan.
He really is similar...
Even the way he says my name....
......

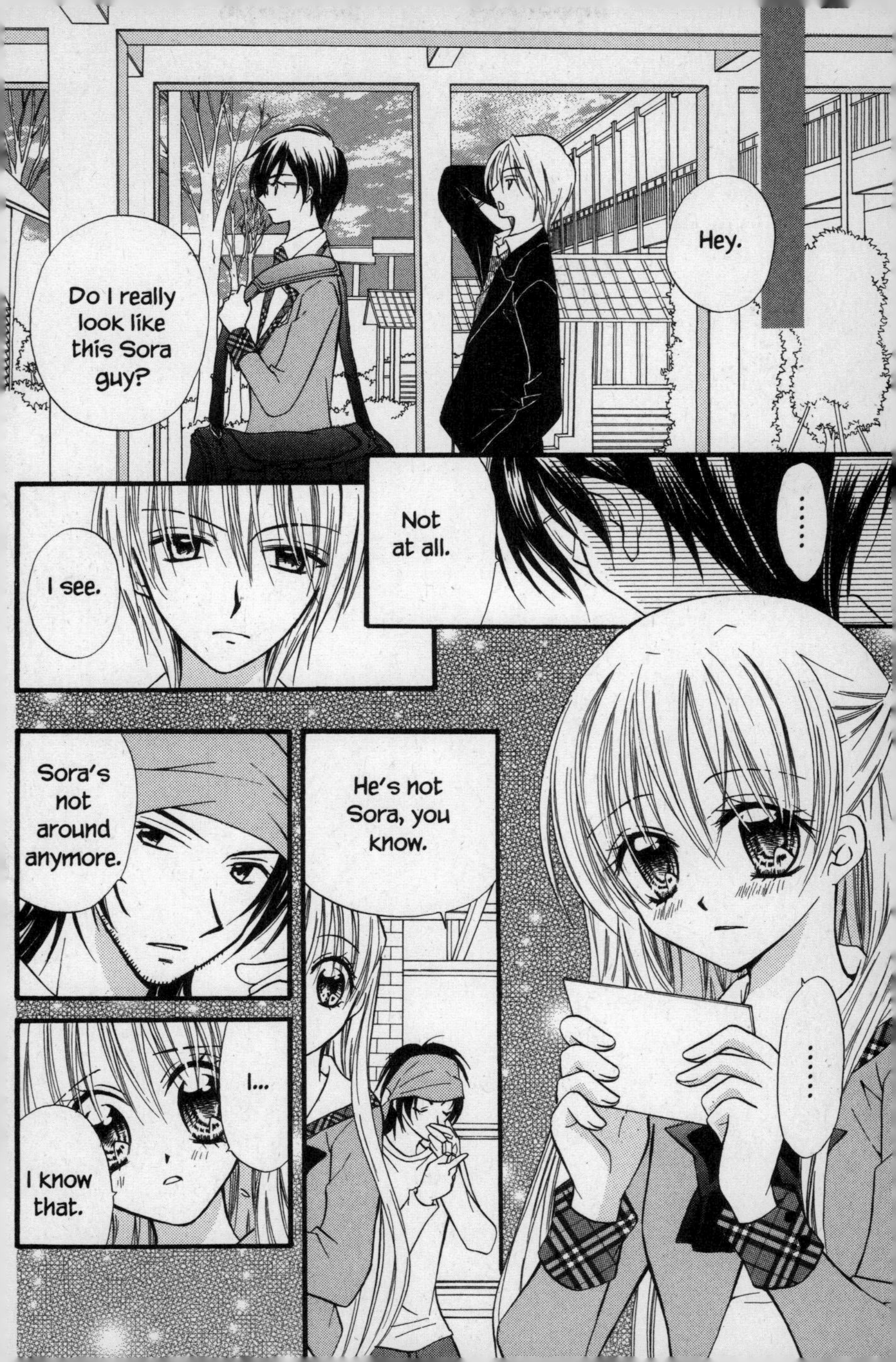
Hey.
Do I really look like this Sora guy?
......
Not at all.
I see.
......
He's not Sora, you know.
Sora's not around anymore.
I...
I know that.

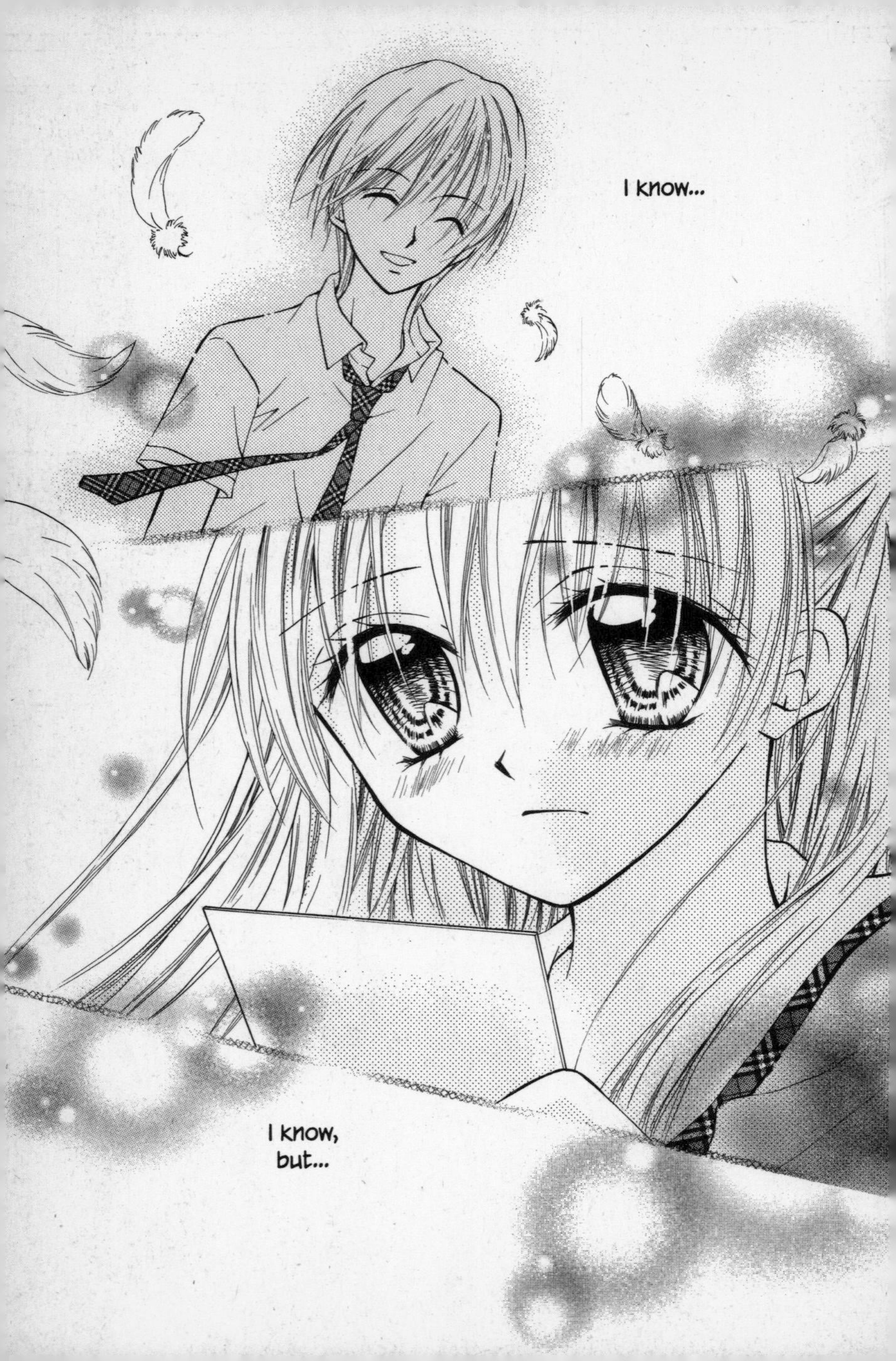
I know...
I know, but...

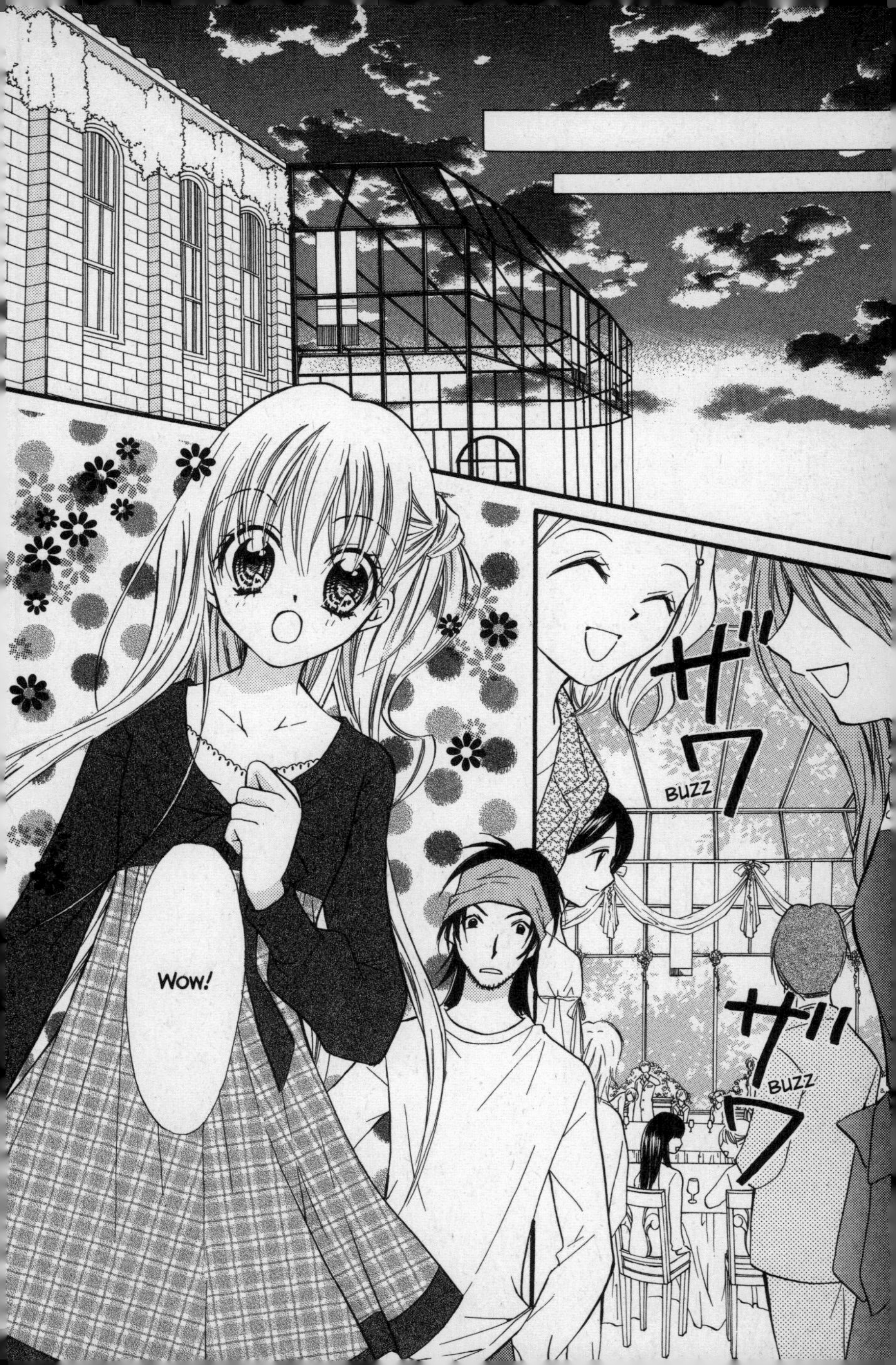
ザワ
BUZZ
ザワ
BUZZ
WOW!

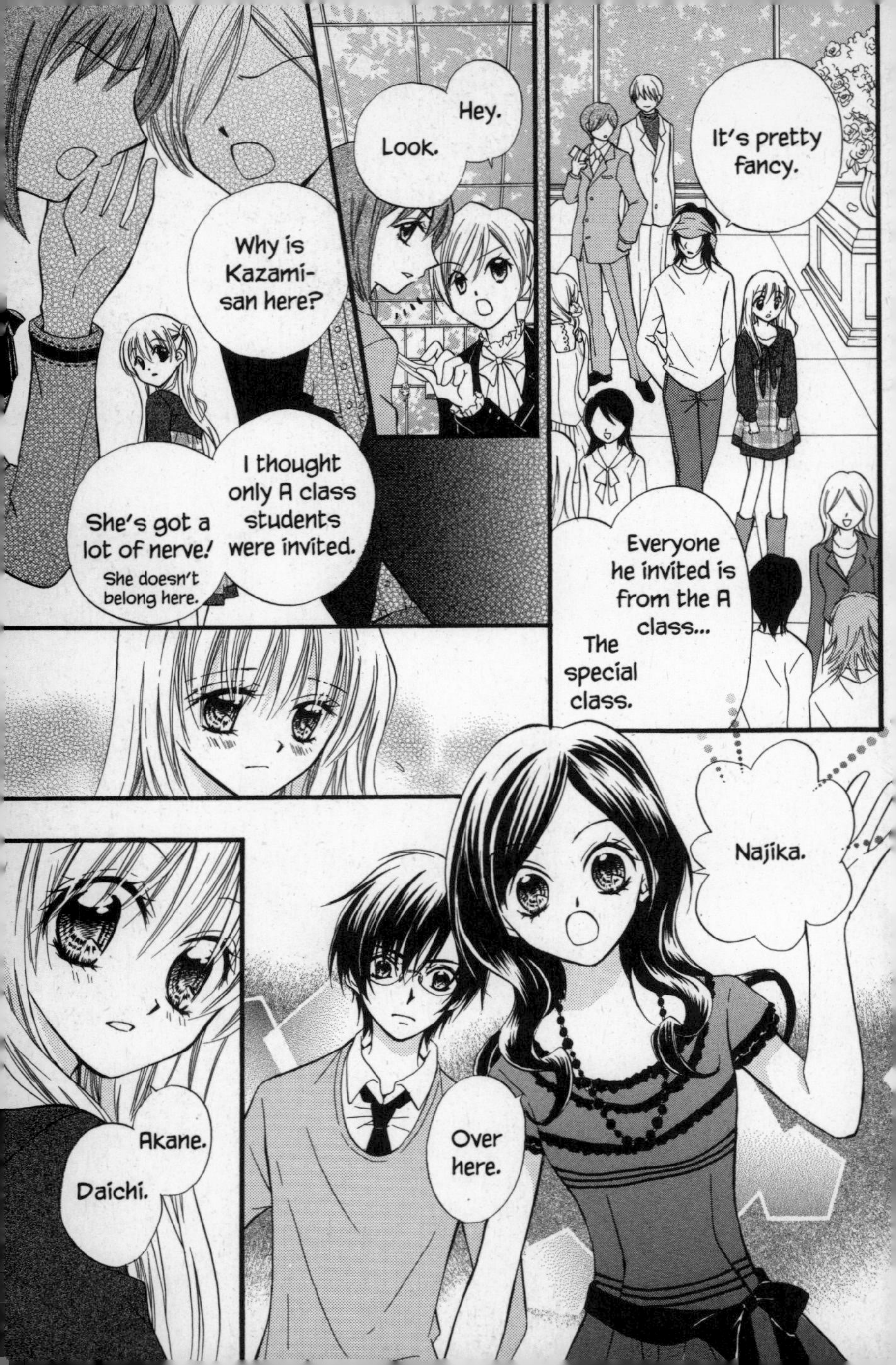
It's pretty fancy.
Everyone he invited is from the A class...
The special class.
Hey.
Look.
Why is Kazami-san here?
I thought only A class students were invited.
She's got a lot of nerve!
She doesn't belong here.
Najika.
Over here.
Akane.
Daichi.

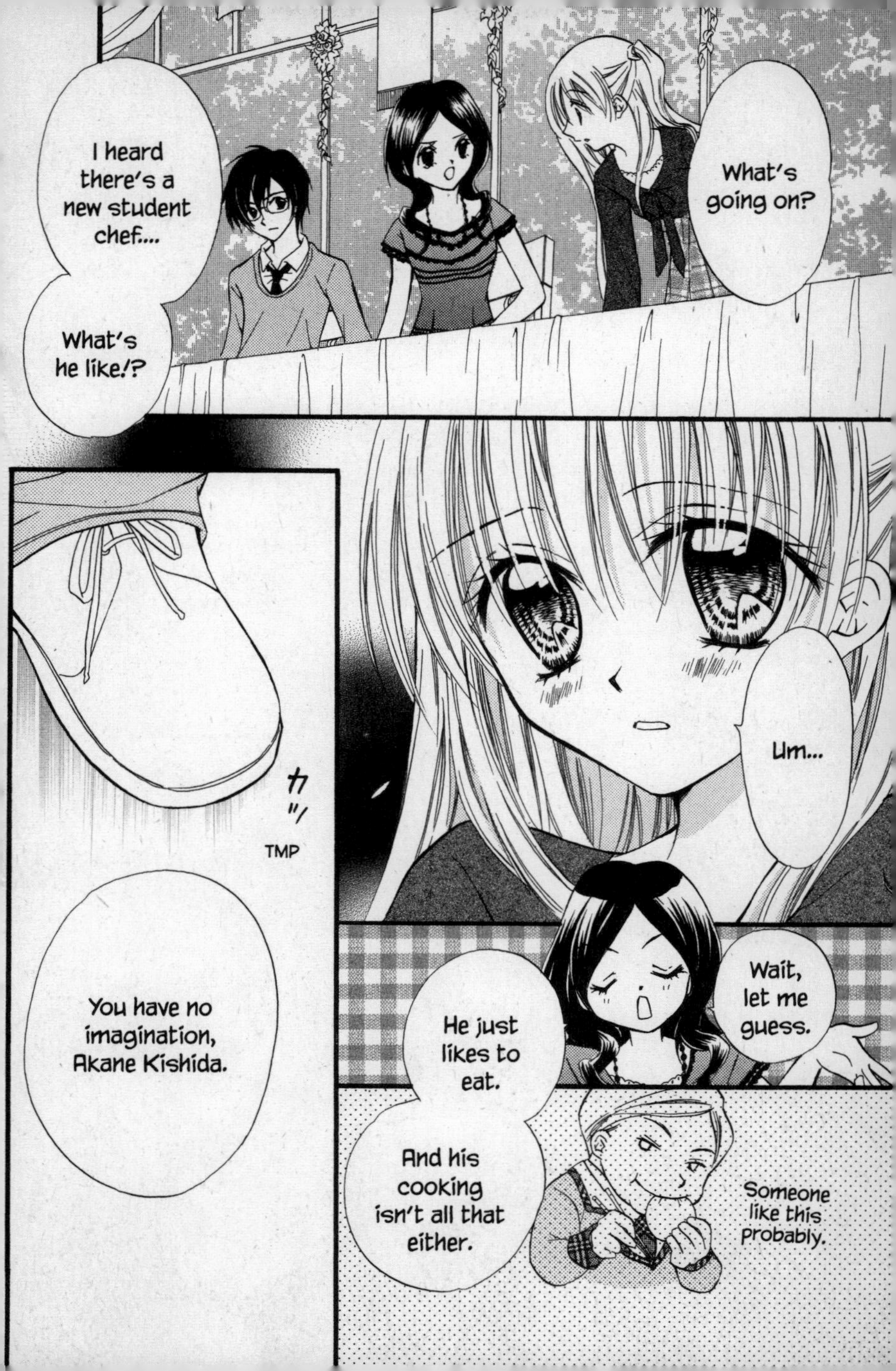
What's going on?
I heard there's a new student chef....
What's he like!?
Um...
Wait, let me guess.
He just likes to eat.
And his cooking isn't all that either.
Someone like this probably.
カツ
TMP
You have no imagination, Akane Kishida.

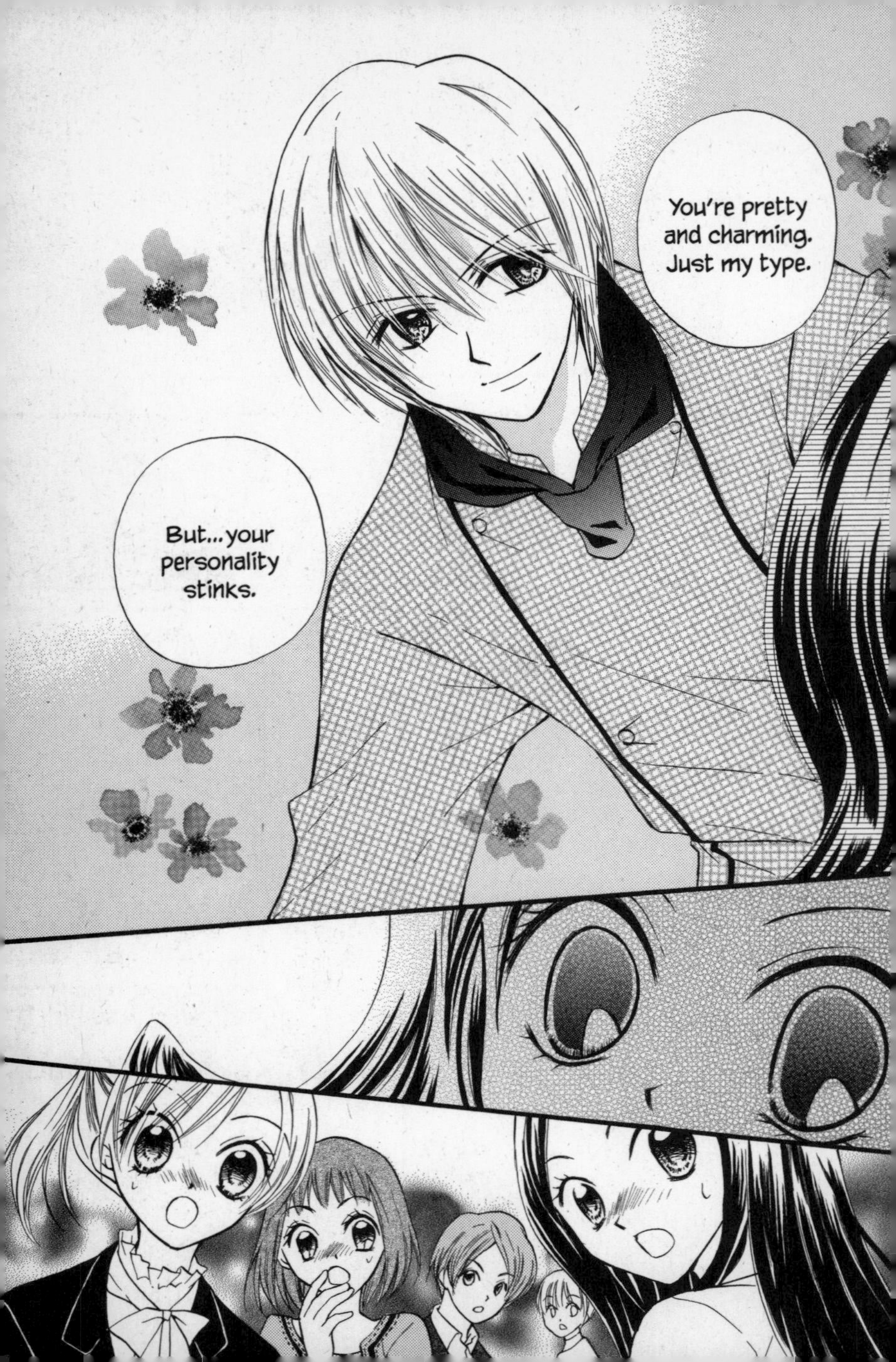
You're pretty and charming. Just my type.
But...your personality stinks.

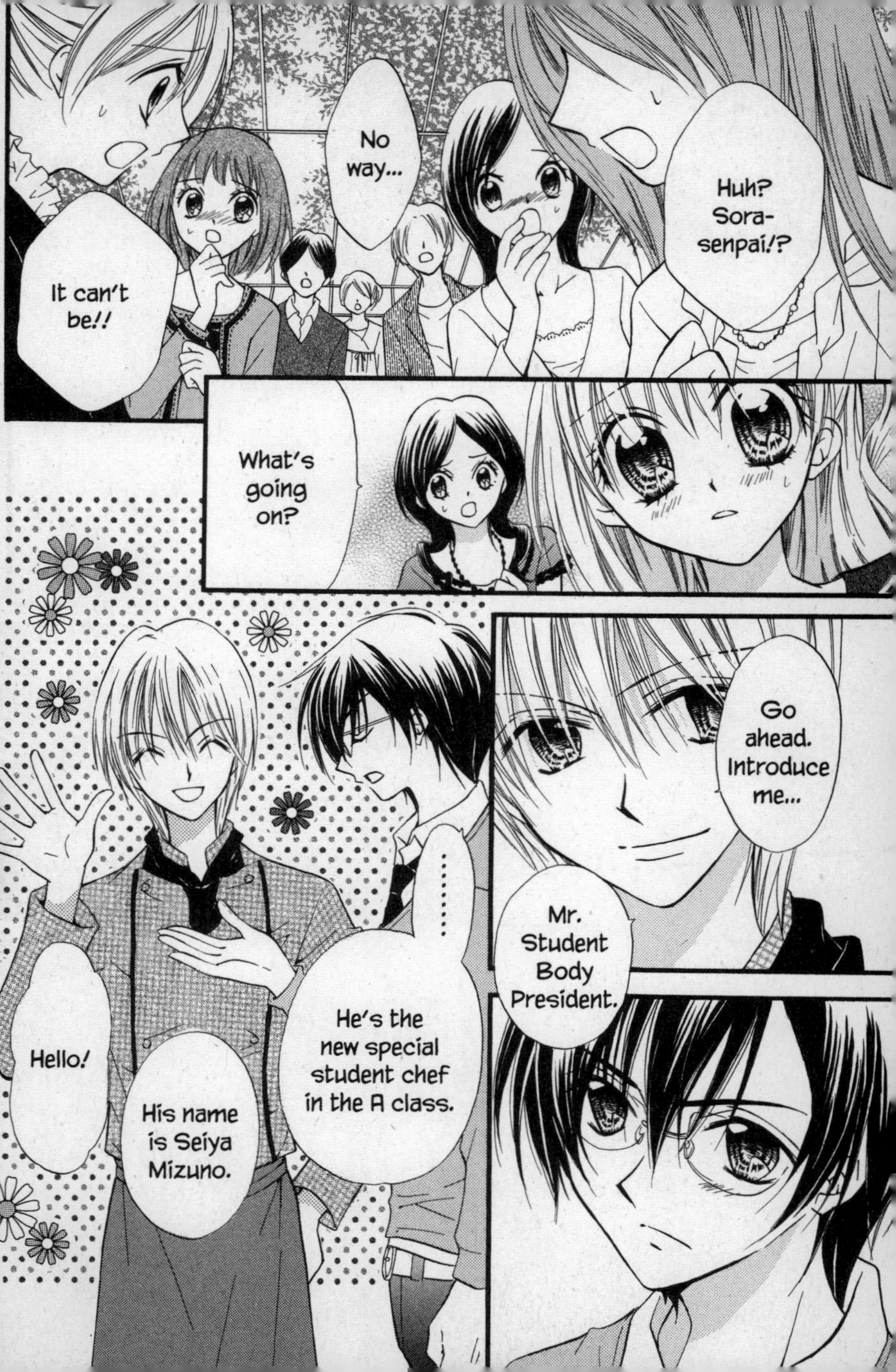
Huh? Sora-senpai!?
No way...
It can't be!!
What's going on?
Go ahead. Introduce me...
Mr. Student Body President.
......
He's the new special student chef in the A class.
His name is Seiya Mizuno.
Hello!

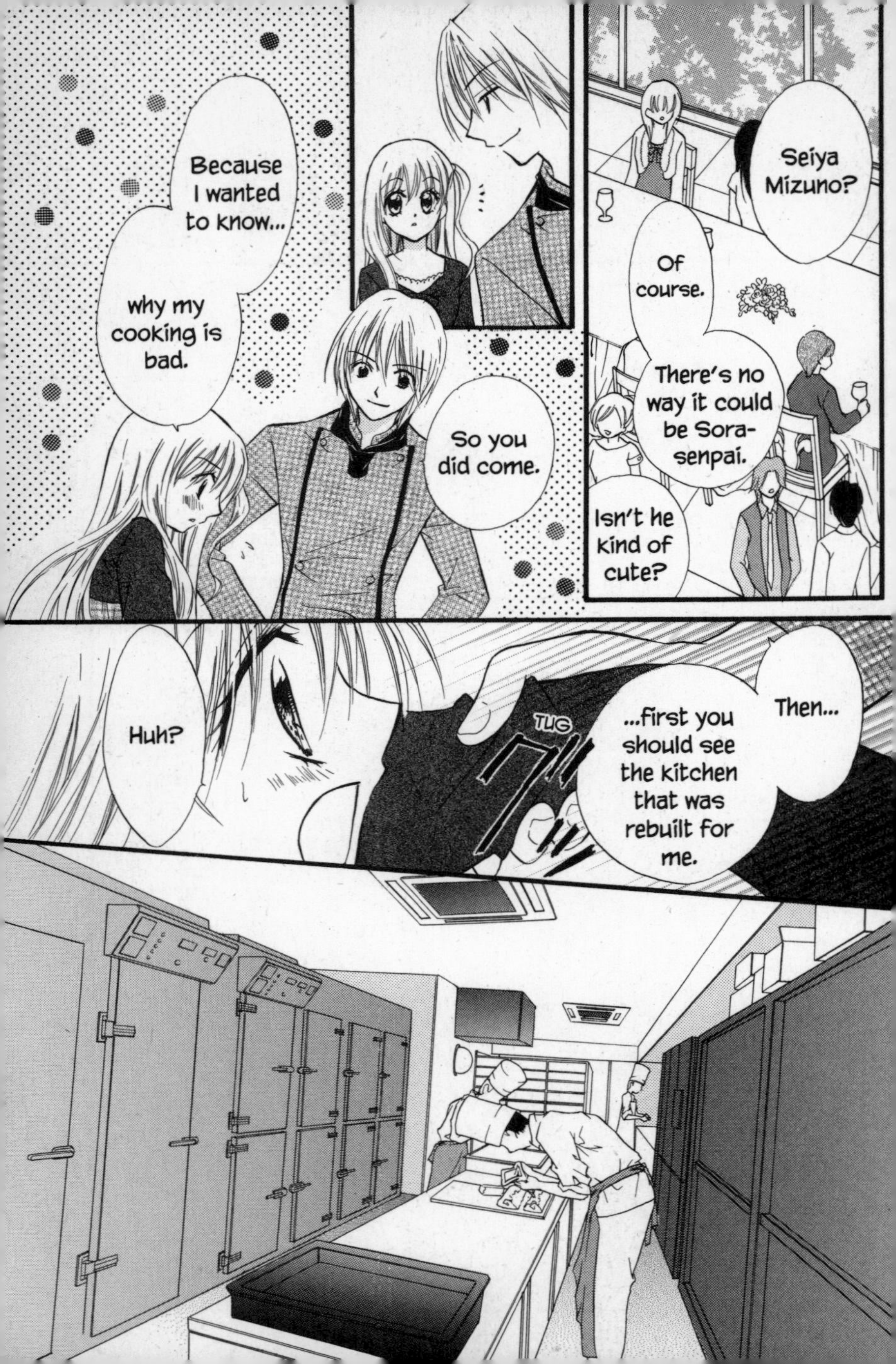
Seiya Mizuno?
Of course.
There's no way it could be Sora-senpai.
Isn't he kind of cute?
So you did come.
Because I wanted to know...
why my cooking is bad.
Then...
...first you should see the kitchen that was rebuilt for me.
TUG
Huh?

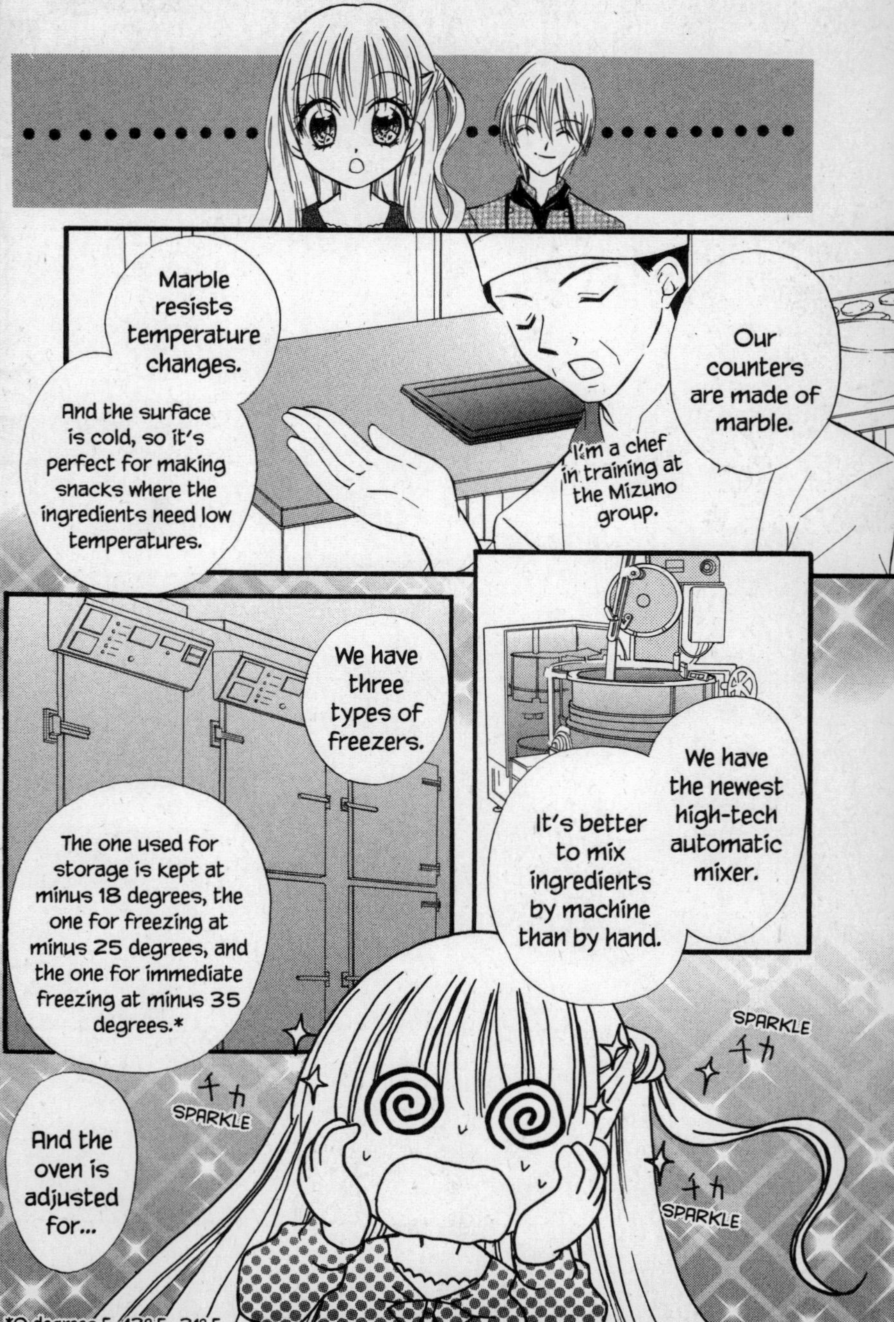
Our counters are made of marble.
I'm a chef in training at the Mizuno group.
Marble resists temperature changes.
And the surface is cold, so it's perfect for making snacks where the ingredients need low temperatures.
We have the newest high-tech automatic mixer.
It's better to mix ingredients by machine than by hand.
We have three types of freezers.
The one used for storage is kept at minus 18 degrees, the one for freezing at minus 25 degrees, and the one for immediate freezing at minus 35 degrees.*
SPARKLE
SPARKLE
SPARKLE
And the oven is adjusted for...

*0 degrees F, -13° F, -31° F

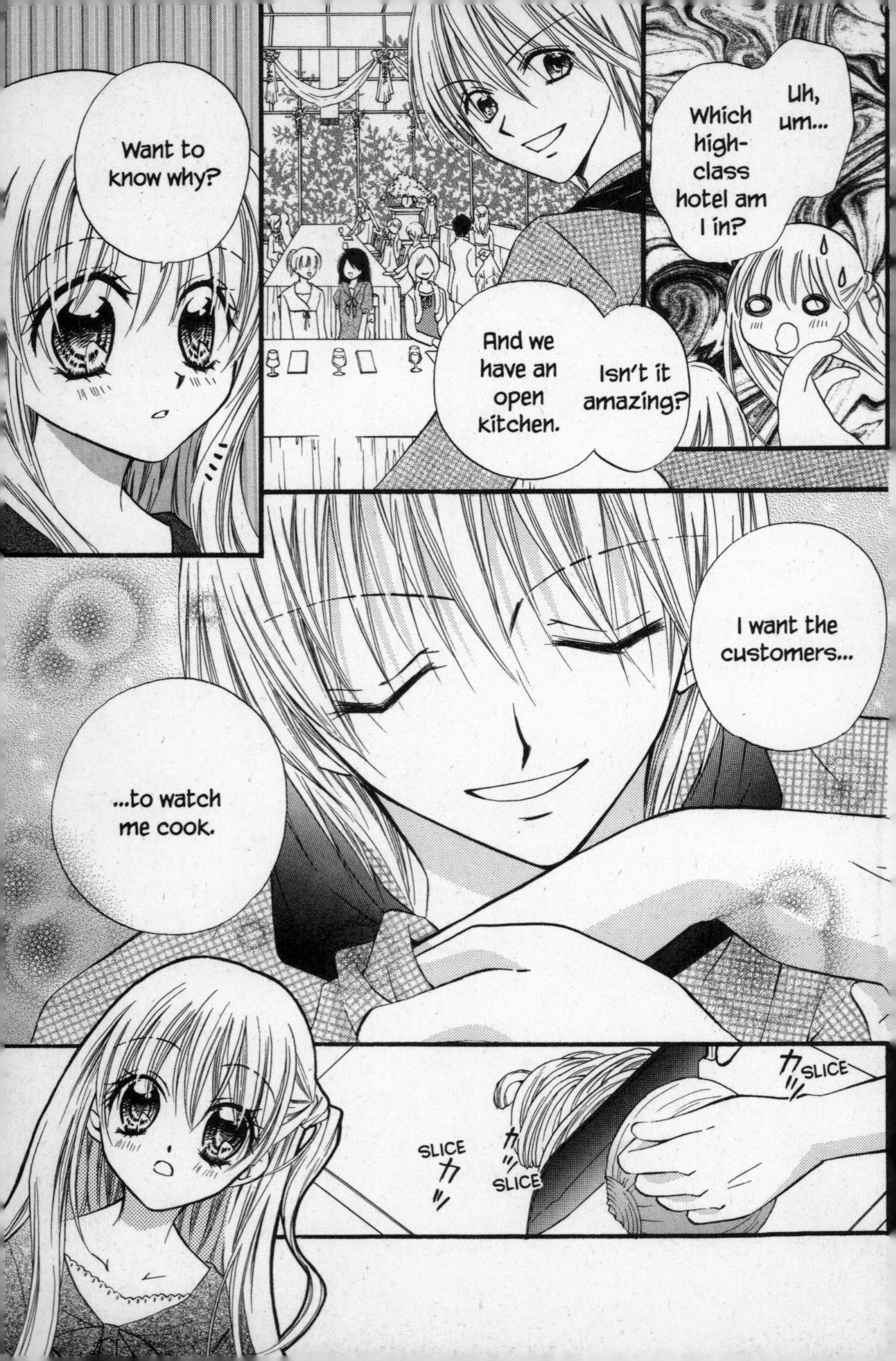
Uh, um...
Which high-class hotel am I in?
And we have an open kitchen.
Isn't it amazing?
Want to know why?
I want the customers...
...to watch me cook.
カ SLICE
カ SLICE
SLICE カ

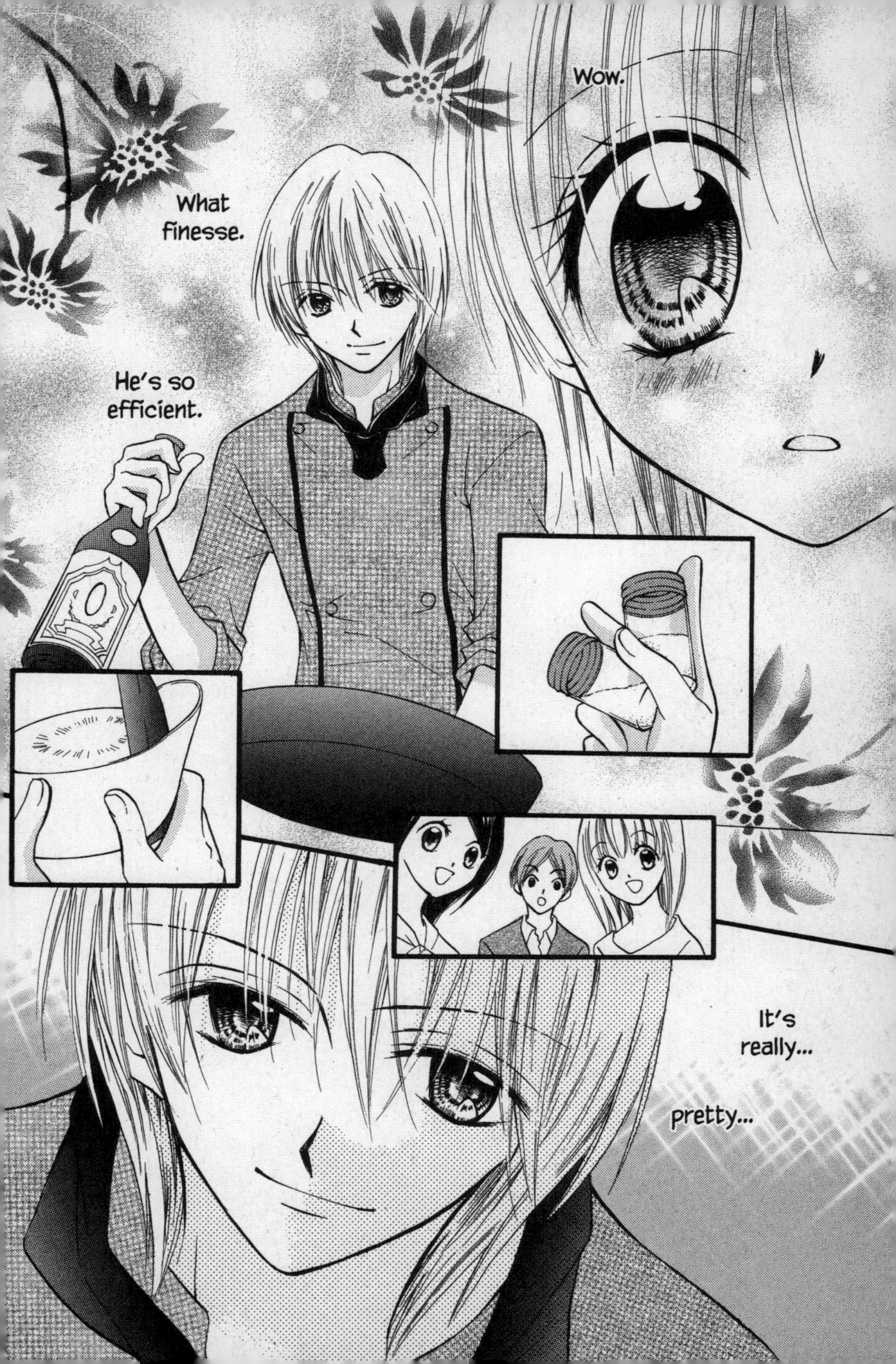
Wow.
What finesse.
He's so efficient.
It's really...
pretty...

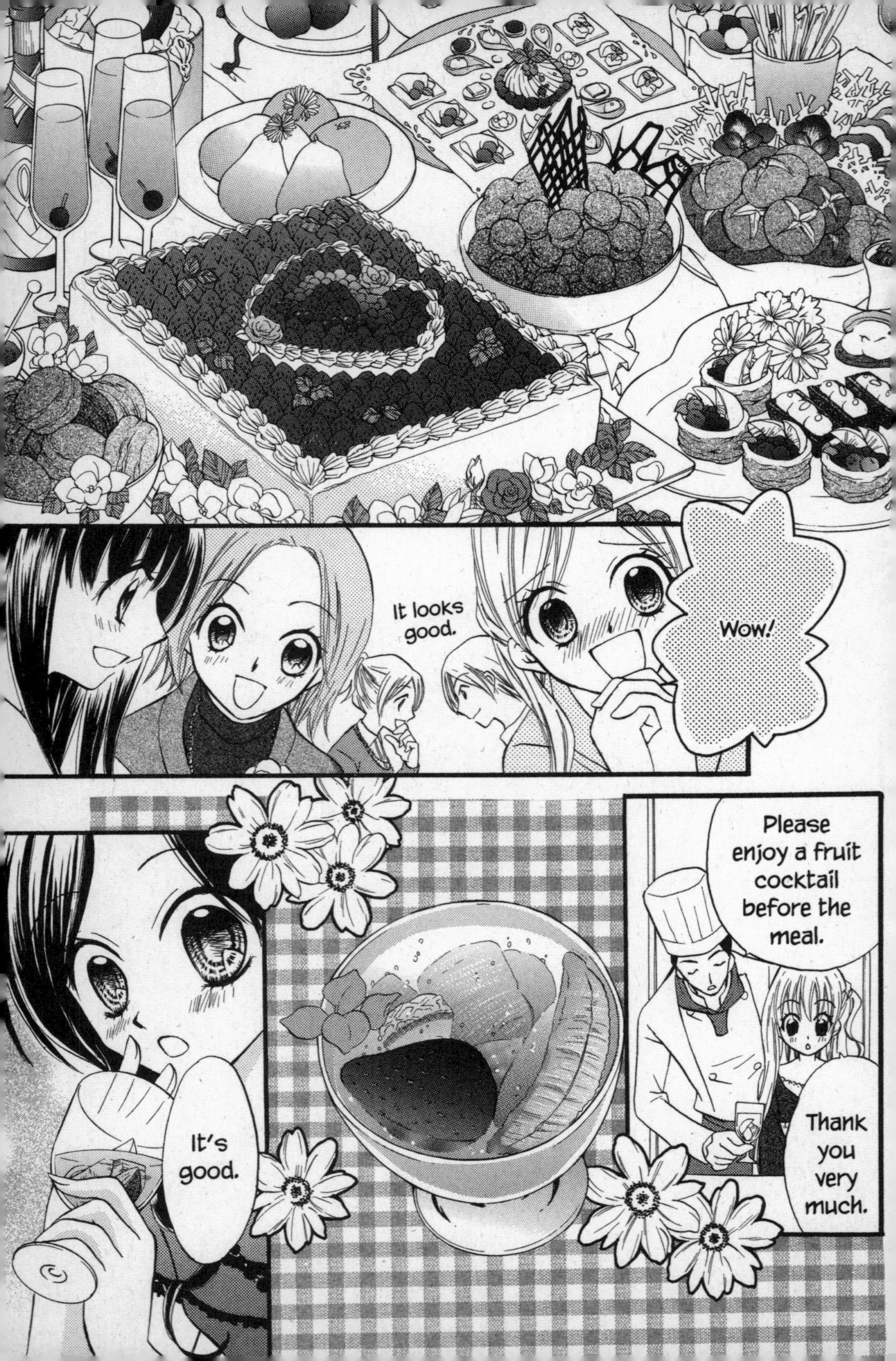
Wow!
It looks good.
Please enjoy a fruit cocktail before the meal.
Thank you very much.
It's good.

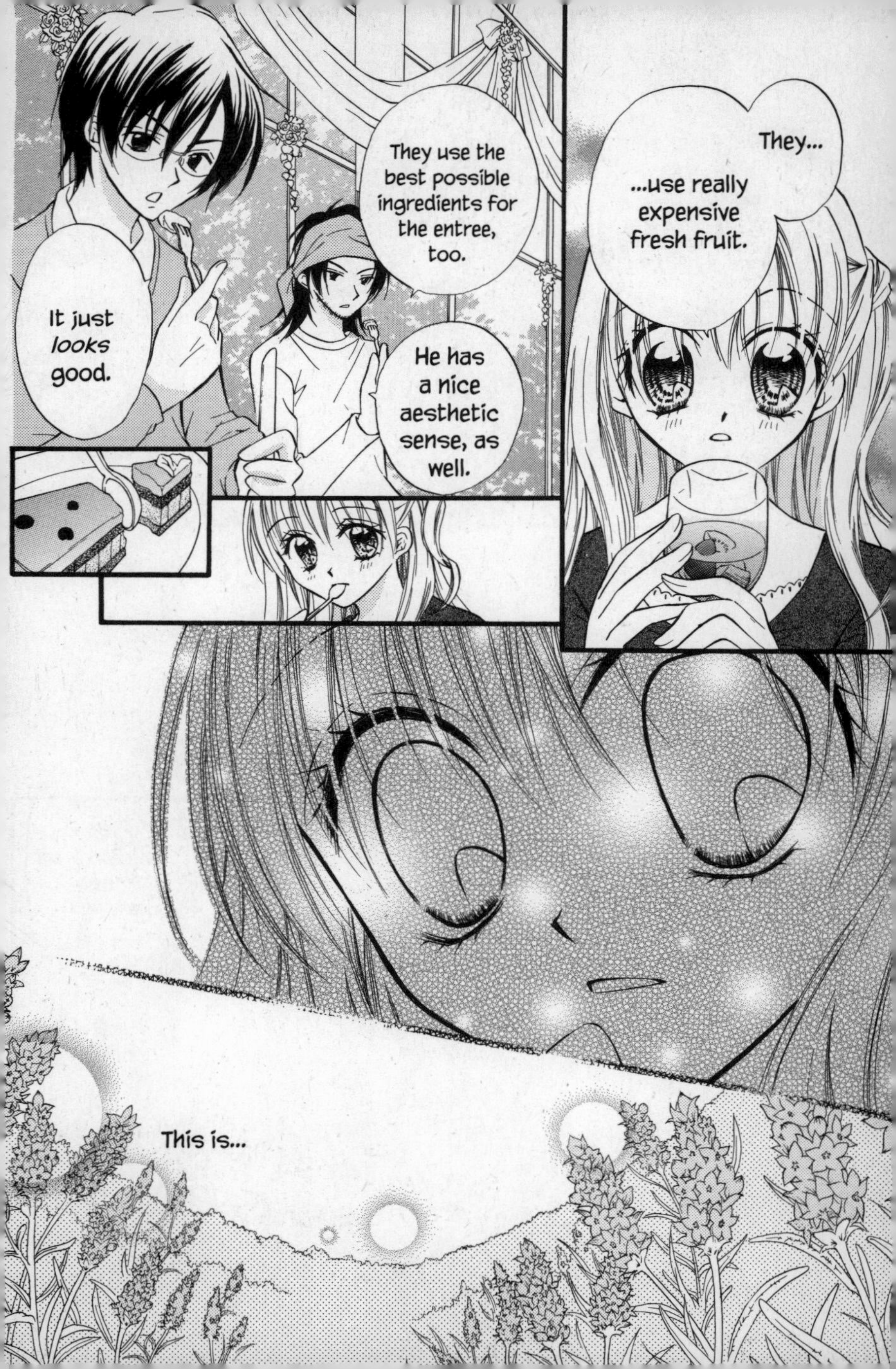
They...
...use really expensive fresh fruit.
They use the best possible ingredients for the entree, too.
It just *looks* good.
He has a nice aesthetic sense, as well.
This is...

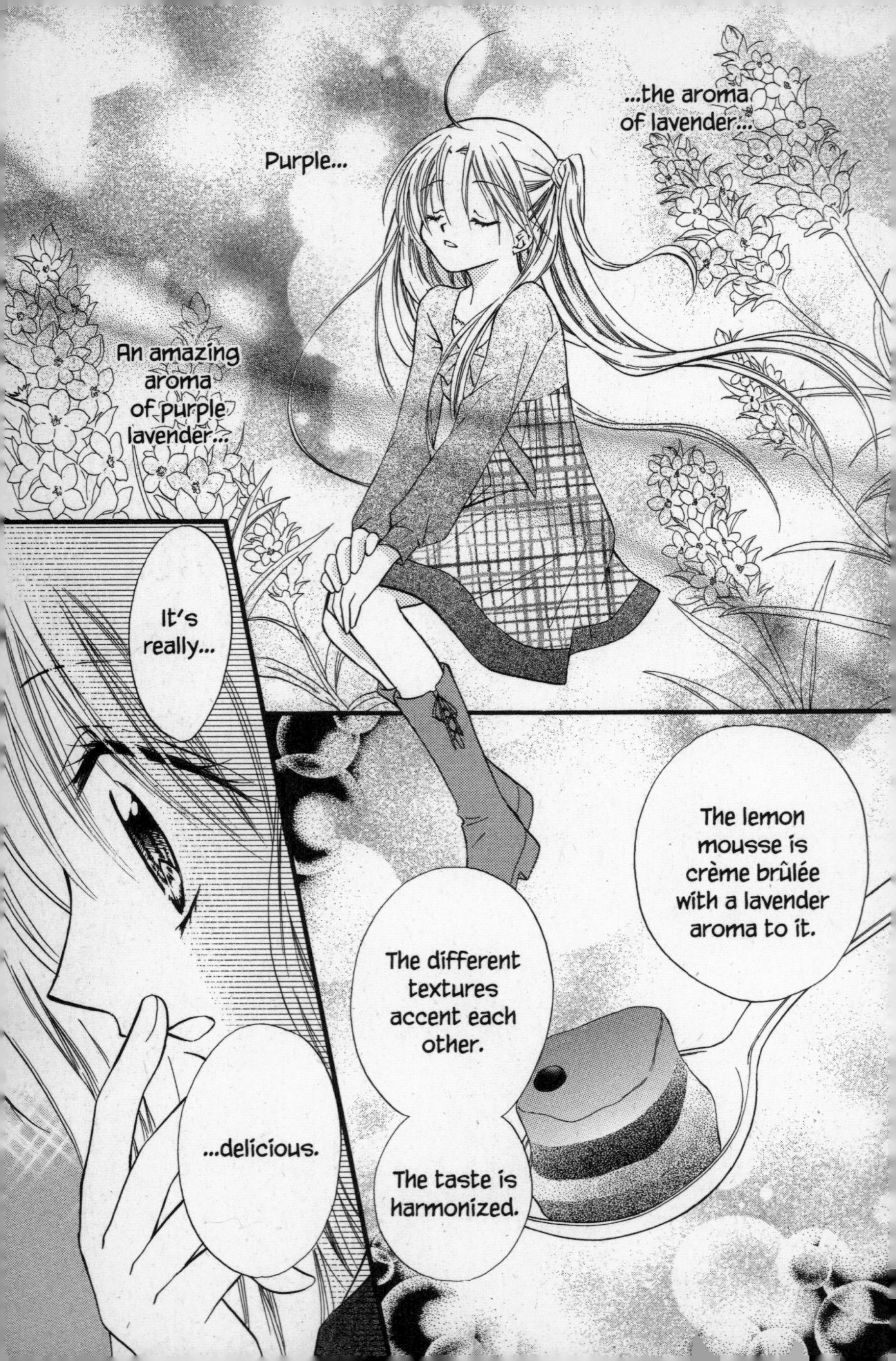
...the aroma of lavender...
Purple...
An amazing aroma of purple lavender...
The lemon mousse is crème brûlée with a lavender aroma to it.
The different textures accent each other.
The taste is harmonized.
It's really...
...delicious.

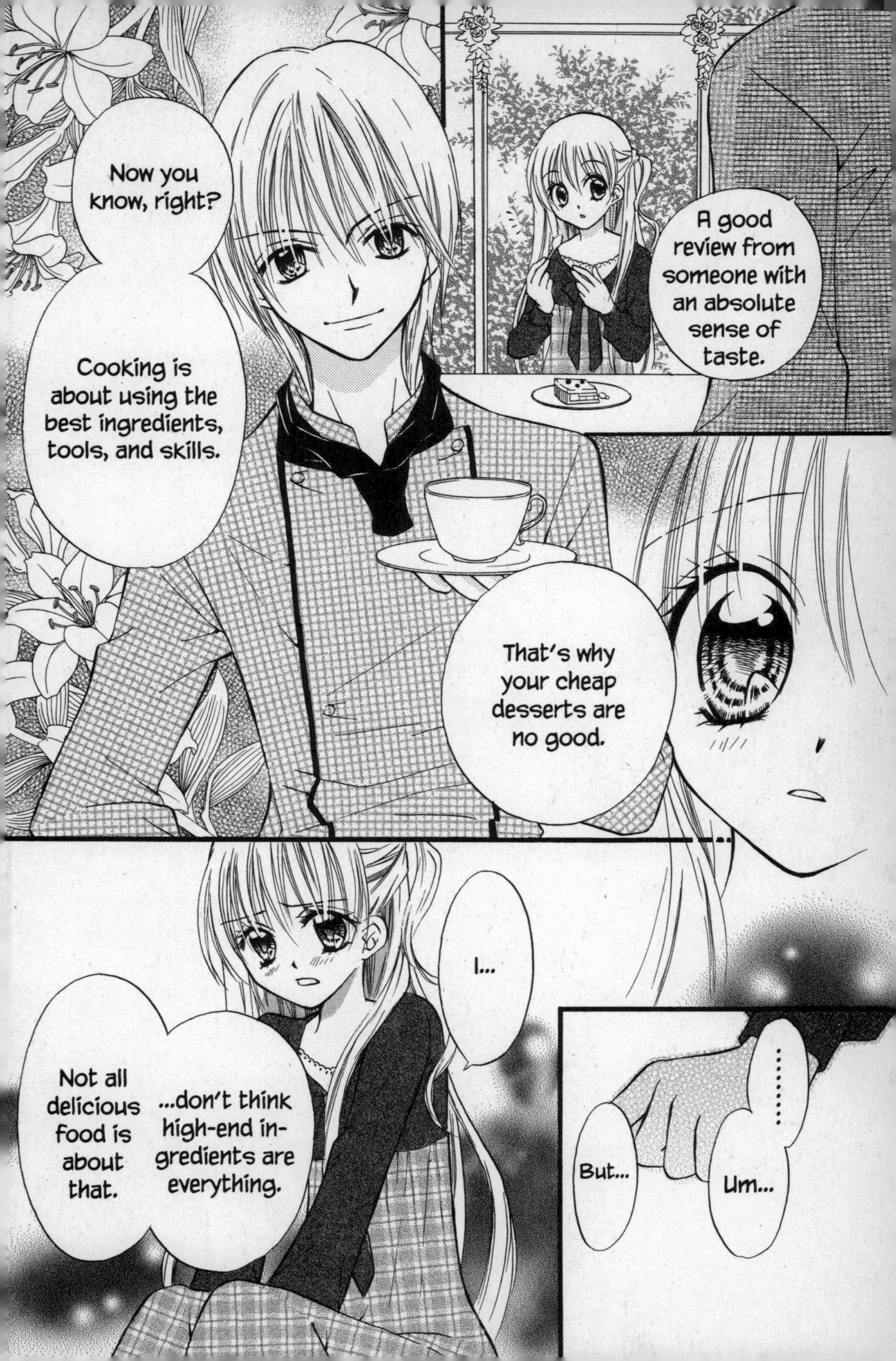
A good review from someone with an absolute sense of taste.
Now you know, right?
Cooking is about using the best ingredients, tools, and skills.
That's why your cheap desserts are no good.
......
Um...
But...
I...
...don't think high-end in-gredients are everything.
Not all delicious food is about that.

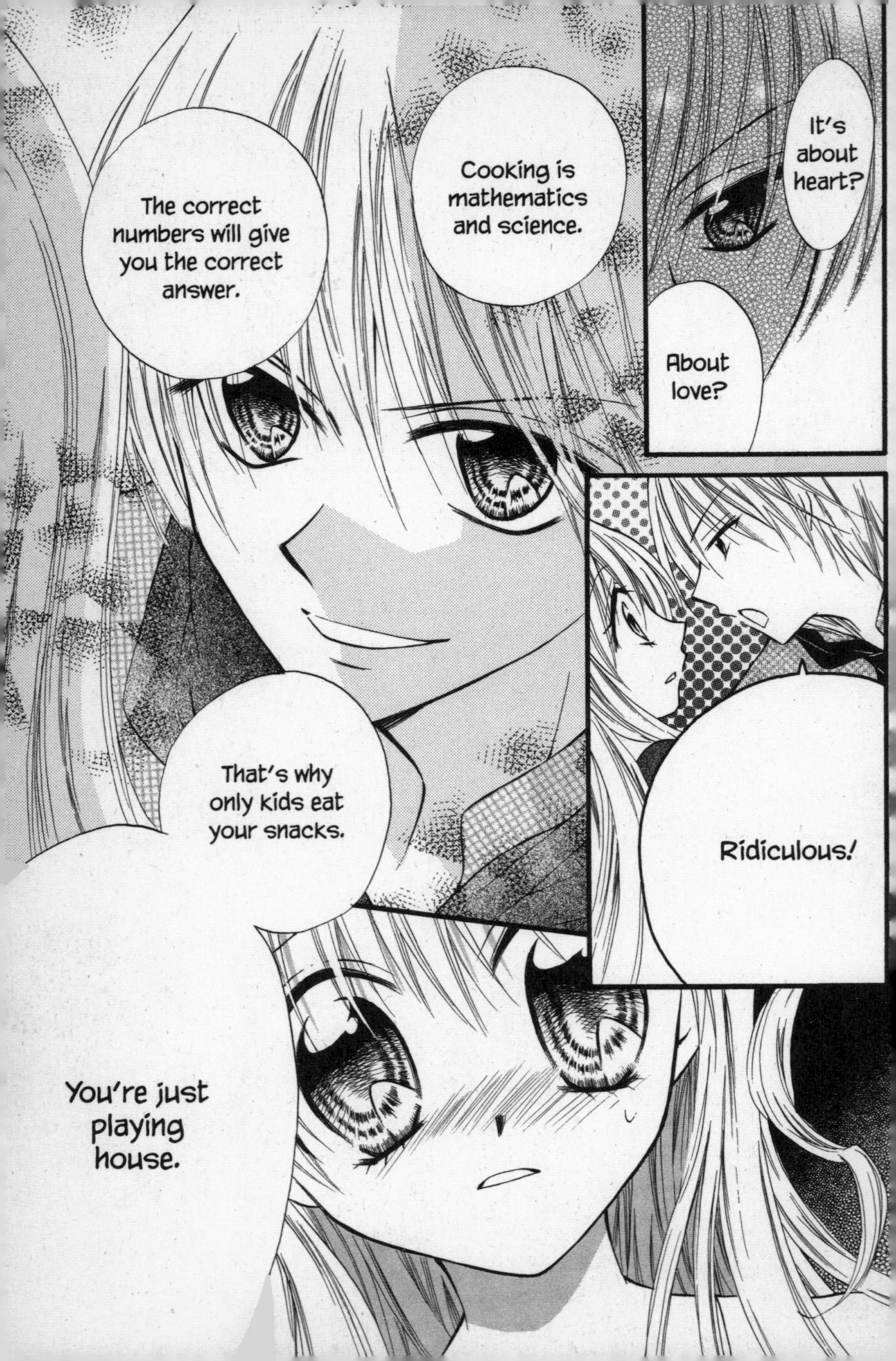

It's about heart?
About love?
Ridiculous!
Cooking is mathematics and science.
The correct numbers will give you the correct answer.
That's why only kids eat your snacks.
You're just playing house.

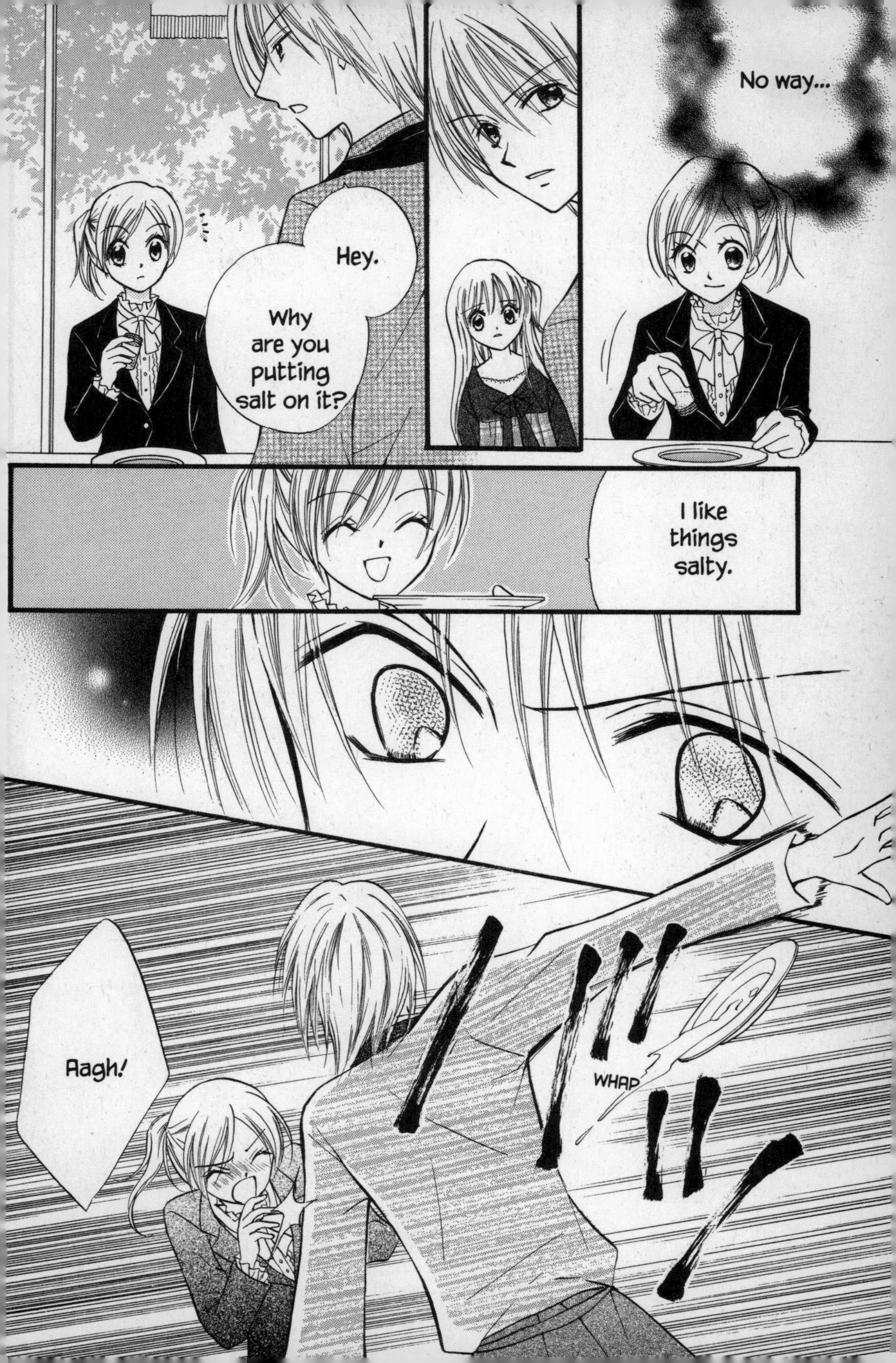
No way...
Hey.
Why are you putting salt on it?
I like things salty.
WHAP
Aagh!

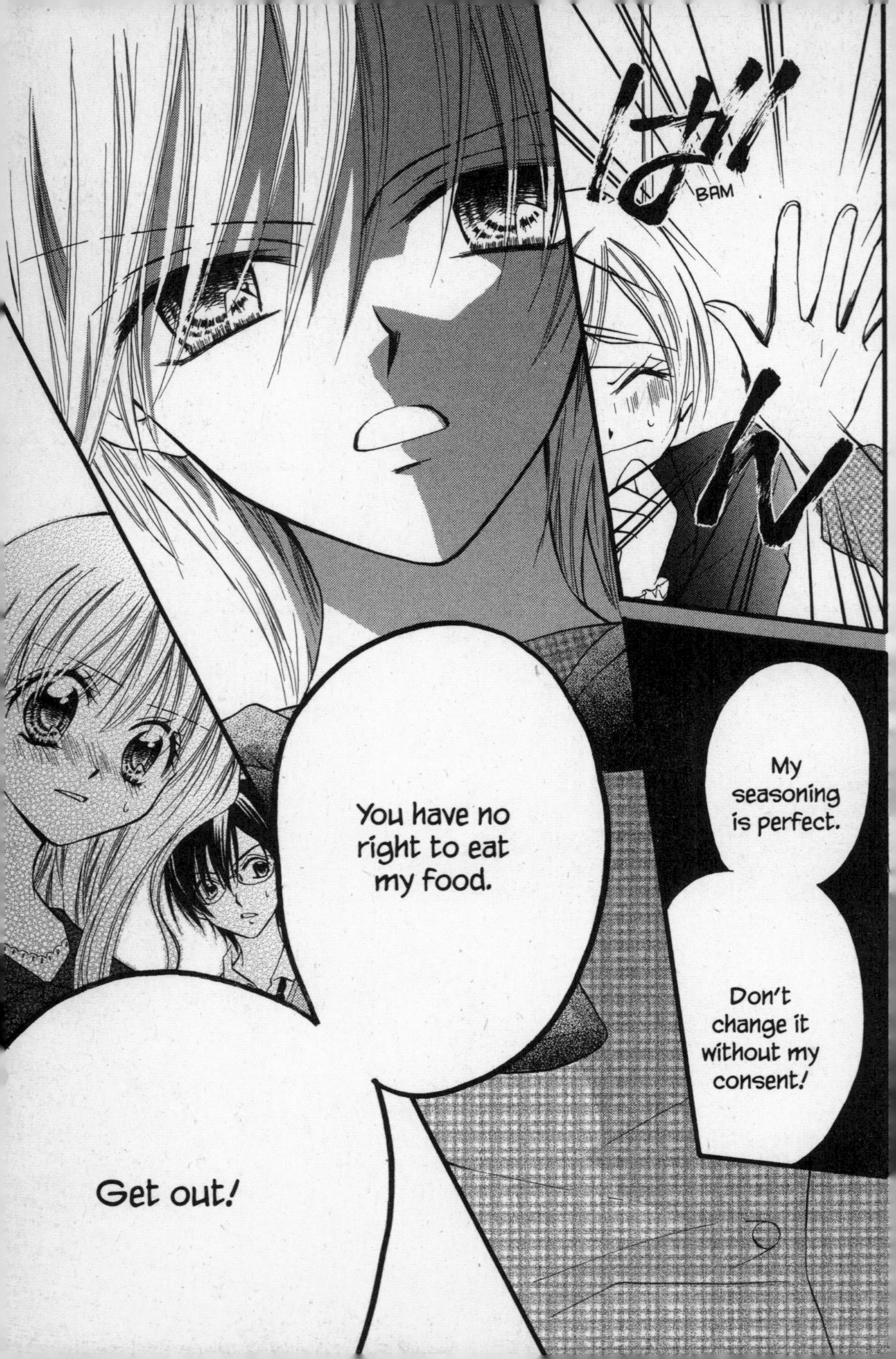
ばん
BAM
My seasoning is perfect.
Don't change it without my consent!
You have no right to eat my food.
Get out!

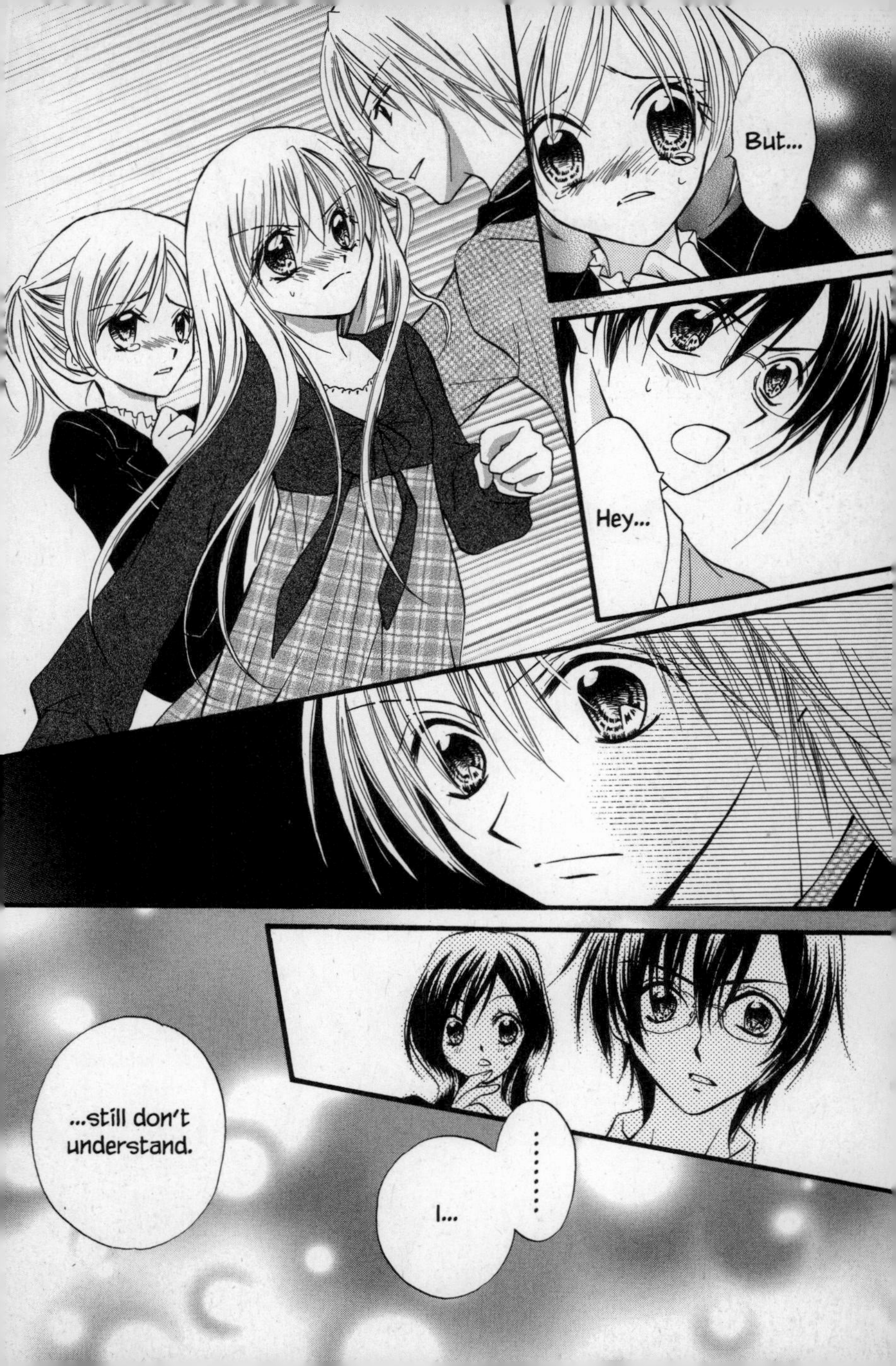
But...
Hey...
......
I...
...still don't understand.

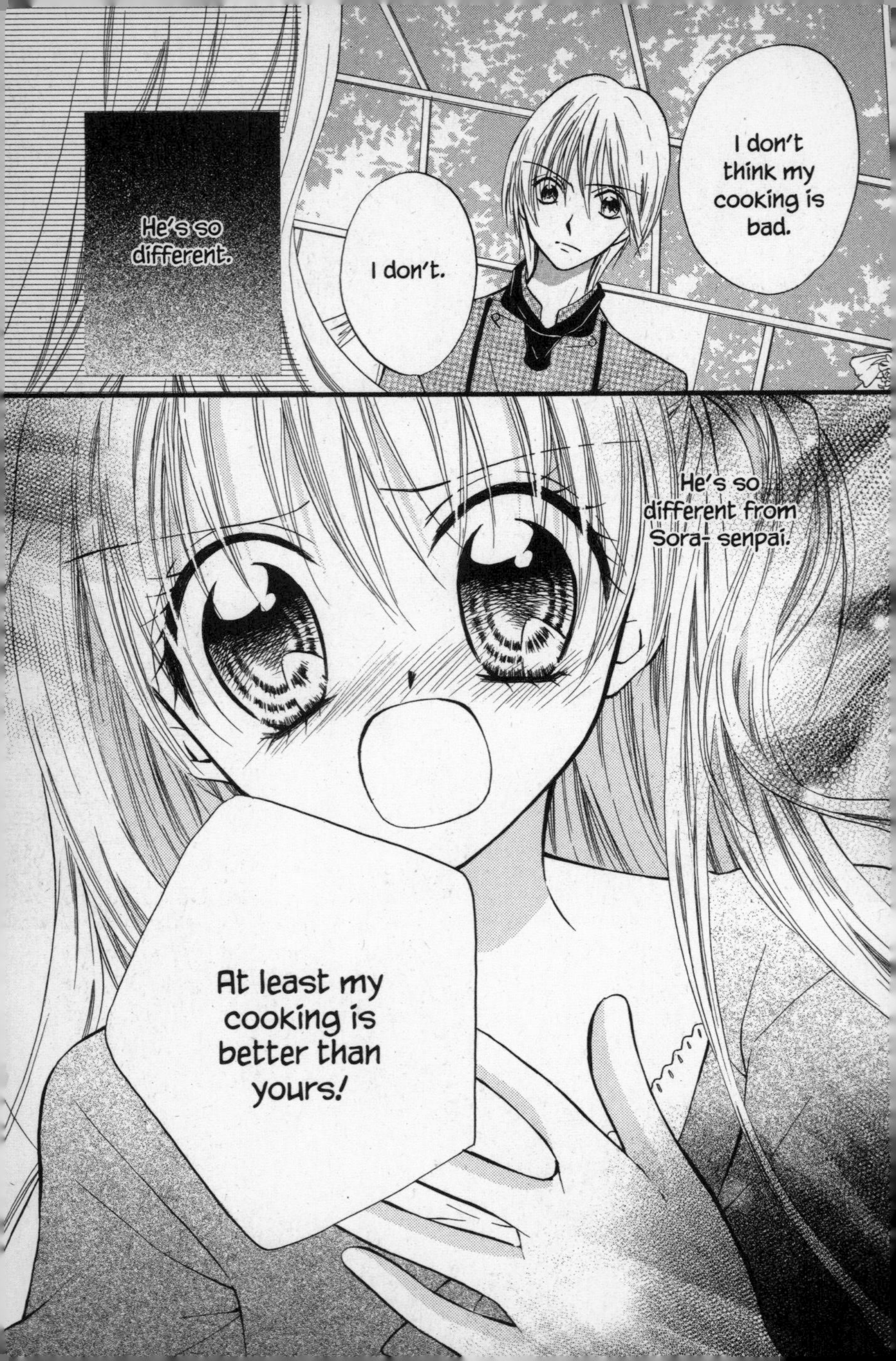
I don't think my cooking is bad.
I don't.
He's so different.
He's so different from Sora- senpai.
At least my cooking is better than yours!

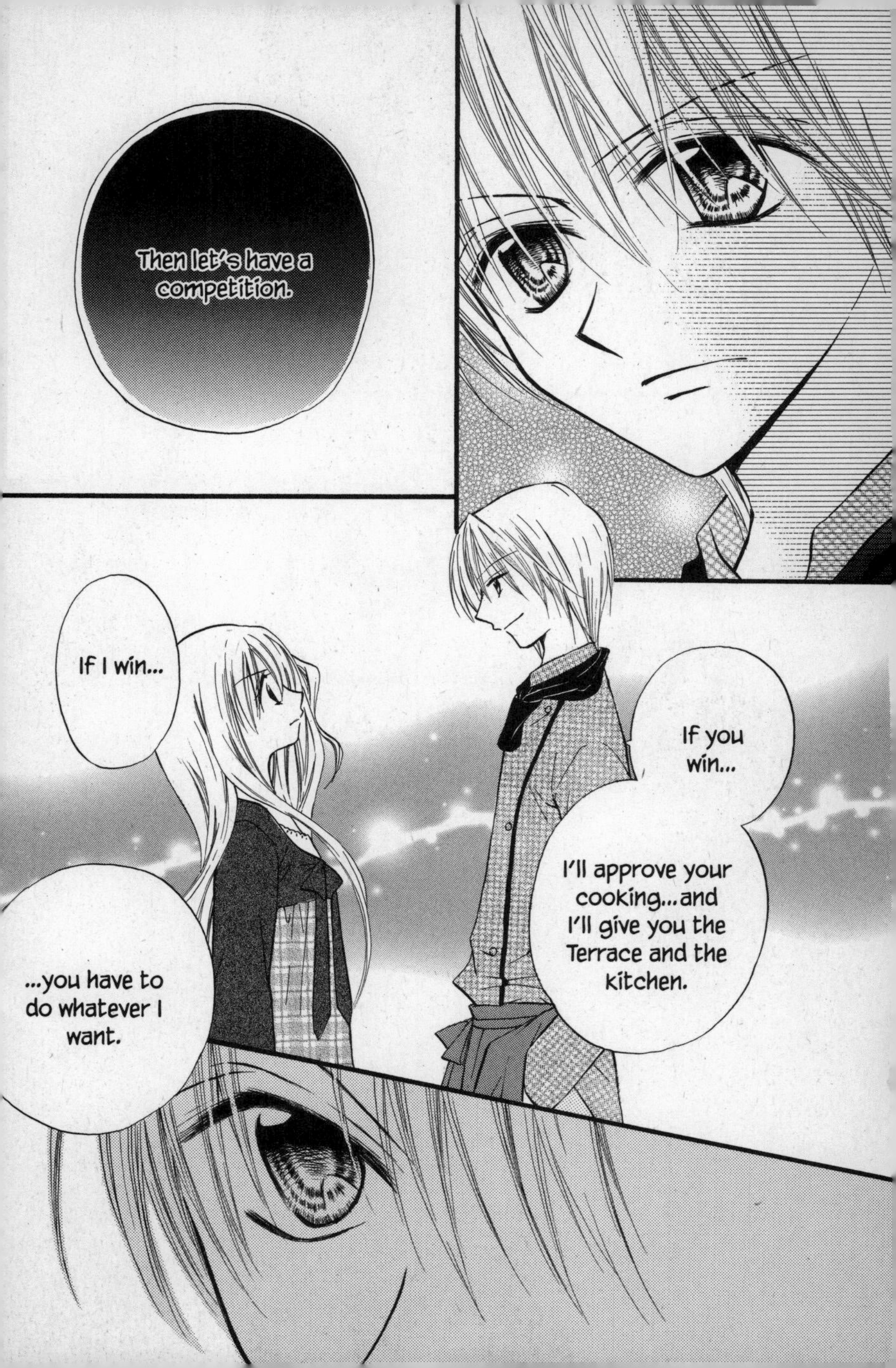
Then let's have a competition.
If you win...
I'll approve your cooking...and I'll give you the Terrace and the kitchen.
If I win...
...you have to do whatever I want.

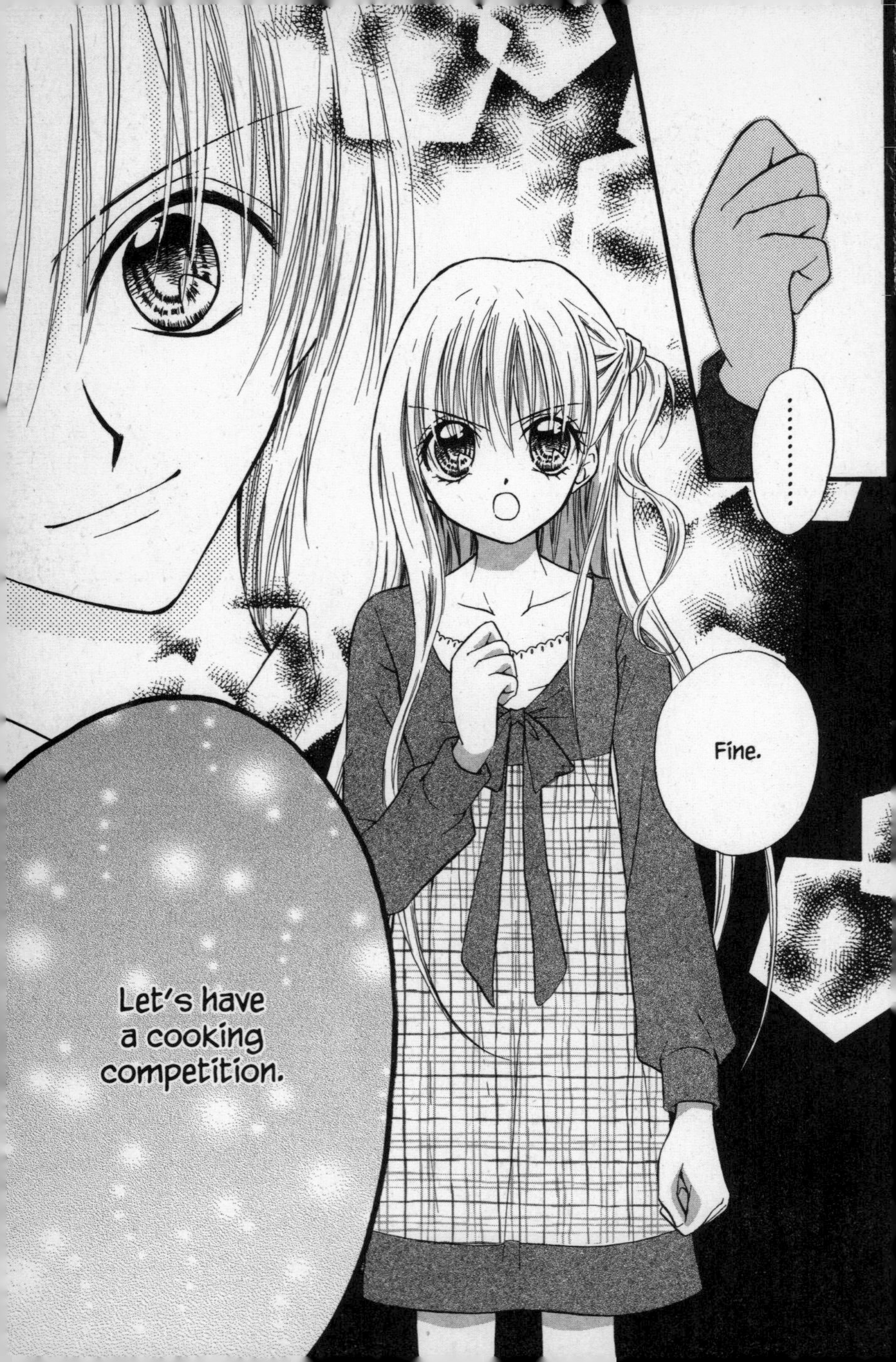
......
Fine.
Let's have a cooking competition.

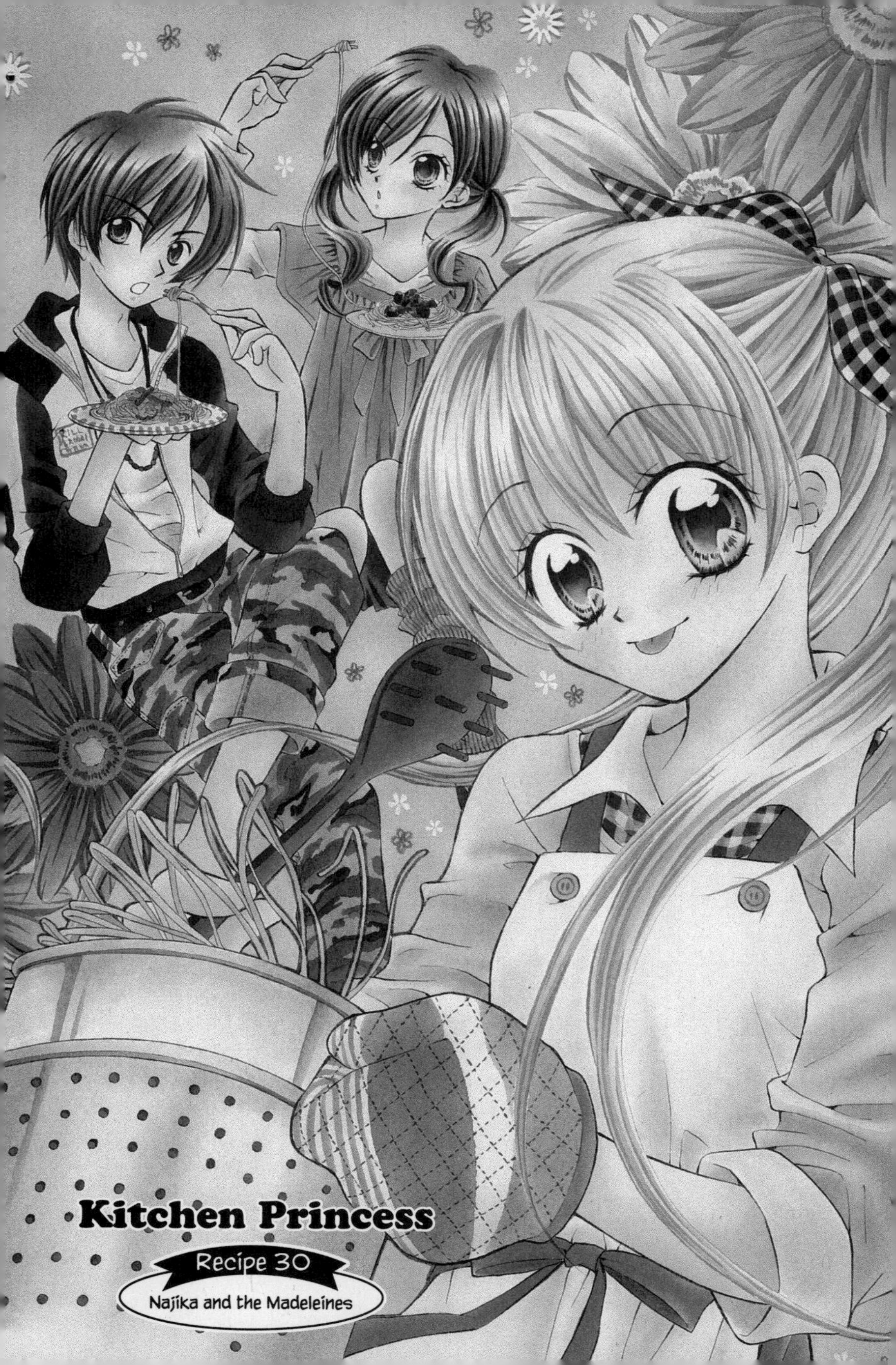
Kitchen Princess
Recipe 30
Najika and the Madeleines

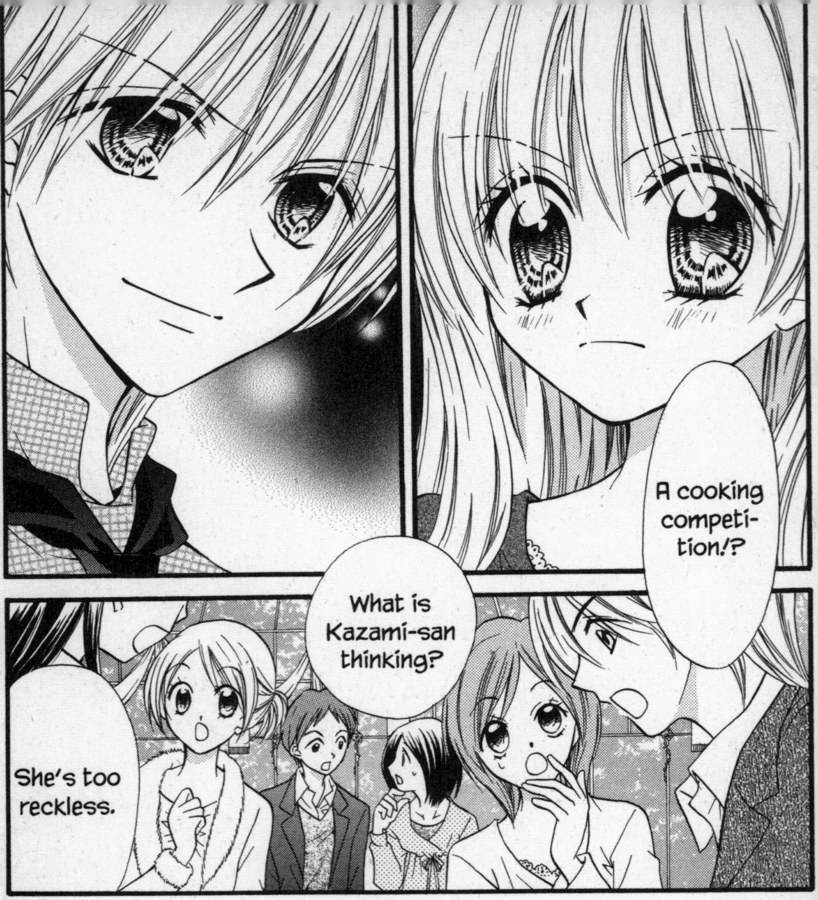
A cooking competi-tion!?
What is Kazami-san thinking?
She's too reckless.

About the Splash pages

- •Recipe 29... Since Daichi was wearing glasses in the story, I wanted to draw him the old way so I put him in the splash page.
- •Recipe 30... I was really into pasta at the time. With pasta, I don't mind eating vegetables I usually avoid. Pasta is great!!
- •Recipe 31... We had a new character but he hadn't been on a splash page yet, so I put him here.
- •Recipe 32... I went to a fancy restaurant where they used a cute combination of colors, so I used the same combination as the background. It's sky blue and turquoise.
- •Recipe 33... I wanted to make it shadowy, so I didn't use screen tones at all. I like drawing the characters in a stylized way.

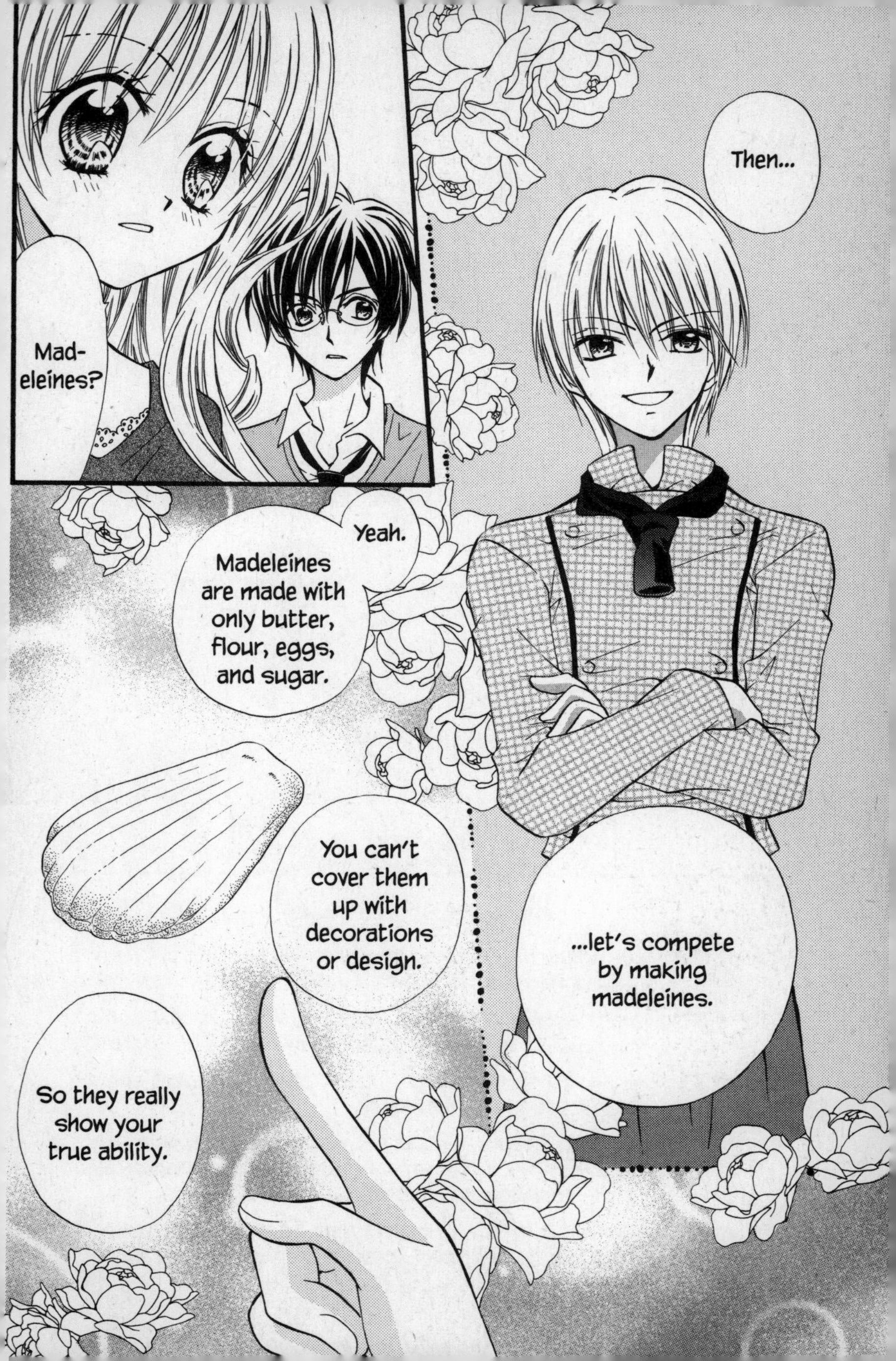

Then...
...let's compete by making madeleines.
Madeleines?
Yeah.
Madeleines are made with only butter, flour, eggs, and sugar.
You can't cover them up with decorations or design.
So they really show your true ability.

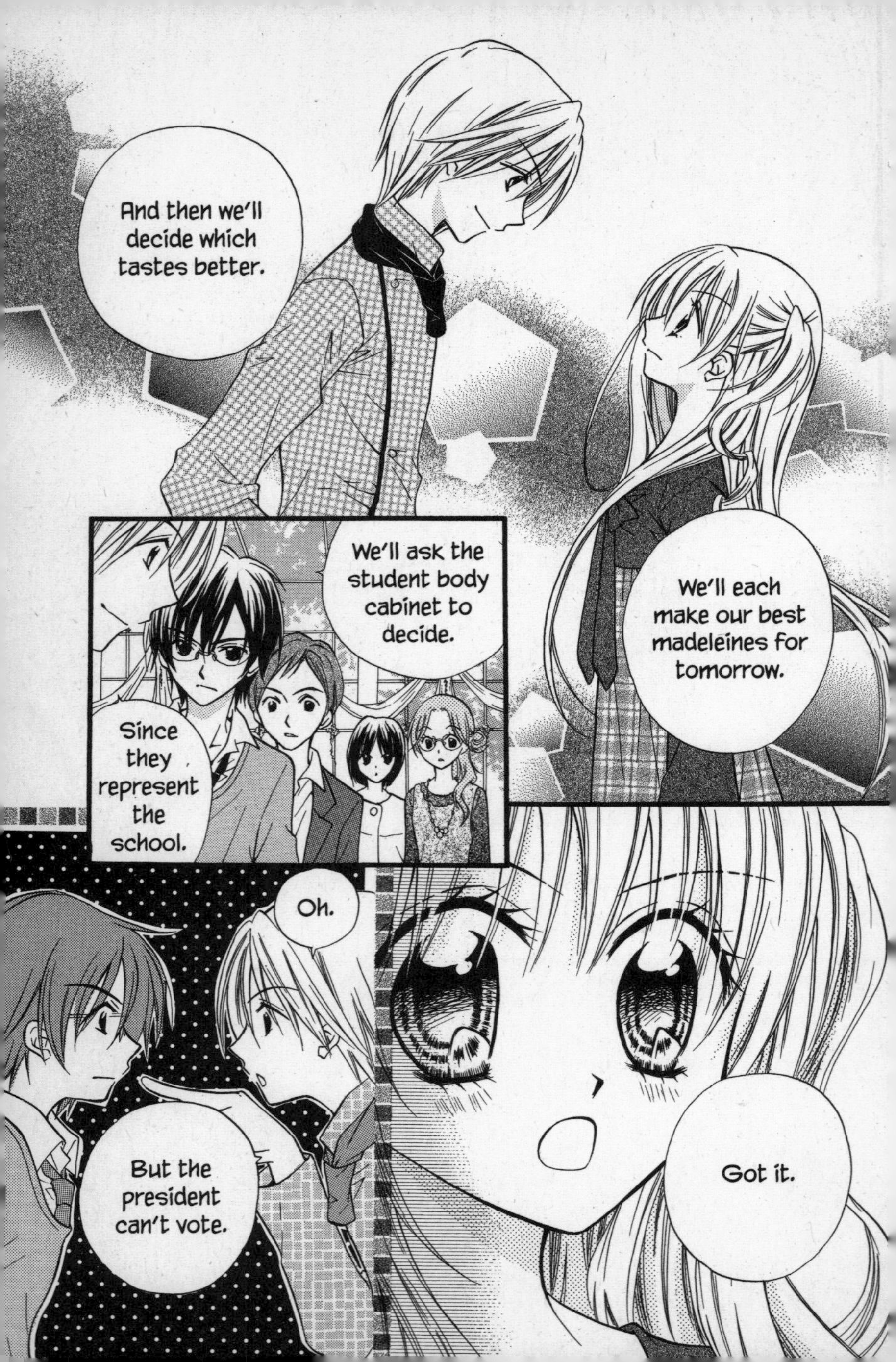

We'll each make our best madeleines for tomorrow.
And then we'll decide which tastes better.
We'll ask the student body cabinet to decide.
Since they represent the school.
Got it.
Oh.
But the president can't vote.

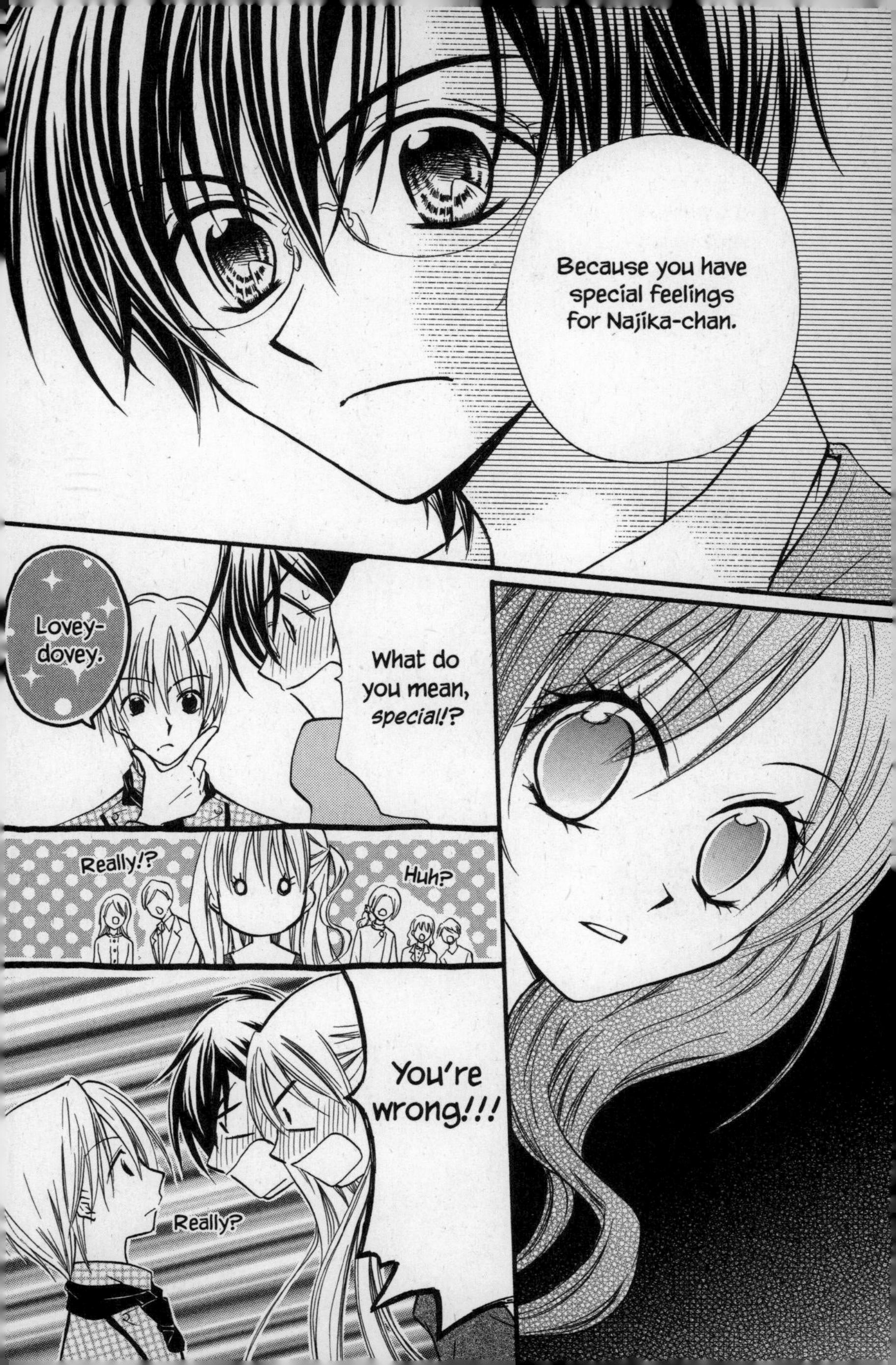
Because you have special feelings for Najika-chan.
What do you mean, *special!?*
Lovey-dovey.
Huh?
Really!?
You're wrong!!!
Really?

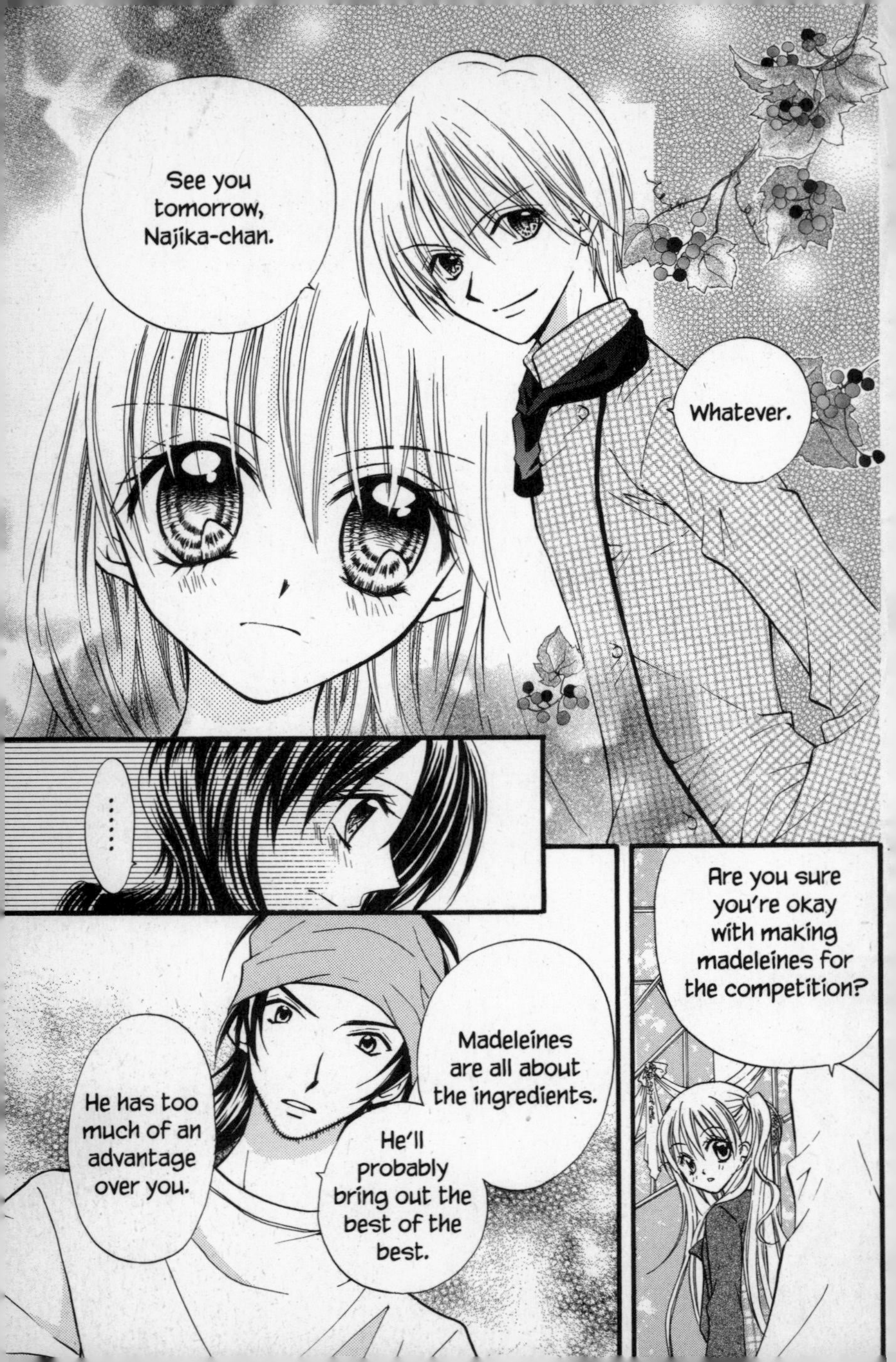
See you tomorrow, Najika-chan.
Whatever.
......
Are you sure you're okay with making madeleines for the competition?
Madeleines are all about the ingredients.
He'll probably bring out the best of the best.
He has too much of an advantage over you.

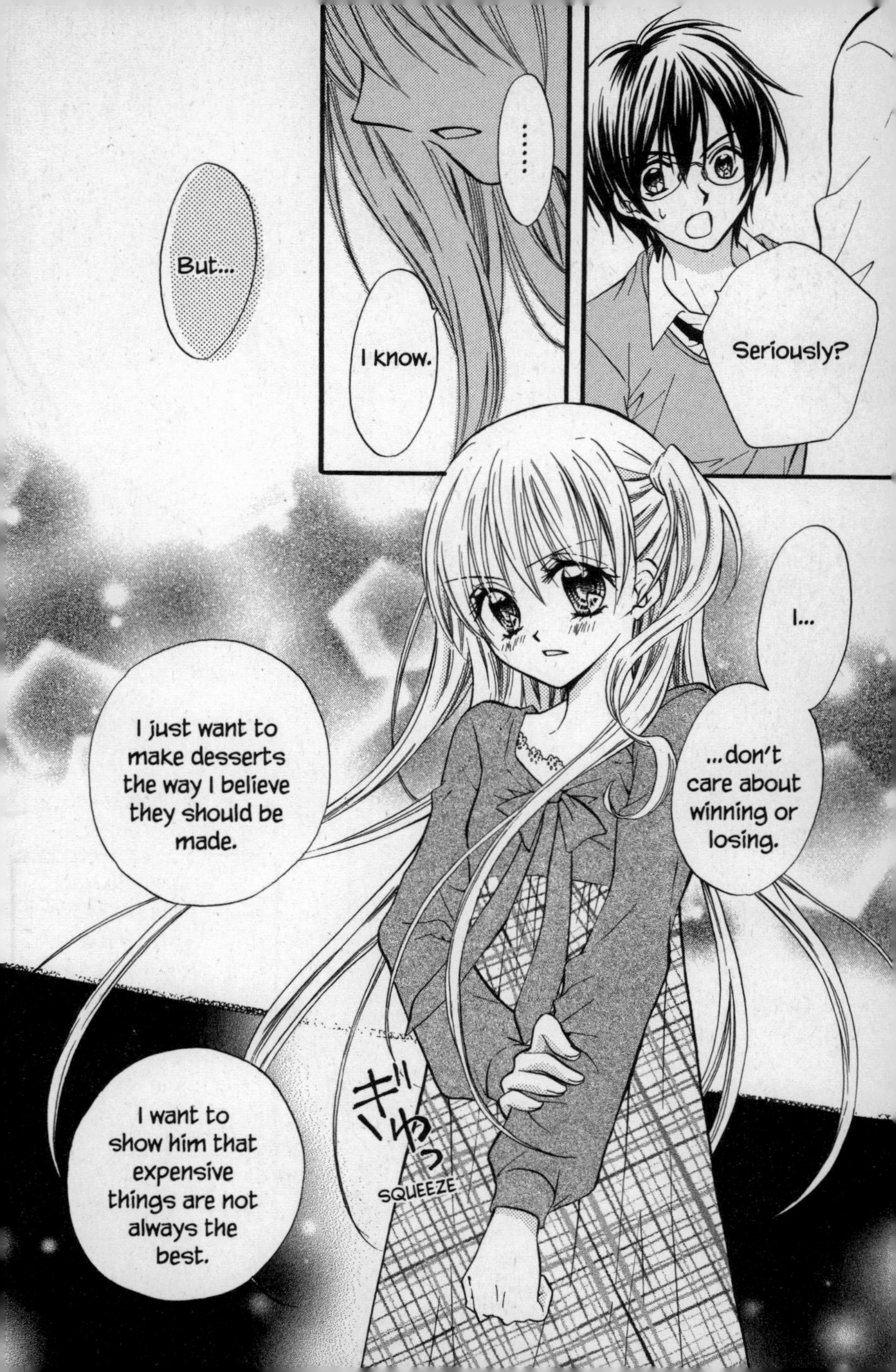
Seriously?
......
I know.
But...
I...
...don't care about winning or losing.
I just want to make desserts the way I believe they should be made.
ぎゅっ
SQUEEZE
I want to show him that expensive things are not always the best.

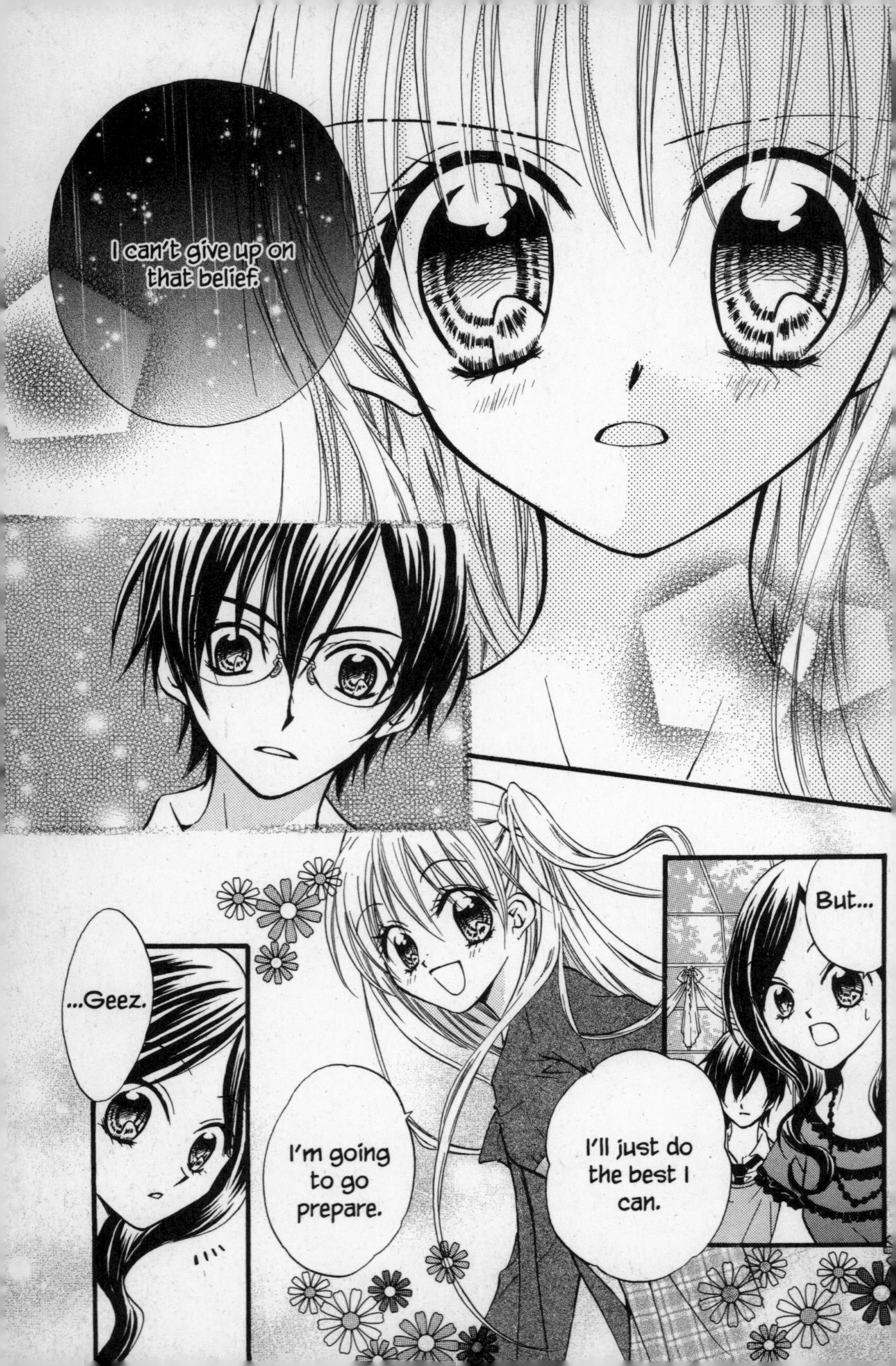
I can't give up on that belief.
But...
I'll just do the best I can.
I'm going to go prepare.
...Geez.

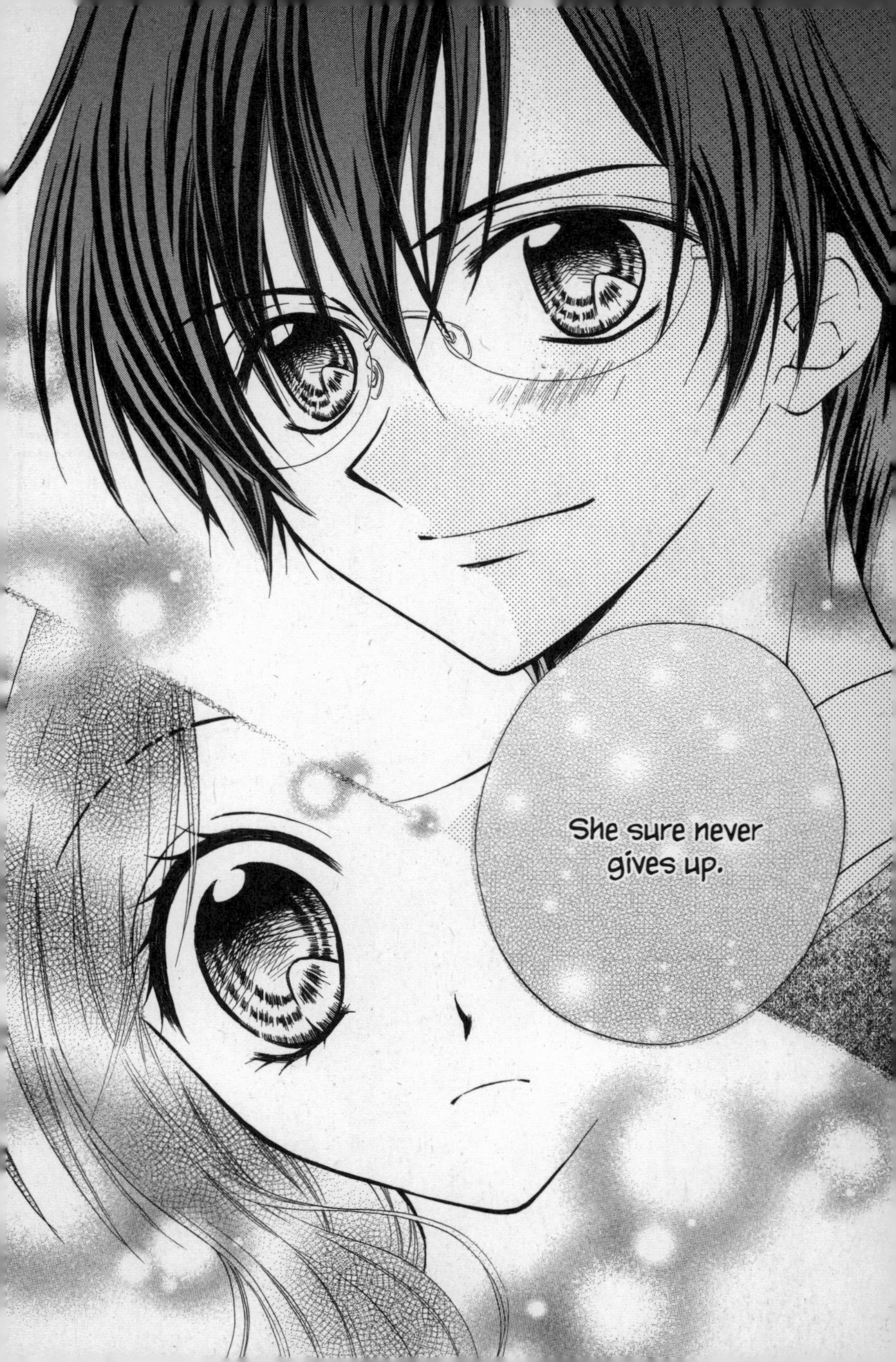
She sure never gives up.

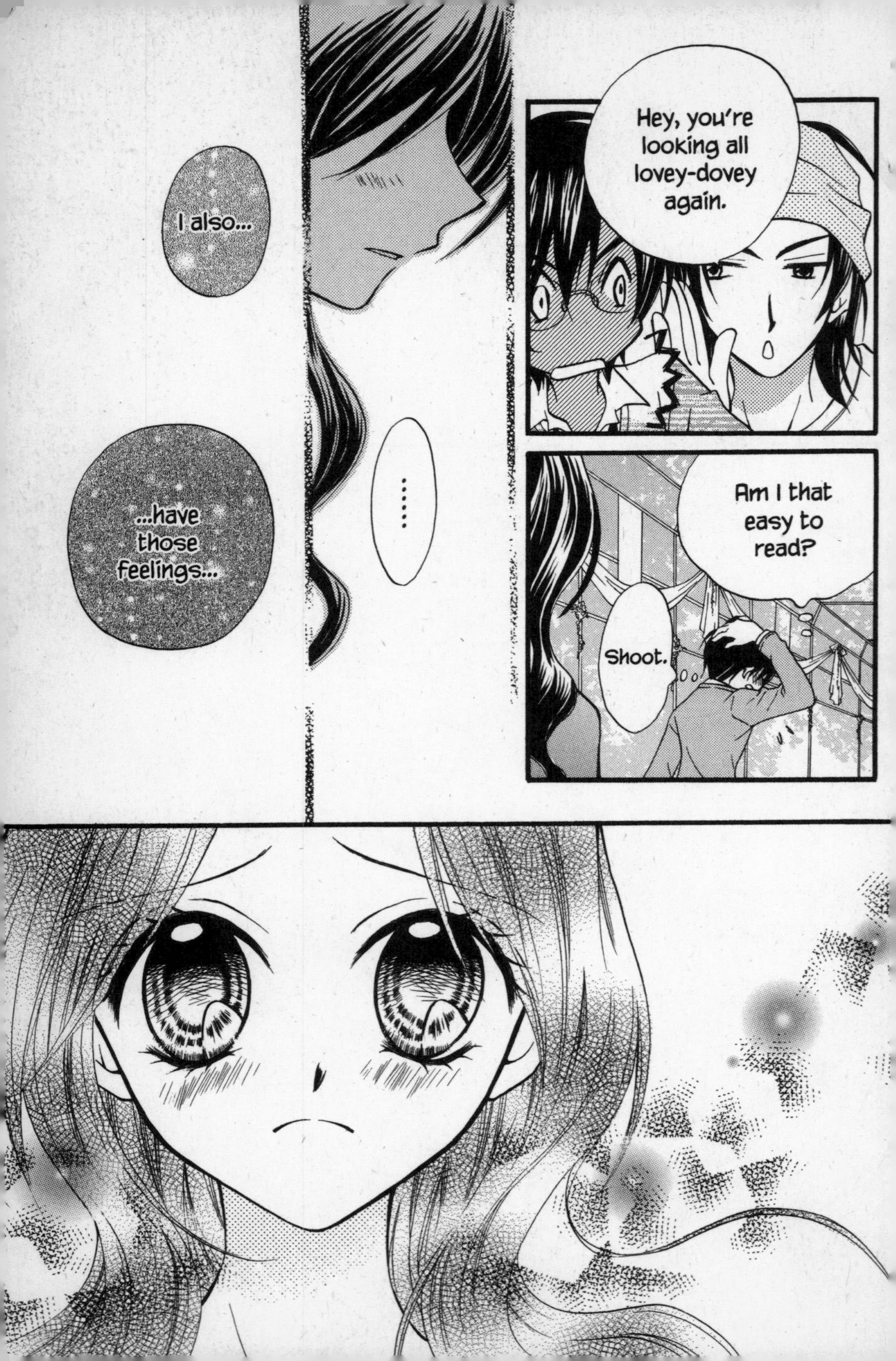
Hey, you're looking all lovey-dovey again.
Am I that easy to read?
Shoot.
......
I also...
...have those feelings...

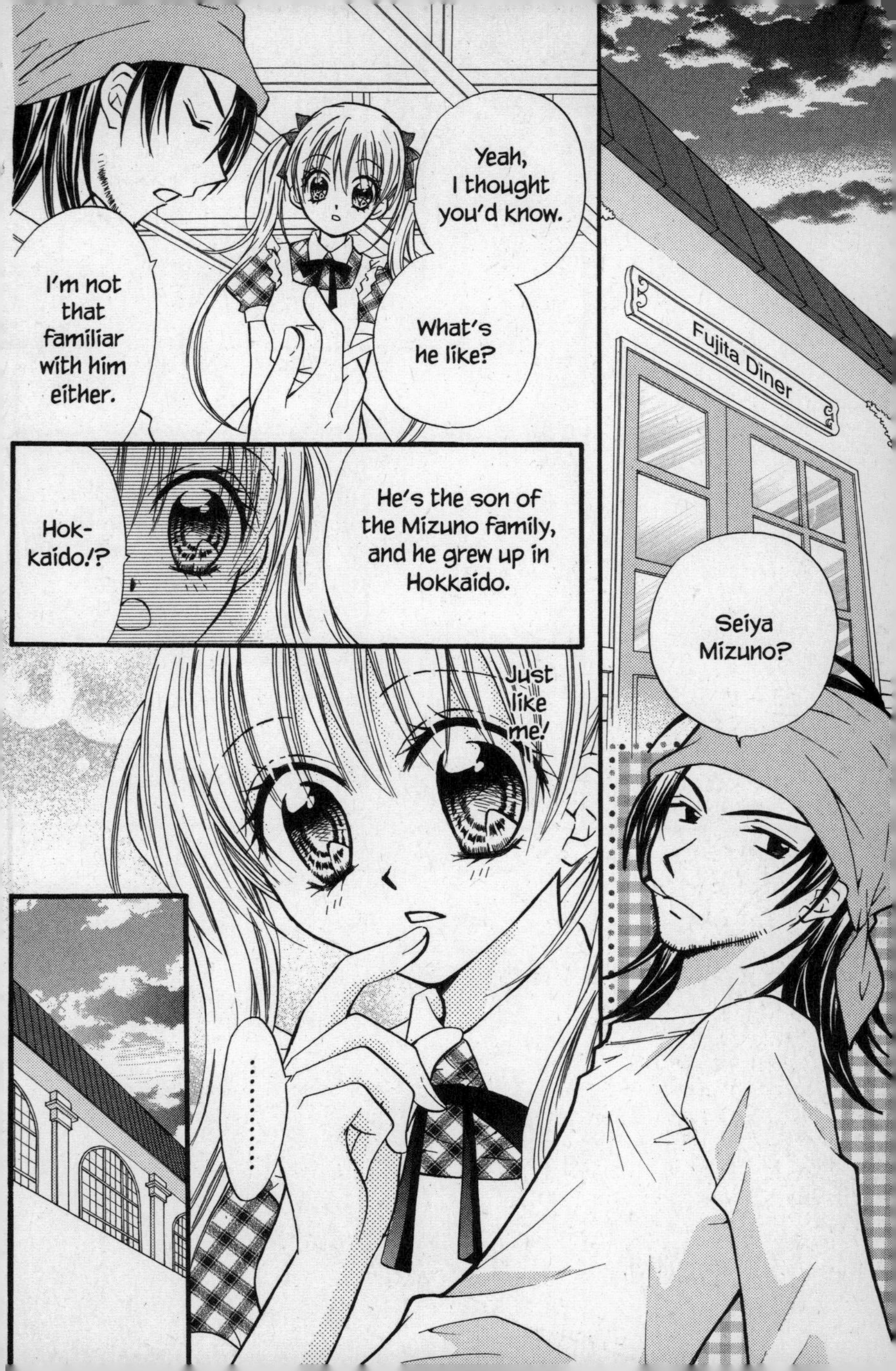

Fujita Diner
Seiya Mizuno?
Yeah, I thought you'd know.
What's he like?
I'm not that familiar with him either.
He's the son of the Mizuno family, and he grew up in Hokkaido.
Hok-kaido!?
Just like me!
......

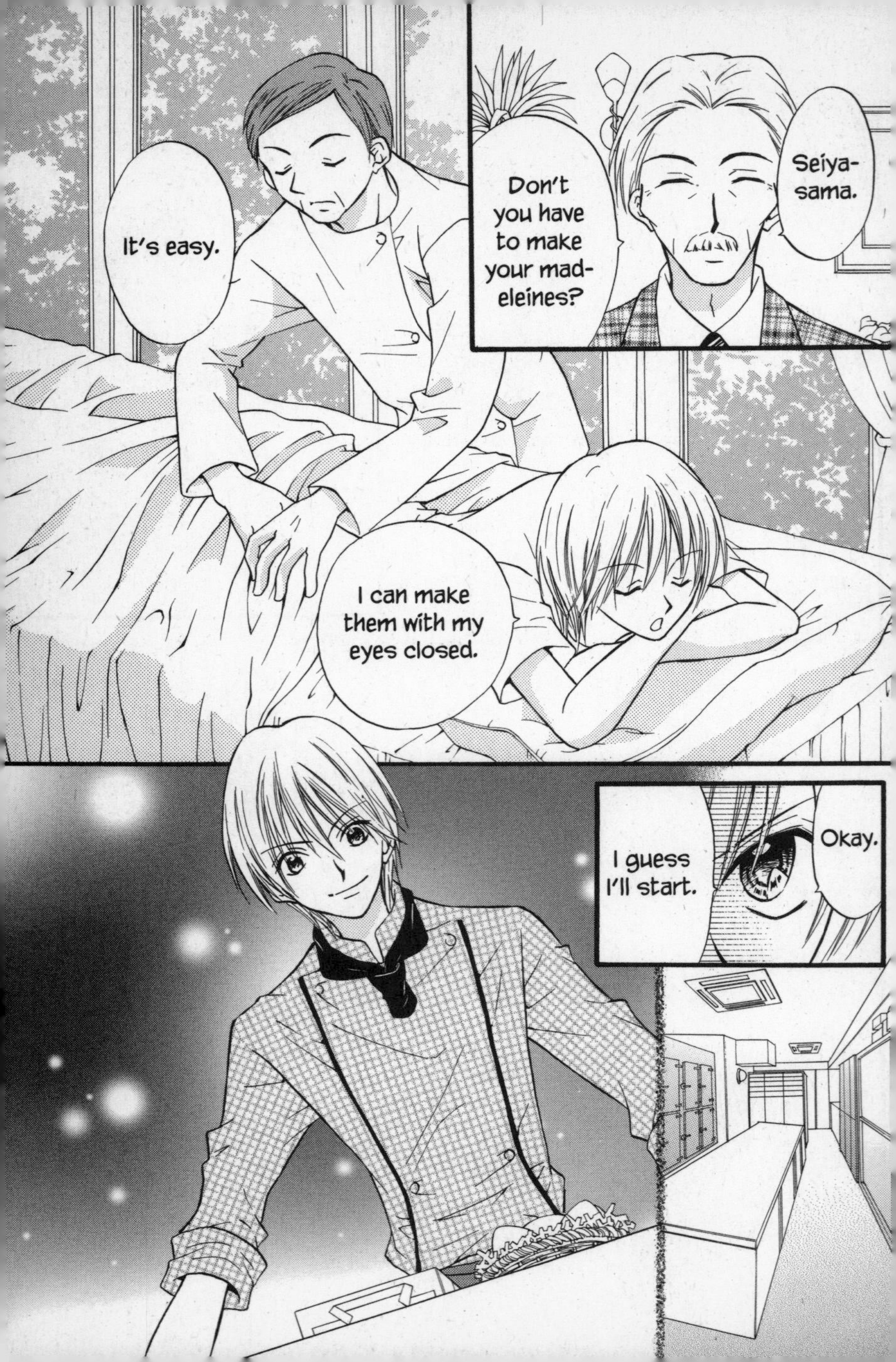
Seiya-sama.
Don't you have to make your mad-eleines?
It's easy.
I can make them with my eyes closed.
Okay.
I guess I'll start.

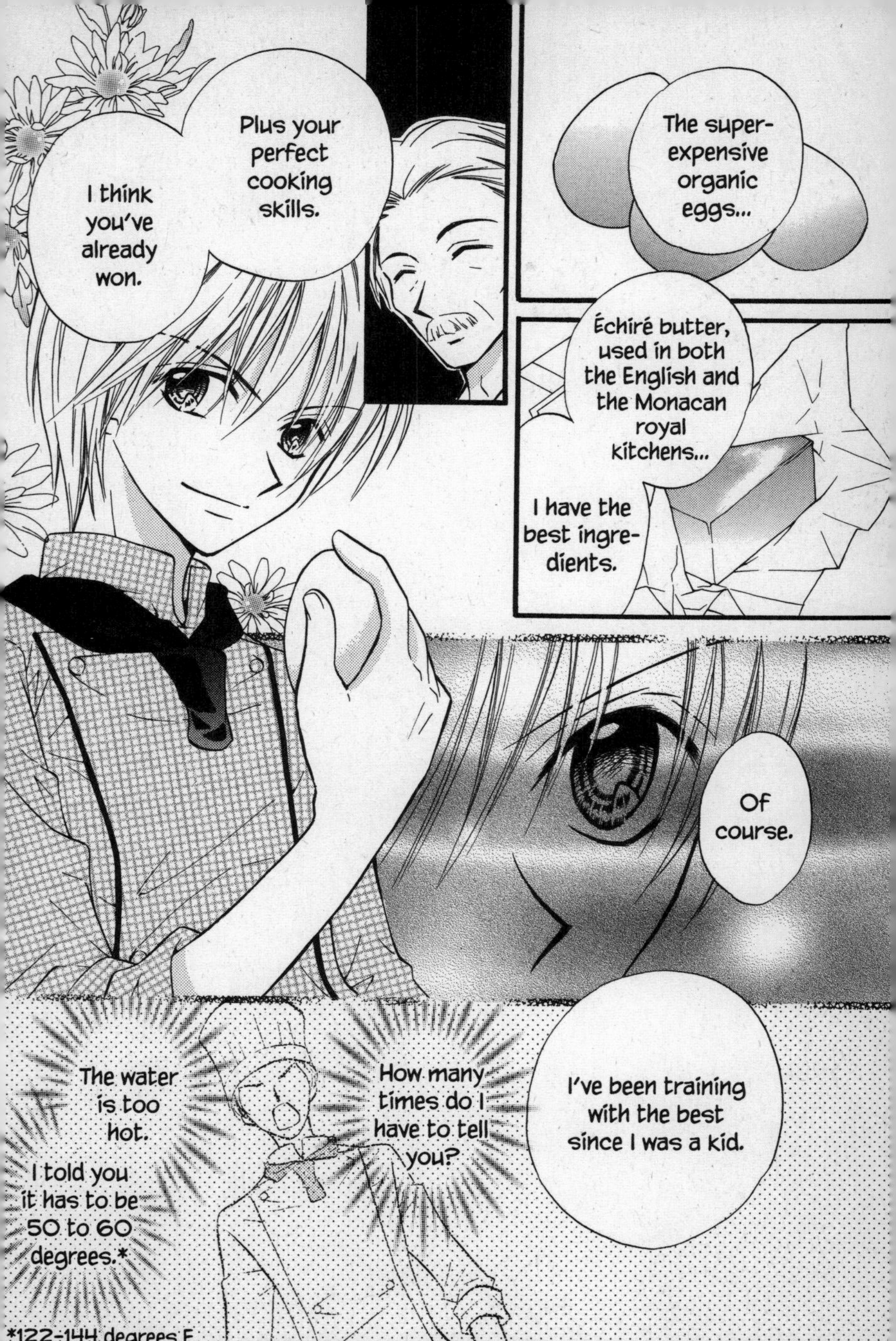
The super-expensive organic eggs...
Échiré butter, used in both the English and the Monacan royal kitchens...
I have the best ingredients.
Plus your perfect cooking skills.
I think you've already won.
Of course.
I've been training with the best since I was a kid.
How many times do I have to tell you?
The water is too hot.
I told you it has to be 50 to 60 degrees.*

*122-144 degrees F

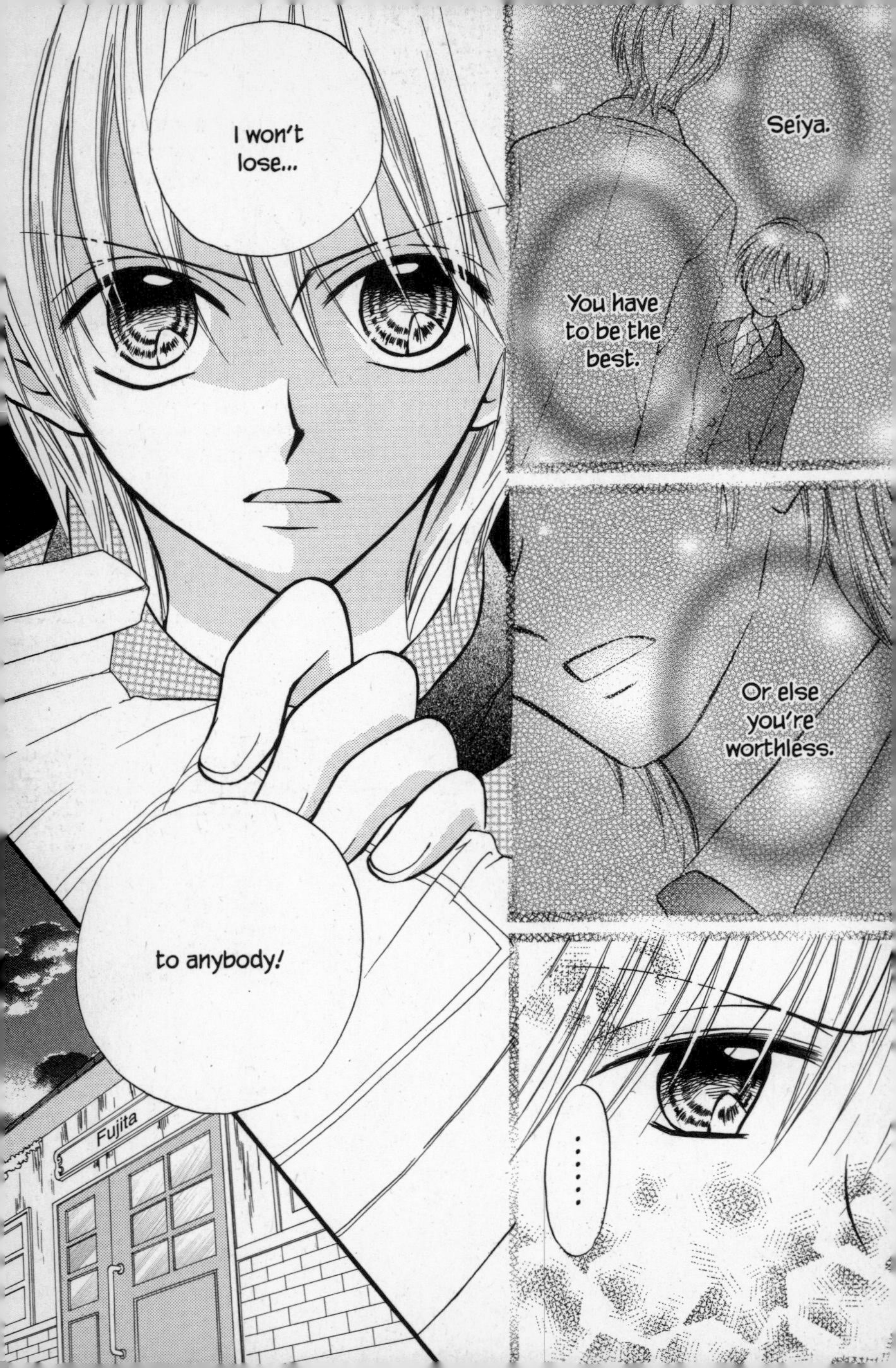
Seiya.
You have to be the best.
Or else you're worthless.
......
I won't lose...
to anybody!
Fujita

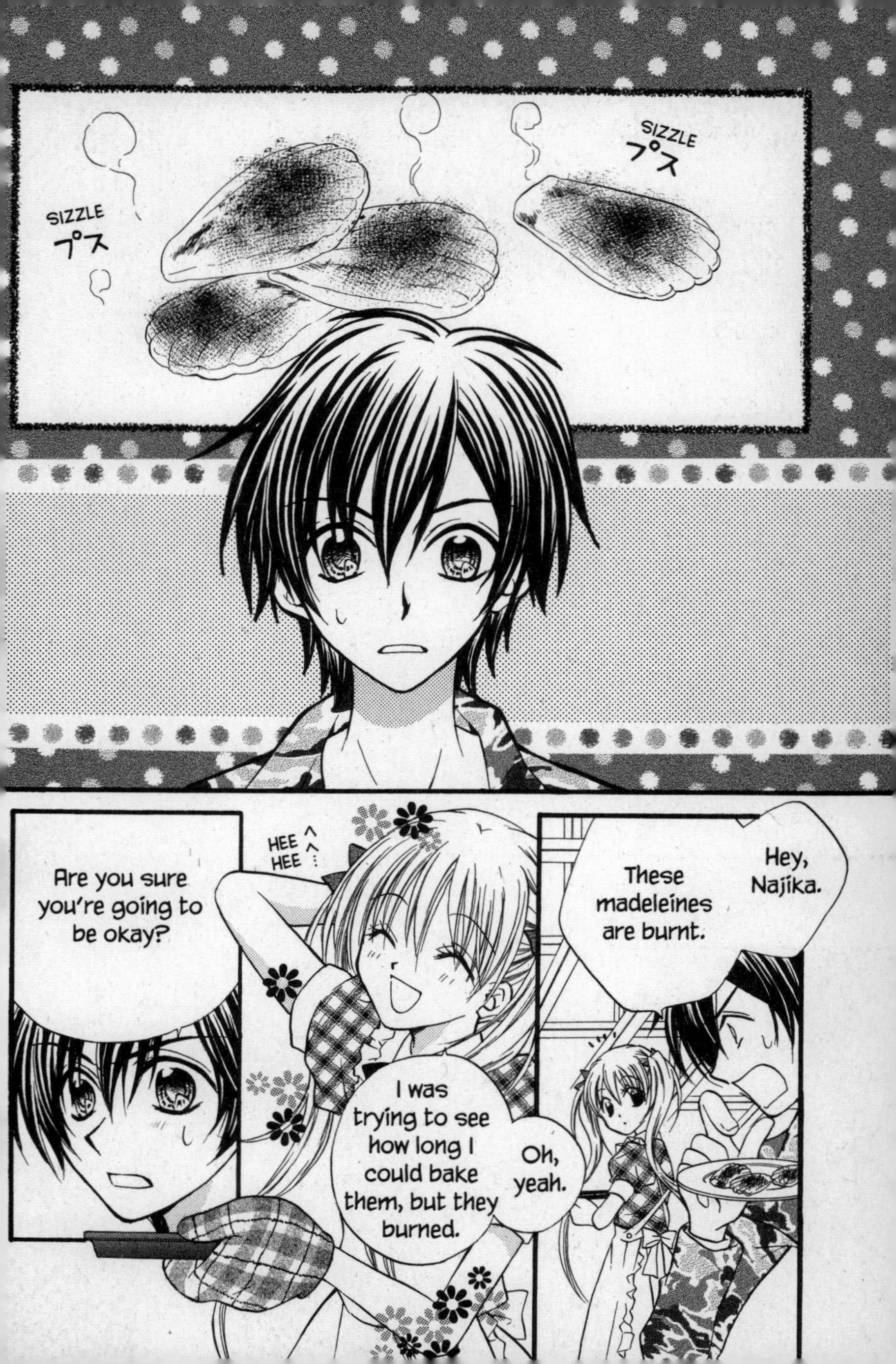
SIZZLE プス
SIZZLE プス
Hey, Najika.
These madeleines are burnt.
HEE HEE
Oh, yeah.
I was trying to see how long I could bake them, but they burned.
Are you sure you're going to be okay?

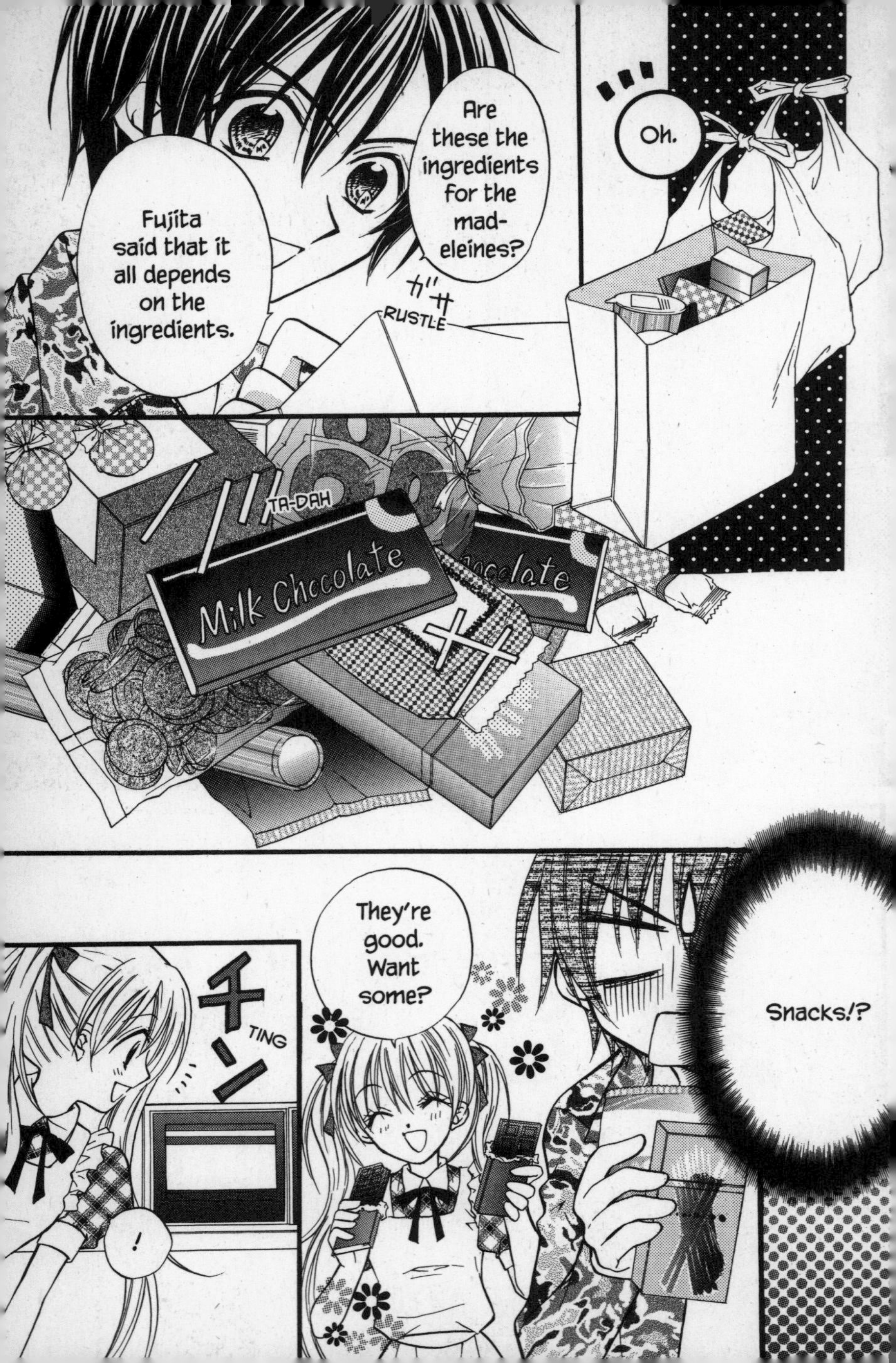

...
Oh.
Are these the ingredients for the mad-eleines?
Fujita said that it all depends on the ingredients.
RUSTLE
TA-DAH
Milk Chocolate
Snacks!?
They're good. Want some?
TING
!

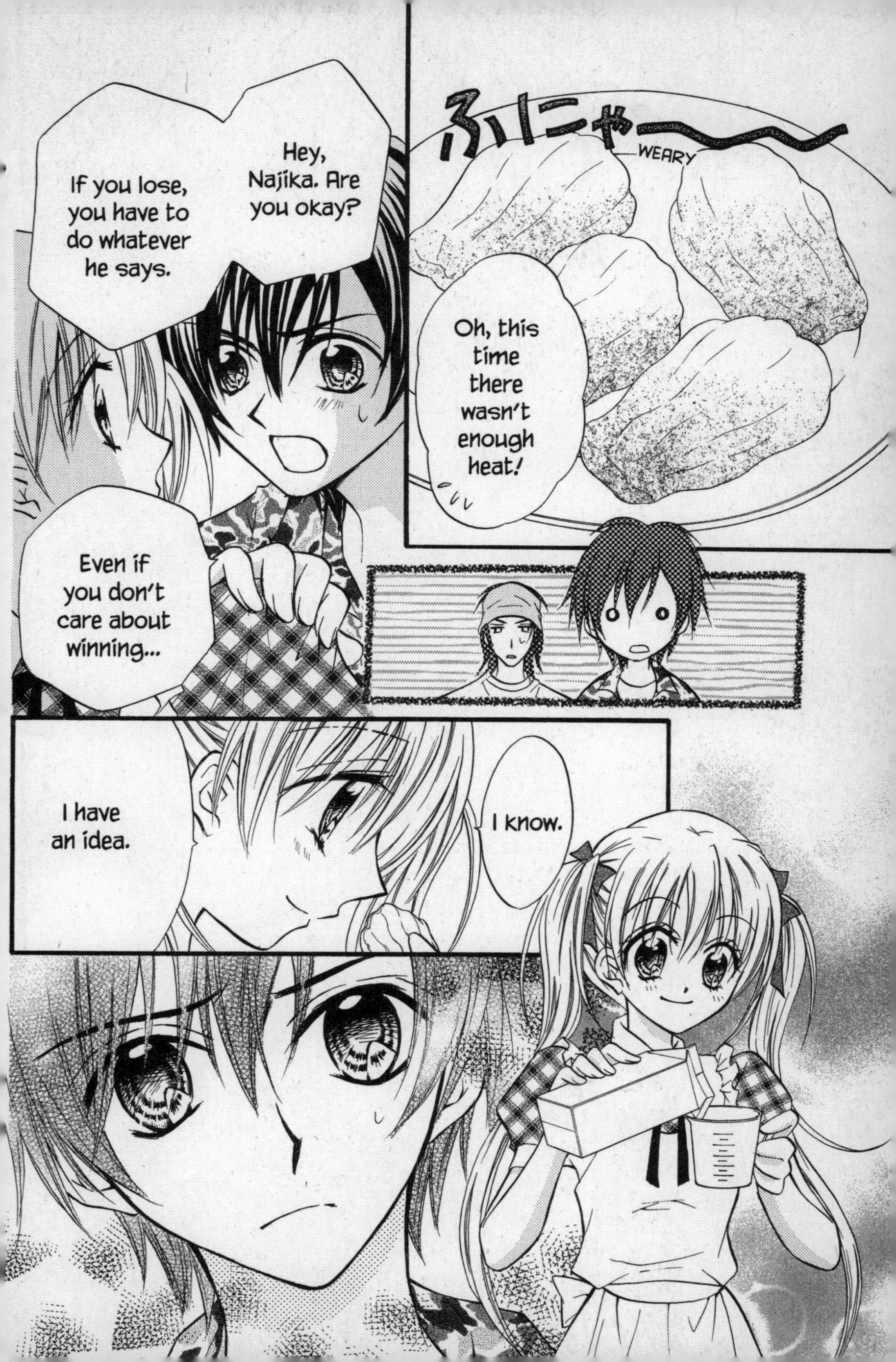

ふにゃ〜〜〜
WEARY
Oh, this time there wasn't enough heat!
Hey, Najika. Are you okay?
If you lose, you have to do whatever he says.
Even if you don't care about winning...
I know.
I have an idea.

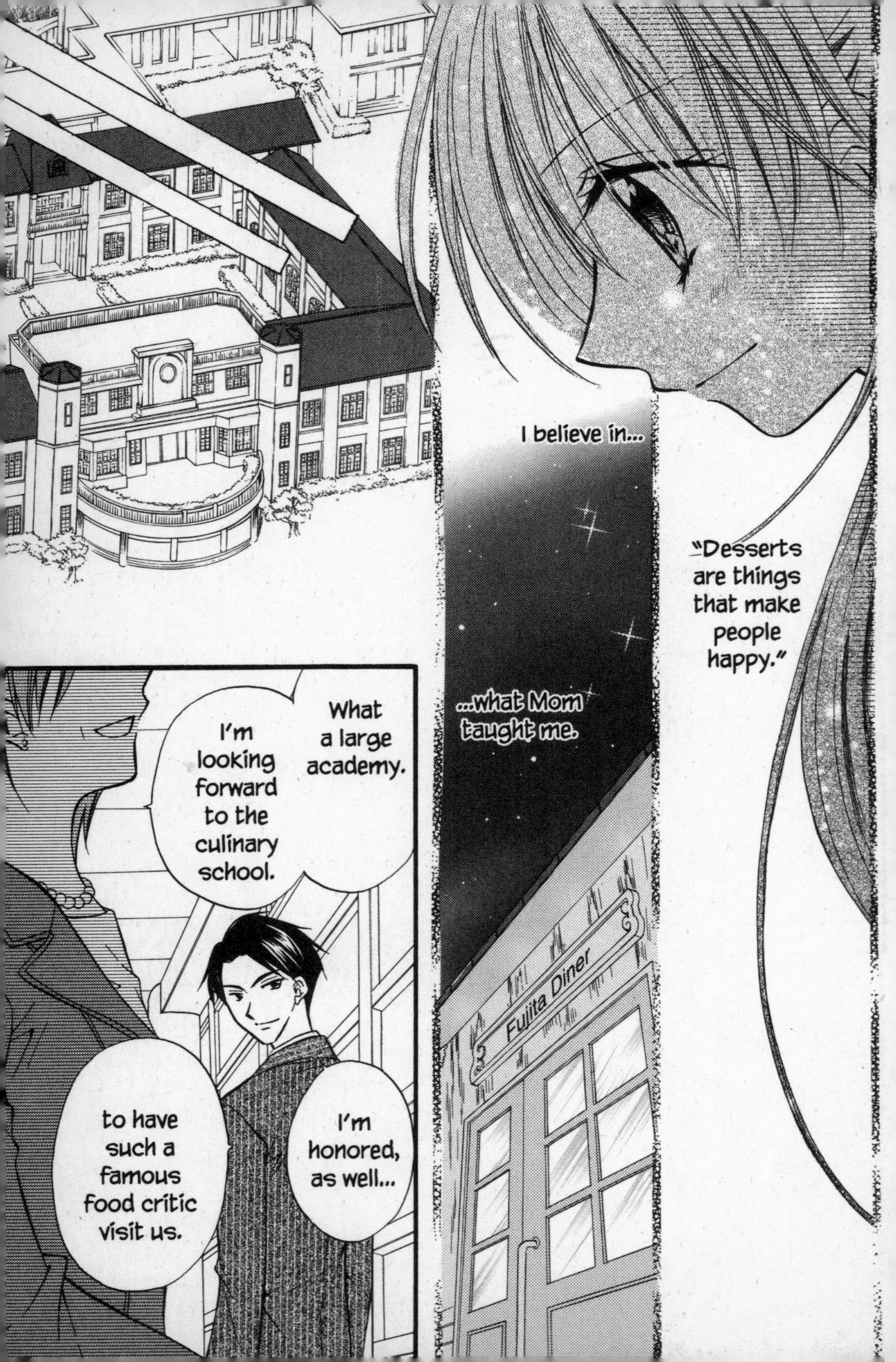
I believe in...
"Desserts are things that make people happy."
...what Mom taught me.
Fujita Diner
What a large academy.
I'm looking forward to the culinary school.
I'm honored, as well...
to have such a famous food critic visit us.

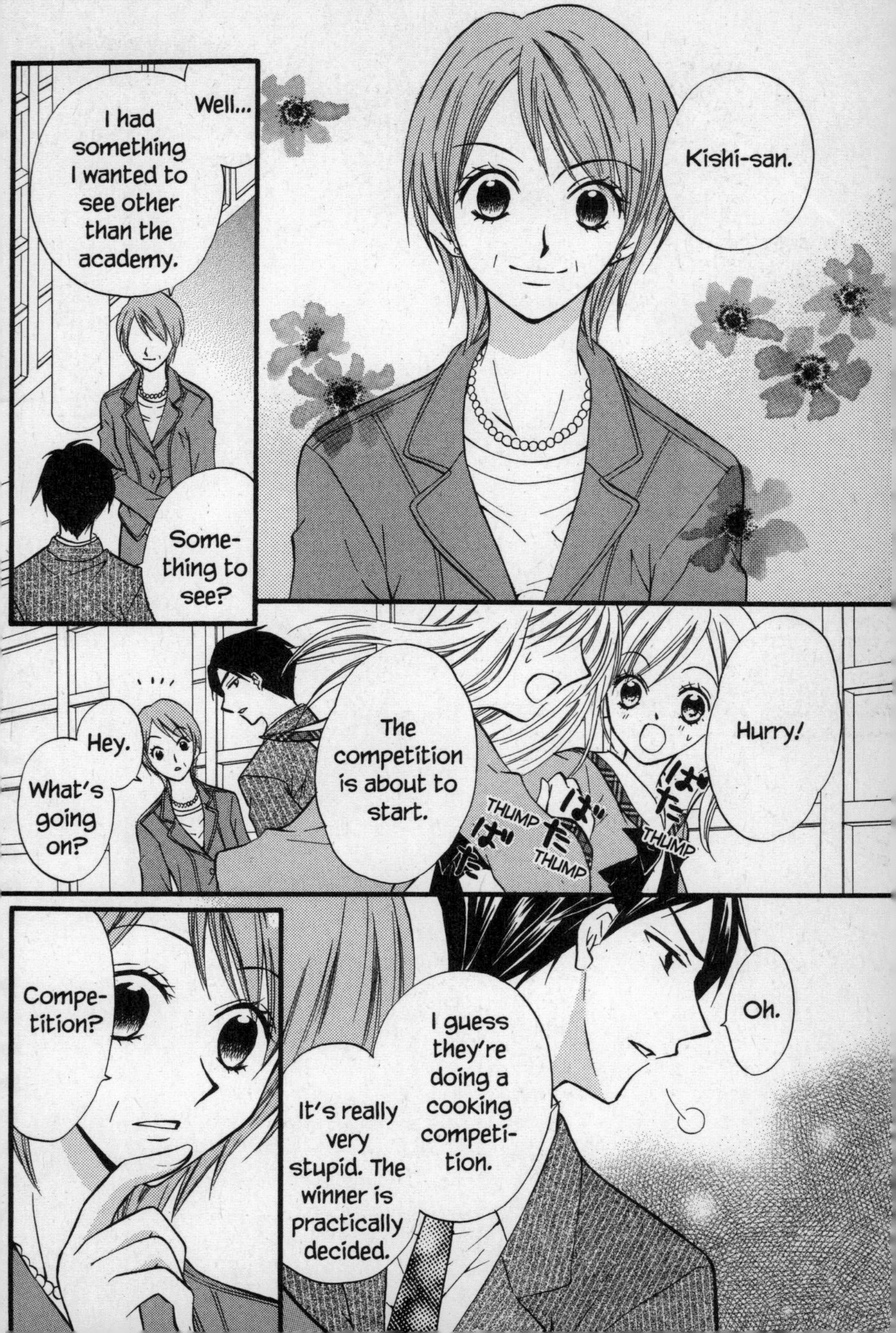
Kishi-san.
Well...
I had something I wanted to see other than the academy.
Some-thing to see?
Hurry!
ばた THUMP
ばた THUMP
ばた THUMP
The competition is about to start.
Hey.
What's going on?
Oh.
I guess they're doing a cooking competition.
It's really very stupid. The winner is practically decided.
Compe-tition?

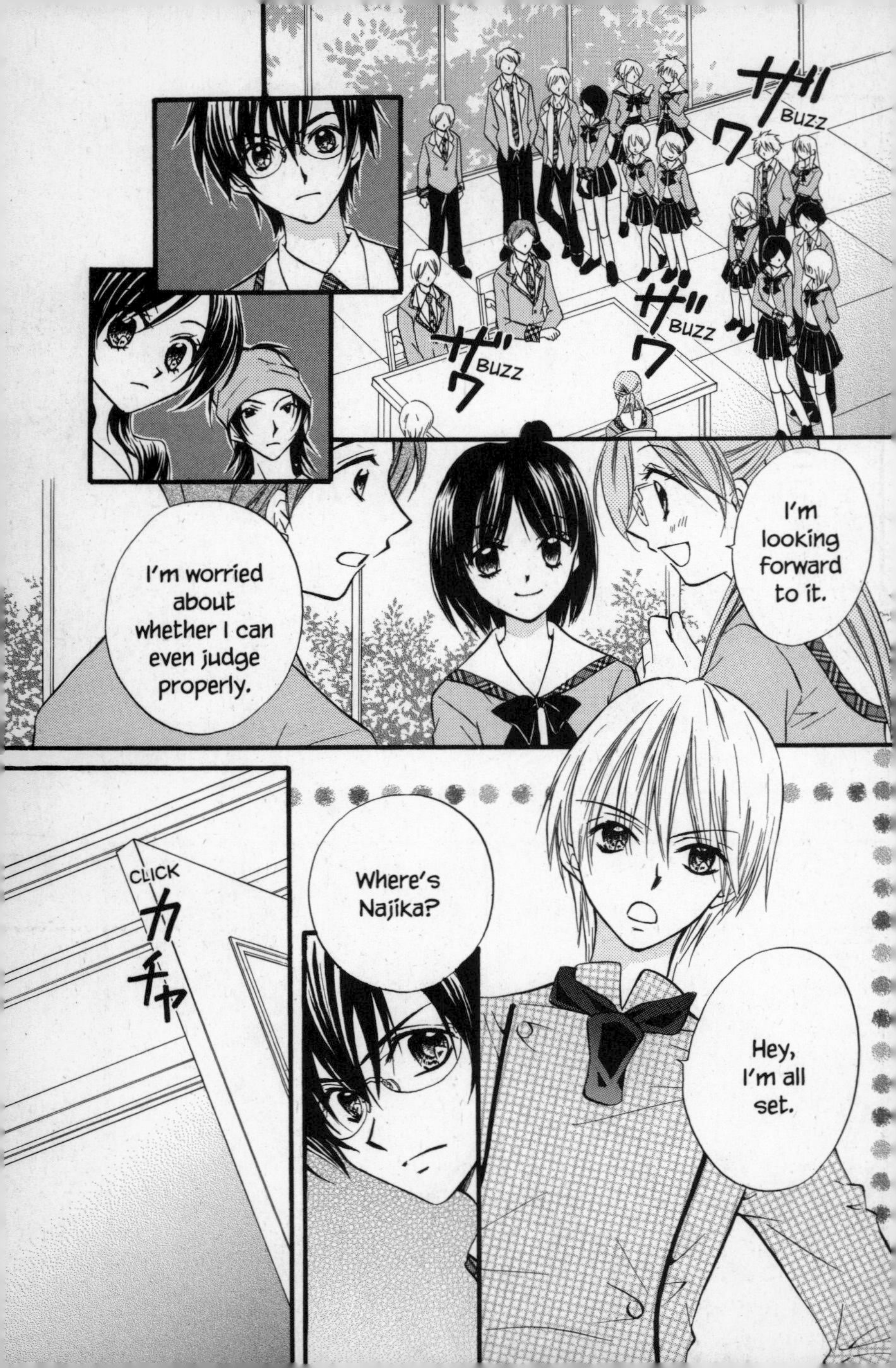
ザワ BUZZ
ザワ BUZZ
ザワ BUZZ
I'm looking forward to it.
I'm worried about whether I can even judge properly.
Where's Najika?
Hey, I'm all set.
CLICK カチャ

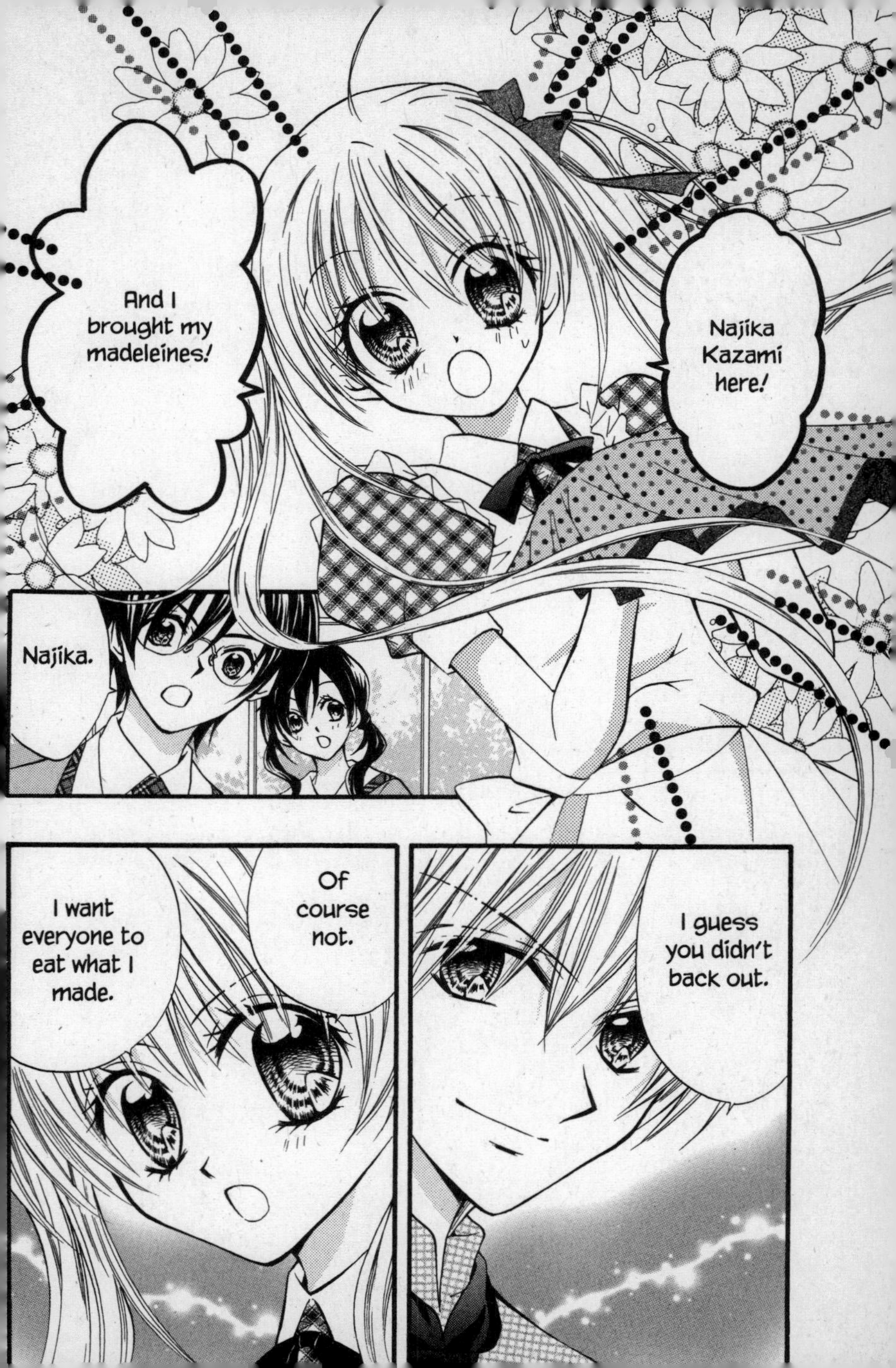
Najika Kazami here!
And I brought my madeleines!
Najika.
I guess you didn't back out.
Of course not.
I want everyone to eat what I made.

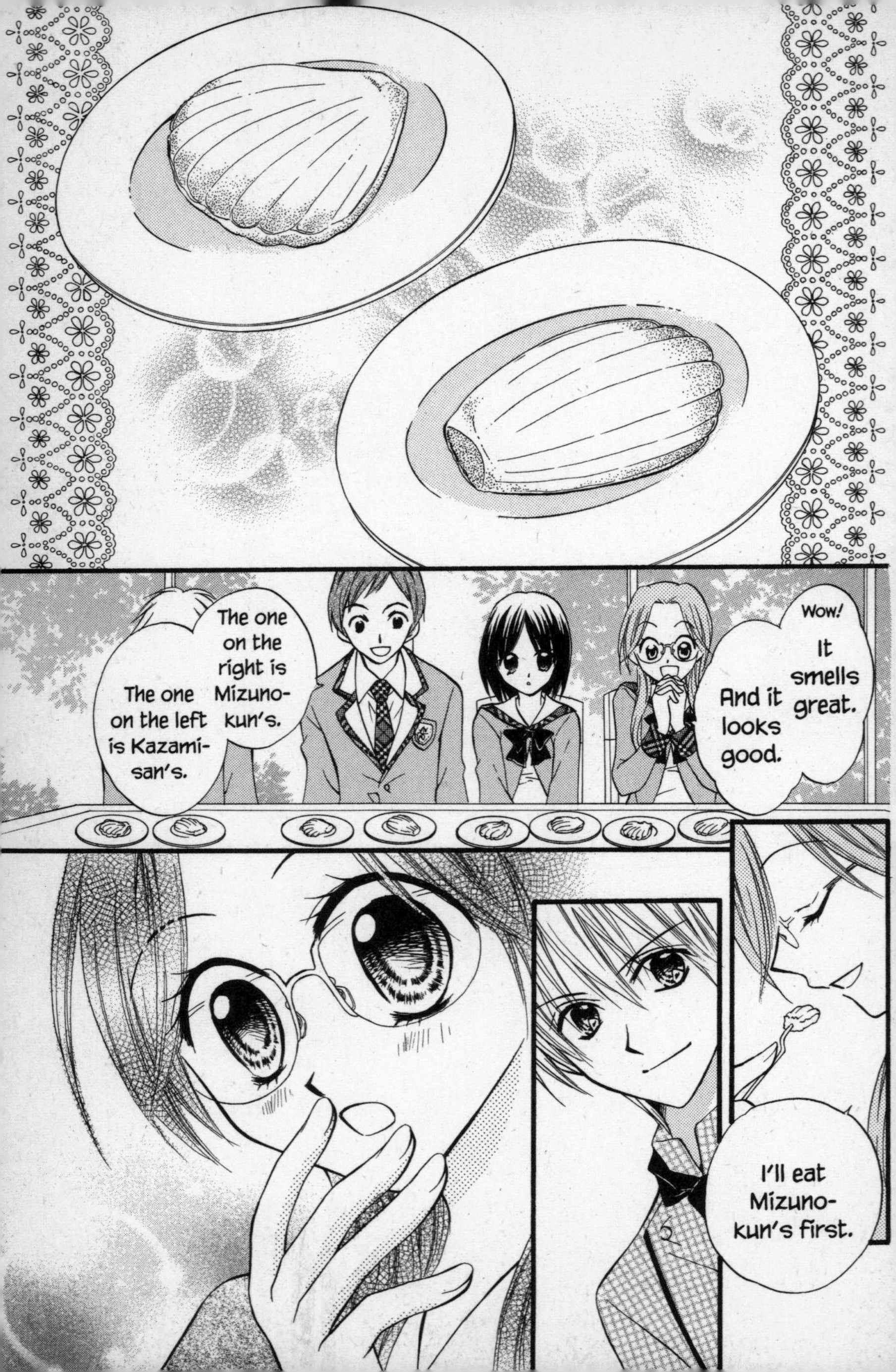
Wow!
It smells great.
And it looks good.
The one on the right is Mizuno-kun's.
The one on the left is Kazami-san's.
I'll eat Mizuno-kun's first.

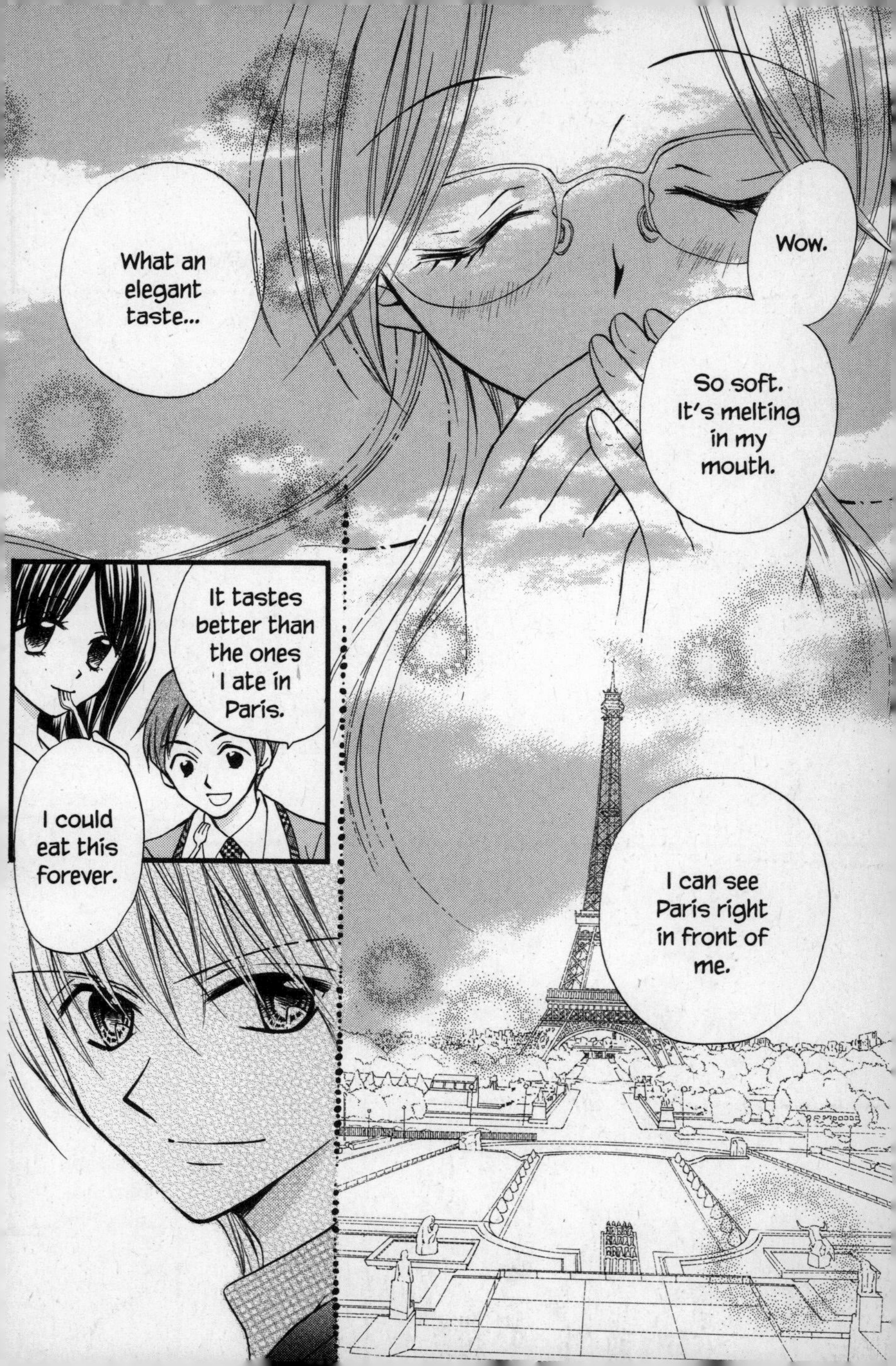
Wow.
So soft. It's melting in my mouth.
What an elegant taste...
I can see Paris right in front of me.
It tastes better than the ones I ate in Paris.
I could eat this forever.

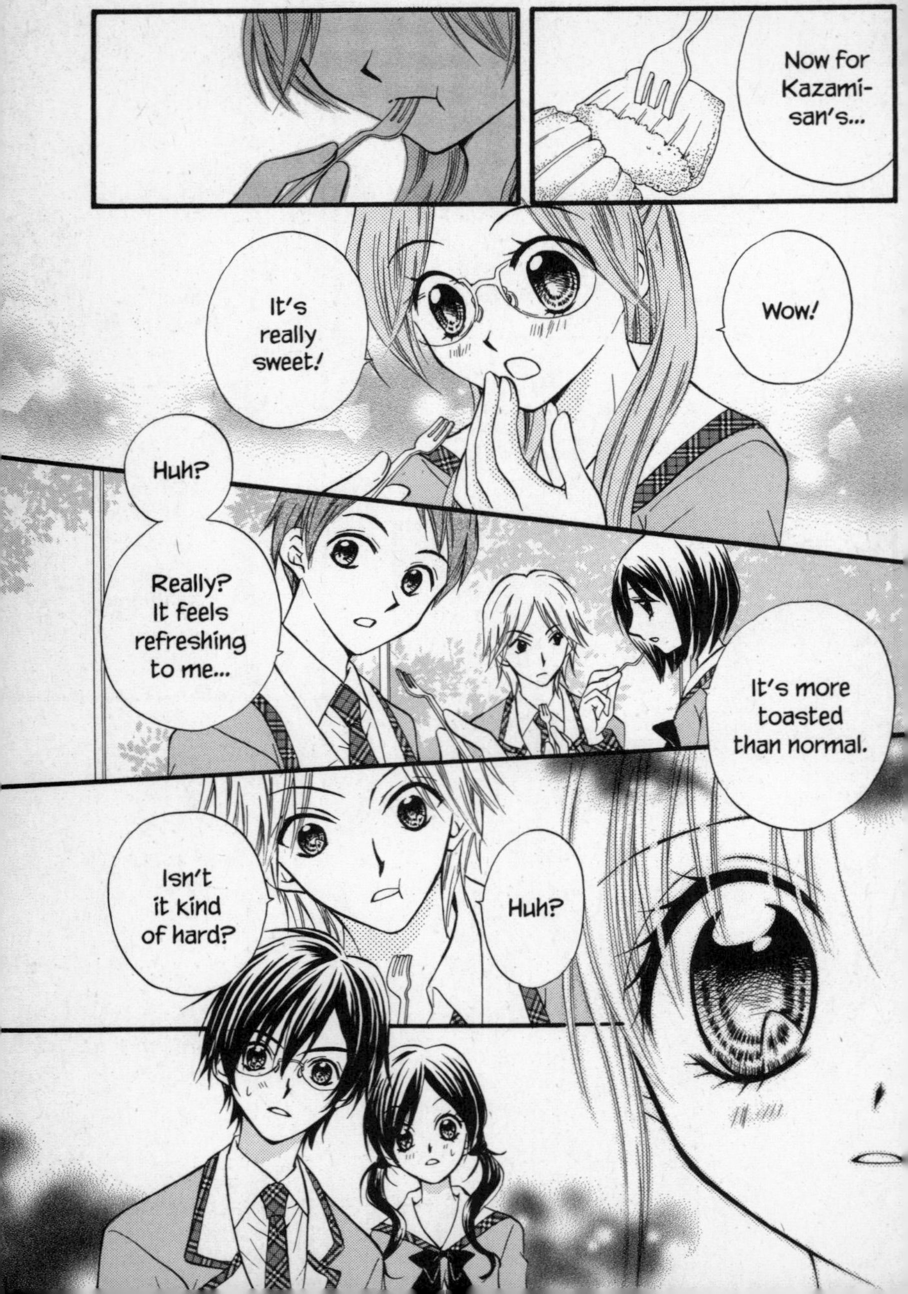
Now for Kazami-san's...
Wow!
It's really sweet!
Huh?
Really? It feels refreshing to me...
It's more toasted than normal.
Isn't it kind of hard?
Huh?

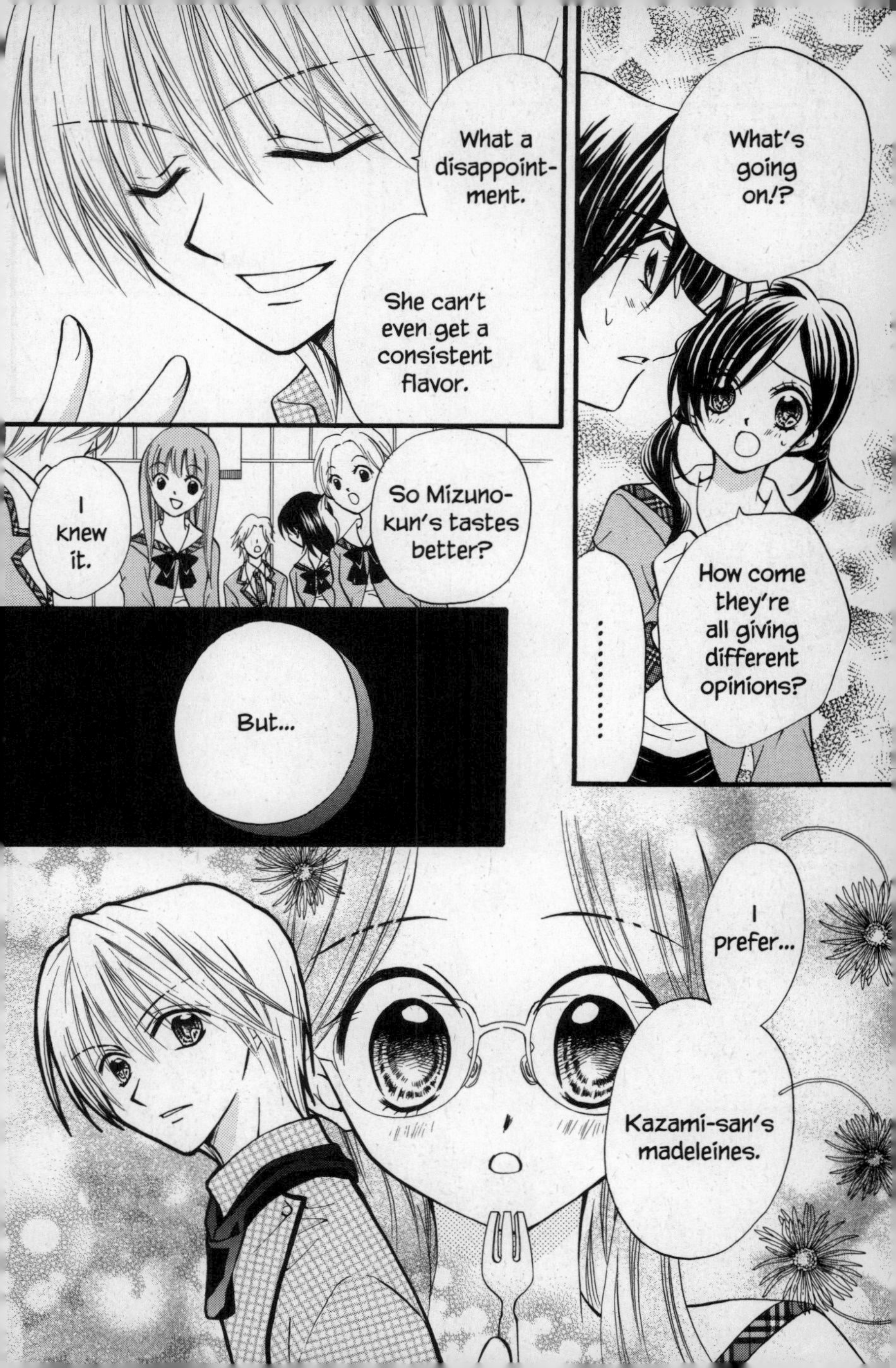
What's going on!?
How come they're all giving different opinions?
......
What a disappointment.
She can't even get a consistent flavor.
So Mizuno-kun's tastes better?
I knew it.
But...
I prefer...
Kazami-san's madeleines.

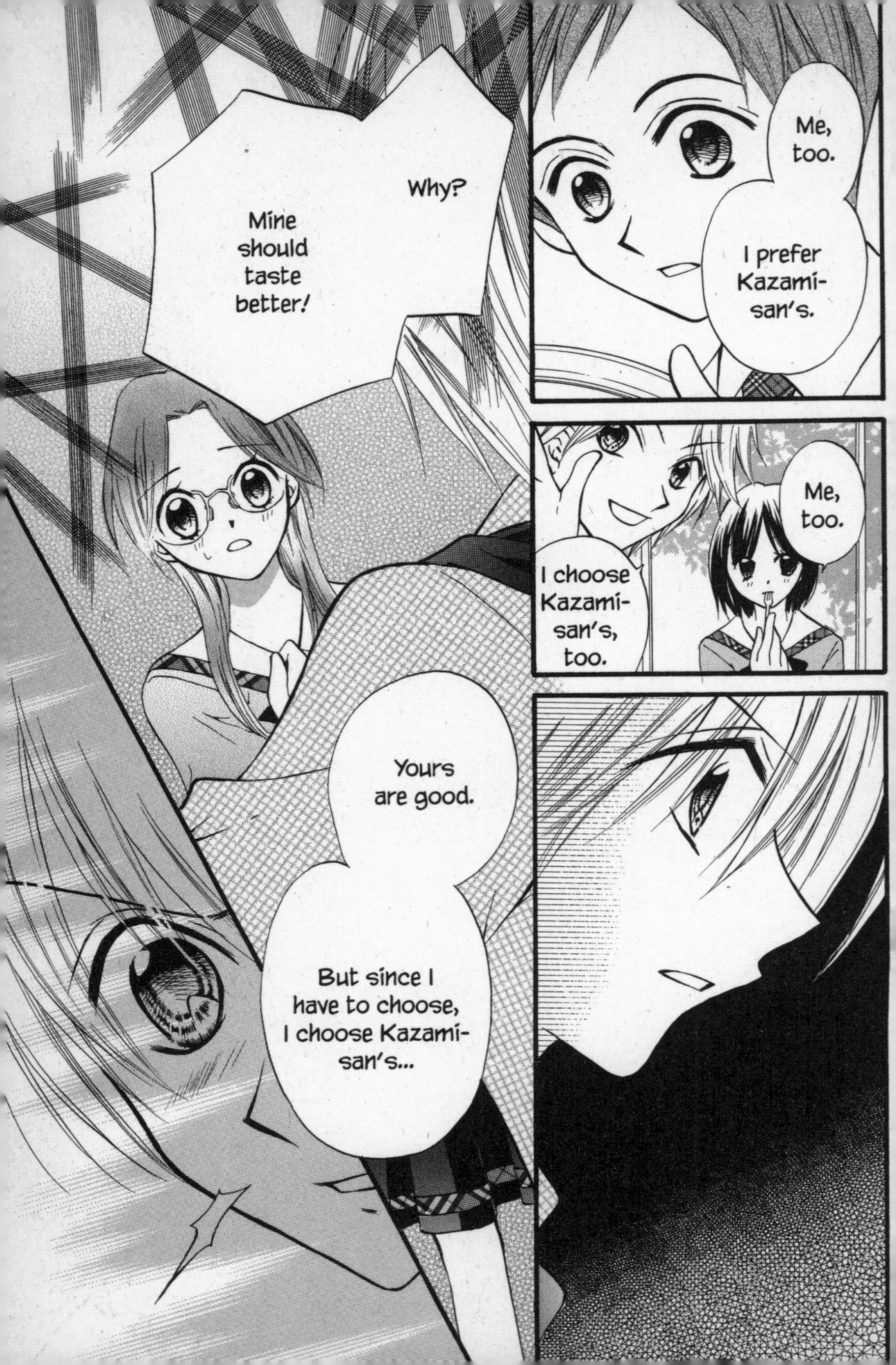
Me, too.
I prefer Kazami-san's.
Me, too.
I choose Kazami-san's, too.
Why?
Mine should taste better!
Yours are good.
But since I have to choose, I choose Kazami-san's...

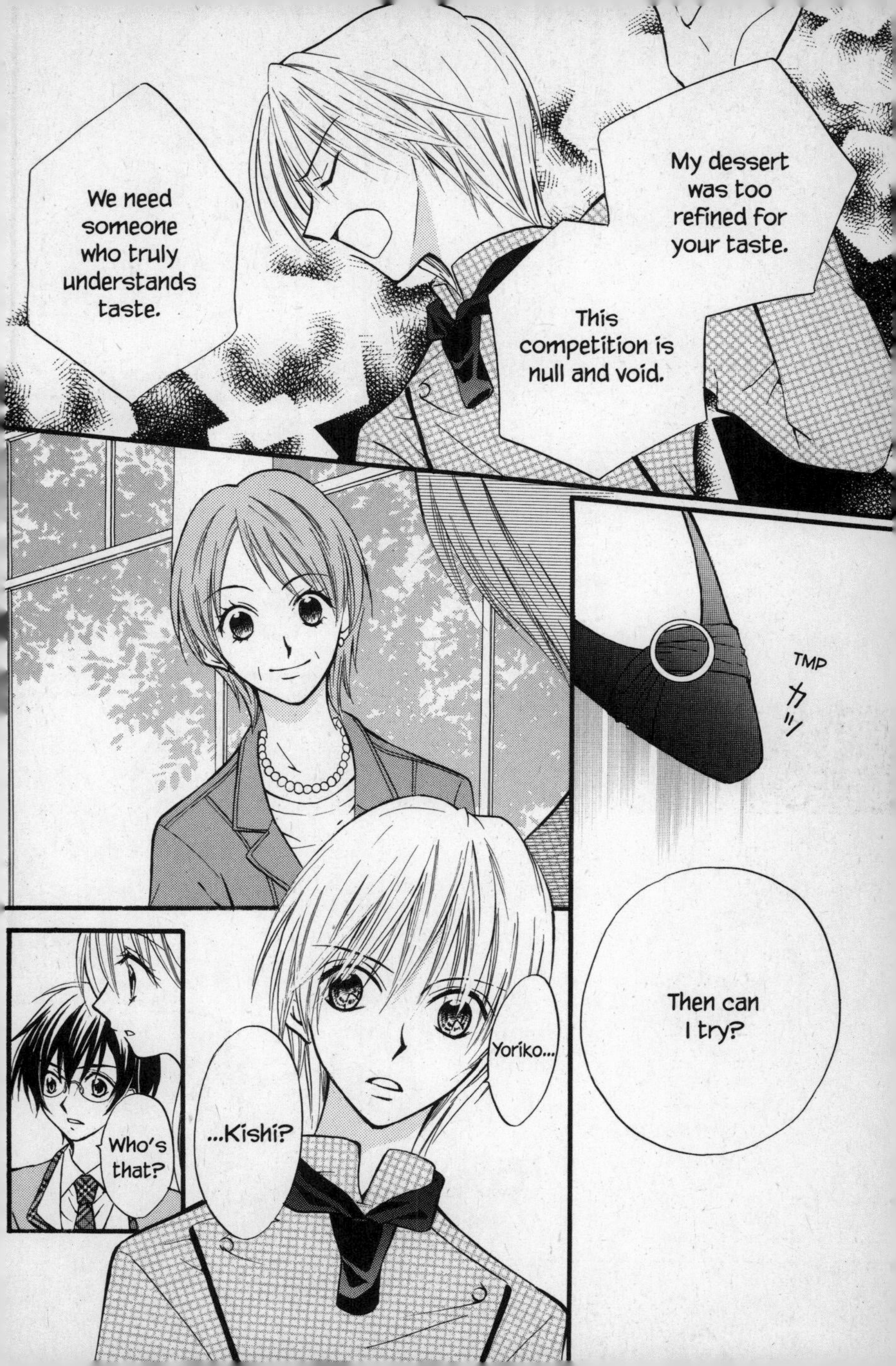
My dessert was too refined for your taste.
This competition is null and void.
We need someone who truly understands taste.
TMP
カッ
Then can I try?
Yoriko...
...Kishi?
Who's that?

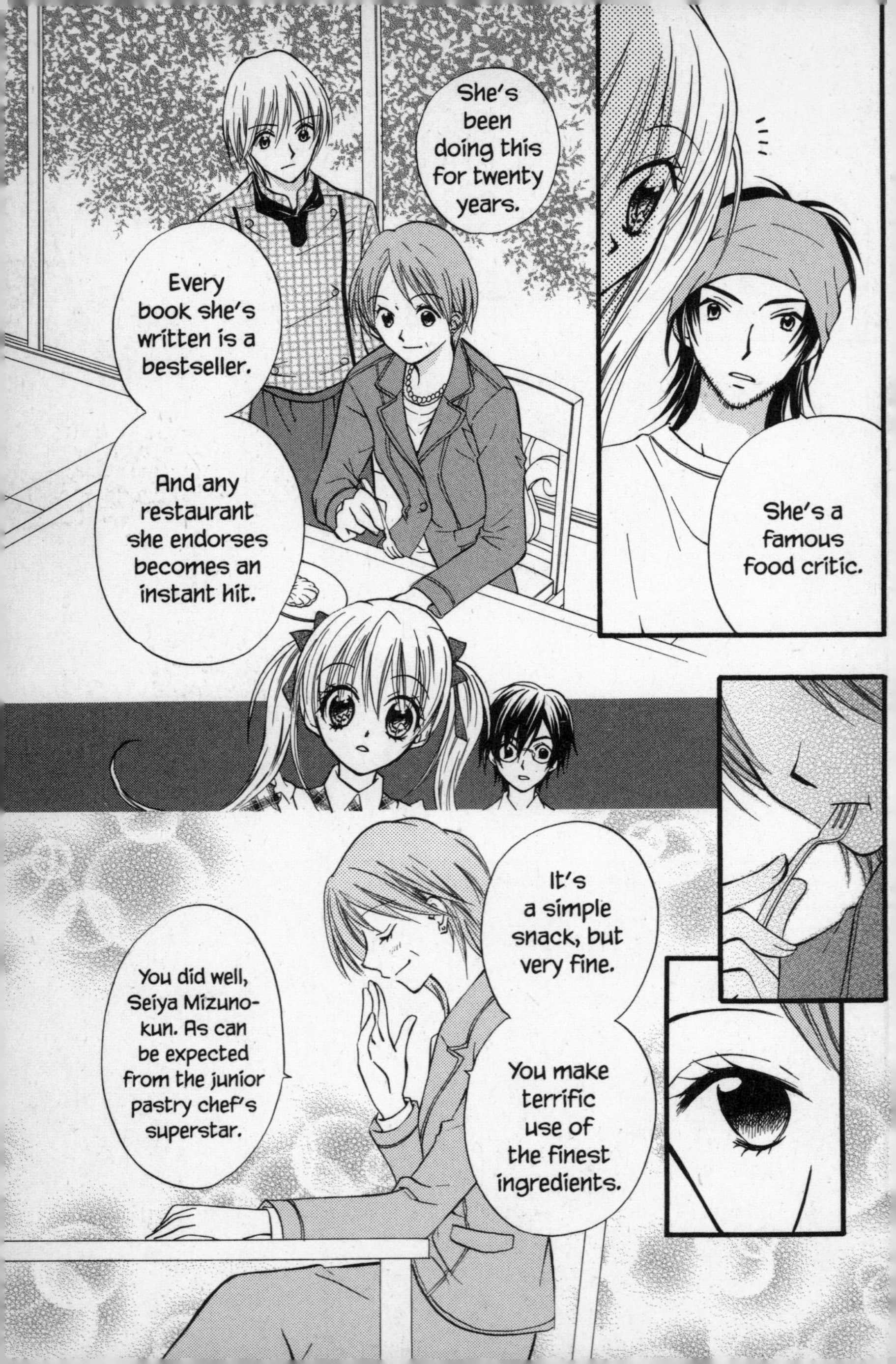
She's a famous food critic.
She's been doing this for twenty years.
Every book she's written is a bestseller.
And any restaurant she endorses becomes an instant hit.
It's a simple snack, but very fine.
You make terrific use of the finest ingredients.
You did well, Seiya Mizuno-kun. As can be expected from the junior pastry chef's superstar.

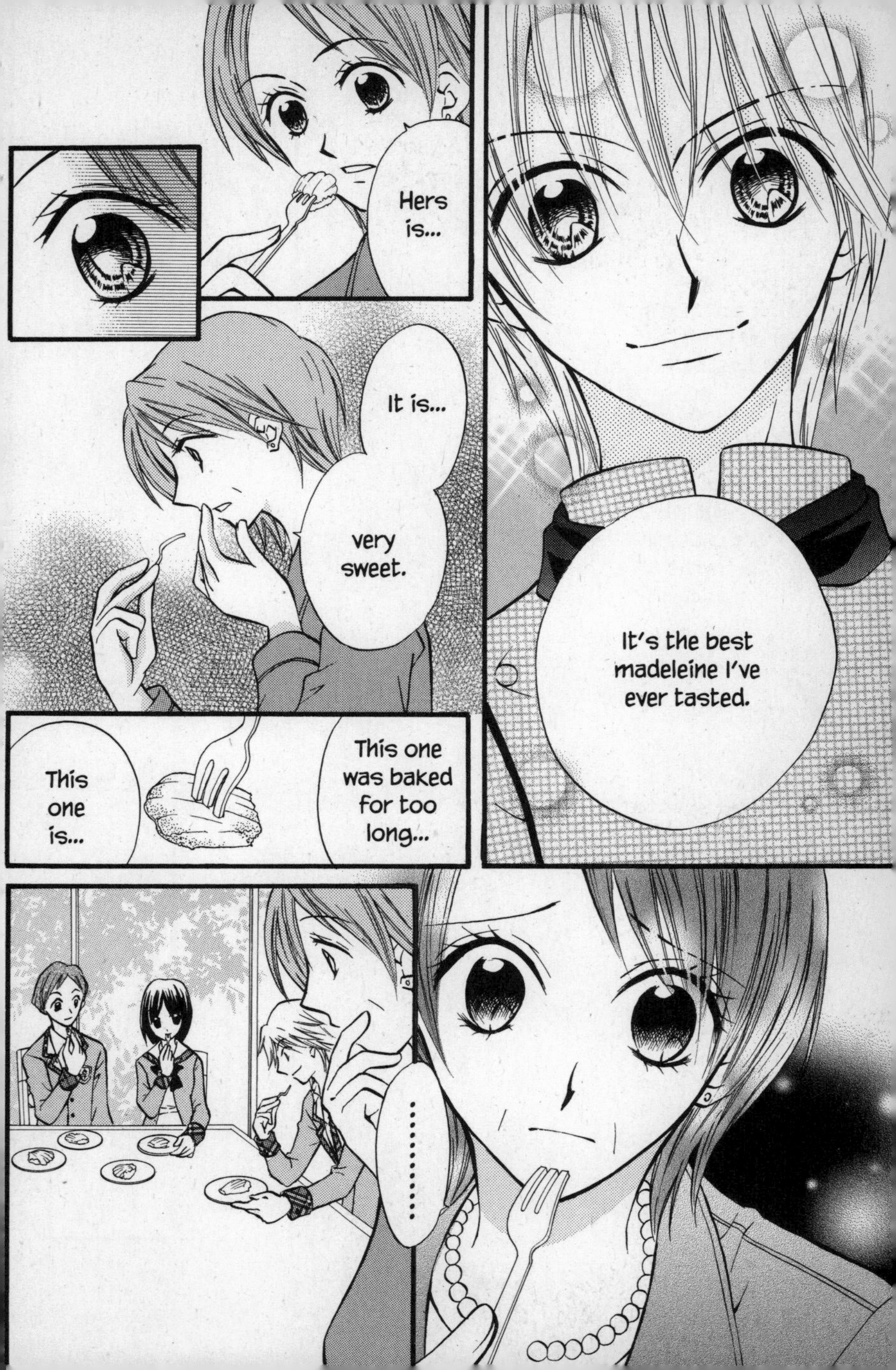
It's the best madeleine I've ever tasted.
Hers is...
It is...
very sweet.
This one was baked for too long...
This one is...
......

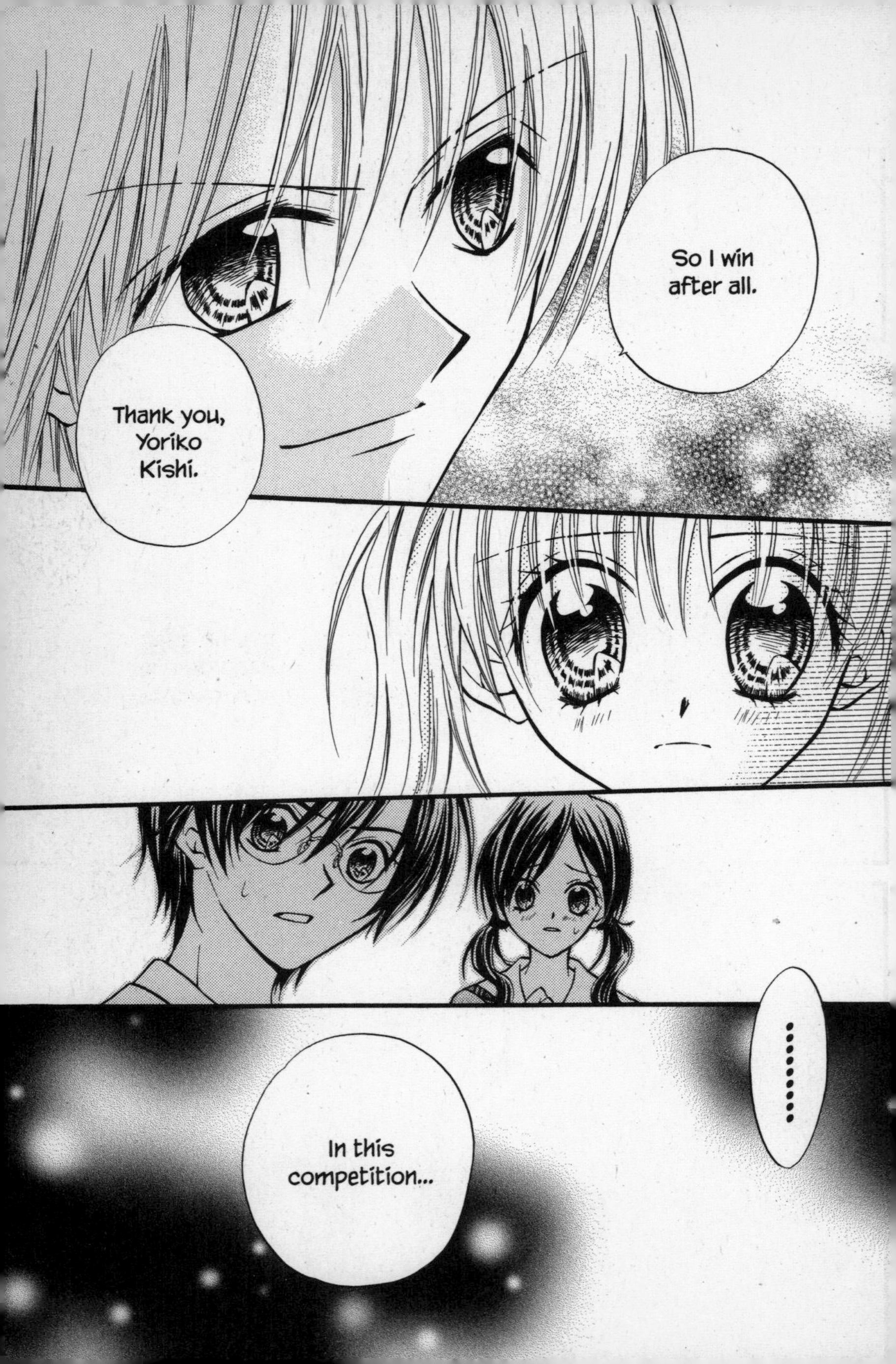
So I win after all.
Thank you, Yoriko Kishi.
....
In this competition...

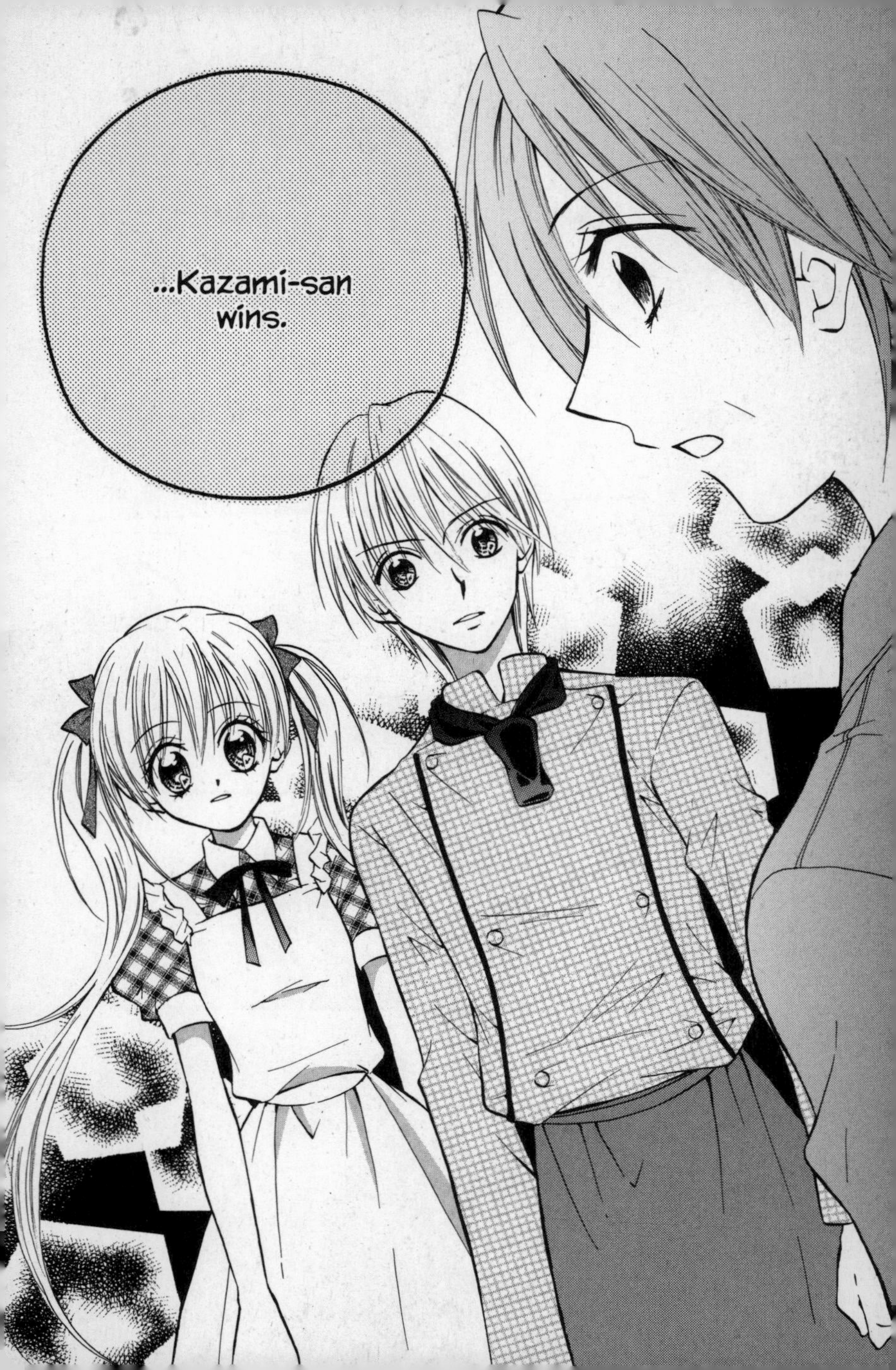
...Kazami-san wins.

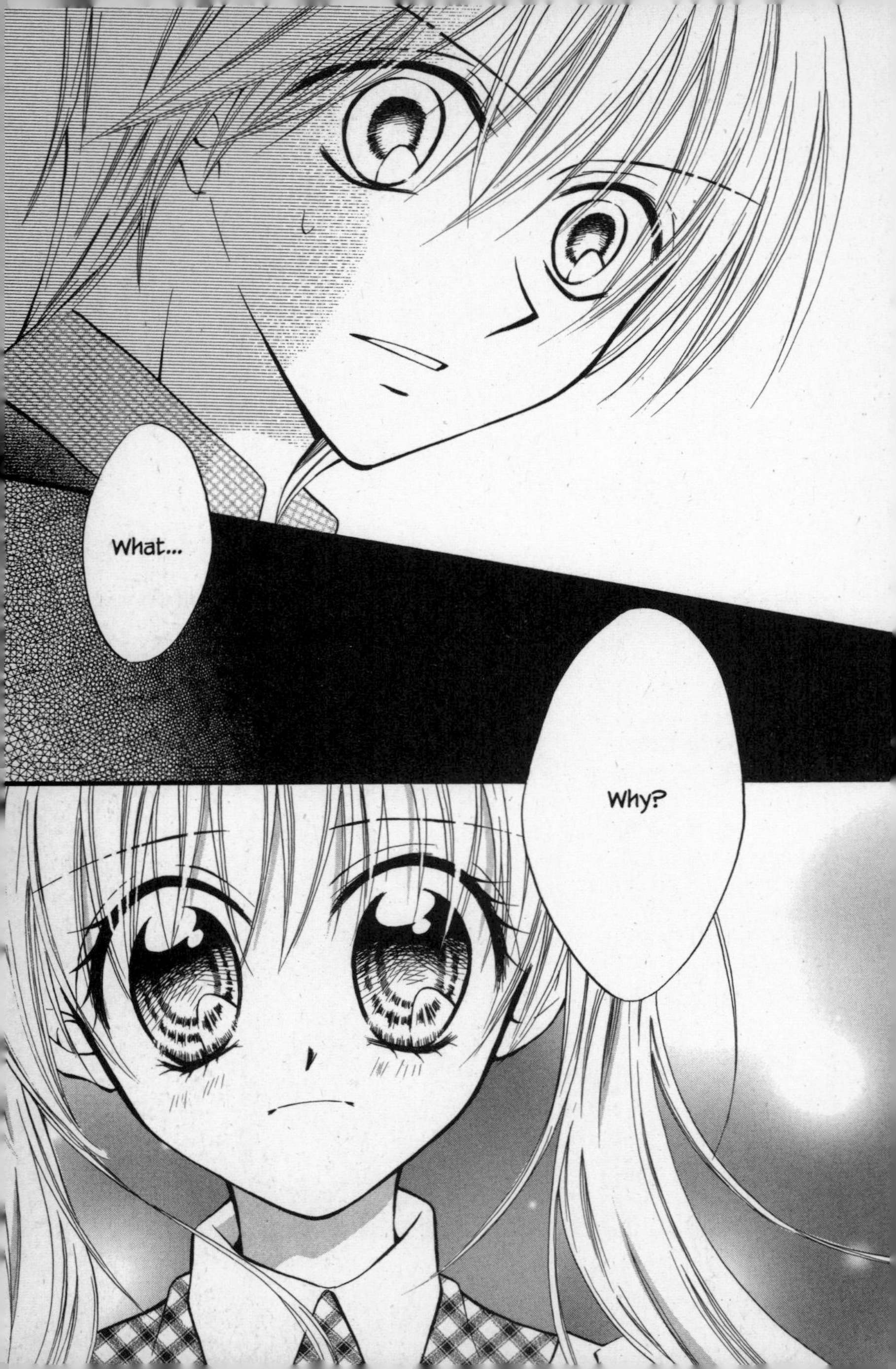
What...
Why?

I love wearing black.

Seiya Mizuno's clothes are mostly black! He would like his chef's uniforms to be black, too. He seems to have a lot of enemies, but no one can stand up to him...

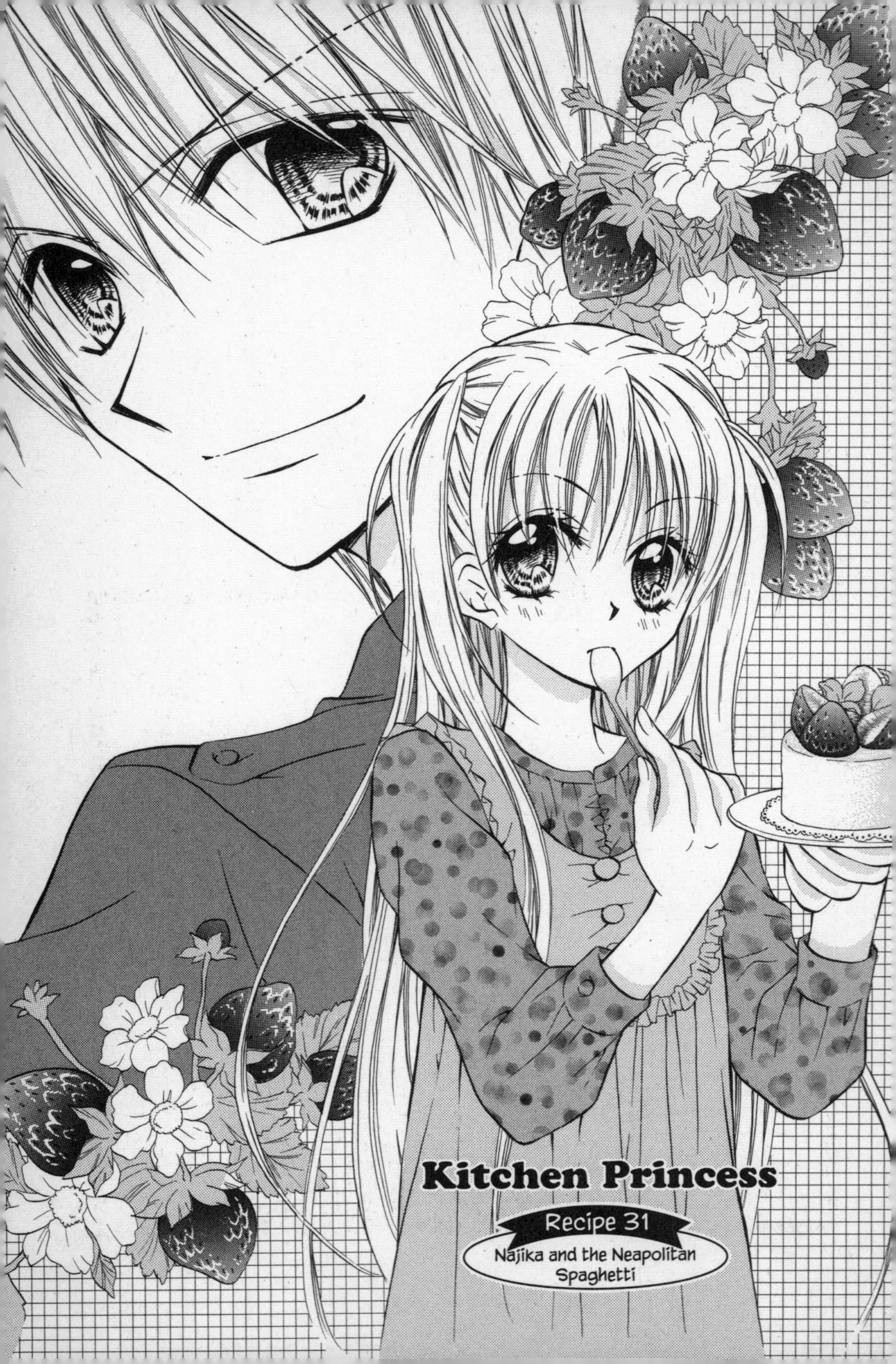
Kitchen Princess
Recipe 31
Najika and the Neapolitan Spaghetti

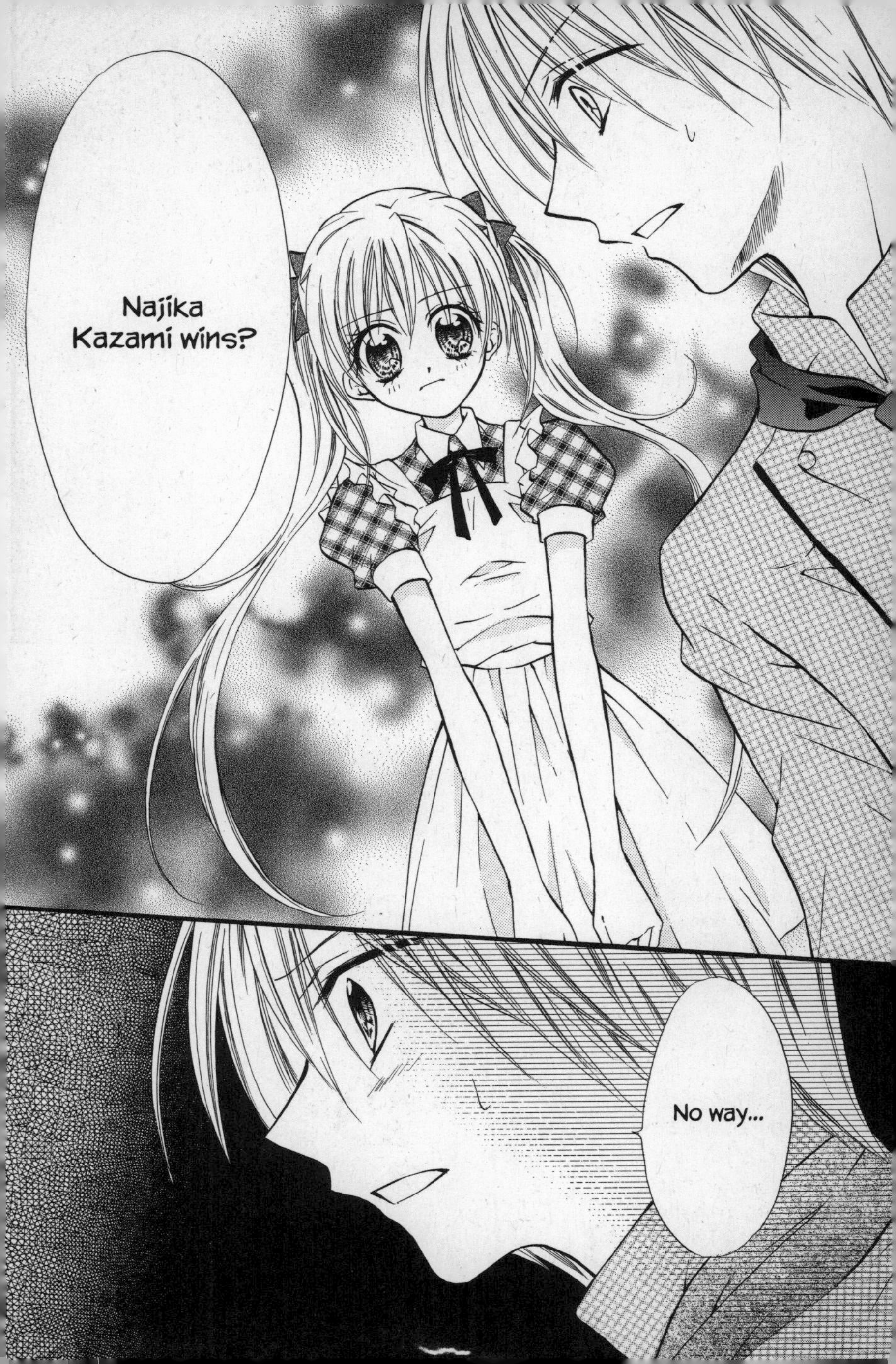
Najika Kazami wins?
No way...

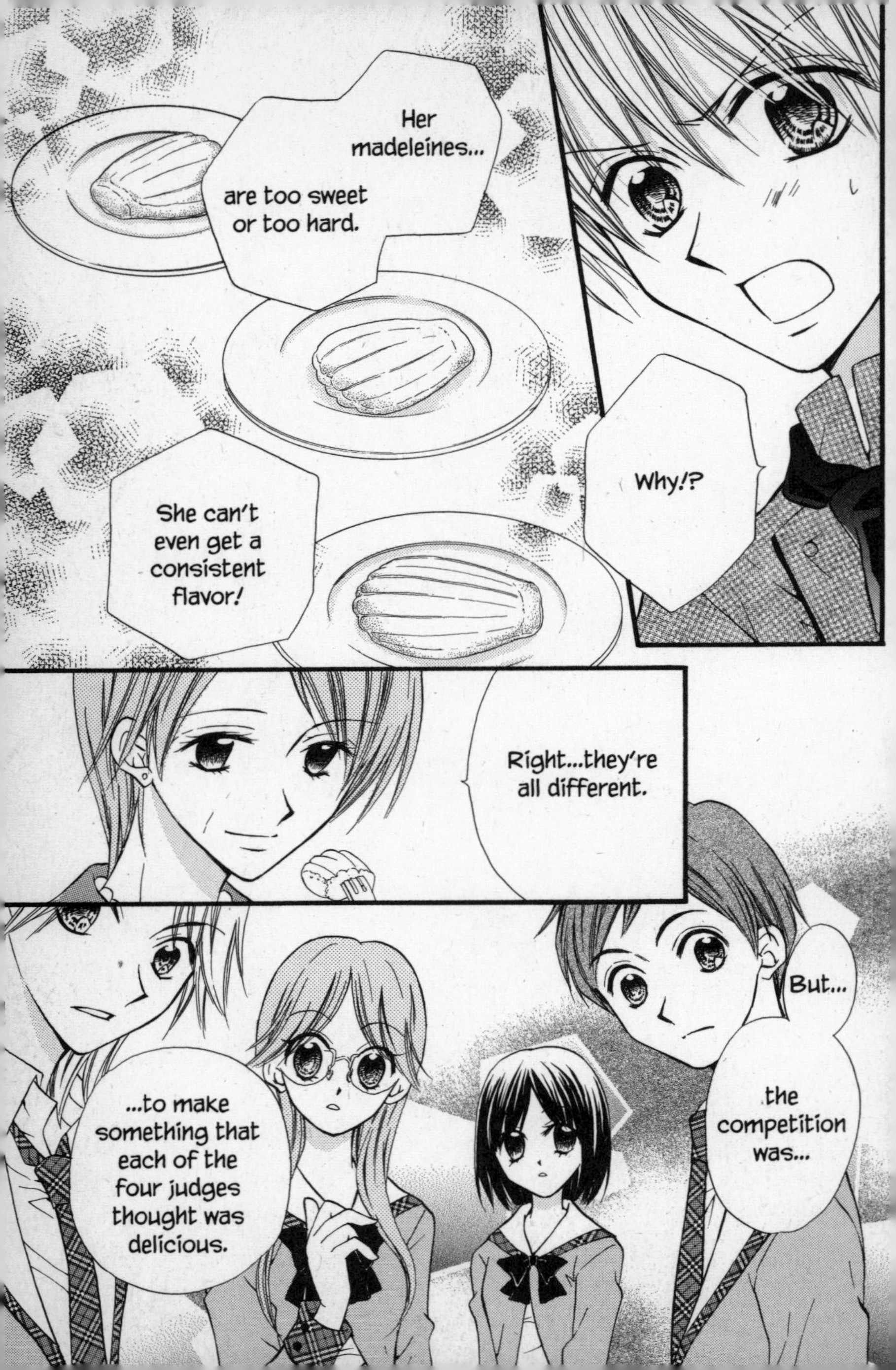
Why!?
Her madeleines...
are too sweet or too hard.
She can't even get a consistent flavor!
Right...they're all different.
But...
the competition was...
...to make something that each of the four judges thought was delicious.

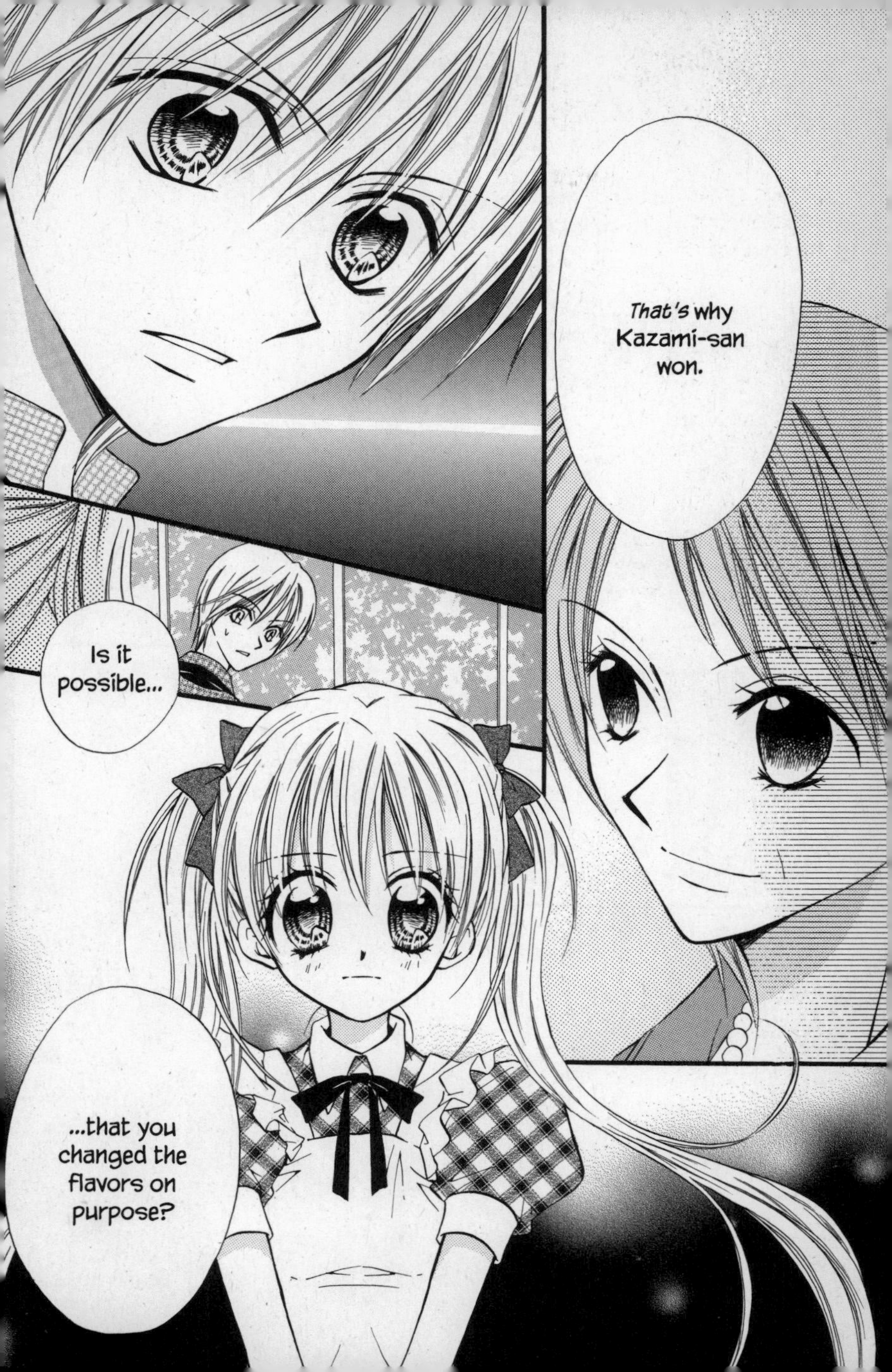
That's why Kazami-san won.
Is it possible...
...that you changed the flavors on purpose?

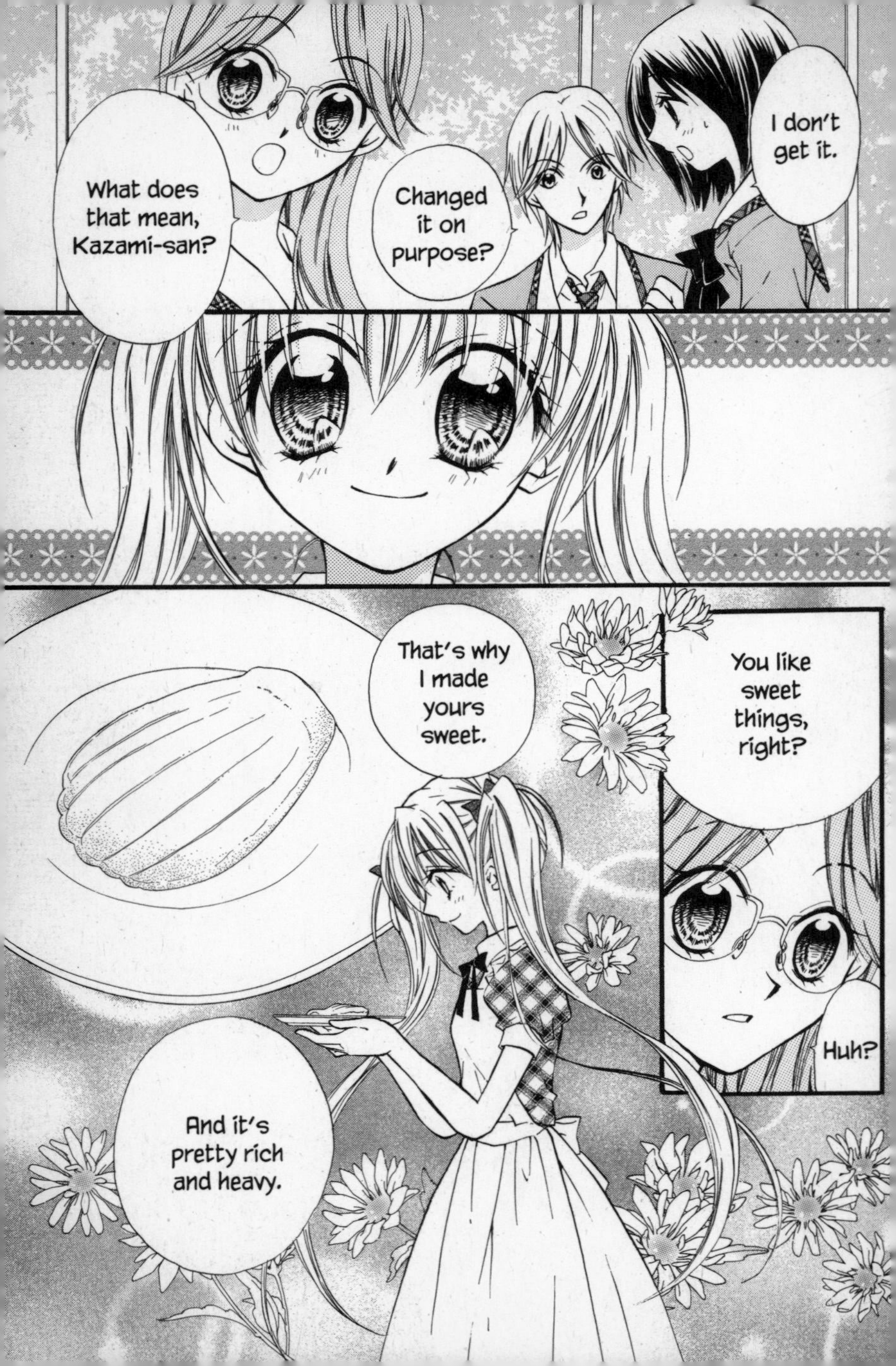
I don't get it.
Changed it on purpose?
What does that mean, Kazami-san?
You like sweet things, right?
Huh?
That's why I made yours sweet.
And it's pretty rich and heavy.

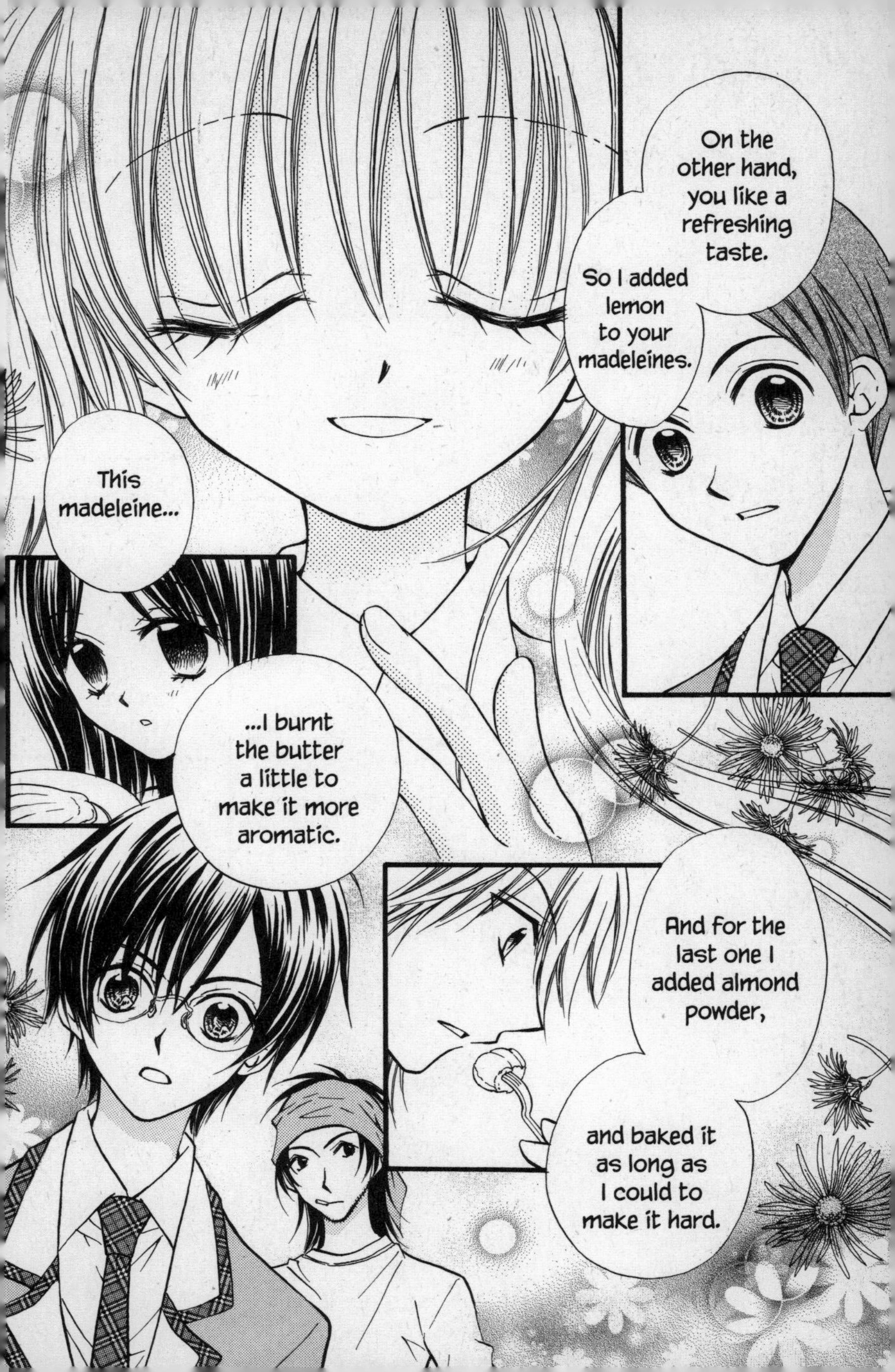
This madeleine...
...I burnt the butter a little to make it more aromatic.
On the other hand, you like a refreshing taste.
So I added lemon to your madeleines.
And for the last one I added almond powder,
and baked it as long as I could to make it hard.

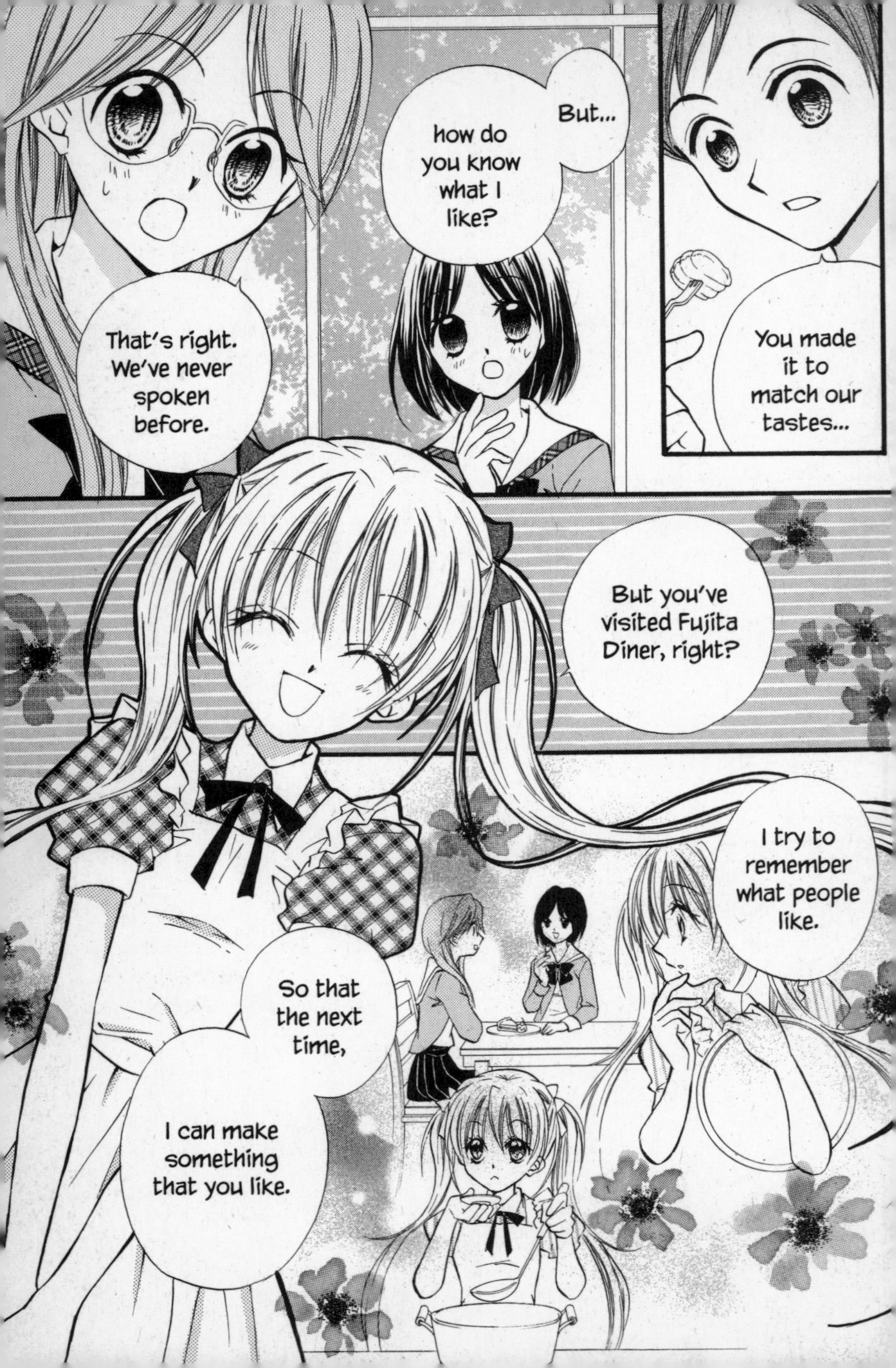
You made it to match our tastes...
But...
how do you know what I like?
That's right. We've never spoken before.
But you've visited Fujita Diner, right?
I try to remember what people like.
So that the next time,
I can make something that you like.

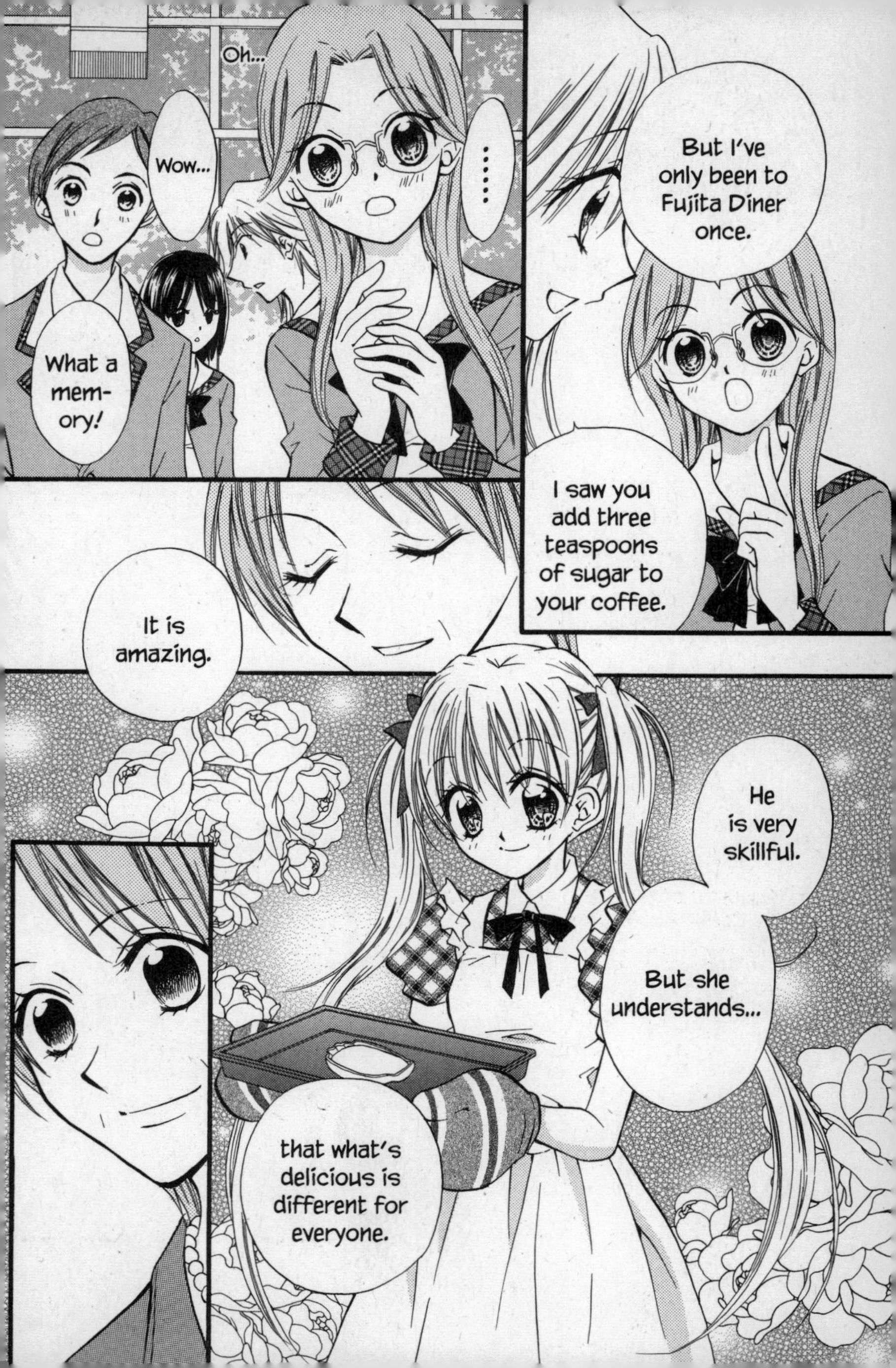

But I've only been to Fujita Diner once.
I saw you add three teaspoons of sugar to your coffee.
Oh...
......
Wow...
What a mem-ory!
It is amazing.
He is very skillful.
But she understands...
that what's delicious is different for everyone.

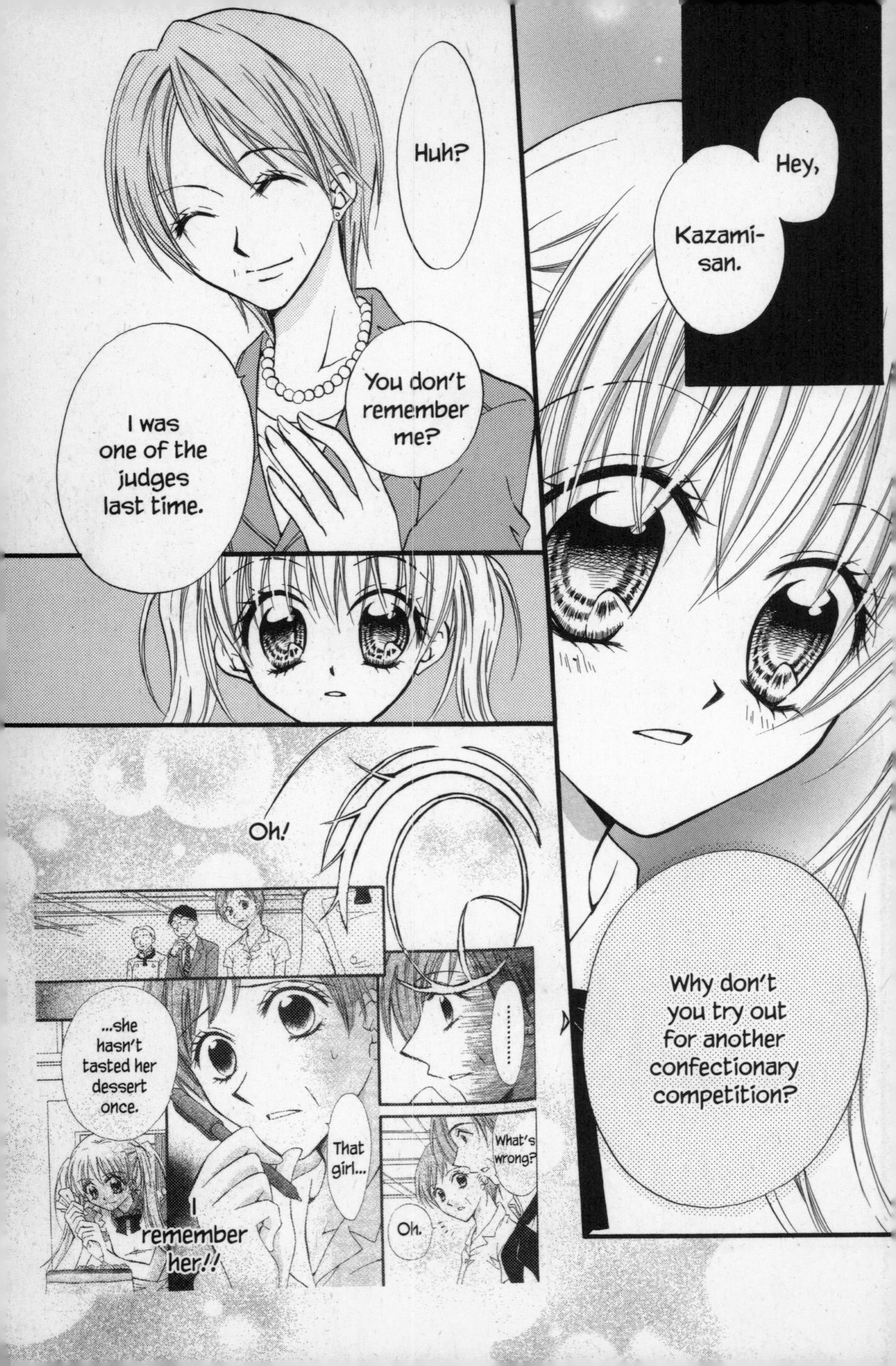
Hey,
Kazami-san.
Why don't you try out for another confectionary competition?
Huh?
You don't remember me?
I was one of the judges last time.
Oh!
......
...she hasn't tasted her dessert once.
What's wrong?
Oh.
That girl...
I remember her!!

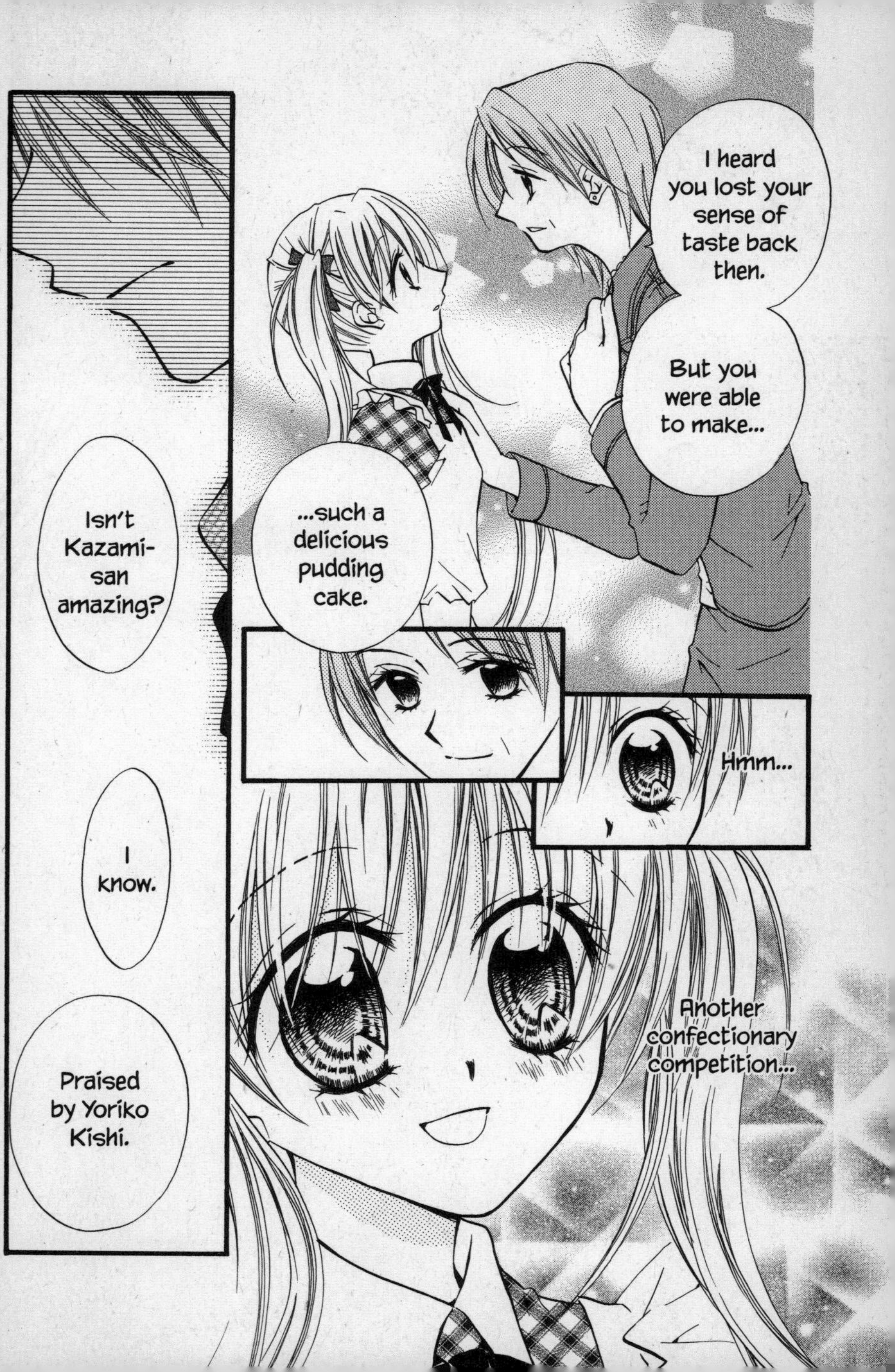
I heard you lost your sense of taste back then.
But you were able to make...
...such a delicious pudding cake.
Hmm...
Another confectionary competition...
Isn't Kazami-san amazing?
I know.
Praised by Yoriko Kishi.

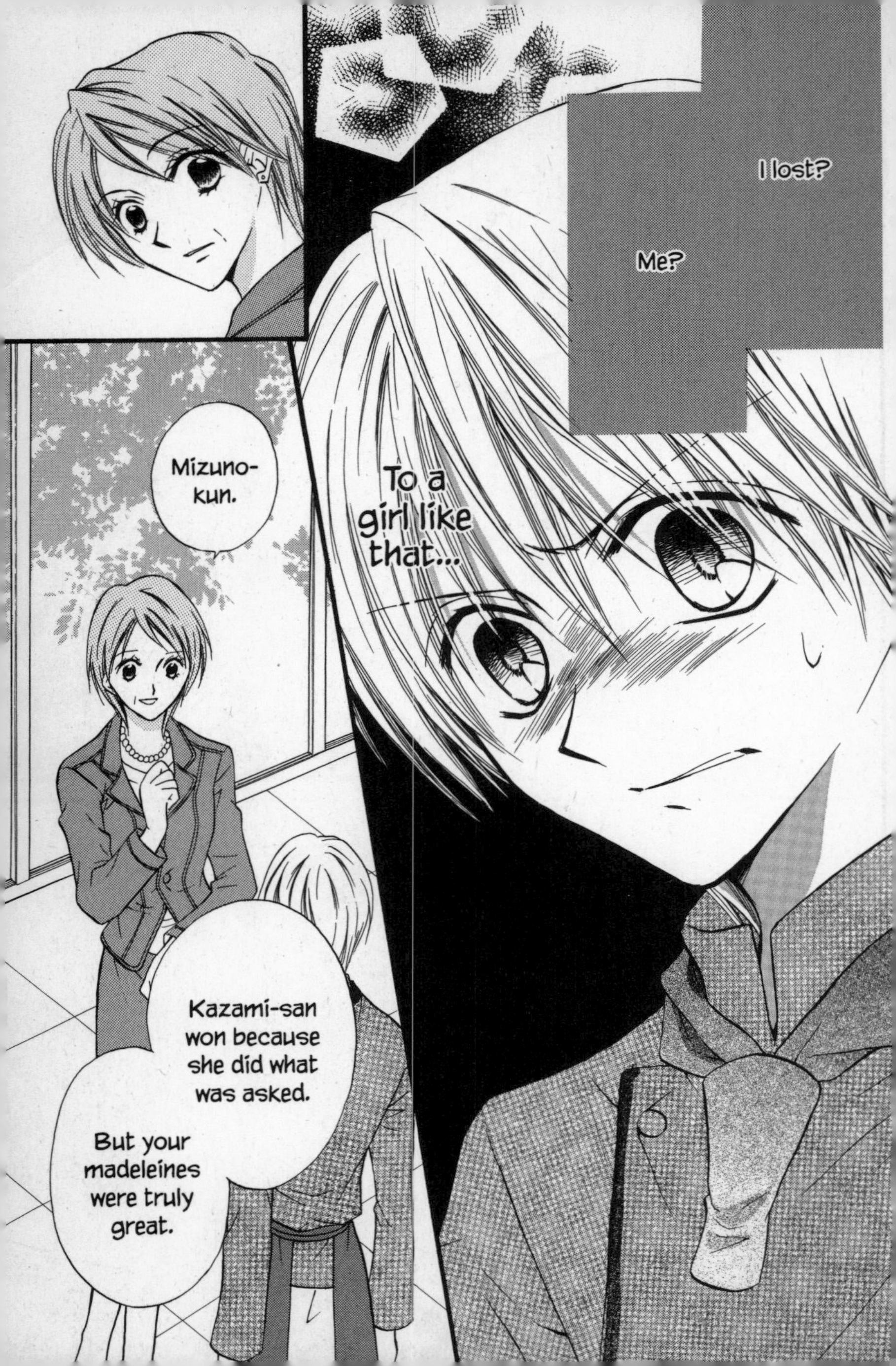
I lost?
Me?
To a girl like that...
Mizuno-kun.
Kazami-san won because she did what was asked.
But your madeleines were truly great.

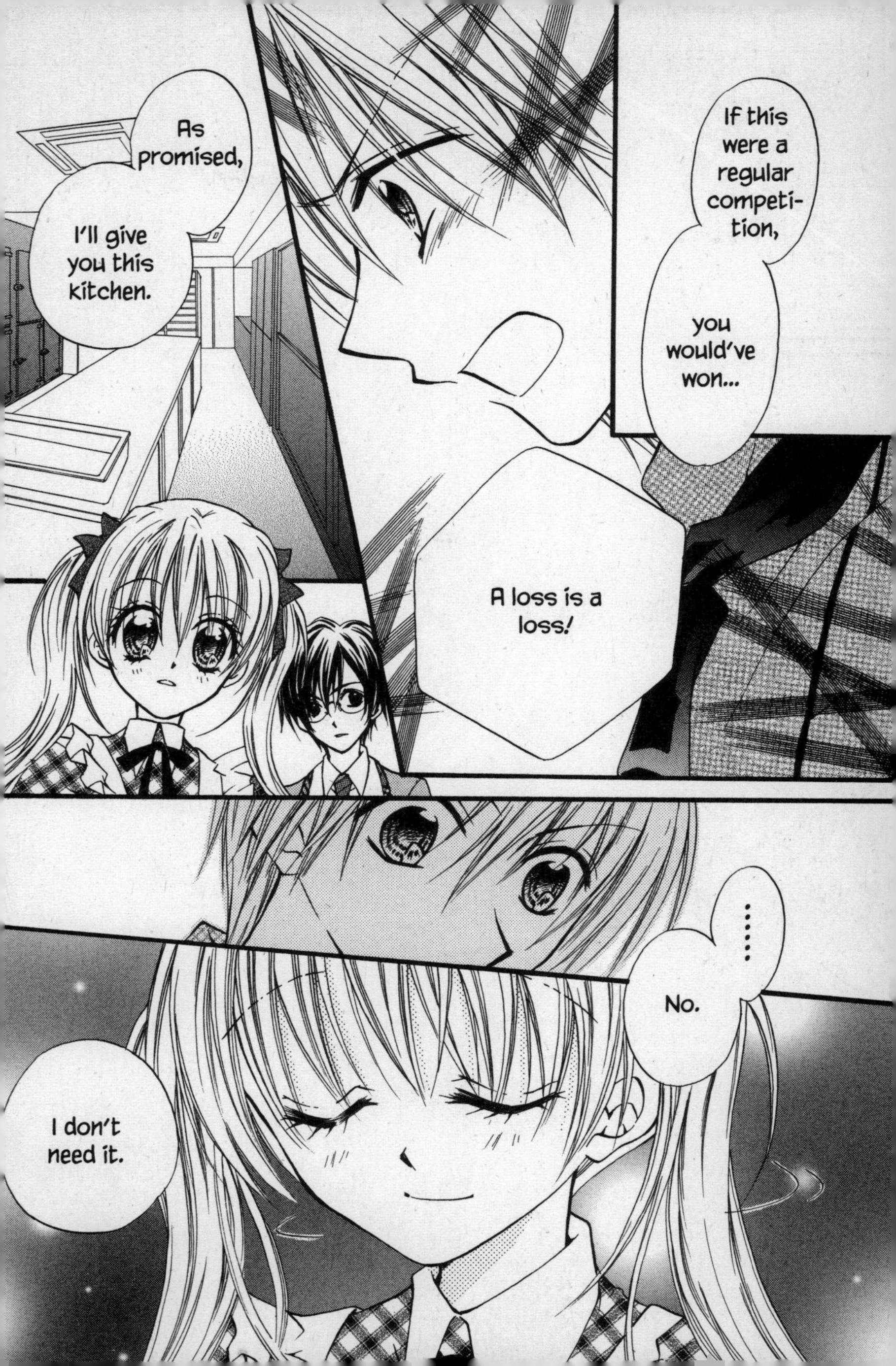
If this were a regular competition,
you would've won...
A loss is a loss!
As promised,
I'll give you this kitchen.
......
No.
I don't need it.

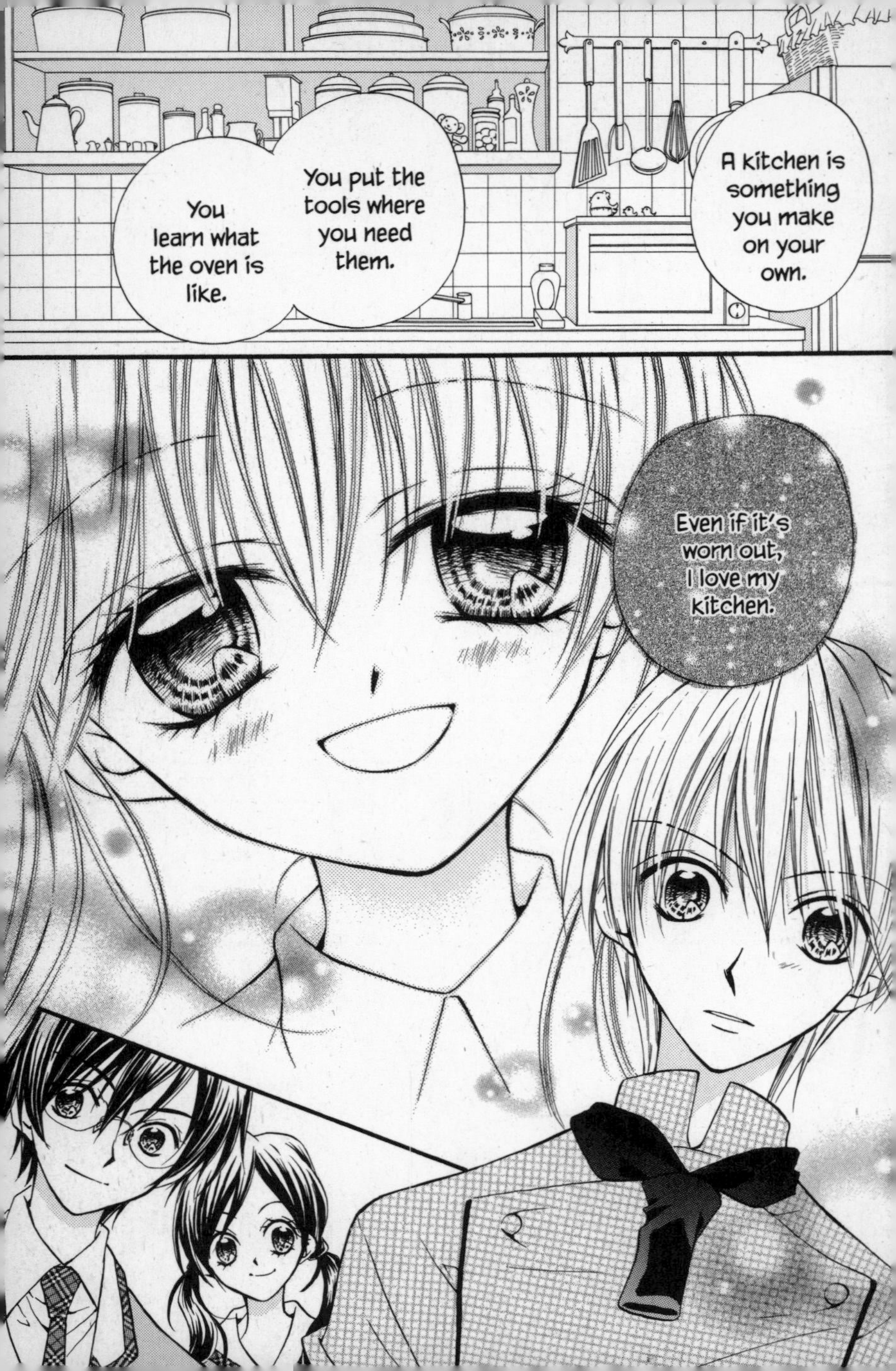
A kitchen is something you make on your own.
You put the tools where you need them.
You learn what the oven is like.
Even if it's worn out, I love my kitchen.

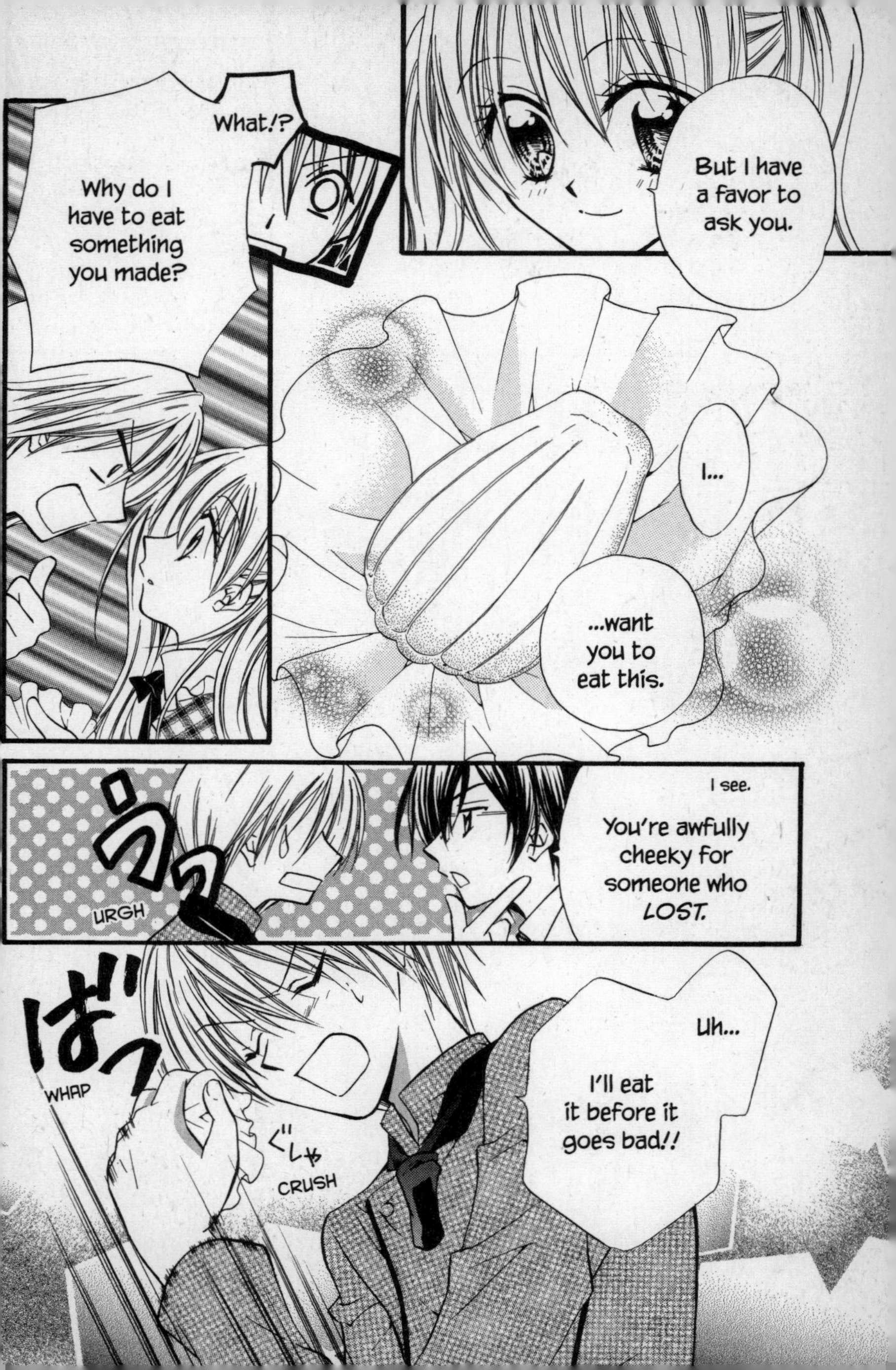
But I have a favor to ask you.
I...
...want you to eat this.
What!?
Why do I have to eat something you made?
I see.
You're awfully cheeky for someone who *LOST.*
URGH
Uh...
I'll eat it before it goes bad!!
CRUSH
WHAP

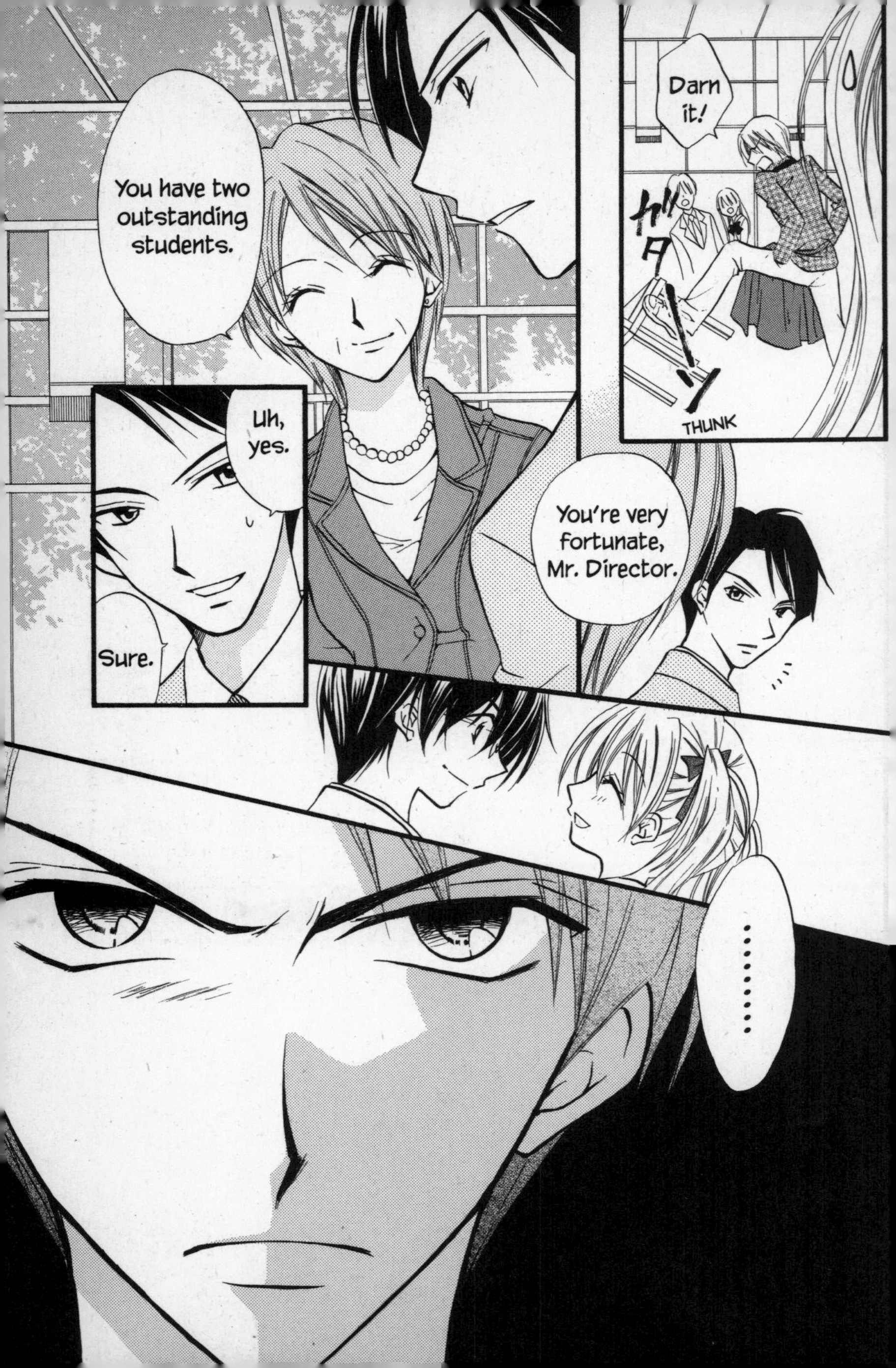
Darn it!
THUNK
You're very fortunate, Mr. Director.
You have two outstanding students.
Uh, yes.
Sure.
......

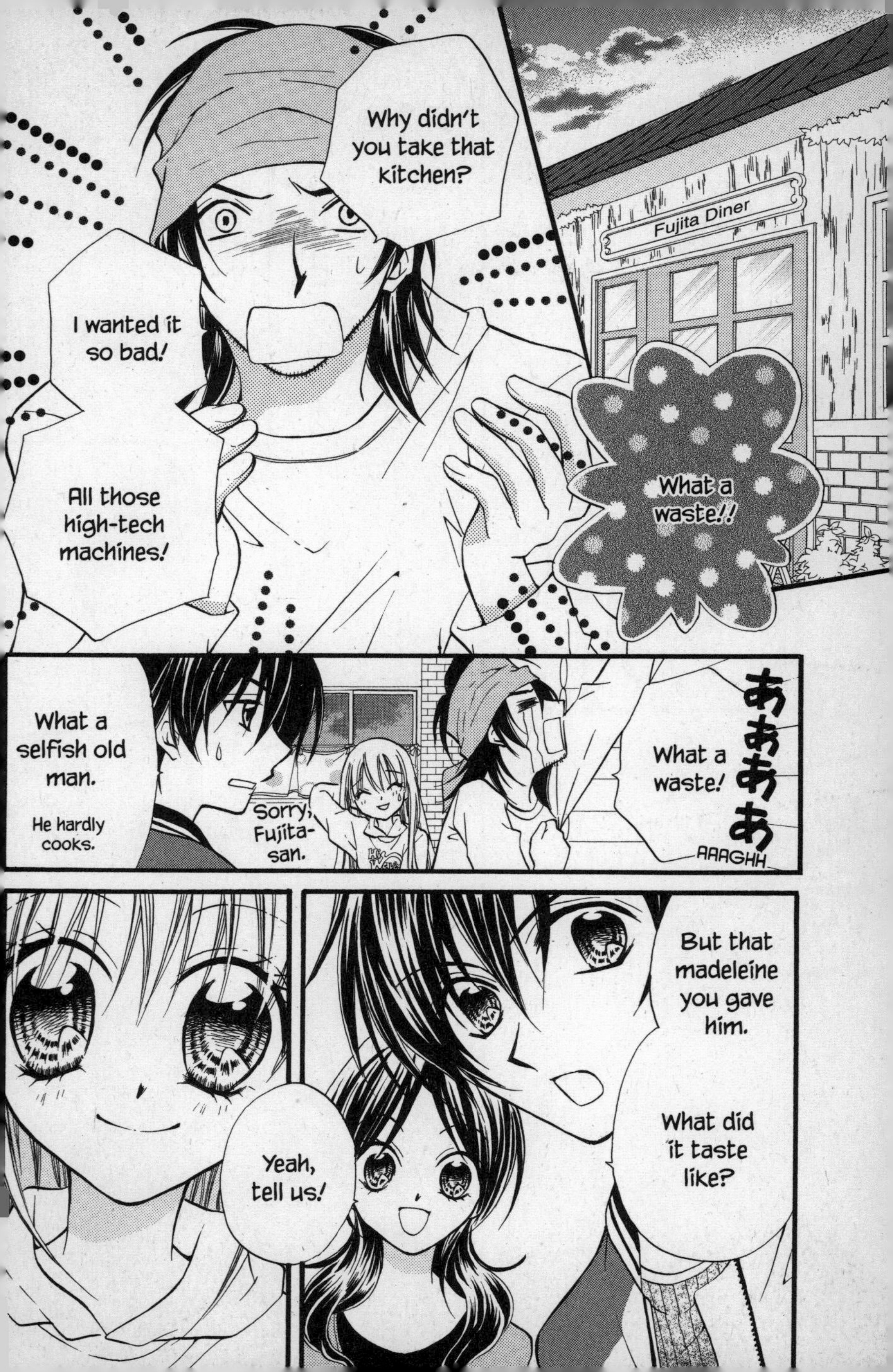
Fujita Diner
Why didn't you take that kitchen?
What a waste!!
I wanted it so bad!
All those high-tech machines!
ああああ
AAAGHH
What a waste!
Sorry, Fujita-san.
What a selfish old man.
He hardly cooks.
But that madeleine you gave him.
What did it taste like?
Yeah, tell us!

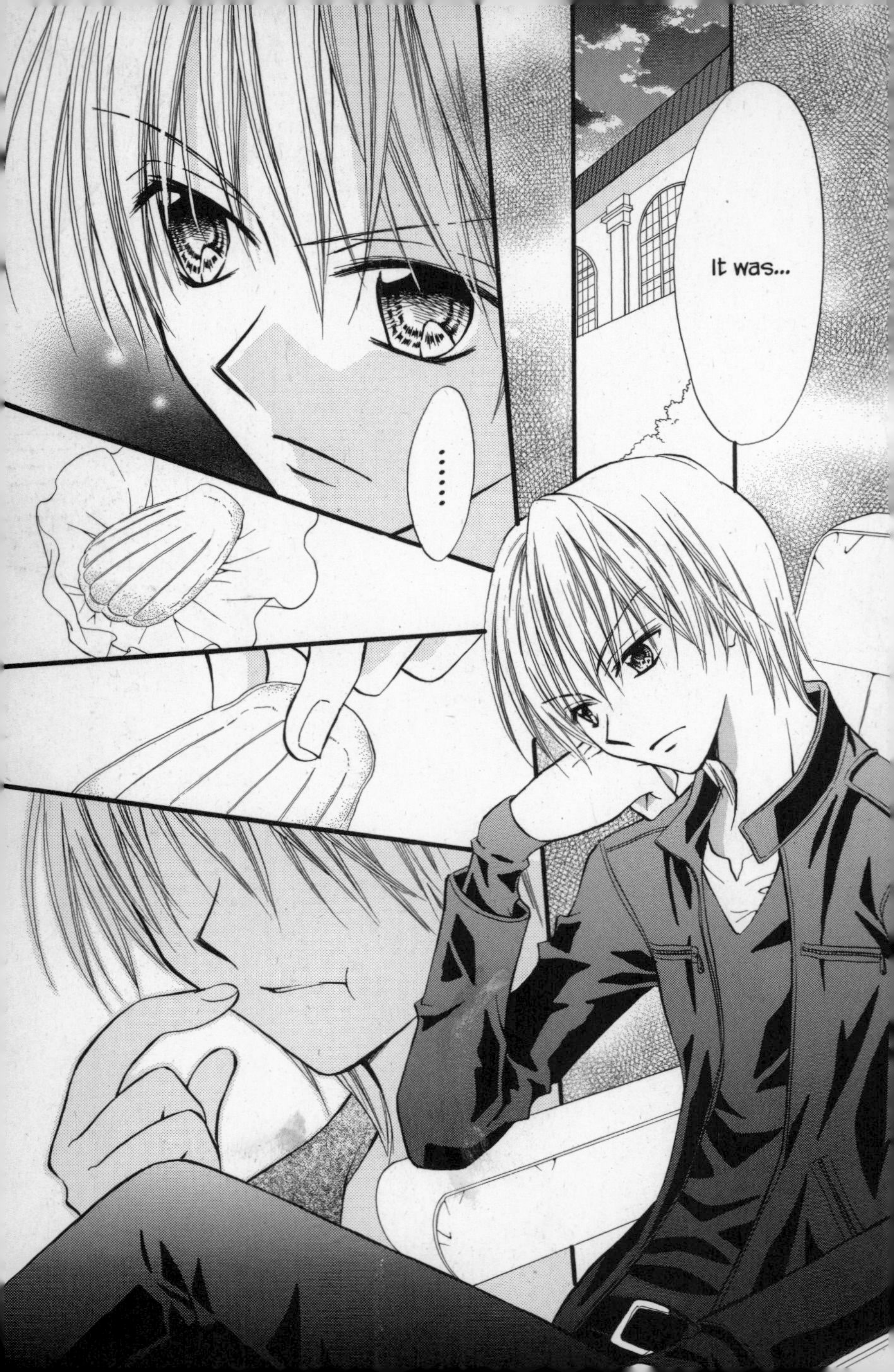
It was...
......

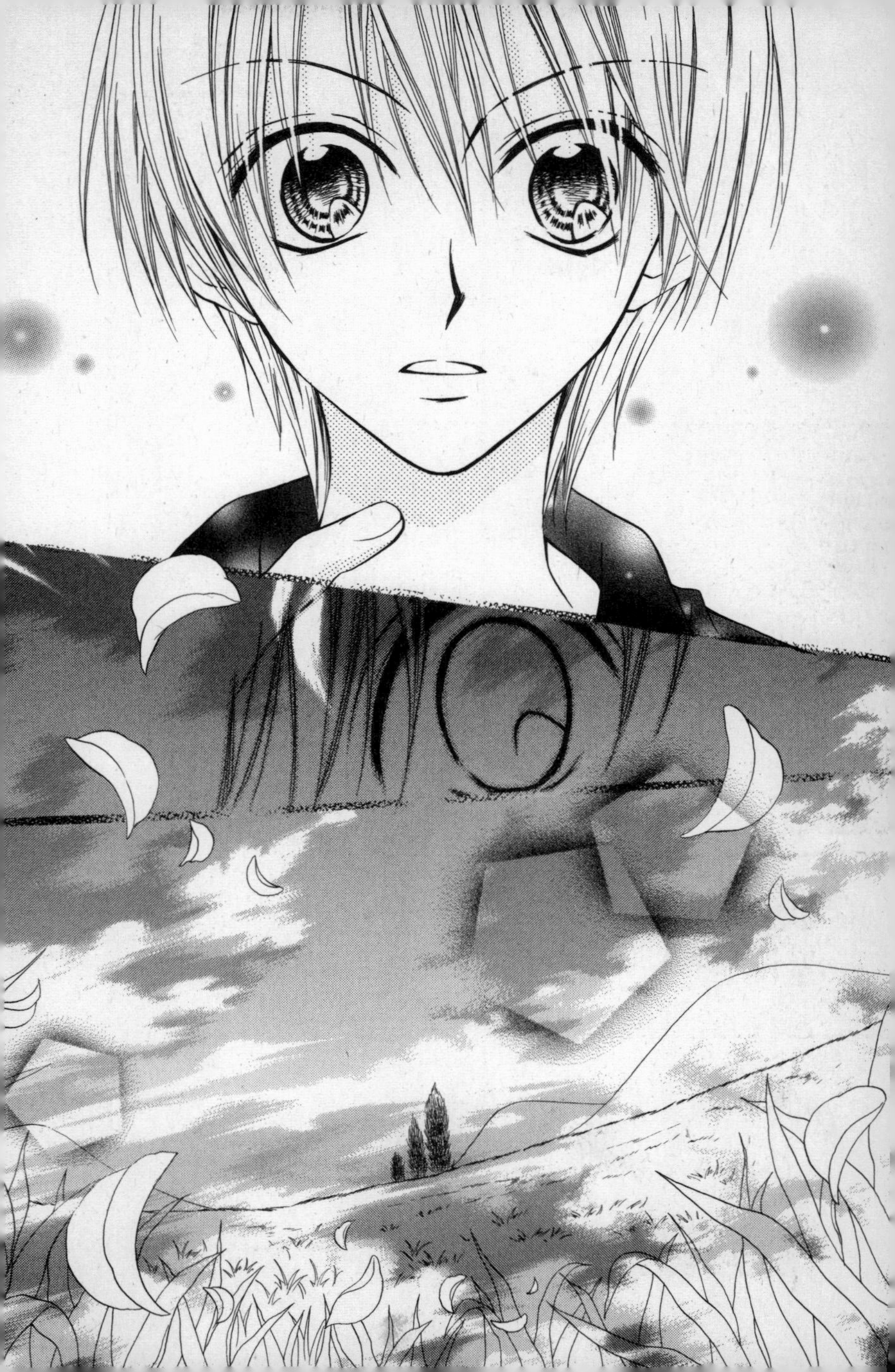

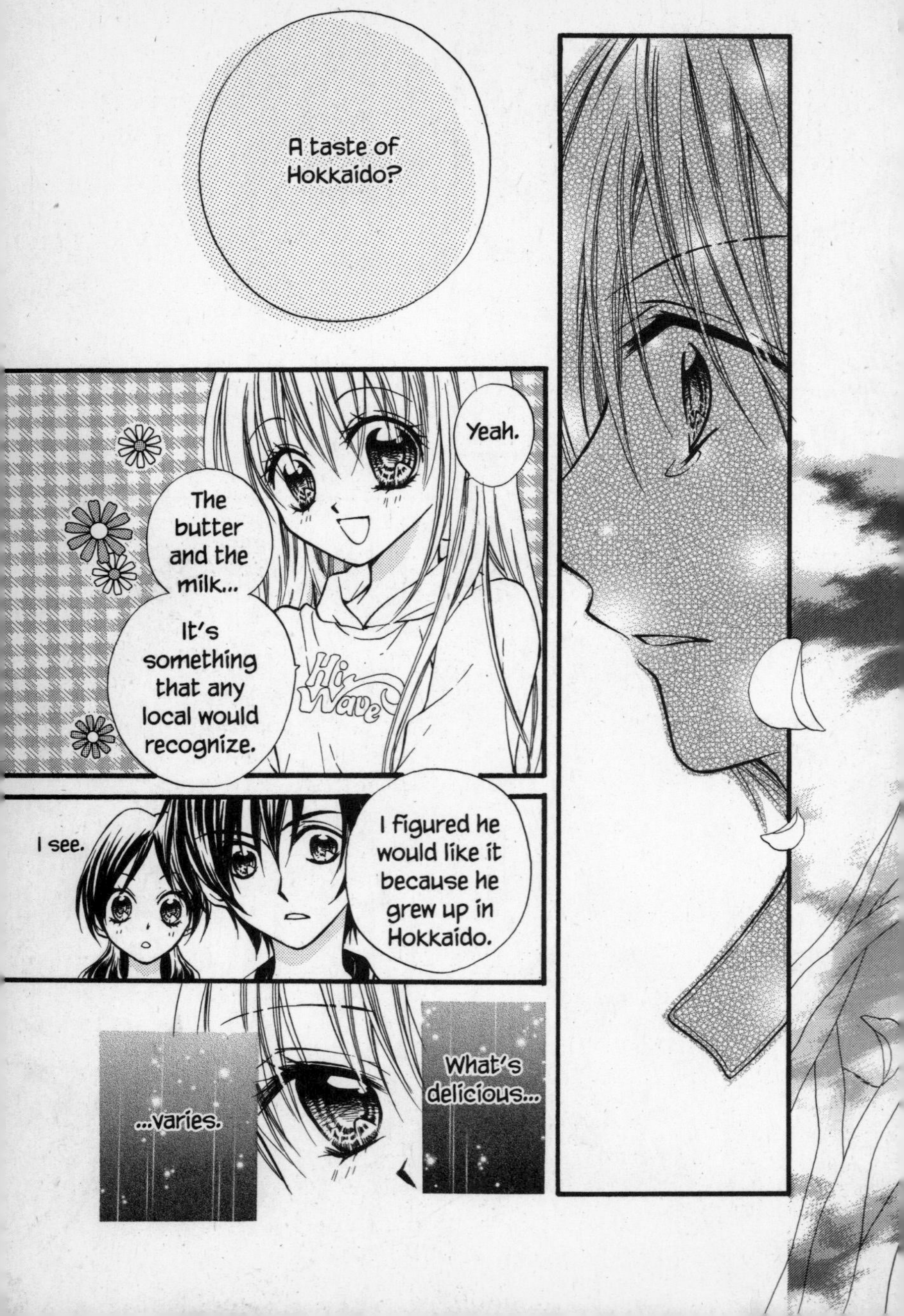
A taste of Hokkaido?
Yeah.
The butter and the milk...
It's something that any local would recognize.
I figured he would like it because he grew up in Hokkaido.
I see.
What's delicious...
...varies.

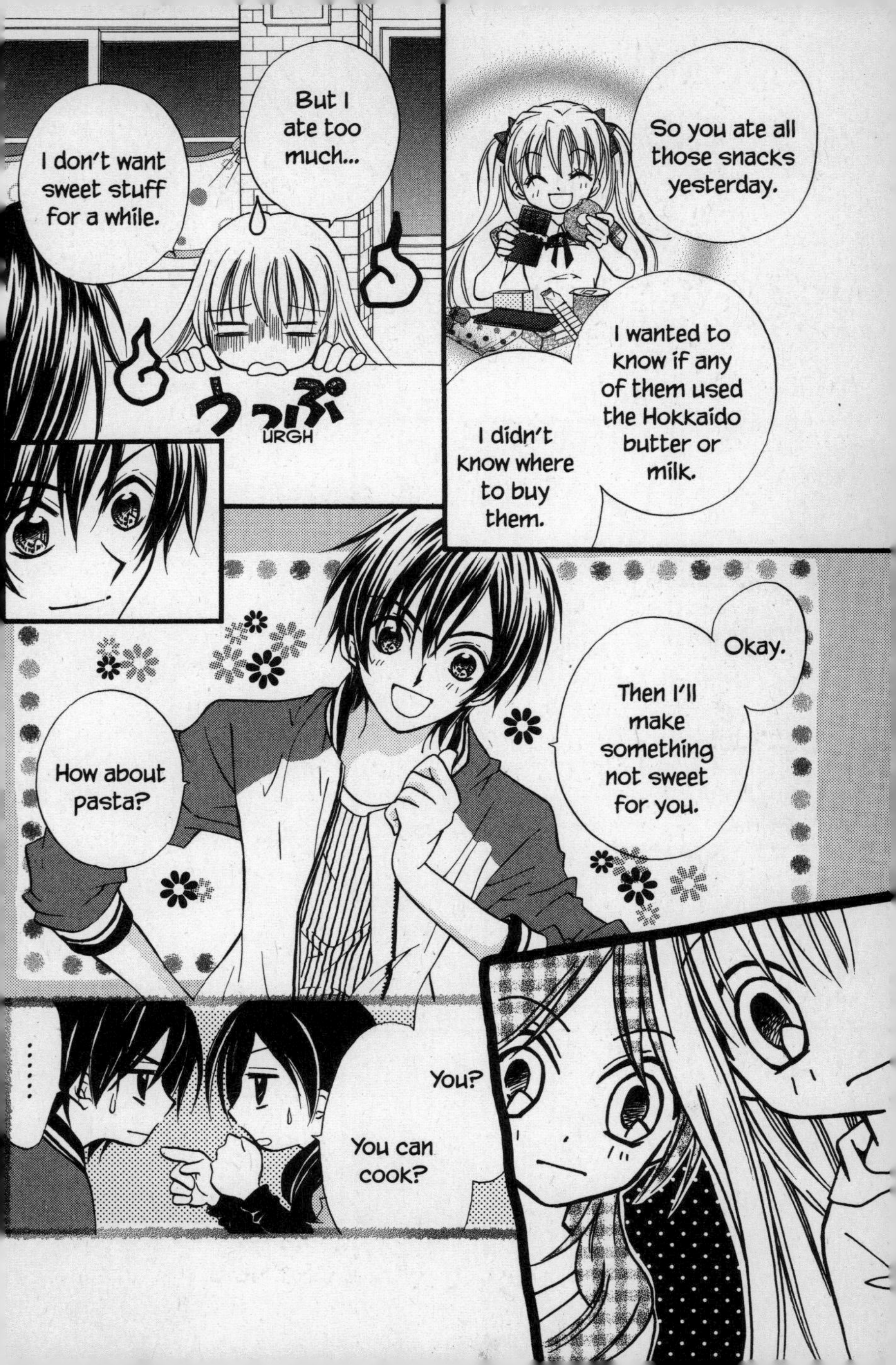
So you ate all those snacks yesterday.
I wanted to know if any of them used the Hokkaido butter or milk.
I didn't know where to buy them.
But I ate too much...
I don't want sweet stuff for a while.
うっぷ
URGH
Okay.
Then I'll make something not sweet for you.
How about pasta?
You?
You can cook?
……

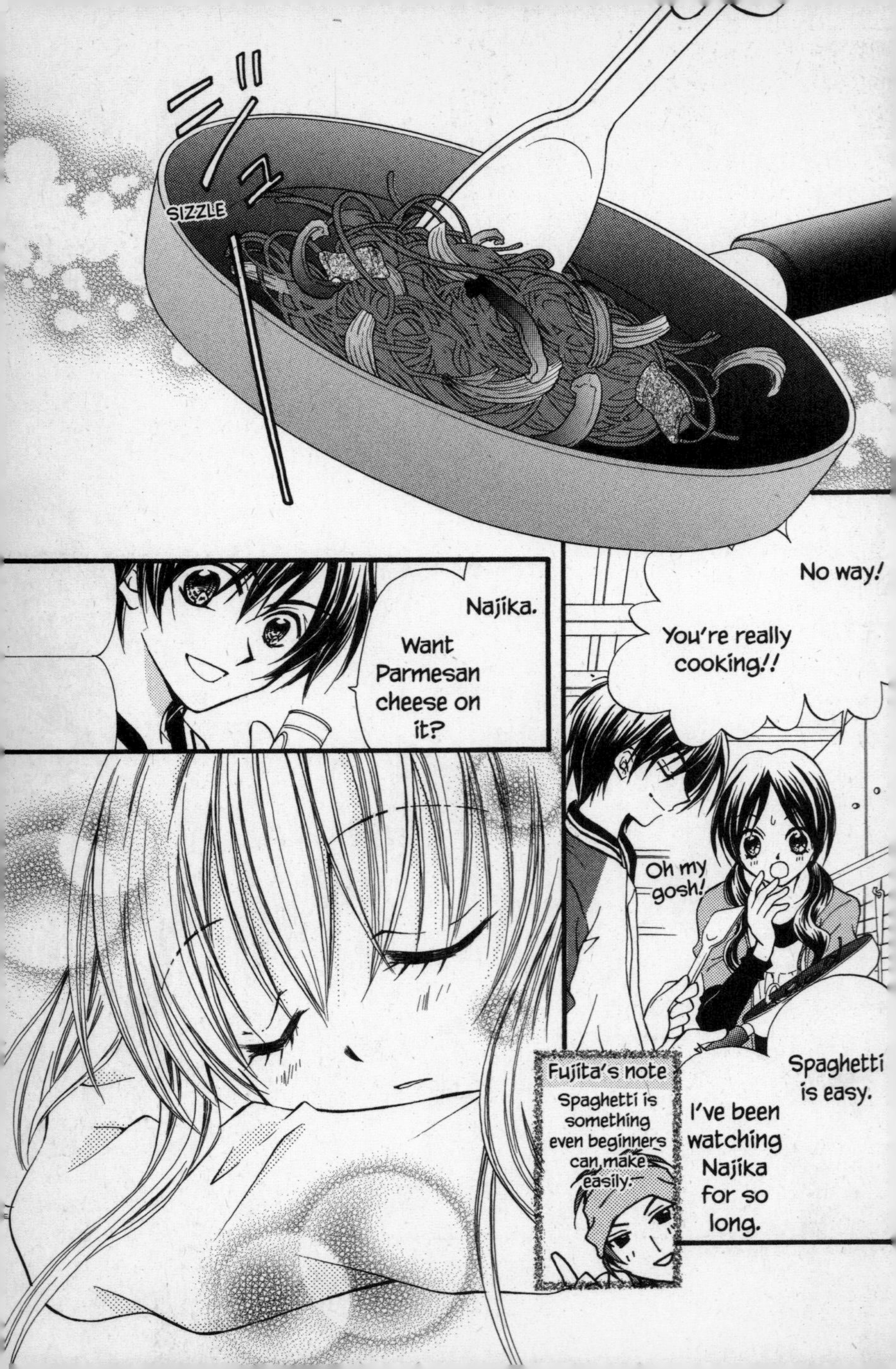

ジュー
SIZZLE
No way!
You're really cooking!!
Oh my gosh!
Spaghetti is easy.
I've been watching Najika for so long.
Najika.
Want Parmesan cheese on it?
Fujita's note
Spaghetti is something even beginners can make easily.

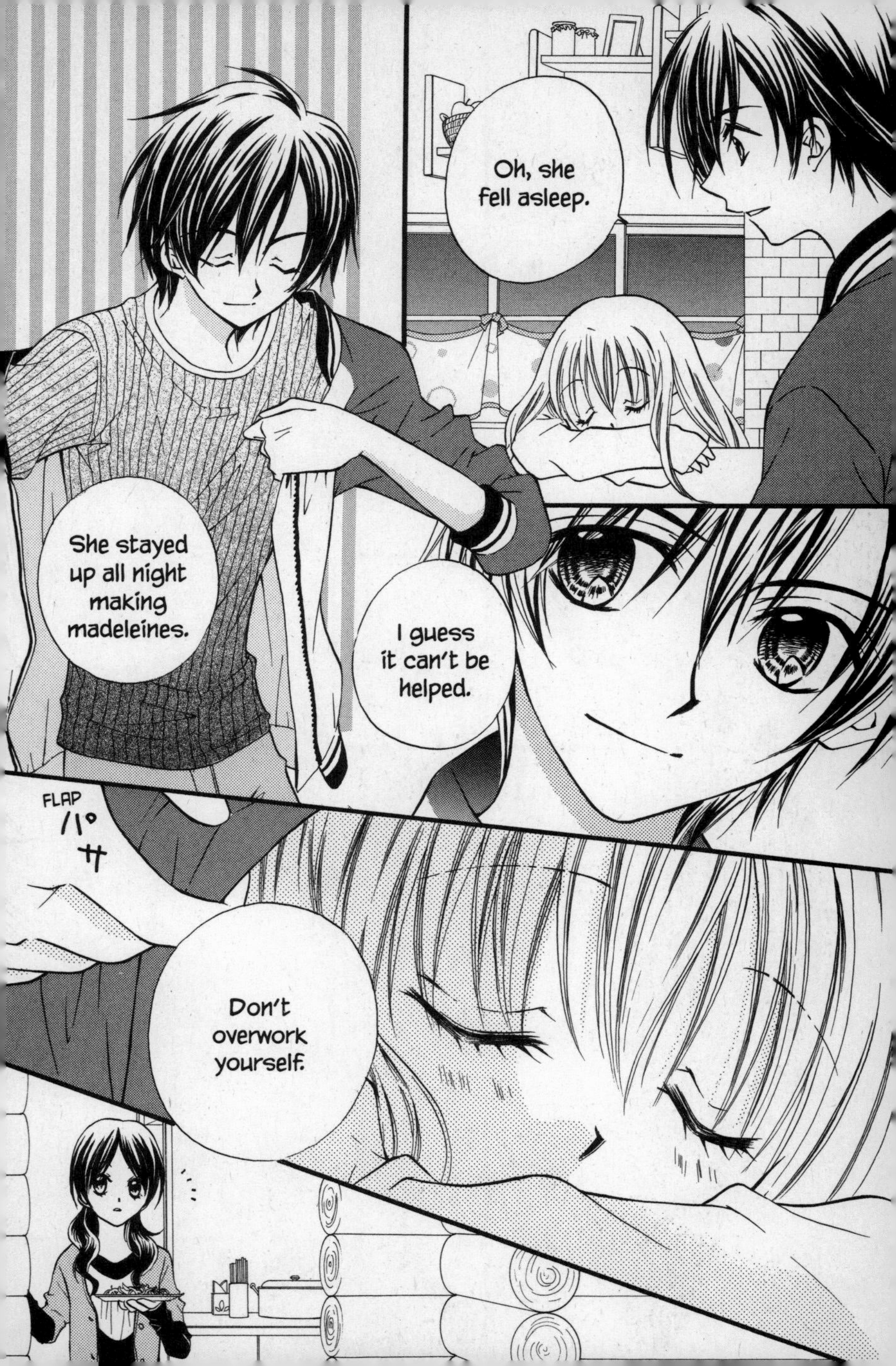
Oh, she fell asleep.
I guess it can't be helped.
She stayed up all night making madeleines.
FLAP
パサ
Don't overwork yourself.

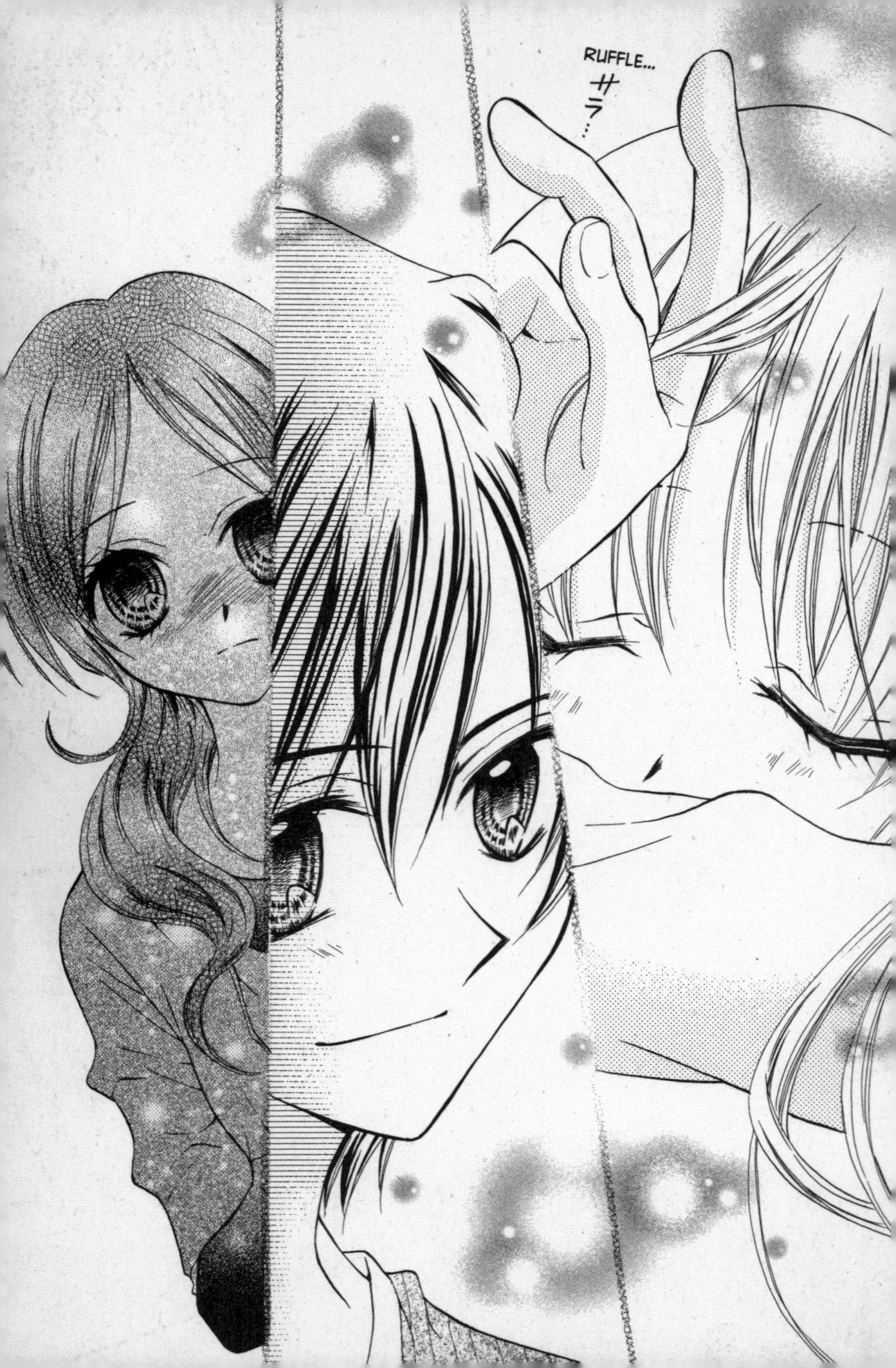
RUFFLE...
サラ…

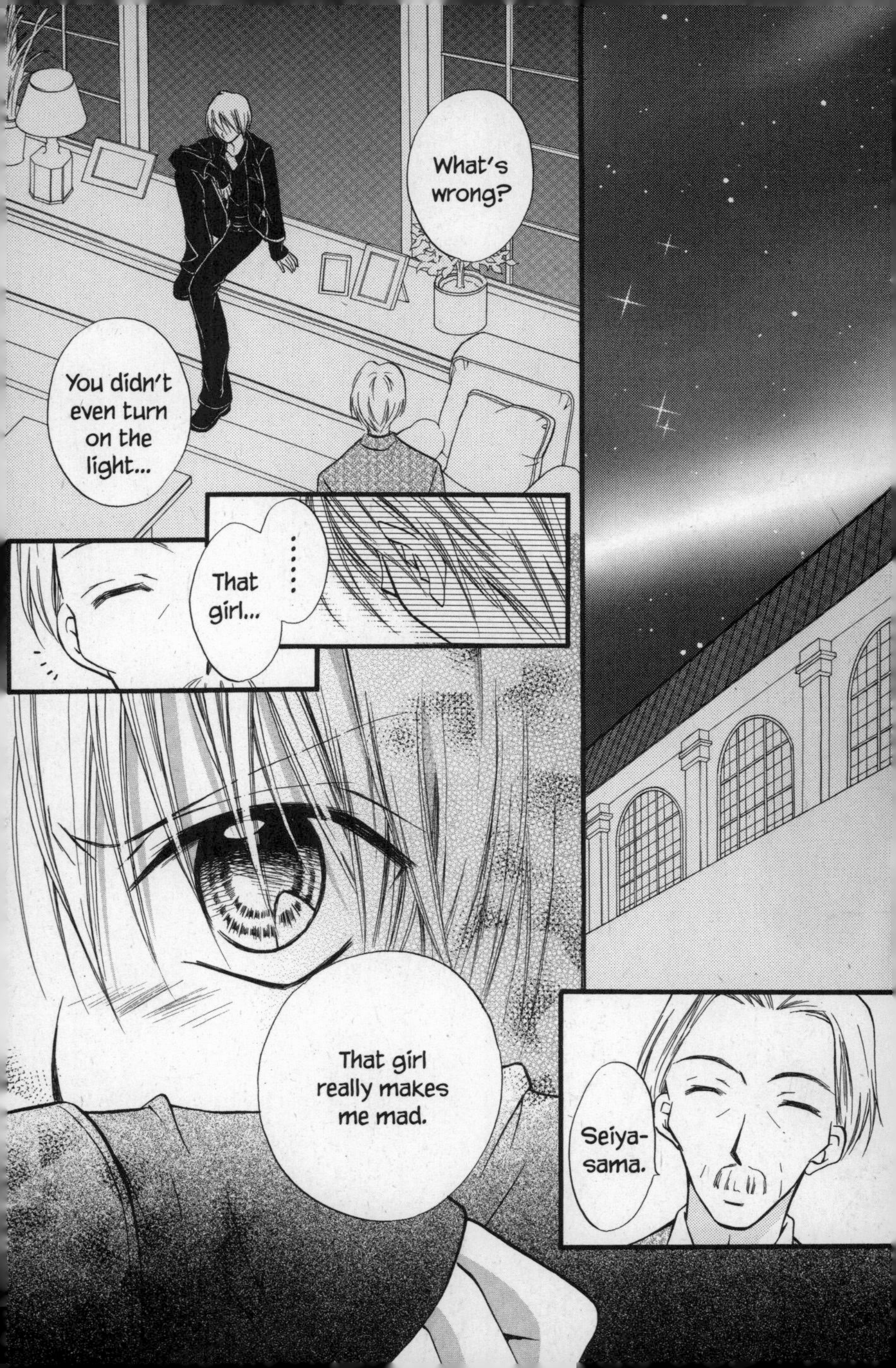
What's wrong?
You didn't even turn on the light...
......
That girl...
That girl really makes me mad.
Seiya-sama.

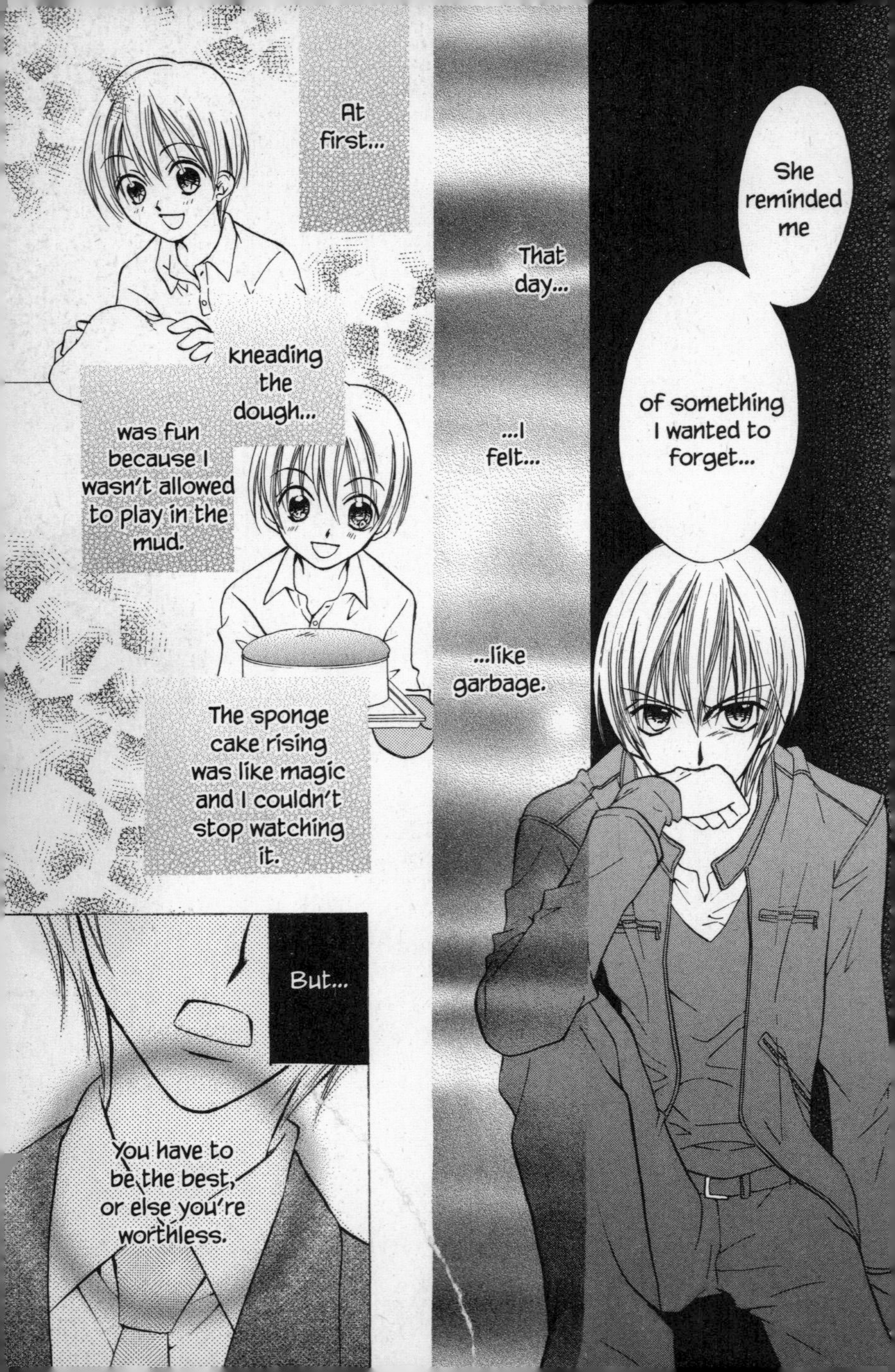
She reminded me
of something I wanted to forget...
That day...
...I felt...
...like garbage.
At first...
kneading the dough...
was fun because I wasn't allowed to play in the mud.
The sponge cake rising was like magic and I couldn't stop watching it.
But...
You have to be the best, or else you're worthless.

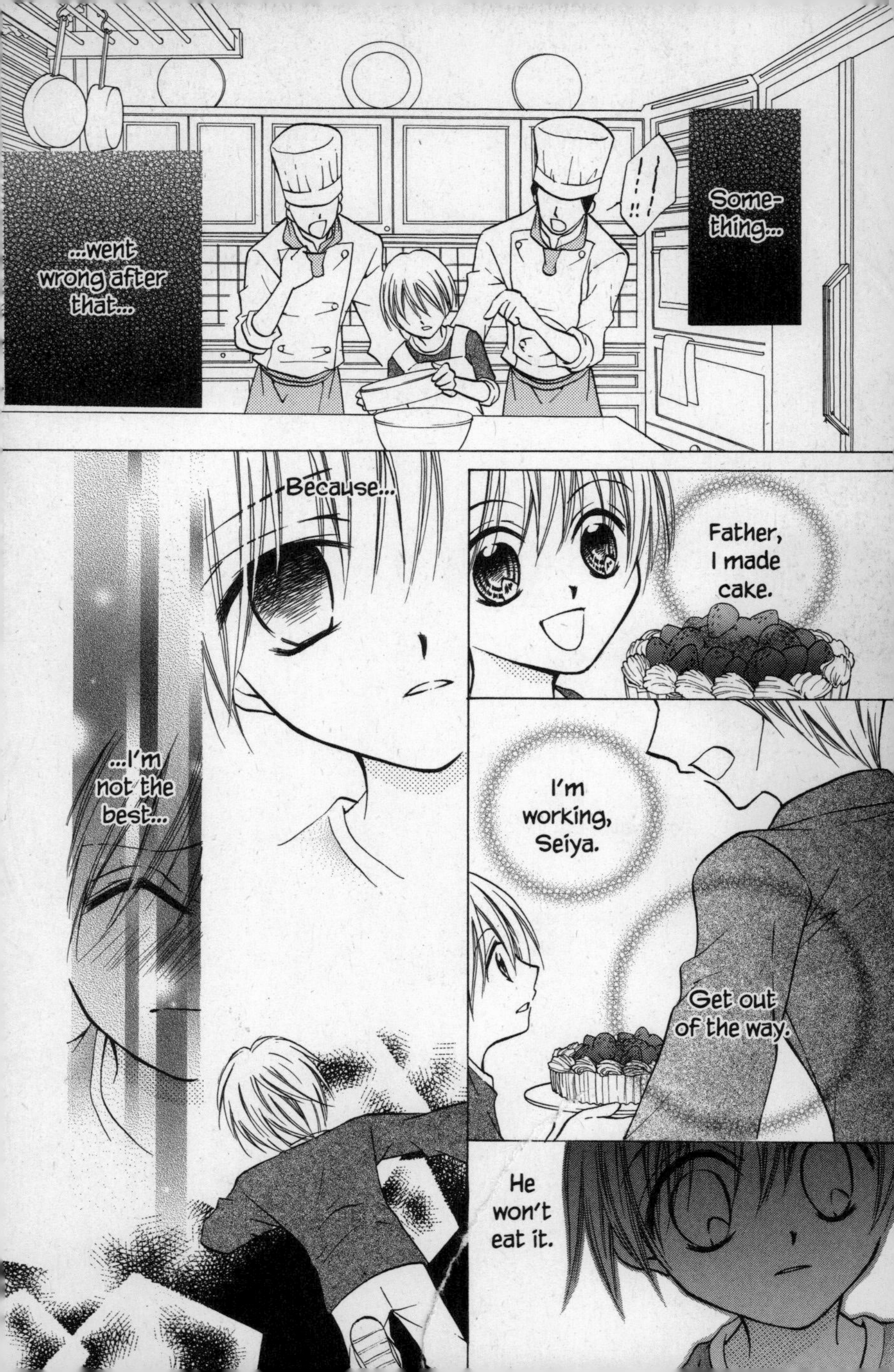
Some-thing...
!!
...went wrong after that...
Father, I made cake.
I'm working, Seiya.
Get out of the way.
He won't eat it.
Because...
...I'm not the best...

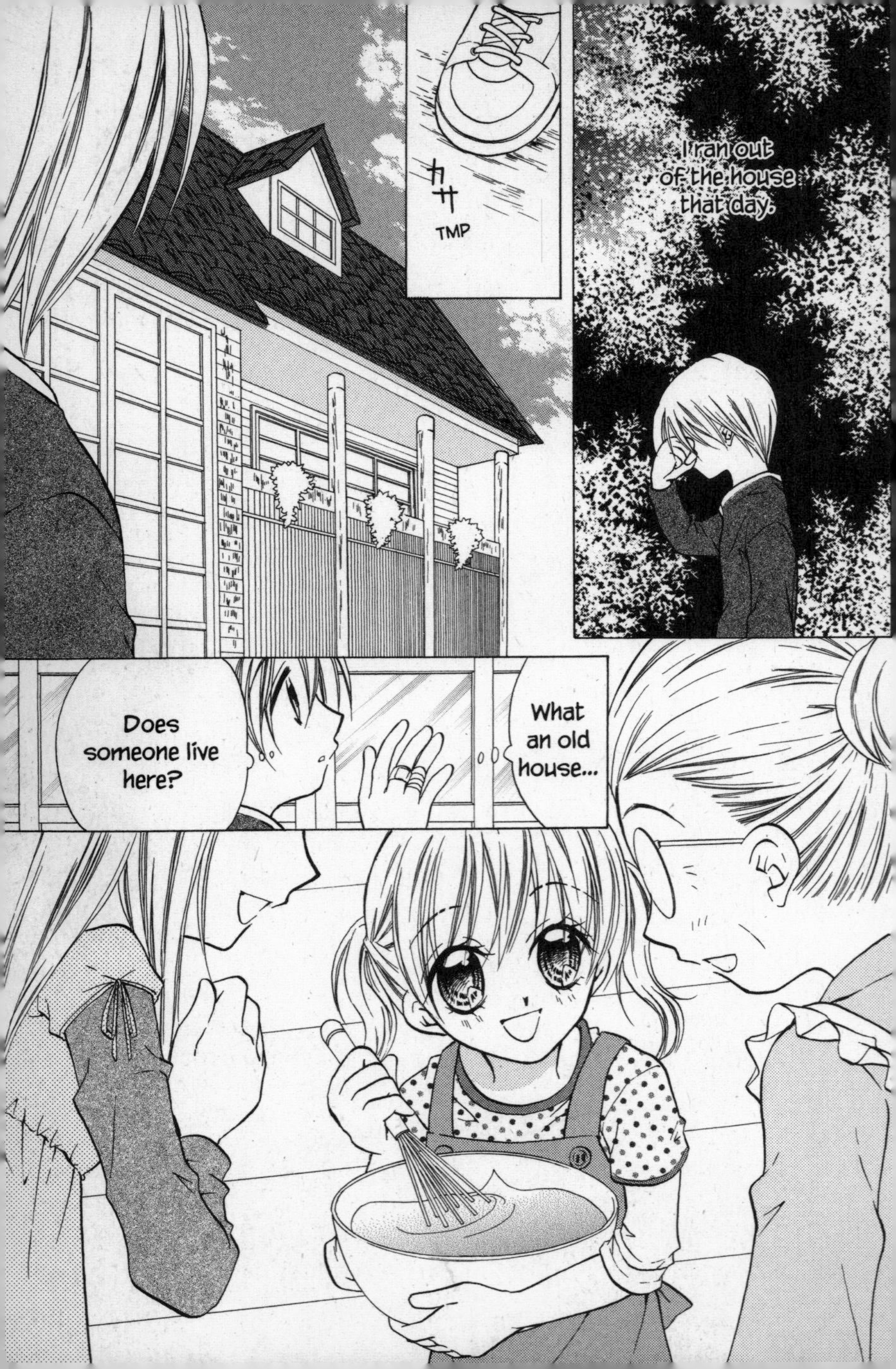
I ran out of the house that day.
カサ
TMP
What an old house...
Does someone live here?

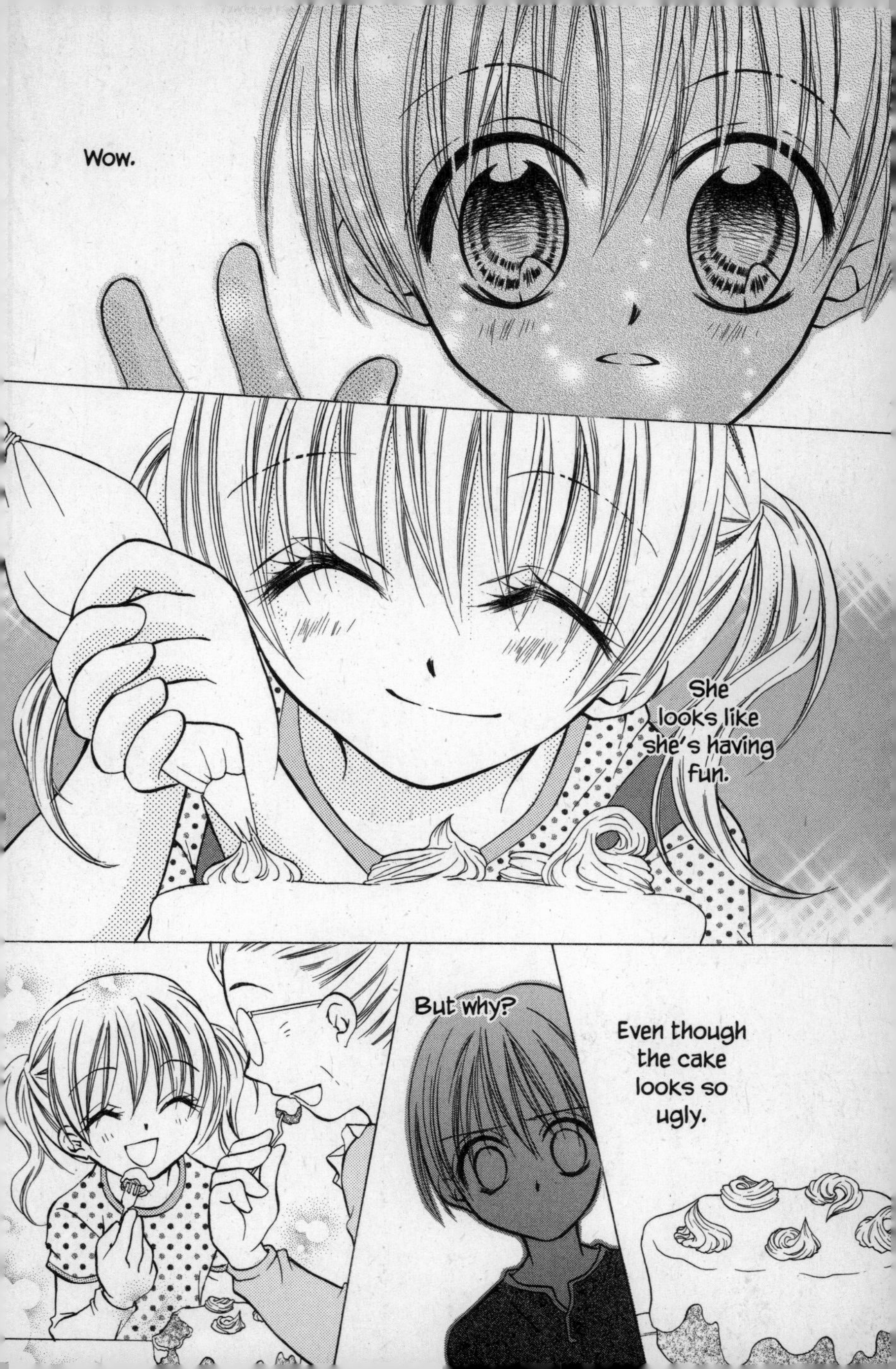
Wow.
She looks like she's having fun.
Even though the cake looks so ugly.
But why?

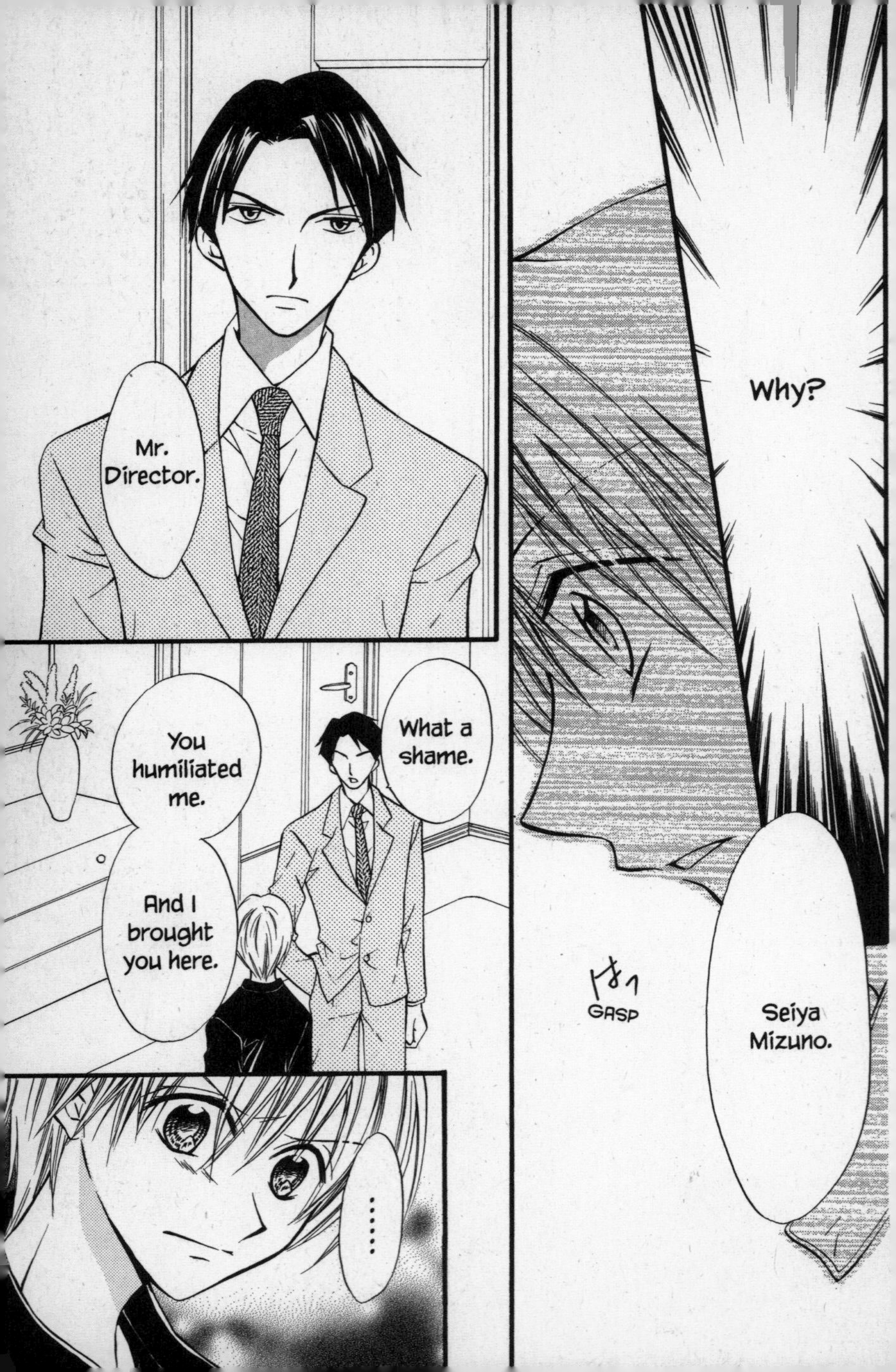
Why?
Seiya Mizuno.
はっ
GASP
Mr. Director.
What a shame.
You humiliated me.
And I brought you here.
......

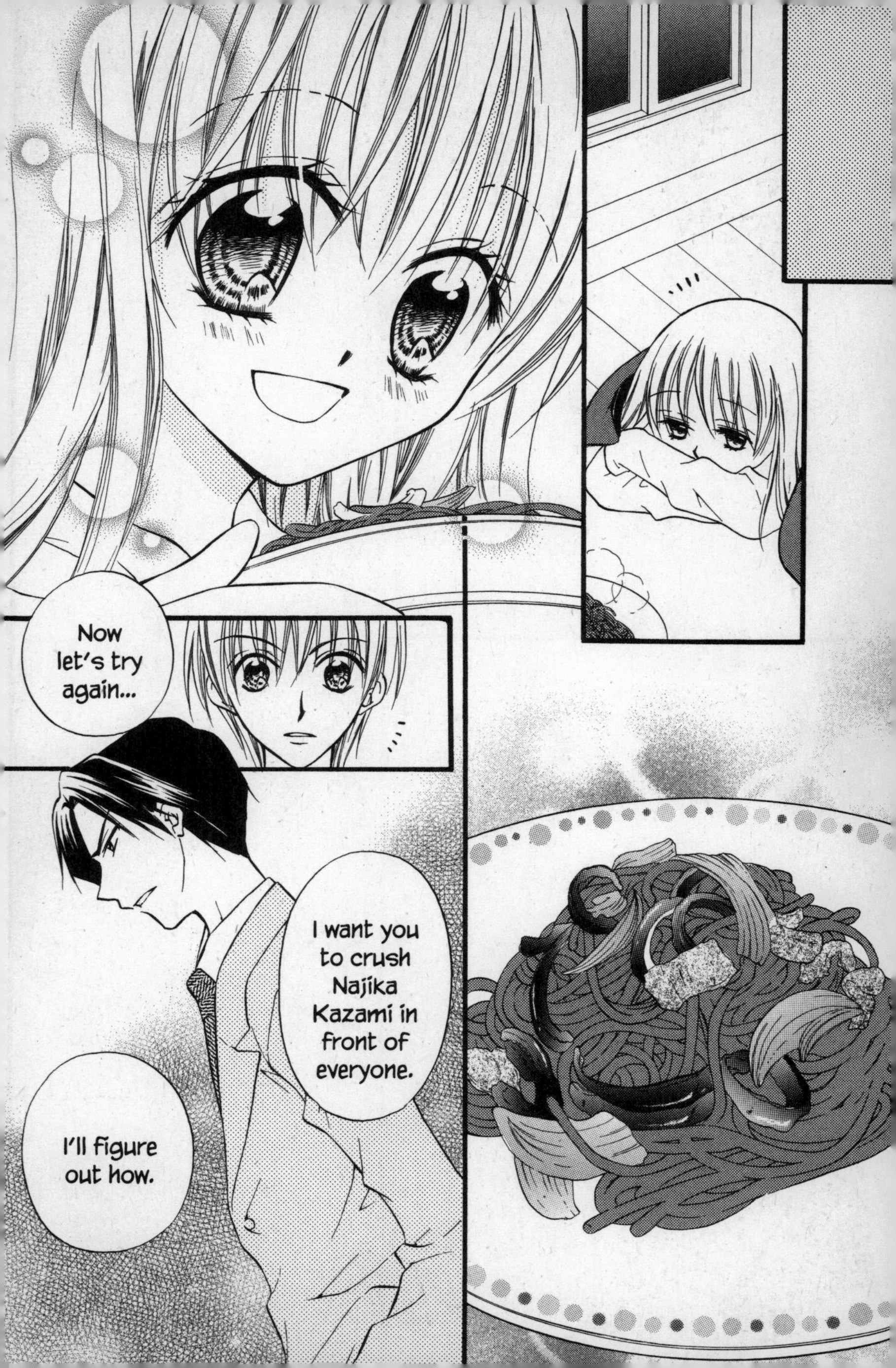
Now let's try again...
I want you to crush Najika Kazami in front of everyone.
I'll figure out how.

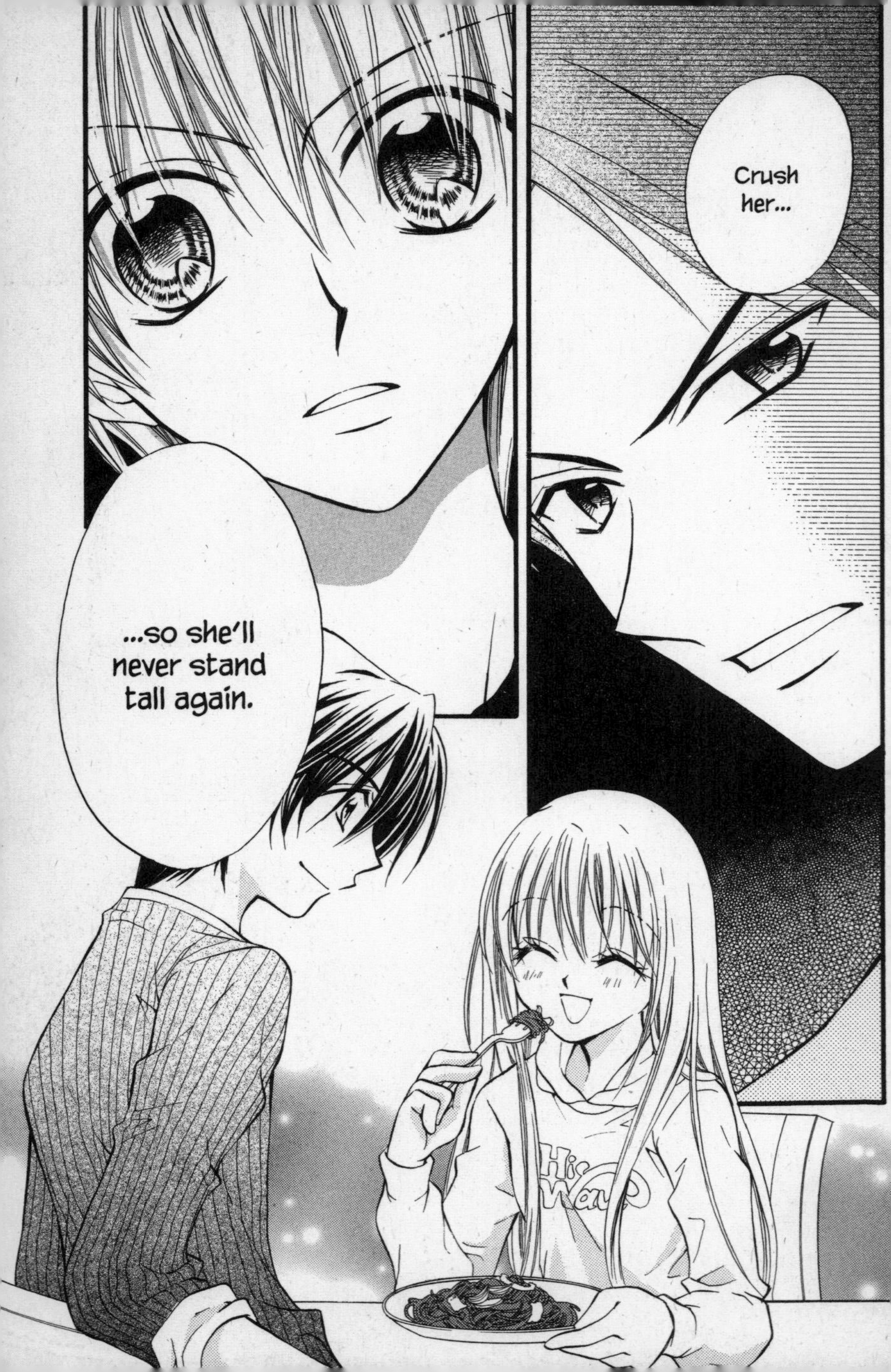
Crush her...
...so she'll never stand tall again.

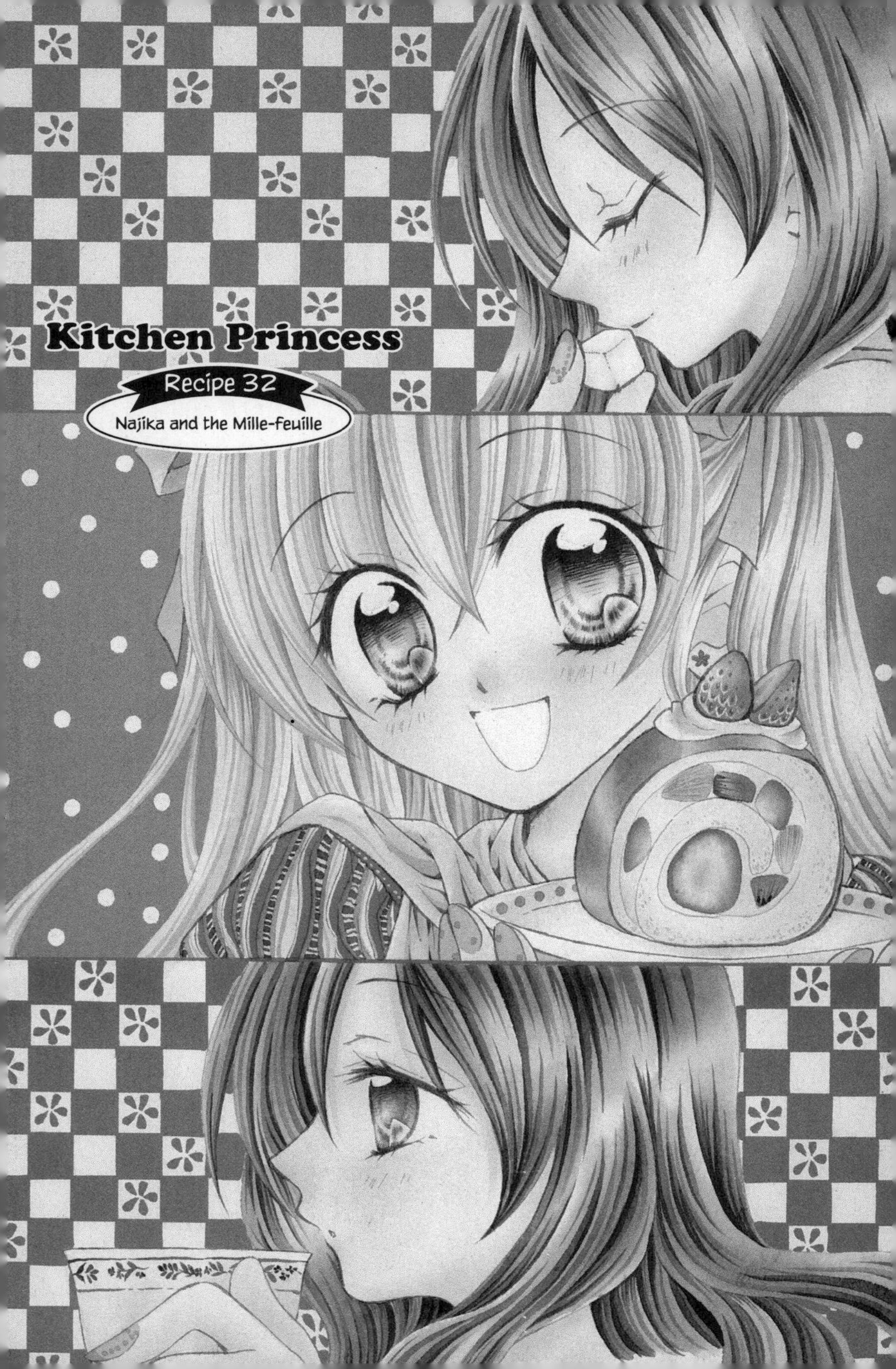
Kitchen Princess
Recipe 32
Najika and the Mille-feuille

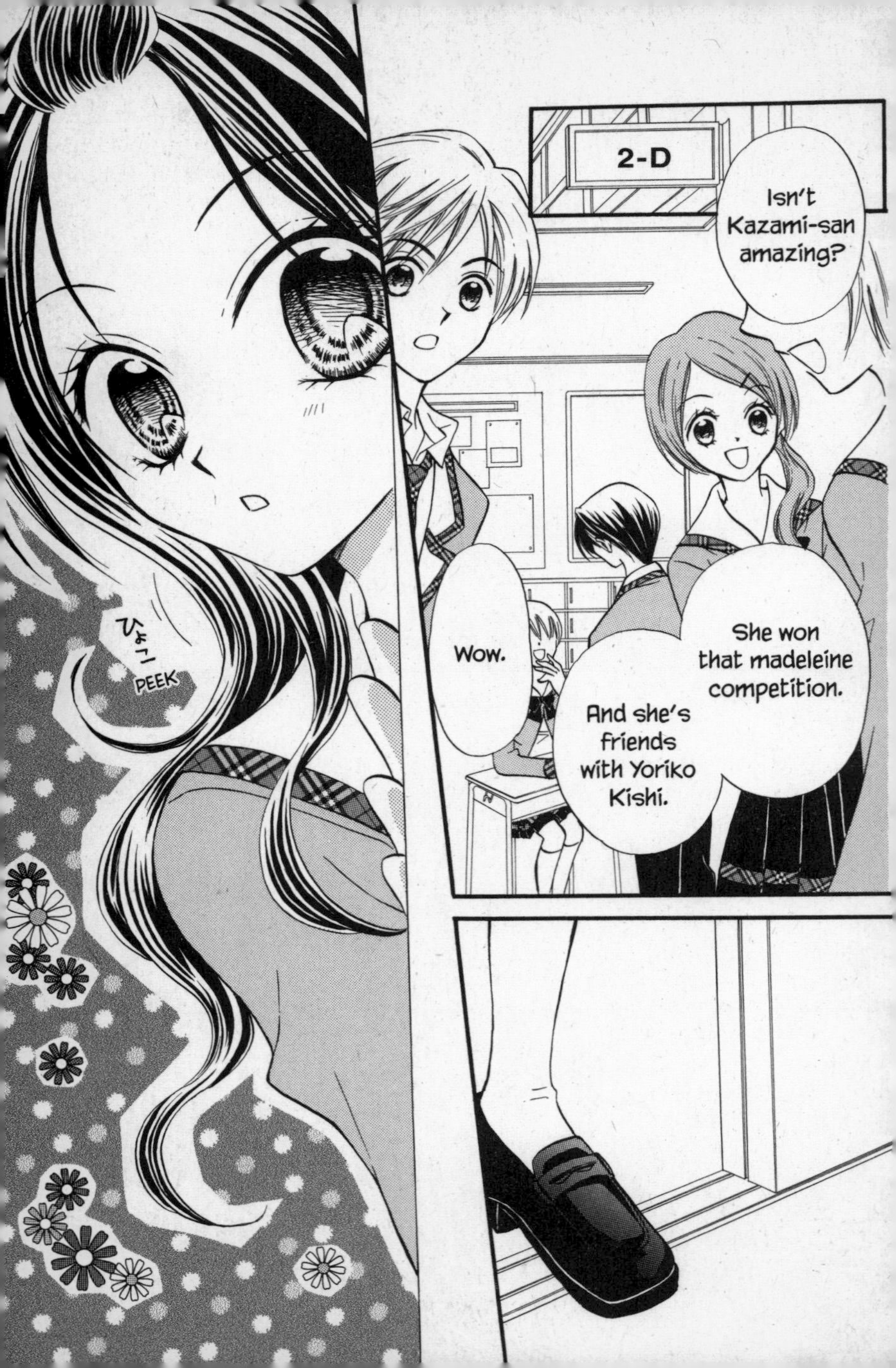
2-D
Isn't Kazami-san amazing?
She won that madeleine competition.
And she's friends with Yoriko Kishi.
Wow.
ひょこ
PEEK

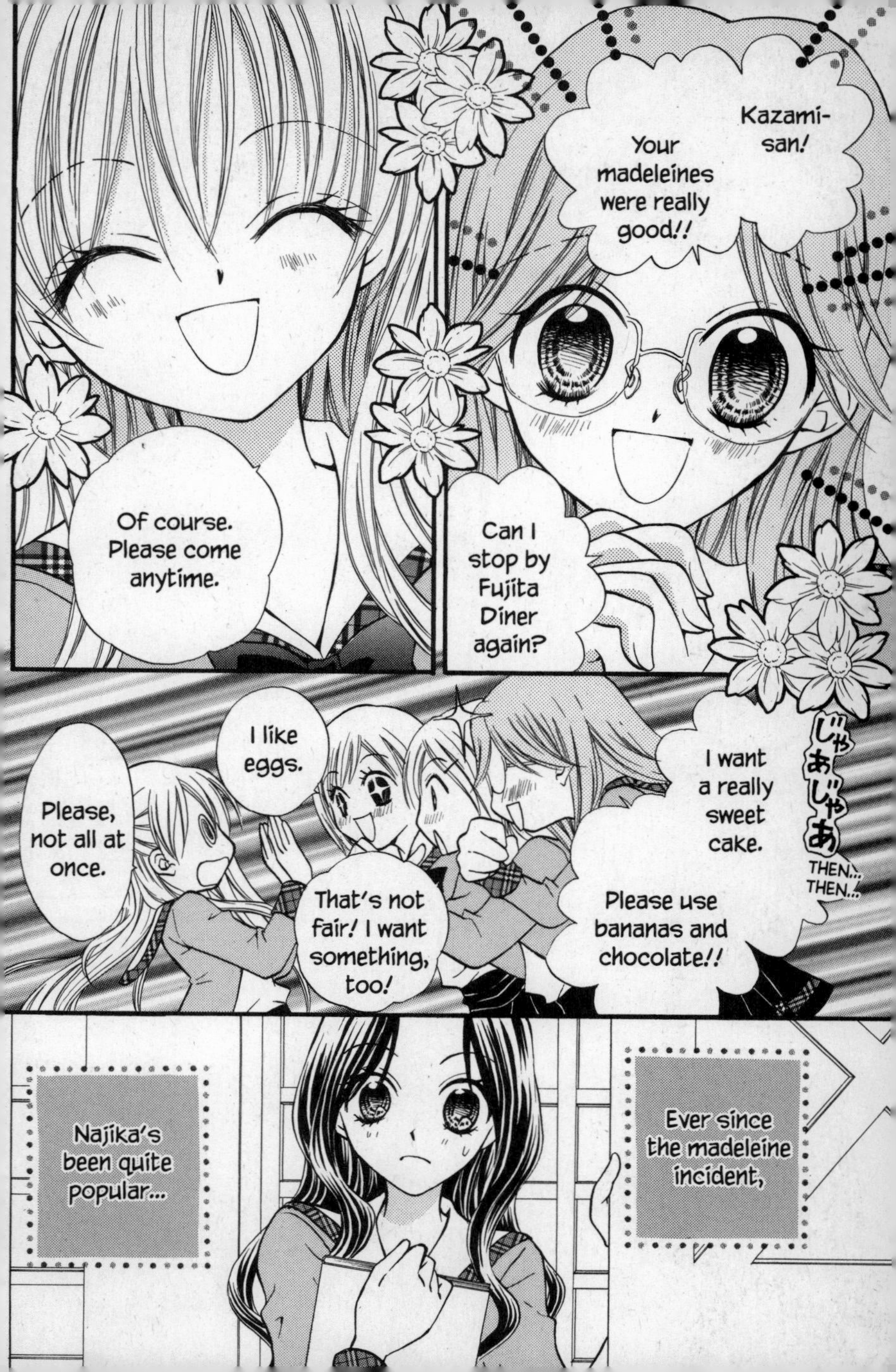

Kazami-san!
Your madeleines were really good!!
Can I stop by Fujita Diner again?
Of course. Please come anytime.
じゃあじゃあ
THEN... THEN...
I want a really sweet cake.
Please use bananas and chocolate!!
That's not fair! I want something, too!
I like eggs.
Please, not all at once.
Ever since the madeleine incident,
Najika's been quite popular...

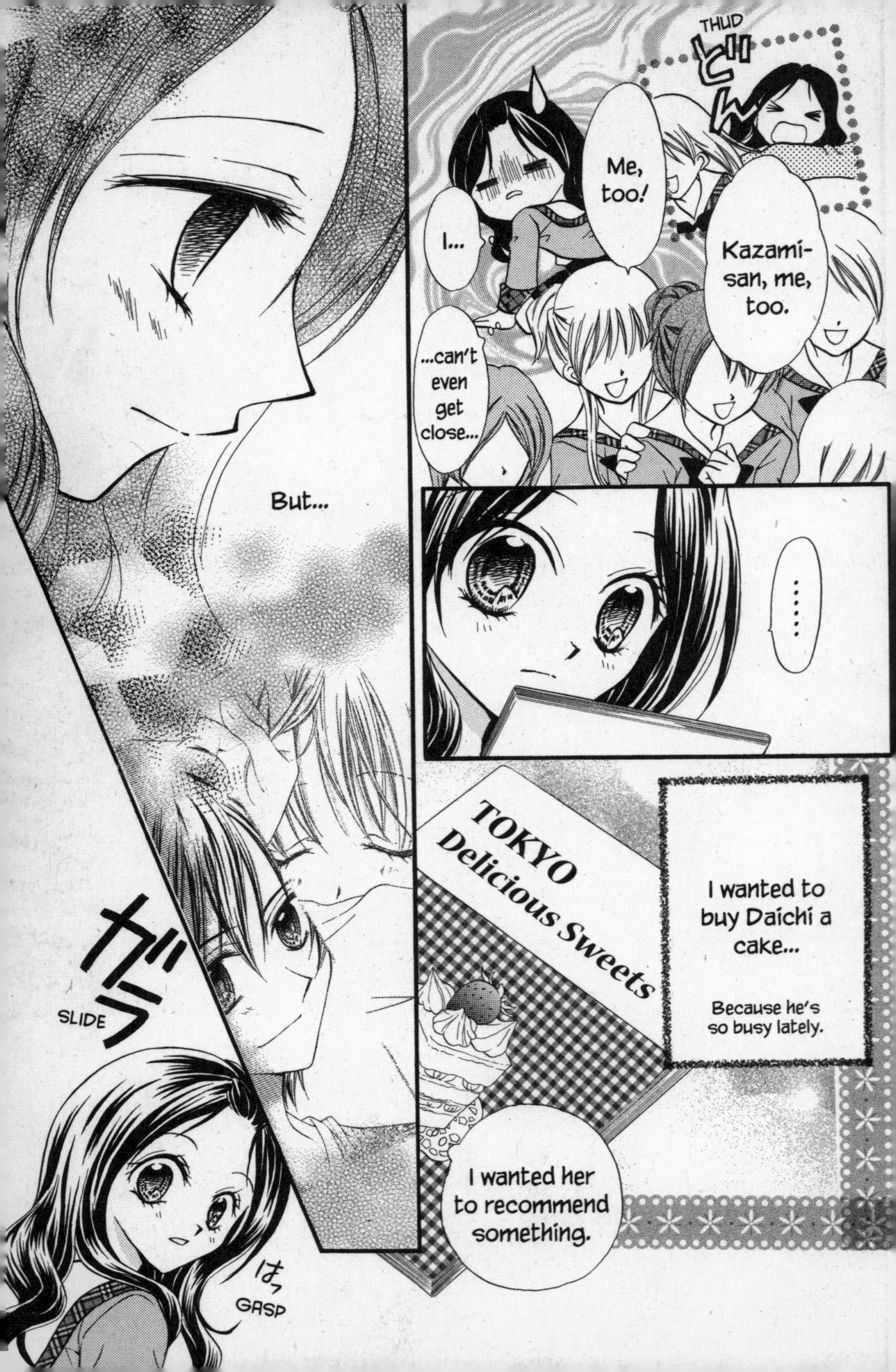

THUD
どん
Kazami-san, me, too.
Me, too!
I...
...can't even get close...
......
I wanted to buy Daichi a cake...
Because he's so busy lately.
TOKYO Delicious Sweets
I wanted her to recommend something.
But...
ガラ
SLIDE
はっ
GASP

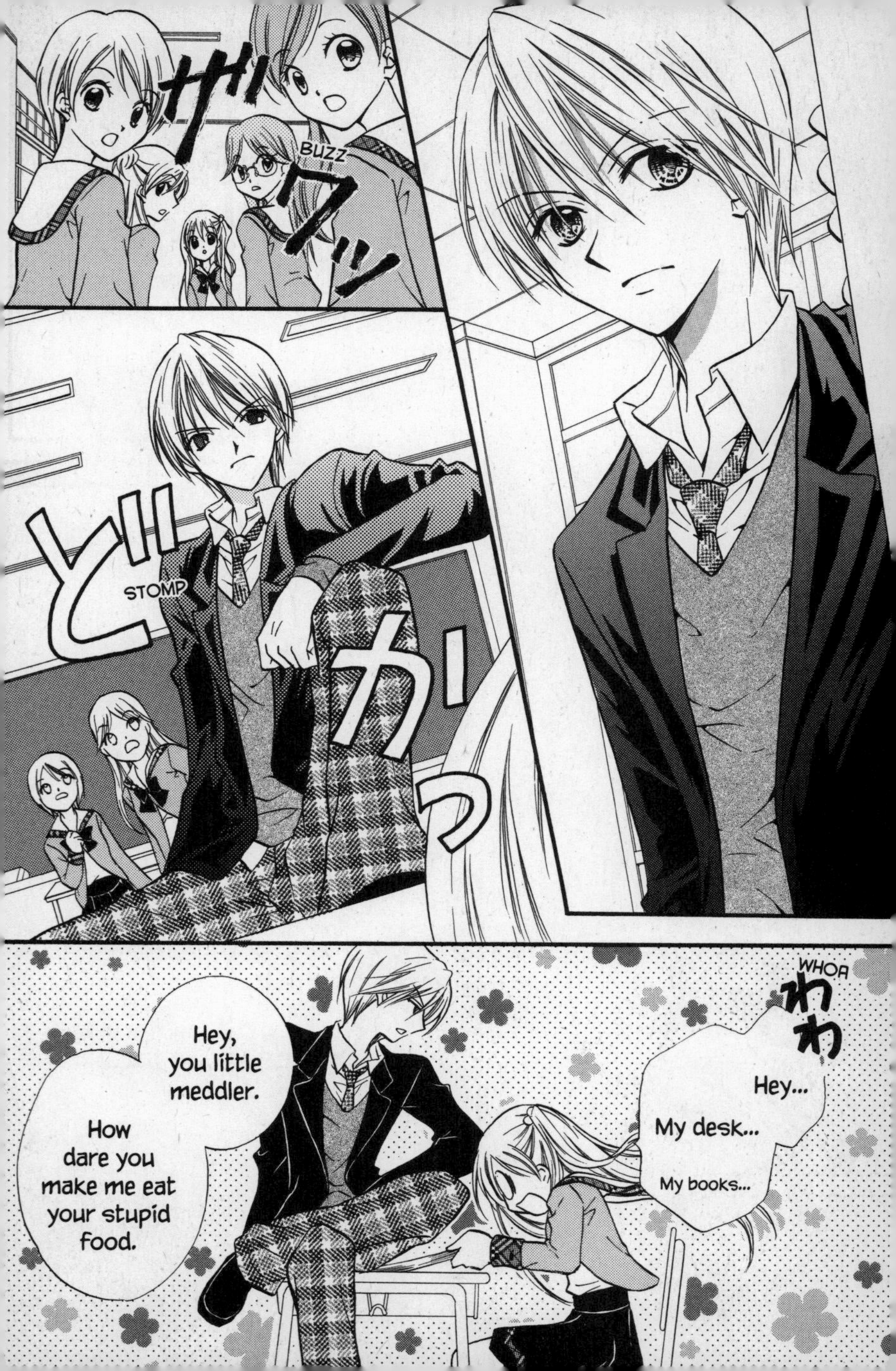
ザワッ
BUZZ
どかっ
STOMP
わわ
WHOA
Hey...
My desk...
My books...
Hey, you little meddler.
How dare you make me eat your stupid food.

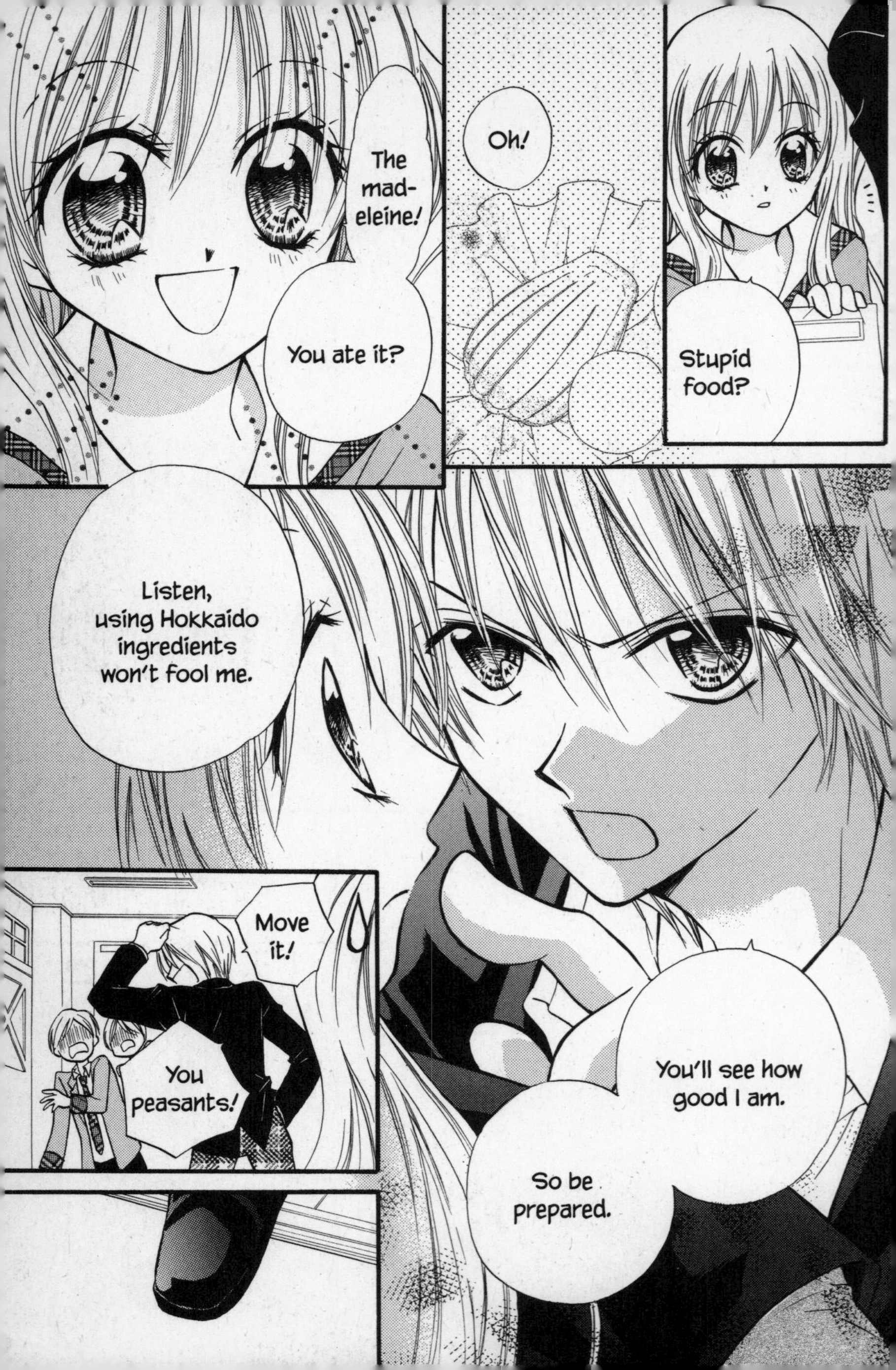
Stupid food?
Oh!
The mad-eleine!
You ate it?
Listen, using Hokkaido ingredients won't fool me.
You'll see how good I am.
So be prepared.
Move it!
You peasants!

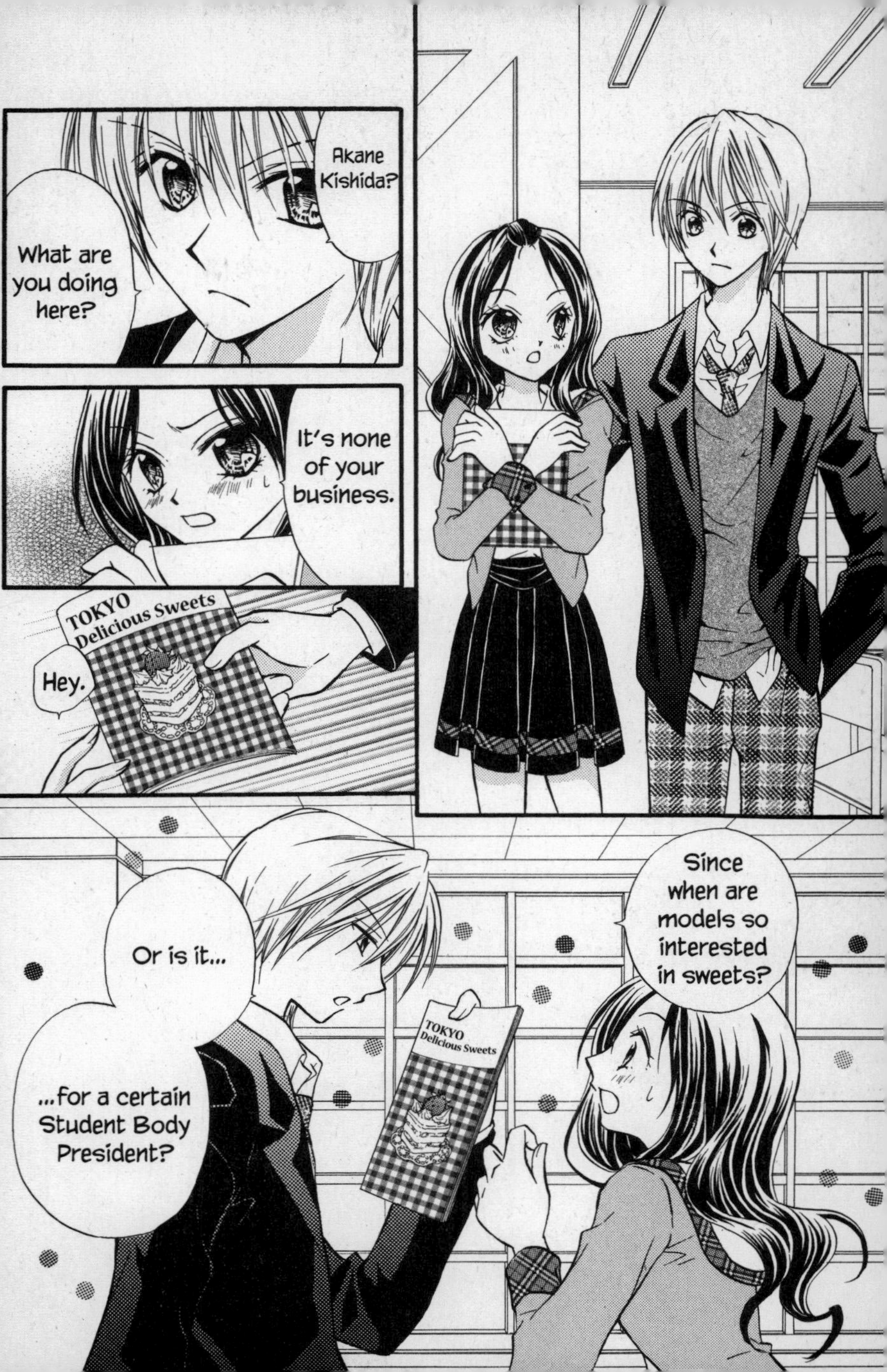
Akane Kishida?
What are you doing here?
It's none of your business.
TOKYO Delicious Sweets
Hey.
Since when are models so interested in sweets?
Or is it...
...for a certain Student Body President?
TOKYO Delicious Sweets

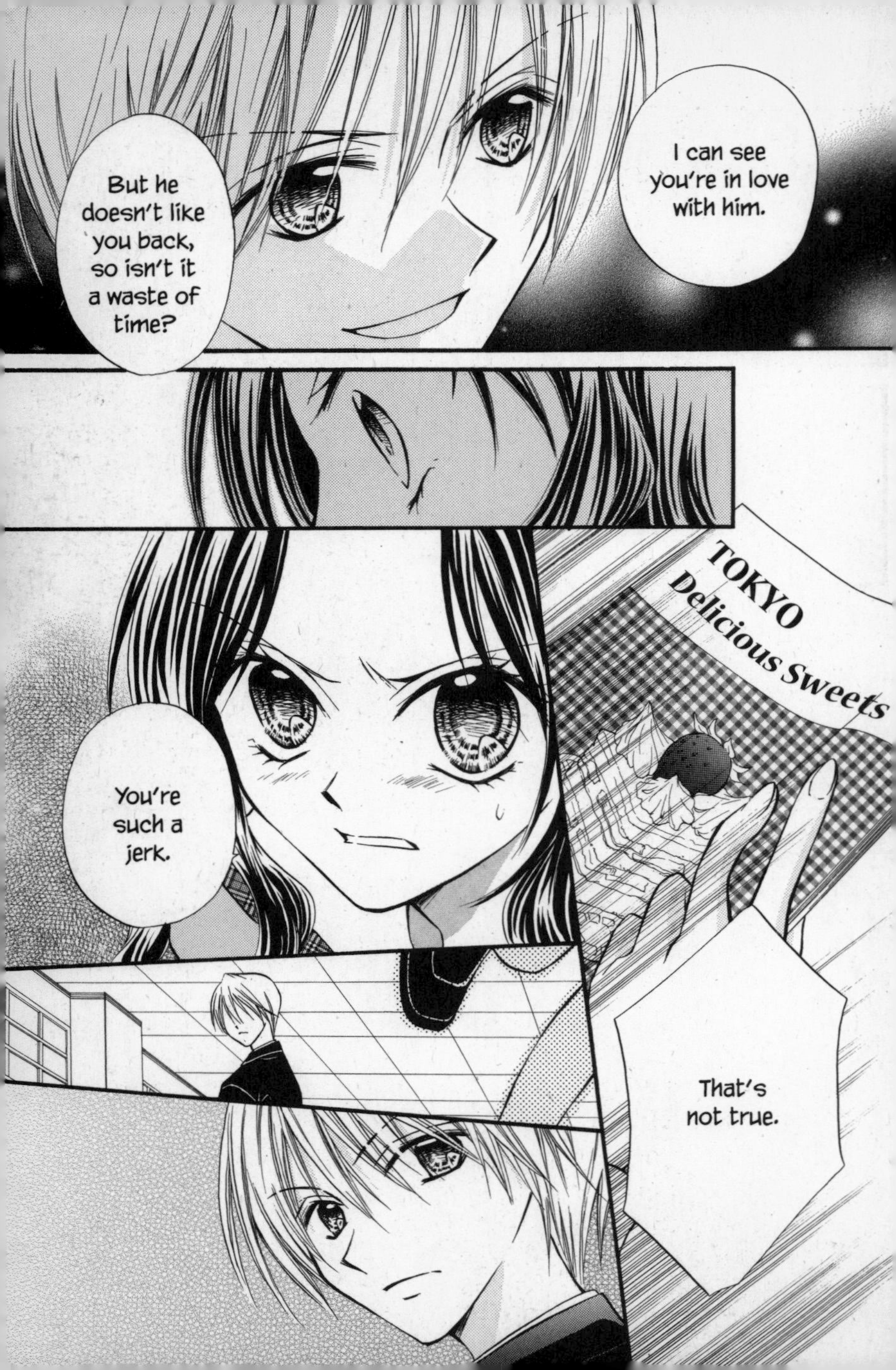
I can see you're in love with him.
But he doesn't like you back, so isn't it a waste of time?
TOKYO Delicious Sweets
You're such a jerk.
That's not true.

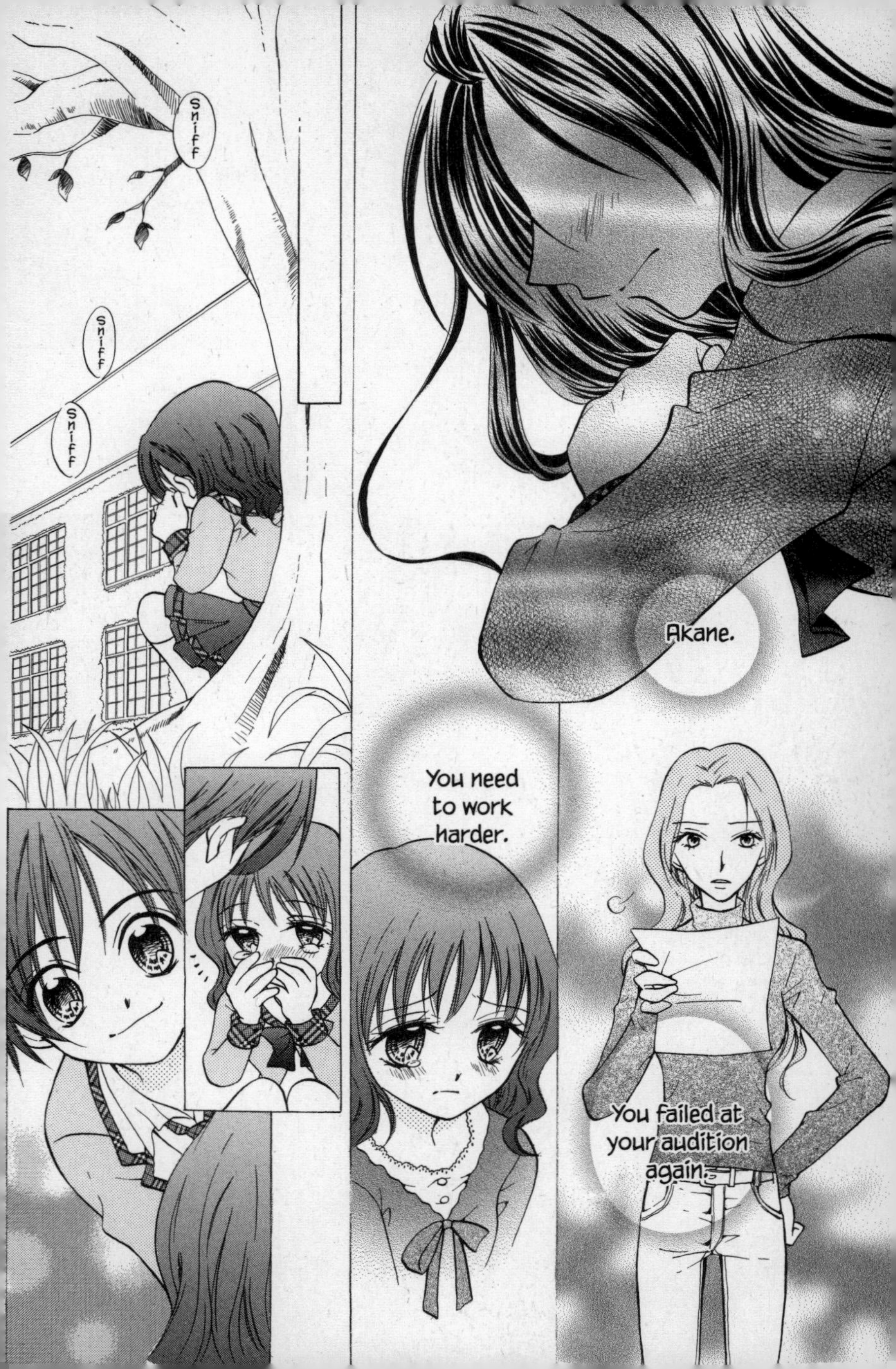
Akane.
You failed at your audition again.
You need to work harder.
Sniff
Sniff
Sniff

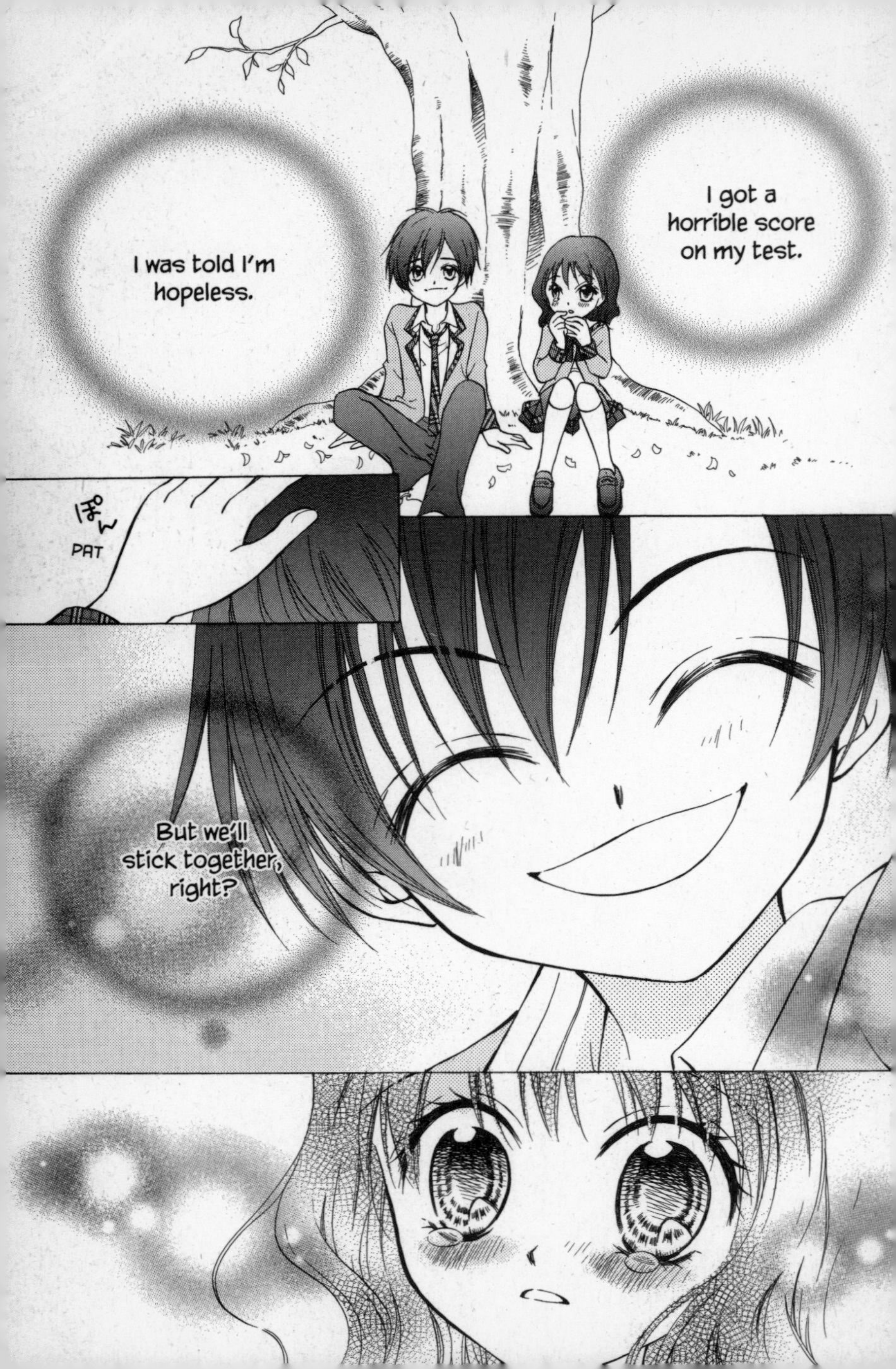
I got a horrible score on my test.
I was told I'm hopeless.
ぽん
PAT
But we'll stick together, right?

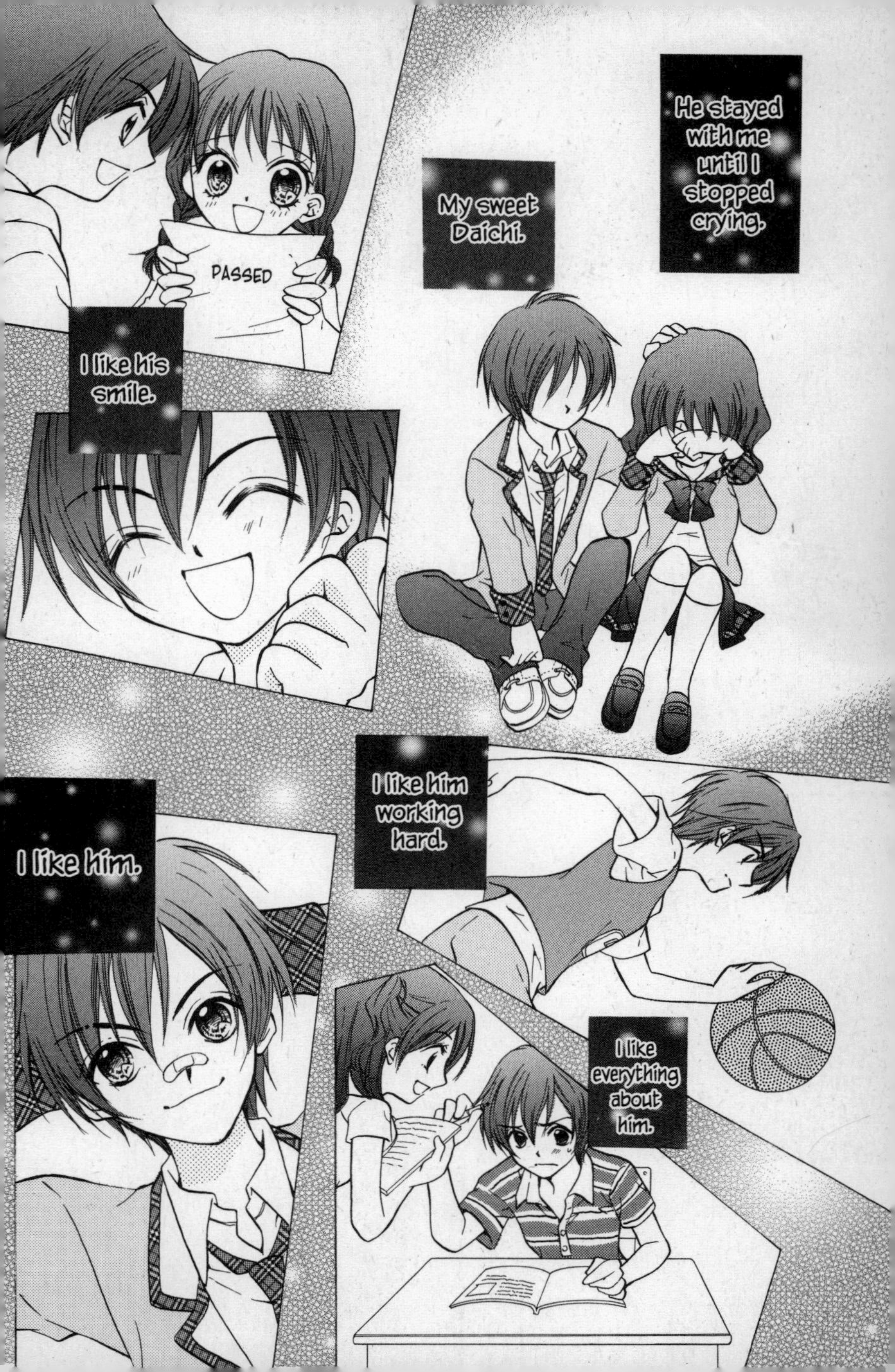
He stayed with me until I stopped crying.
My sweet Daichi.
PASSED
I like his smile.
I like him working hard.
I like everything about him.
I like him.

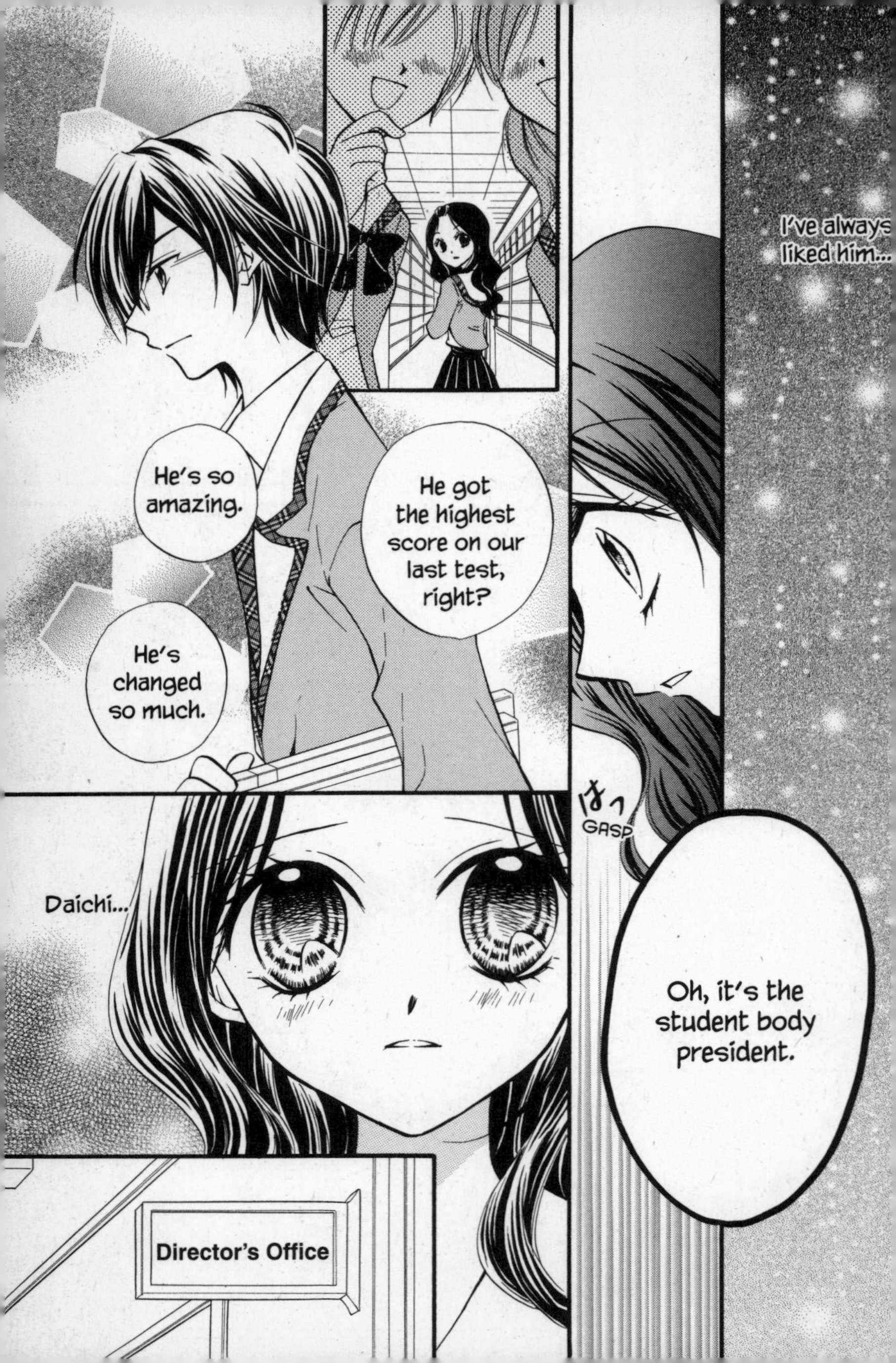

I've always liked him...
Oh, it's the student body president.
はっ
GASP
He got the highest score on our last test, right?
He's so amazing.
He's changed so much.
Daichi...
Director's Office

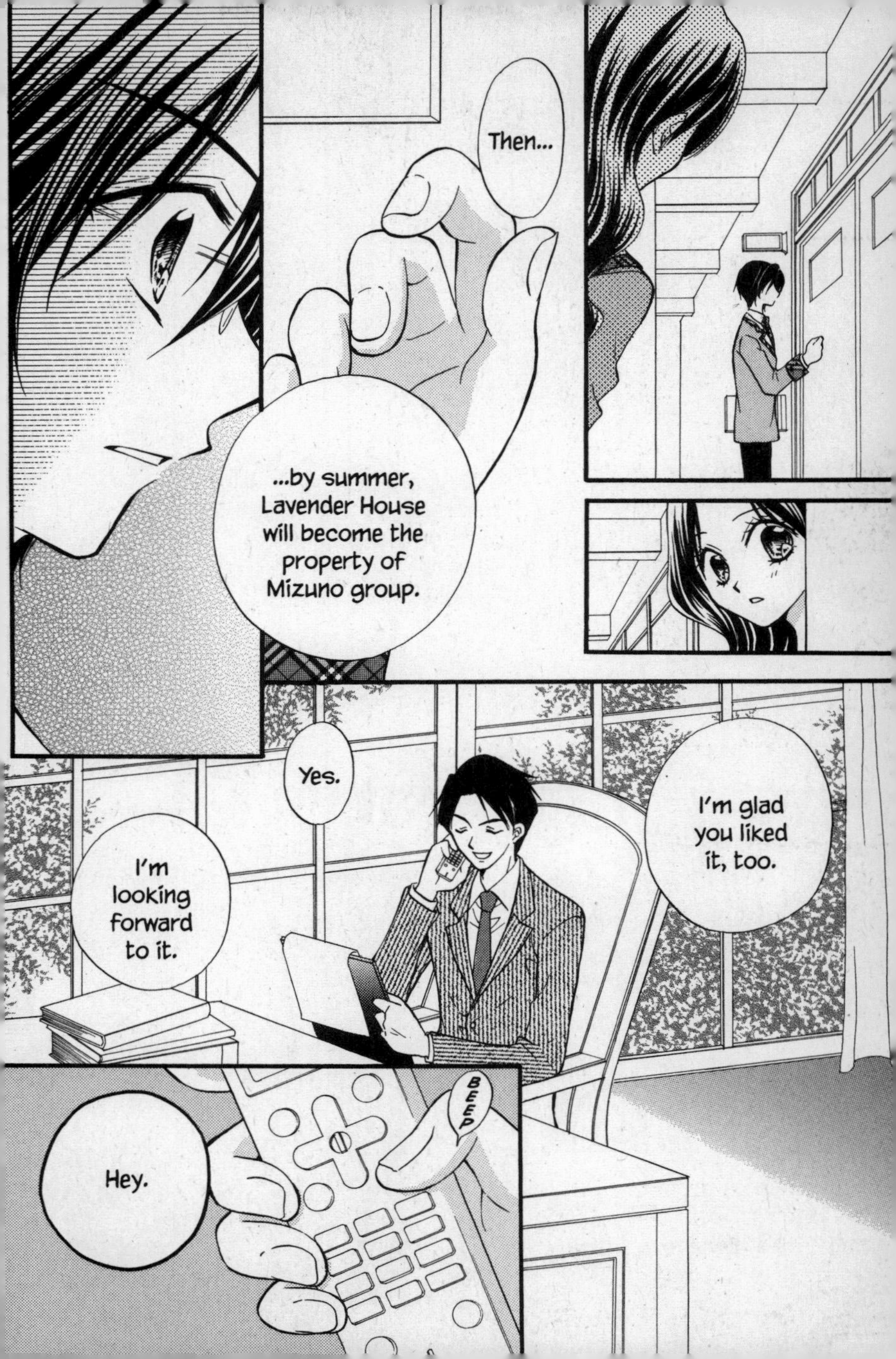
Then...
...by summer, Lavender House will become the property of Mizuno group.
I'm glad you liked it, too.
Yes.
I'm looking forward to it.
BEEP
Hey.

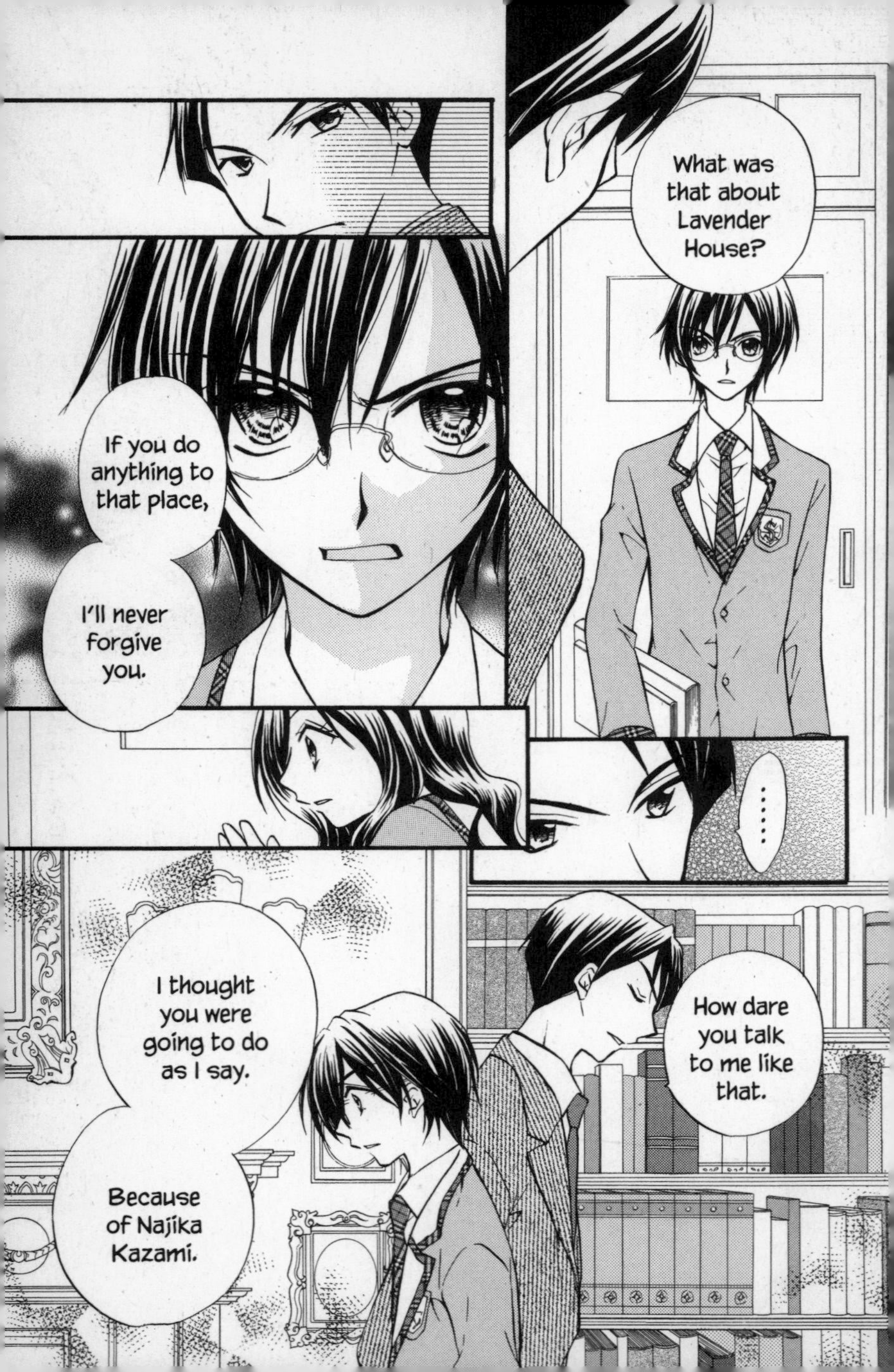
What was that about Lavender House?
If you do anything to that place,
I'll never forgive you.
......
How dare you talk to me like that.
I thought you were going to do as I say.
Because of Najika Kazami.

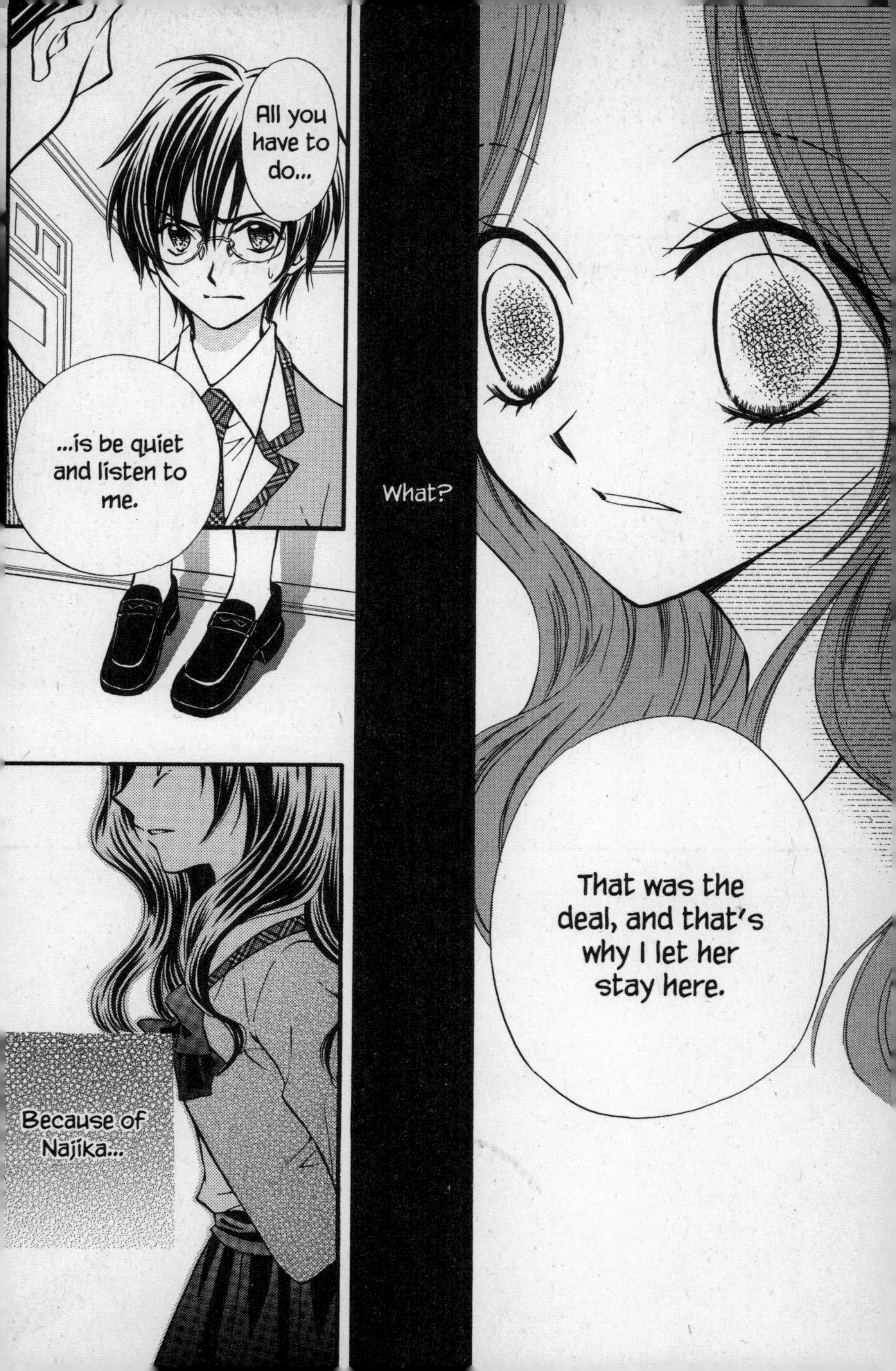
That was the deal, and that's why I let her stay here.
What?
All you have to do...
...is be quiet and listen to me.
Because of Najika...

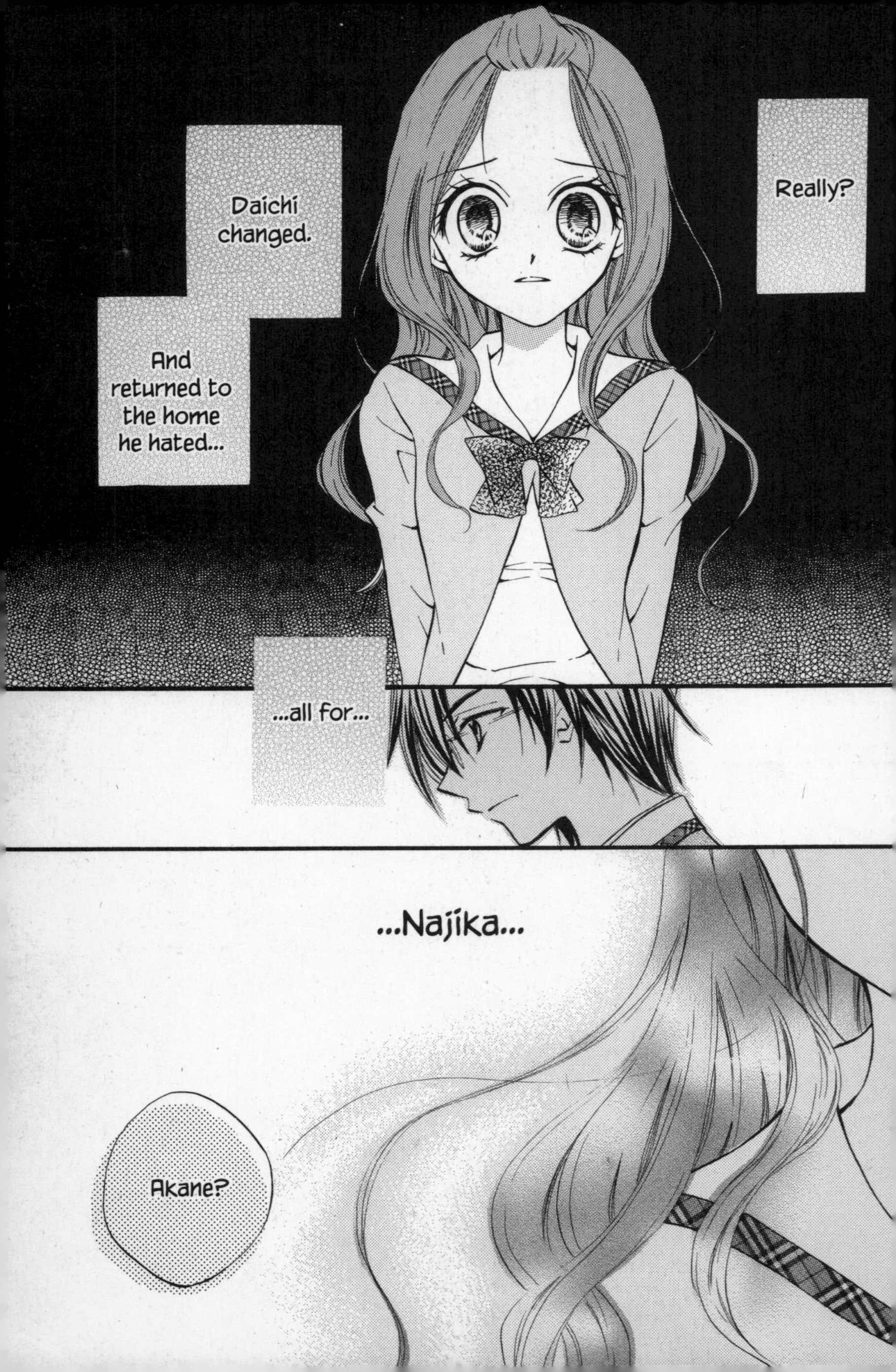
Really?
Daichi changed.
And returned to the home he hated...
...all for...
...Najika...
Akane?

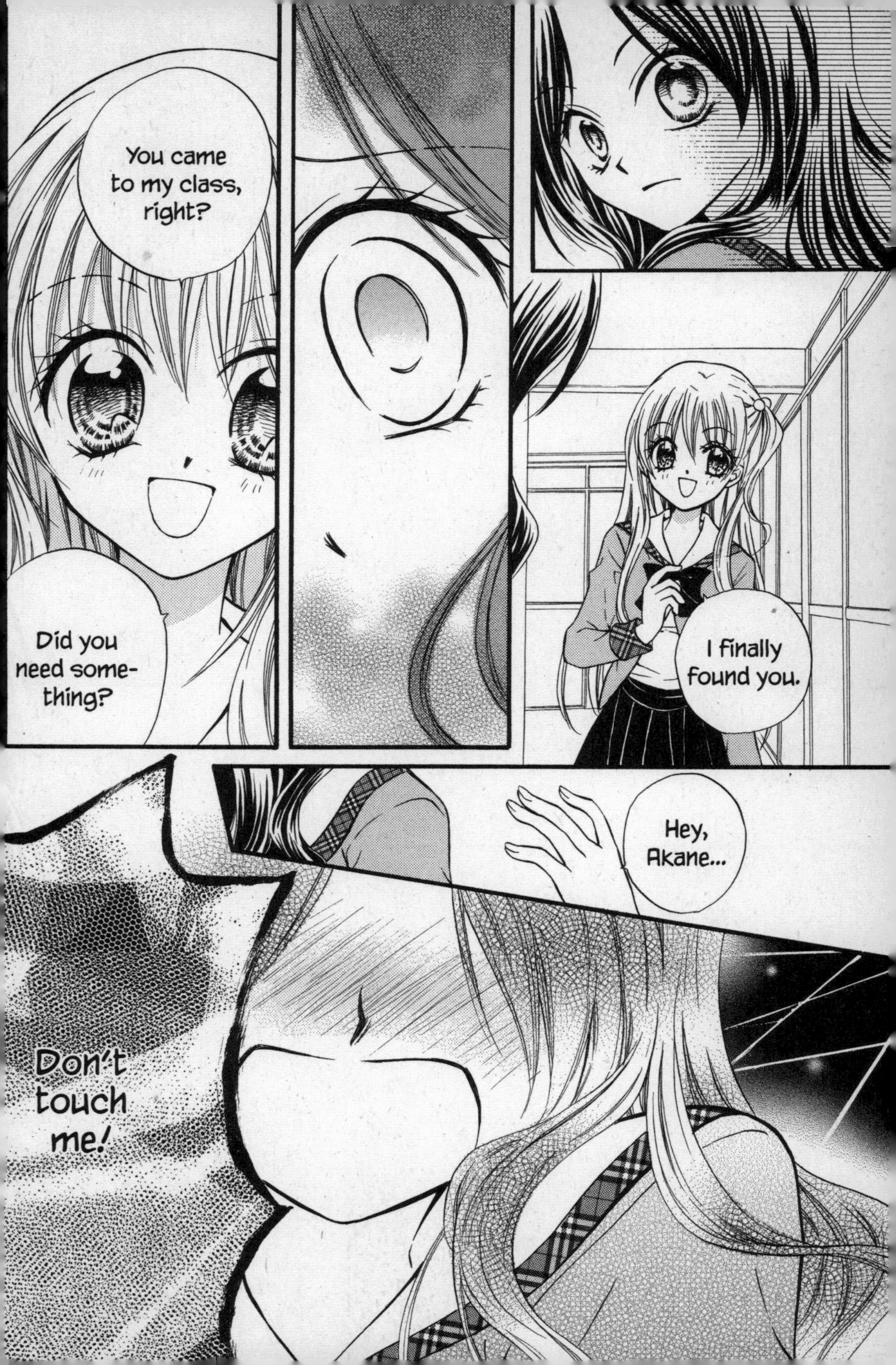
I finally found you.
You came to my class, right?
Did you need some-thing?
Hey, Akane...
Don't touch me!

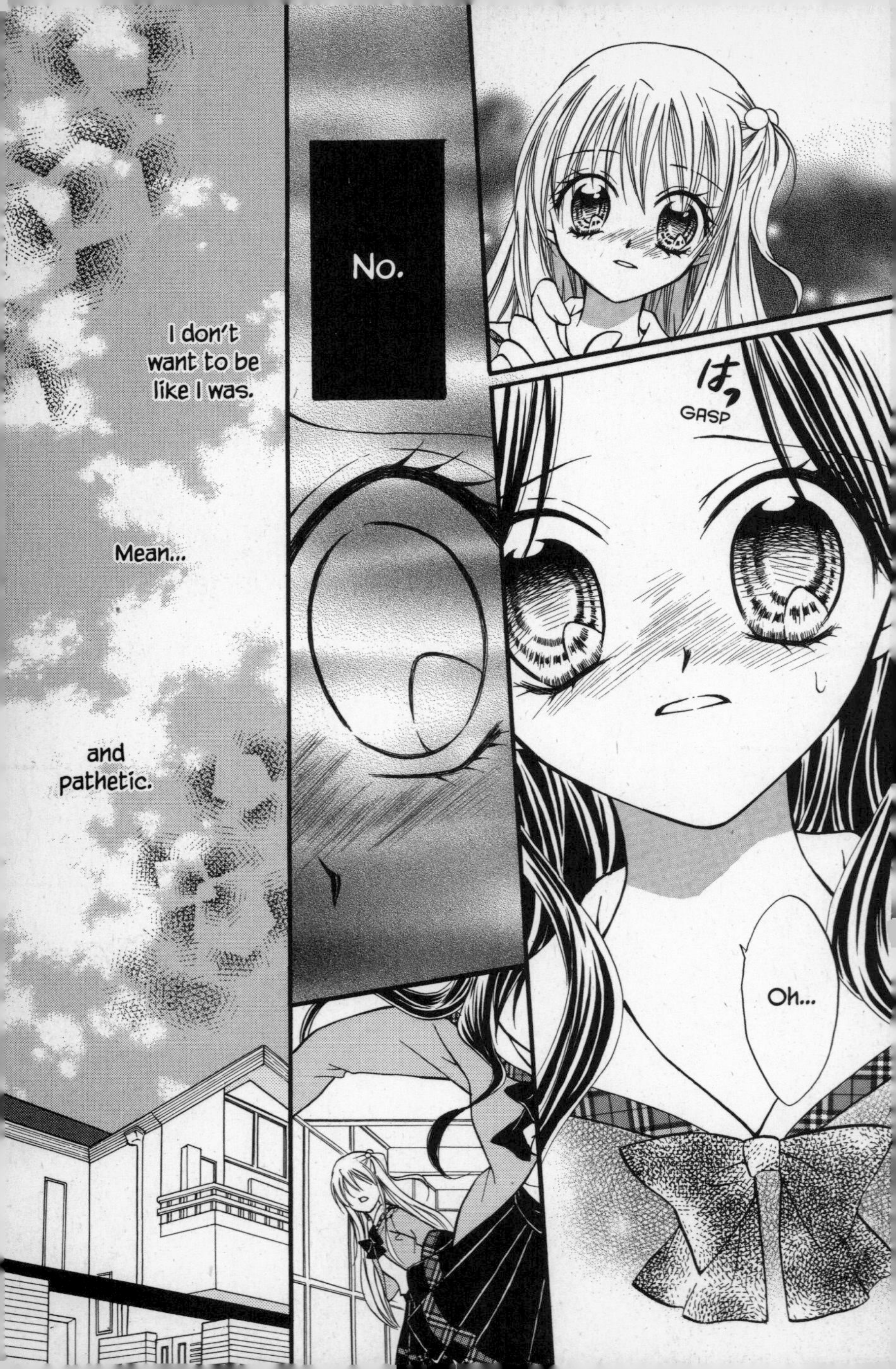
はっ
GASP
Oh...
No.
I don't want to be like I was.
Mean...
and pathetic.

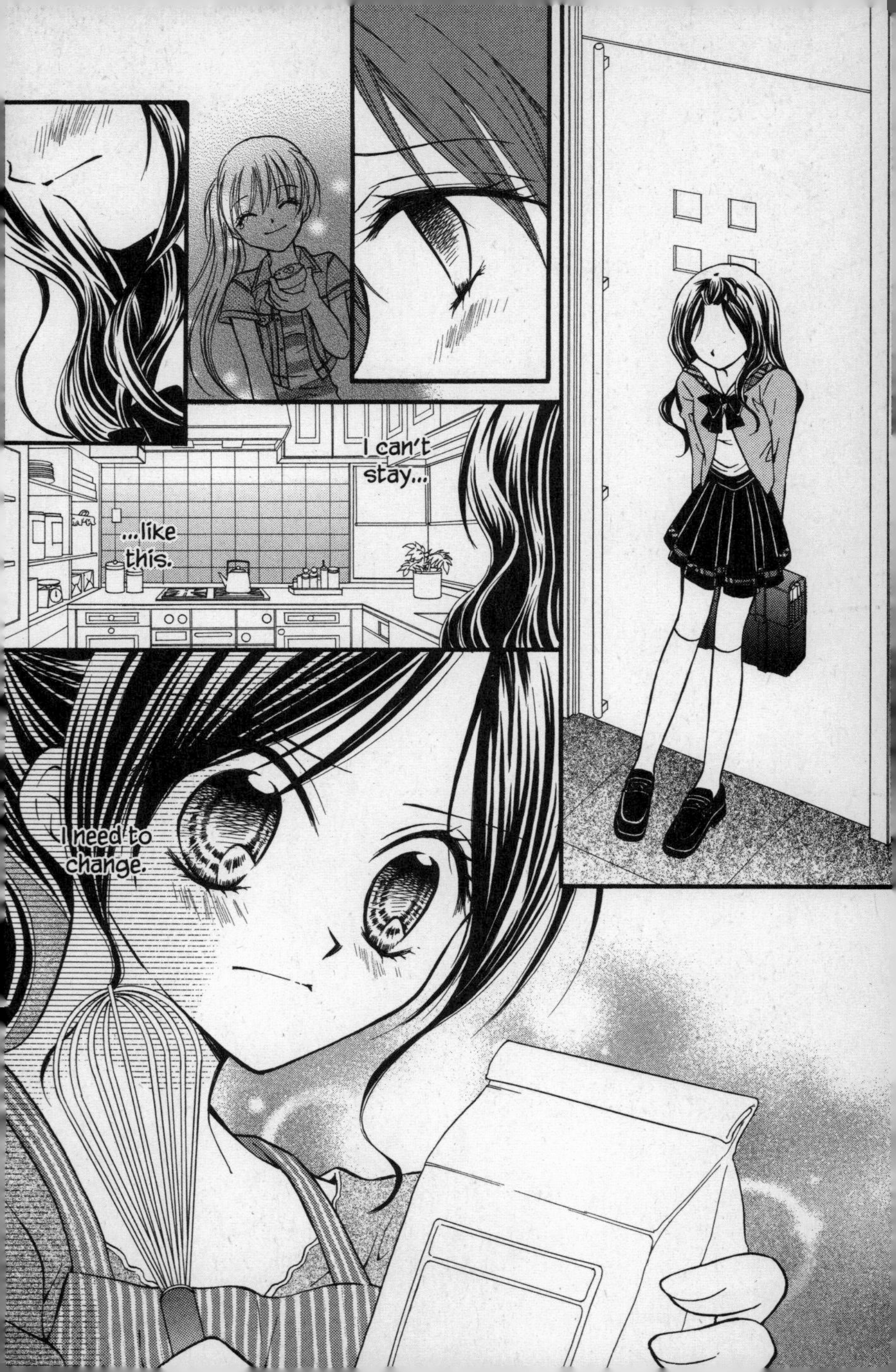
I can't stay...
...like this.
I need to change.

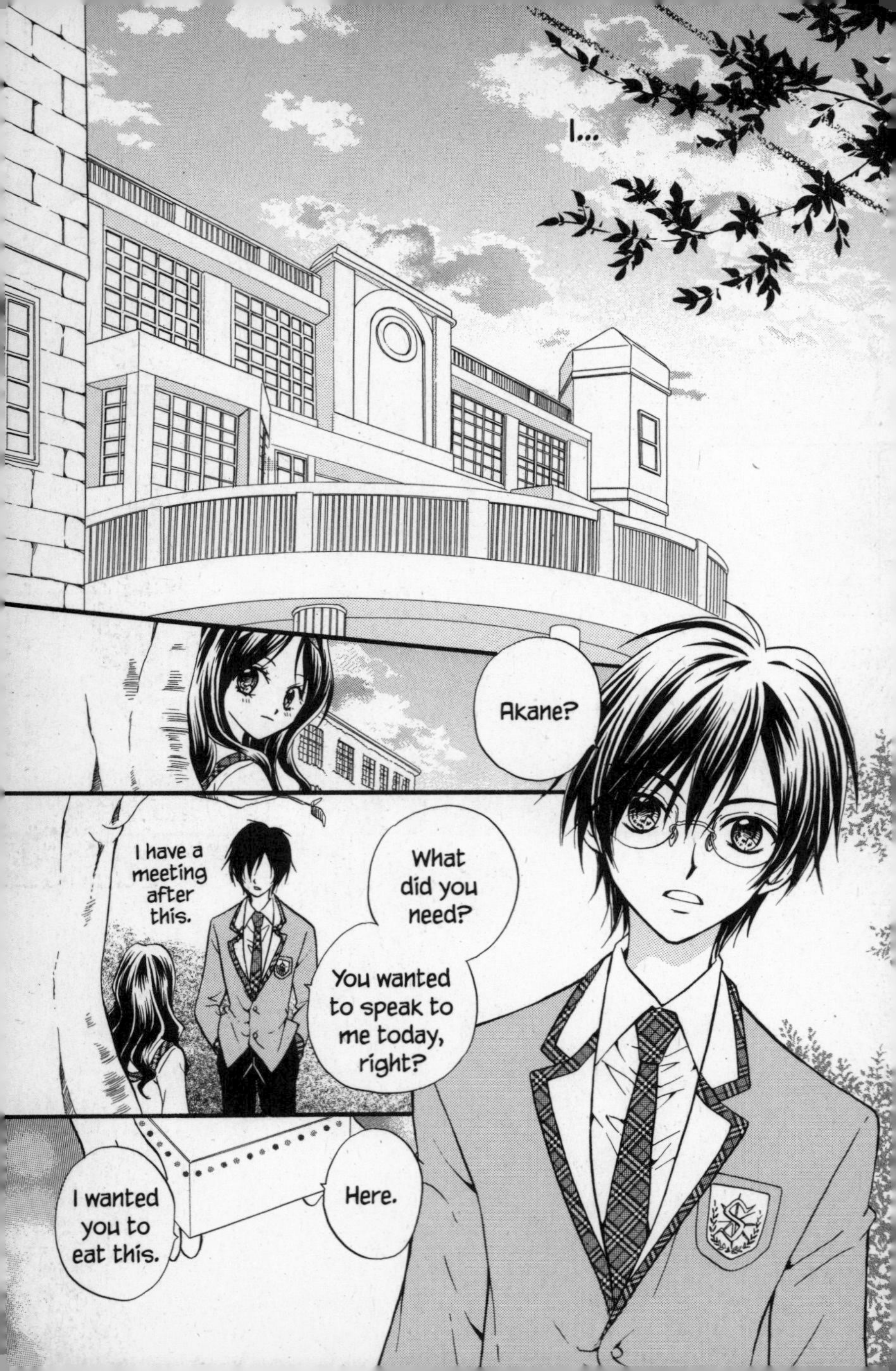
I...
Akane?
What did you need?
I have a meeting after this.
You wanted to speak to me today, right?
Here.
I wanted you to eat this.

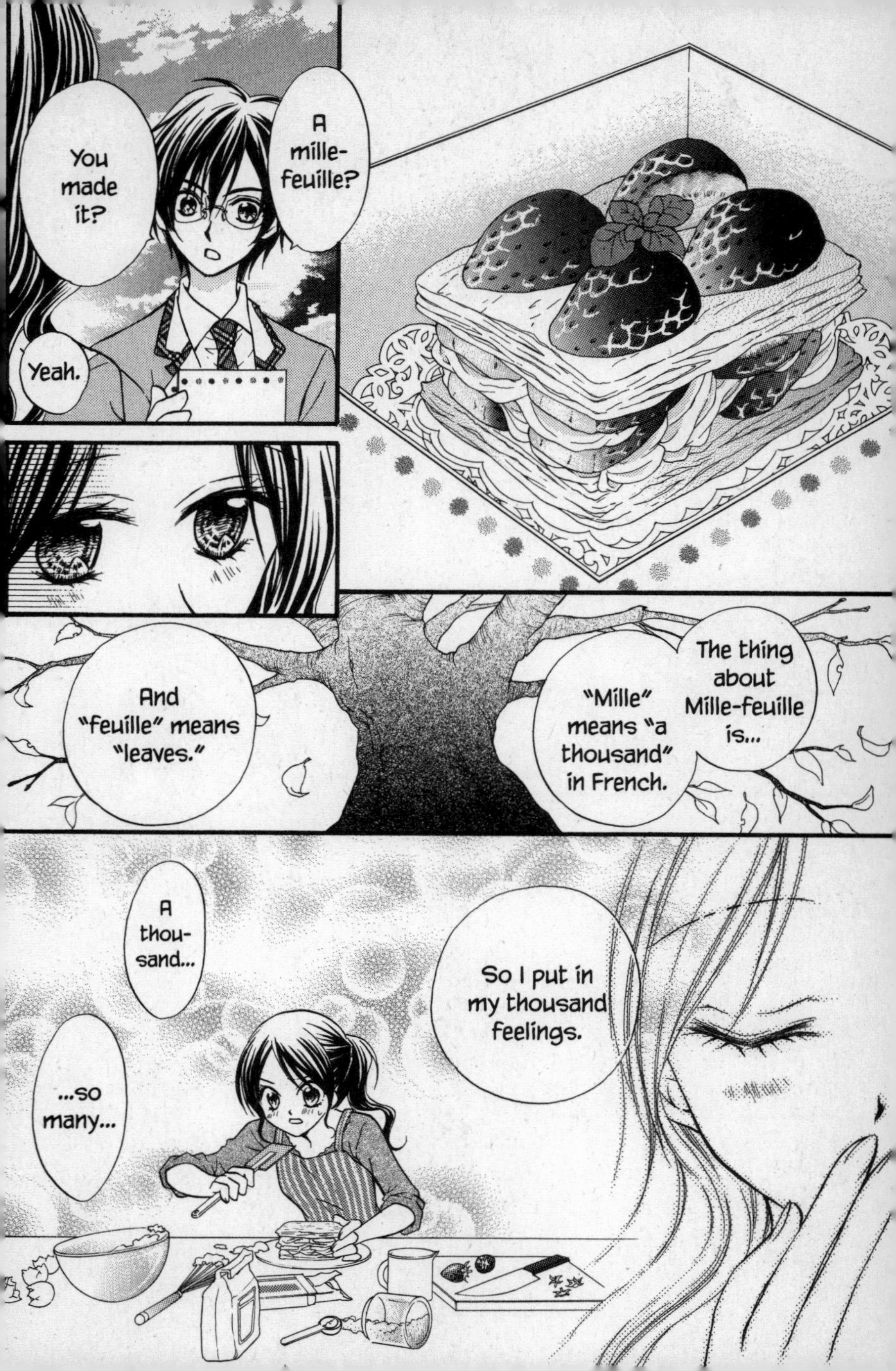
A mille-feuille?
You made it?
Yeah.
The thing about Mille-feuille is...
"Mille" means "a thousand" in French.
And "feuille" means "leaves."
So I put in my thousand feelings.
A thou-sand...
...so many...

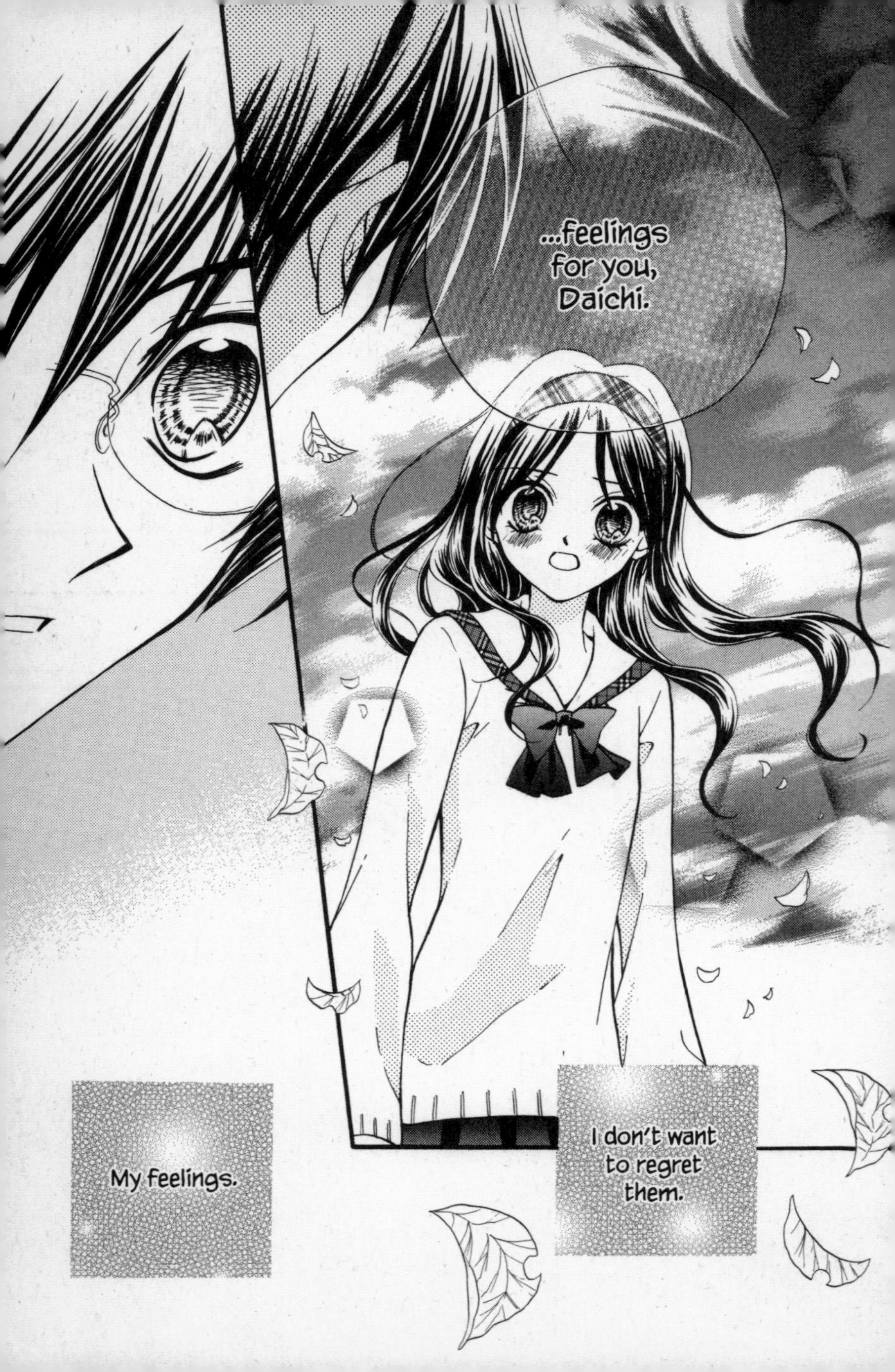
...feelings for you, Daichi.
I don't want to regret them.
My feelings.

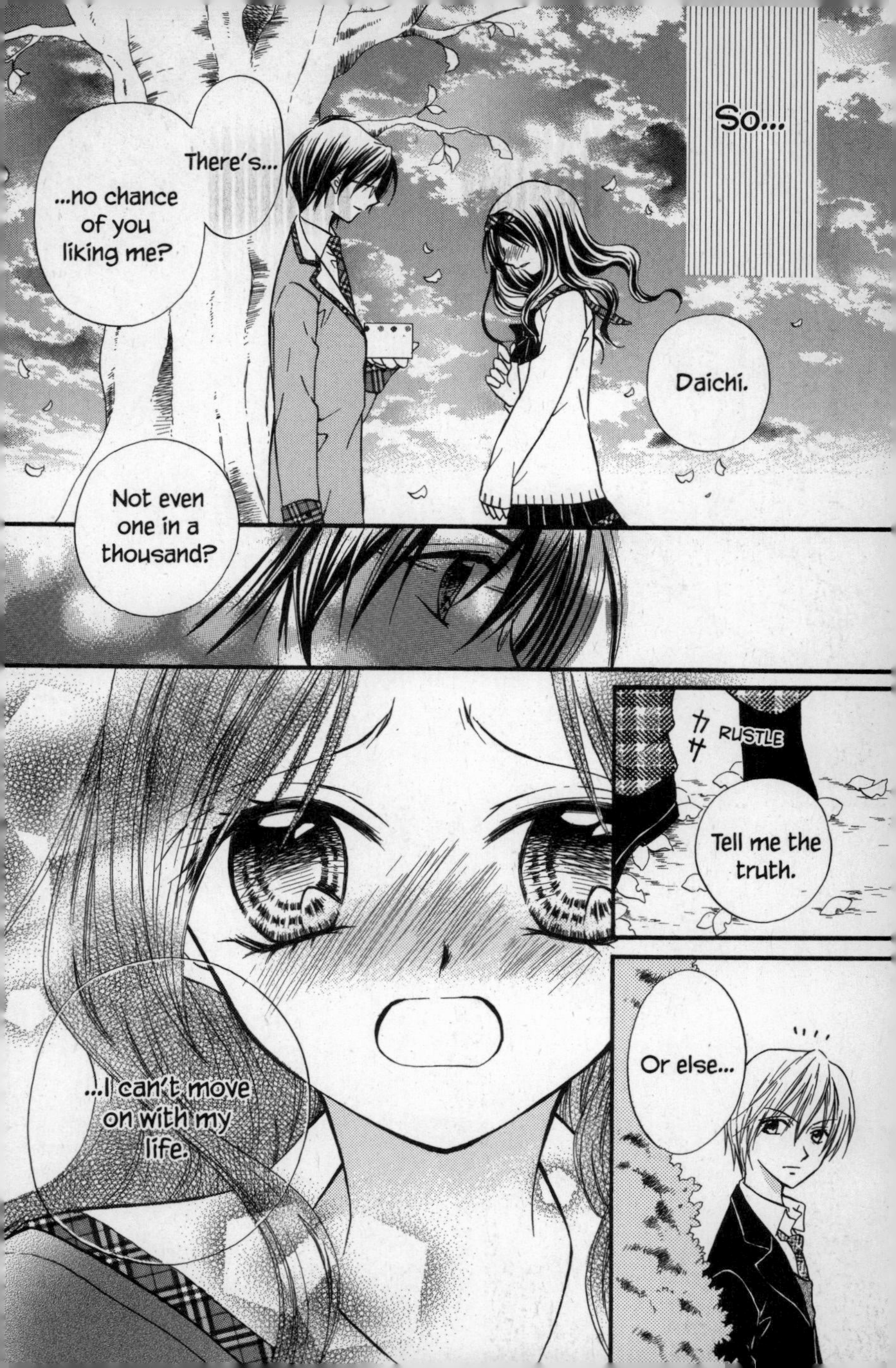
So...
Daichi.
There's...
...no chance of you liking me?
Not even one in a thousand?
カサ
RUSTLE
Tell me the truth.
Or else...
...I can't move on with my life.

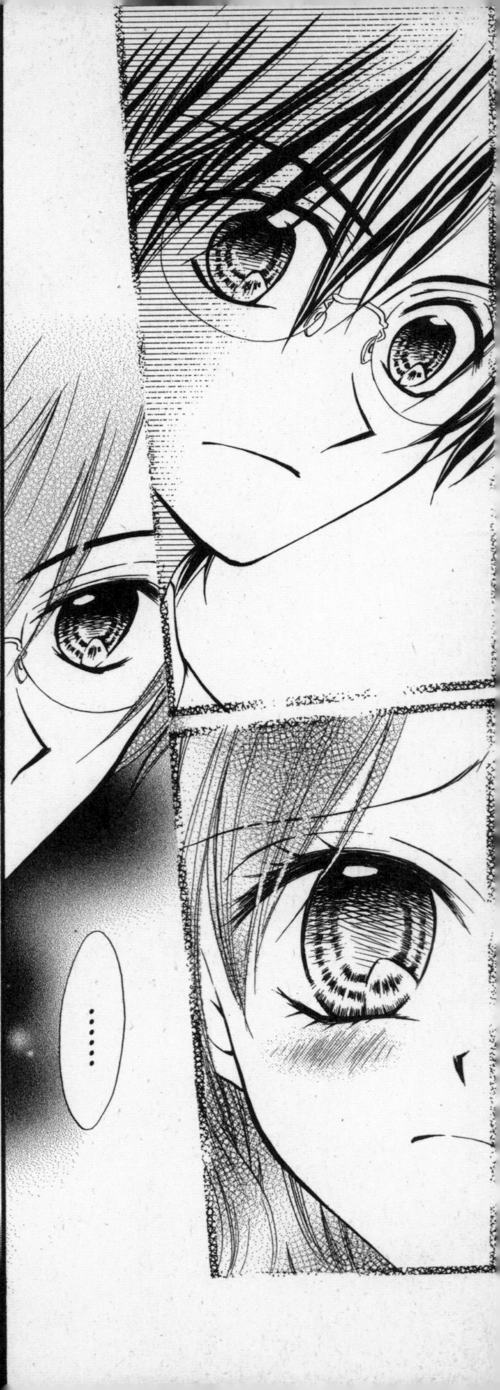
......

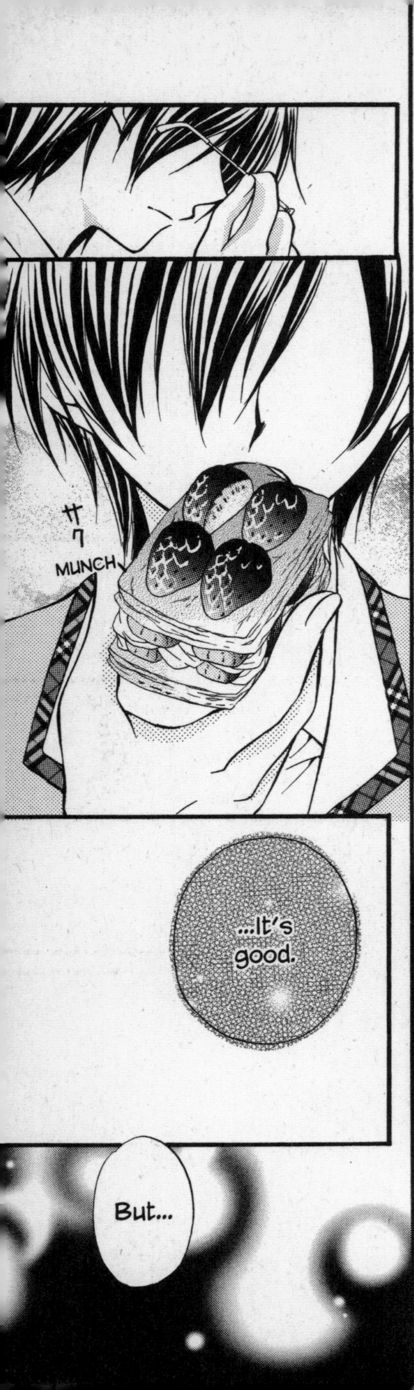
サク
MUNCH
...It's good.
But...

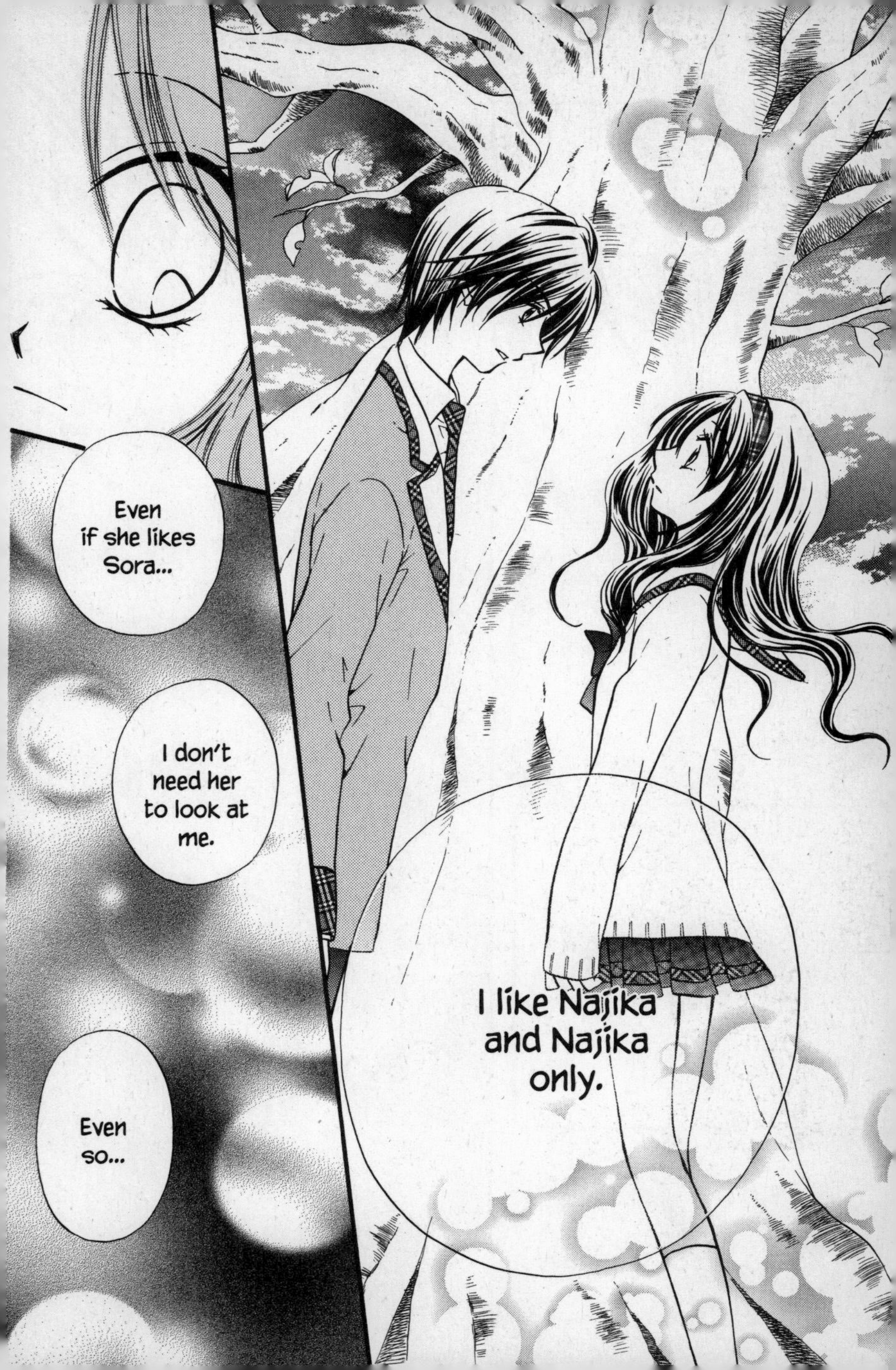

I like Najika and Najika only.
Even if she likes Sora...
I don't need her to look at me.
Even so...

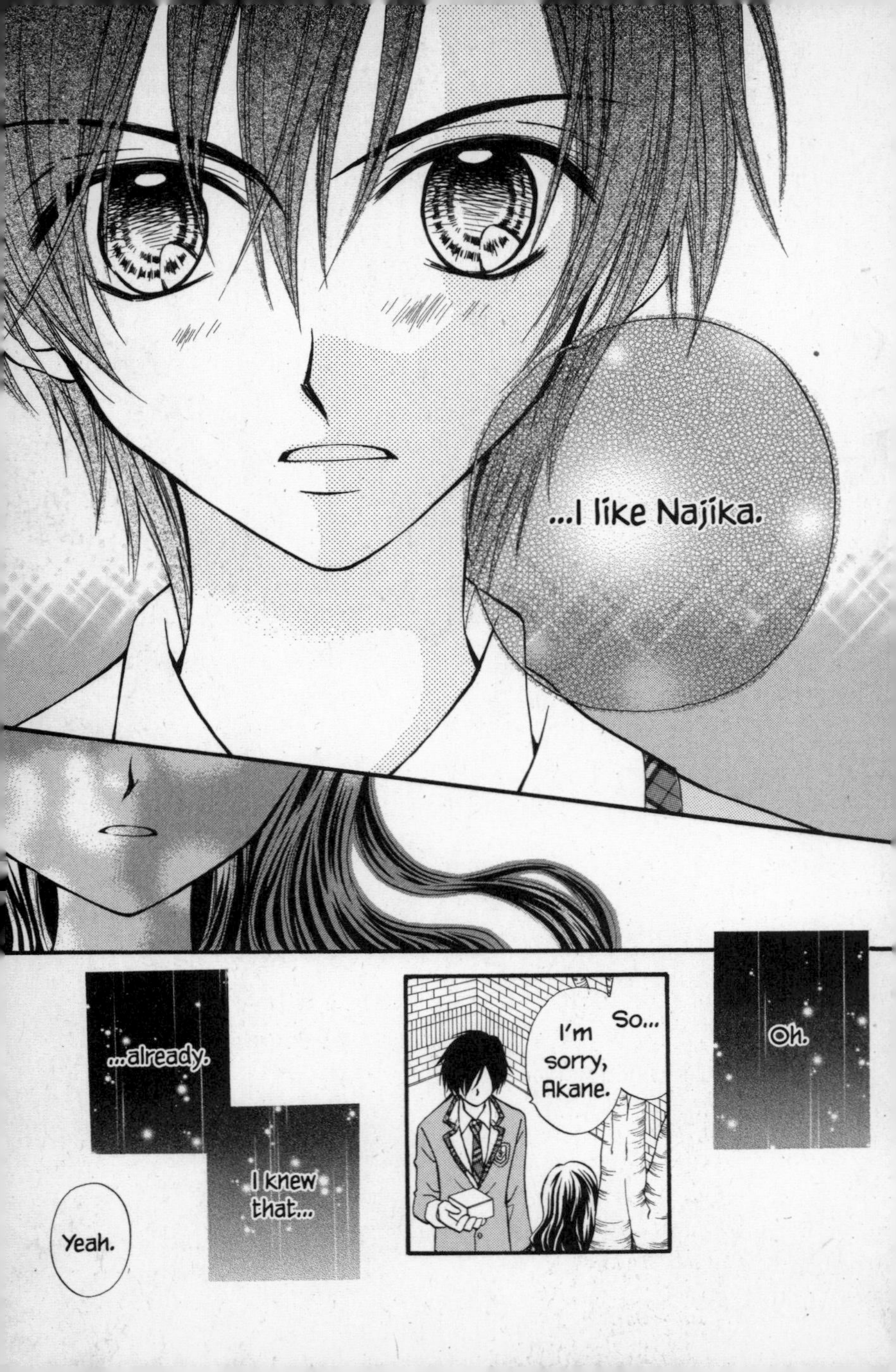
...I like Najika.
Oh.
So...
I'm sorry, Akane.
I knew that...
...already.
Yeah.

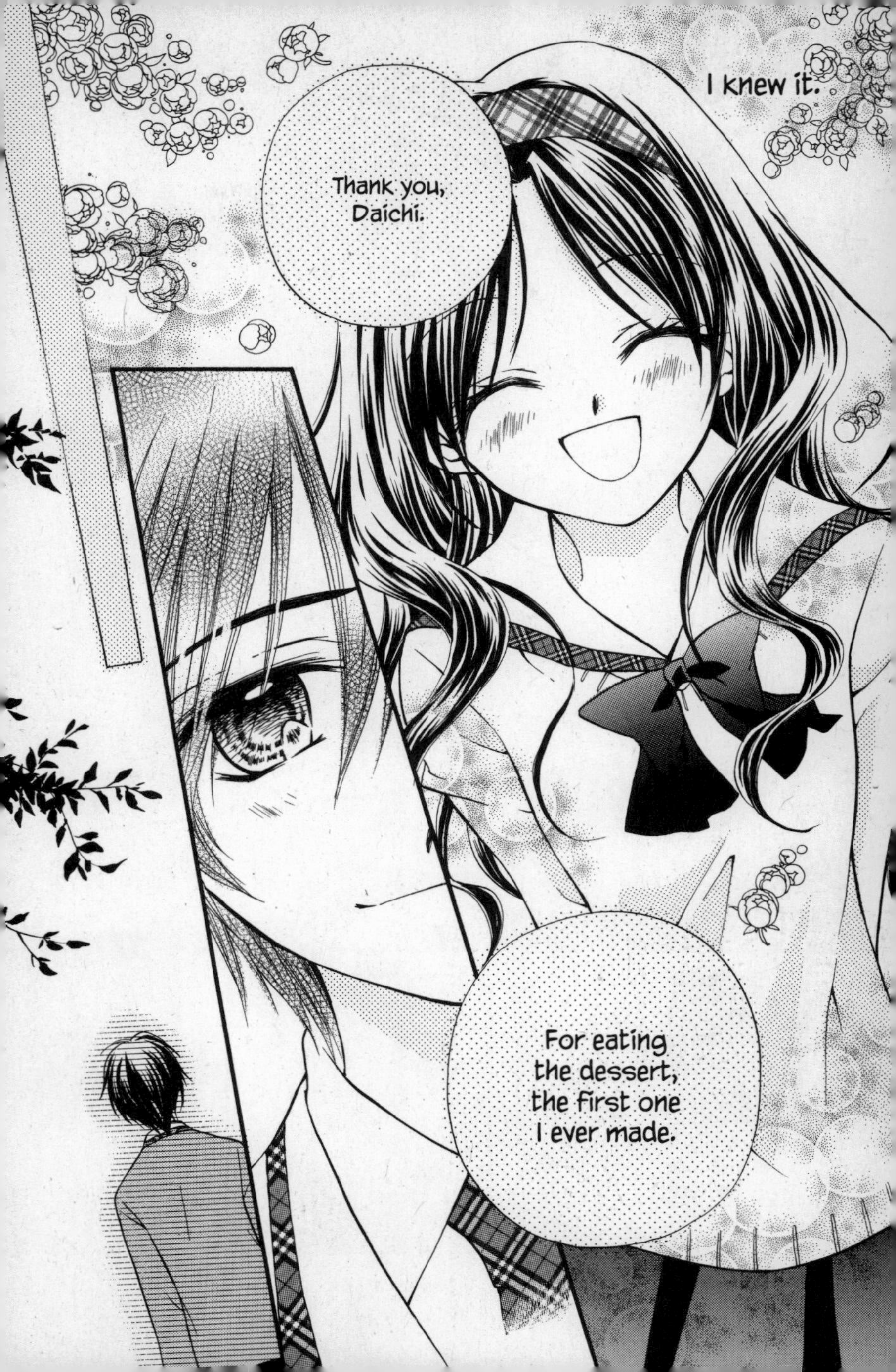
I knew it.
Thank you, Daichi.
For eating the dessert, the first one I ever made.

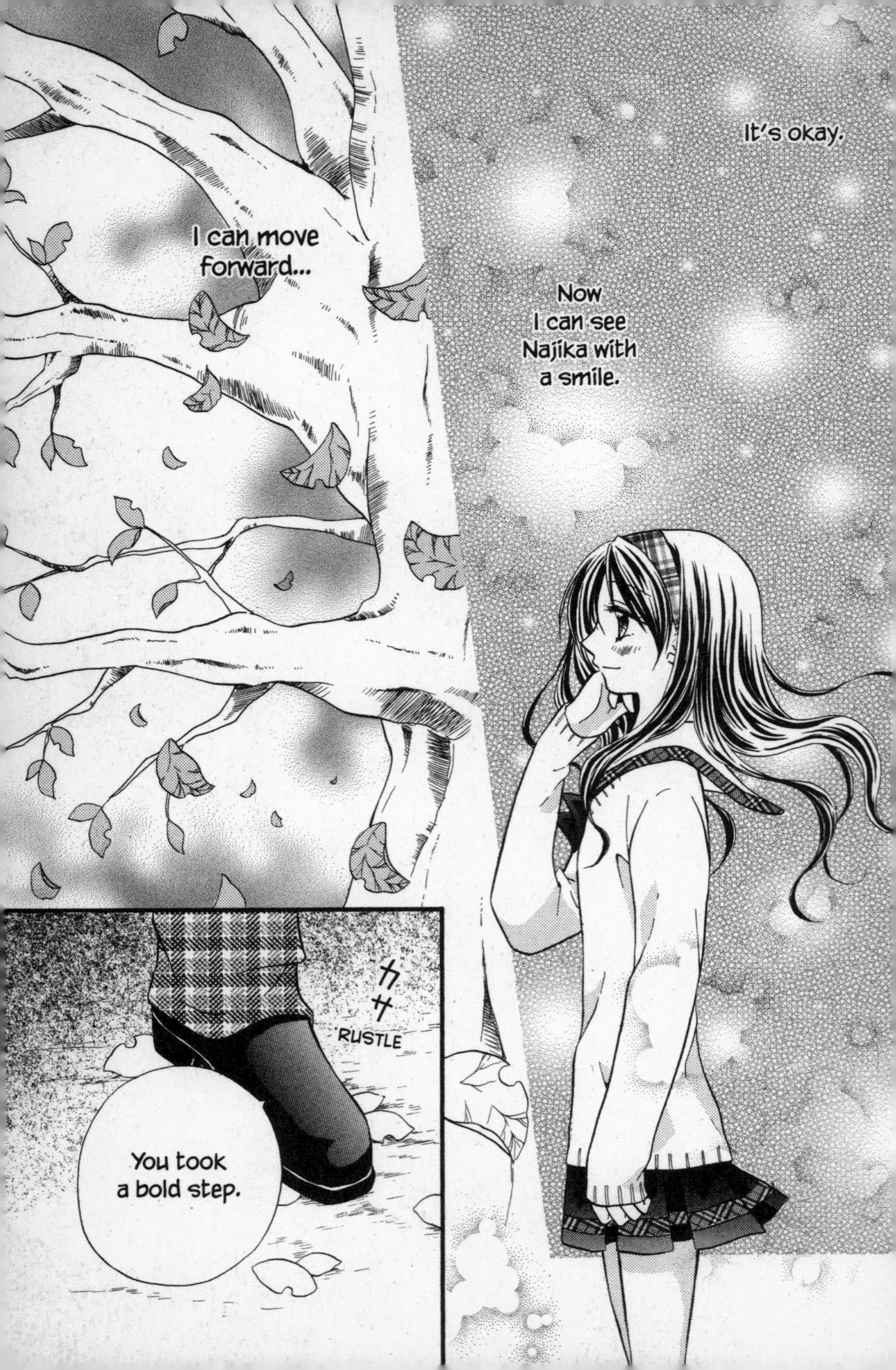
It's okay.
Now I can see Najika with a smile.
I can move forward...
カサ
RUSTLE
You took a bold step.

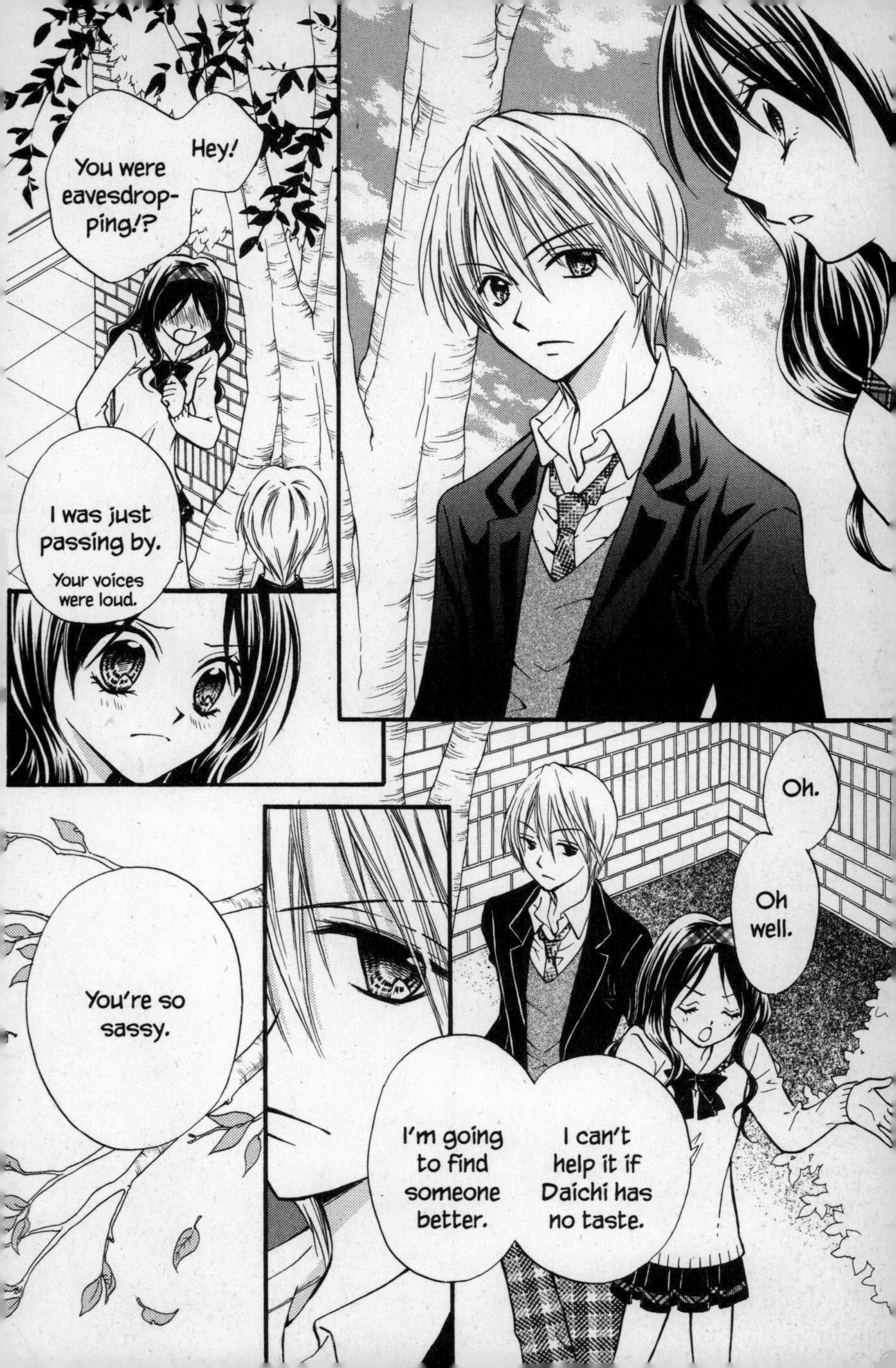

Hey! You were eavesdrop-ping!?
I was just passing by.
Your voices were loud.
Oh.
Oh well.
I can't help it if Daichi has no taste.
I'm going to find someone better.
You're so sassy.

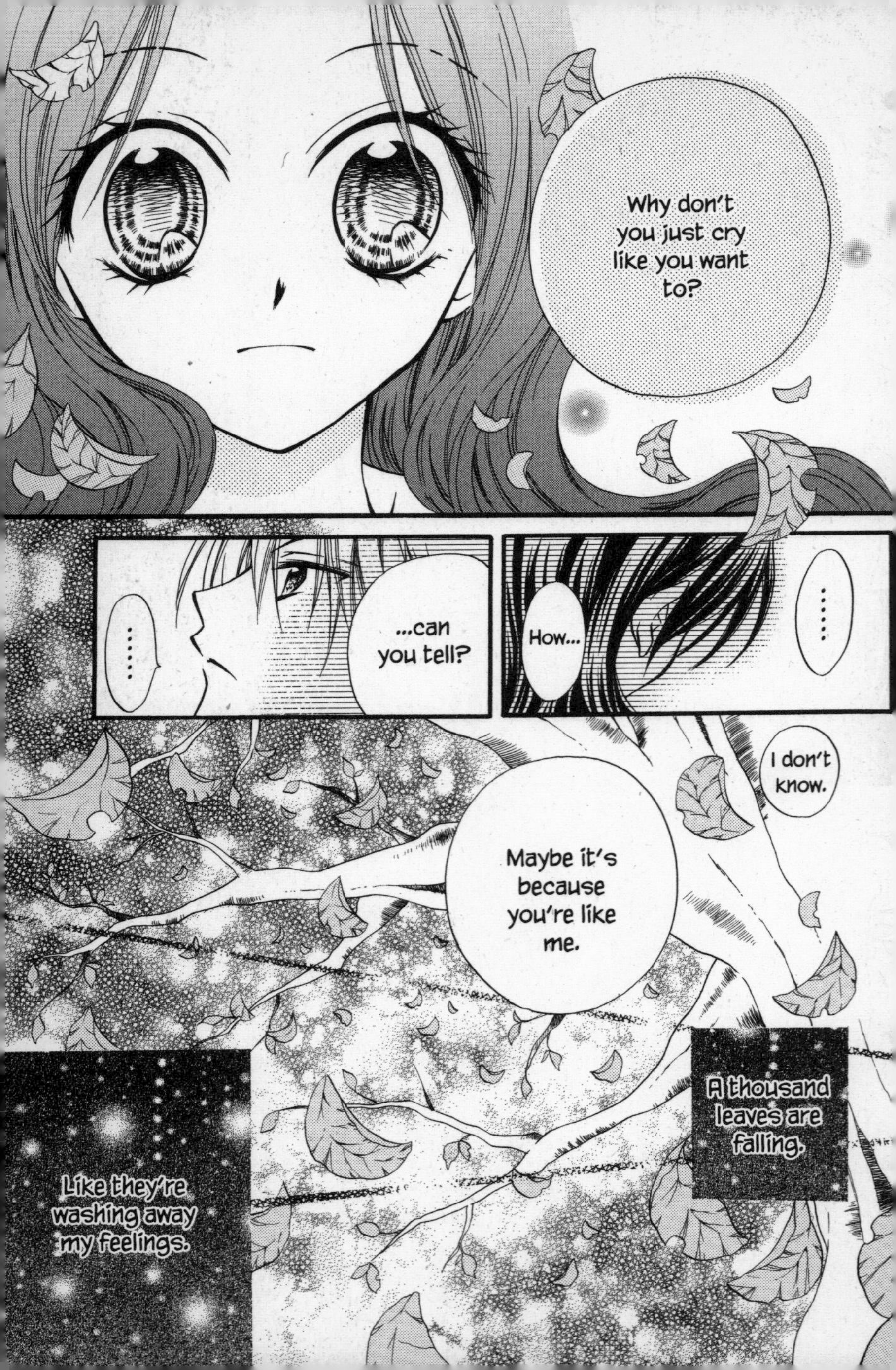
Why don't you just cry like you want to?
......
How...
...can you tell?
......
I don't know.
Maybe it's because you're like me.
A thousand leaves are falling.
Like they're washing away my feelings.

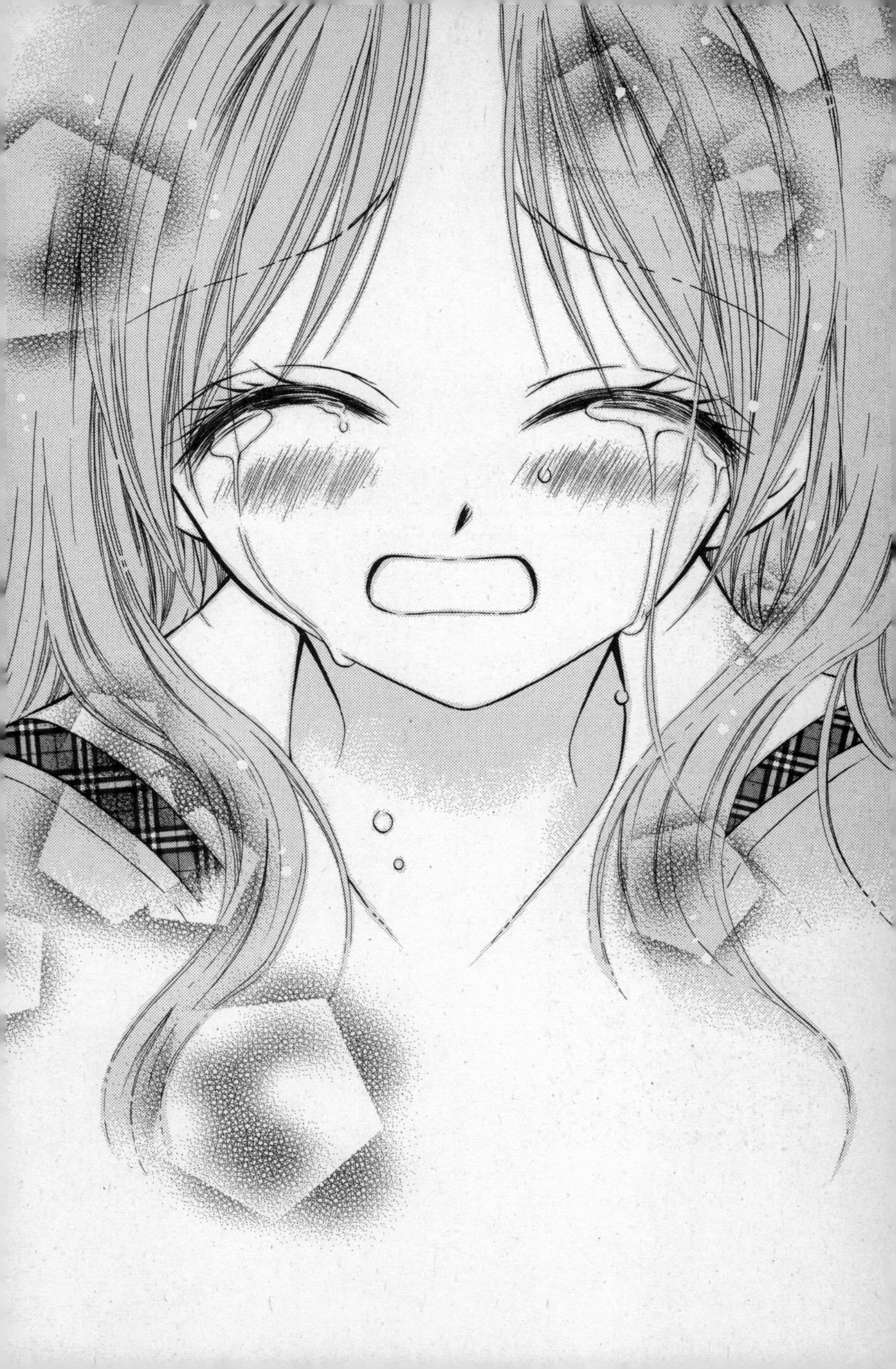

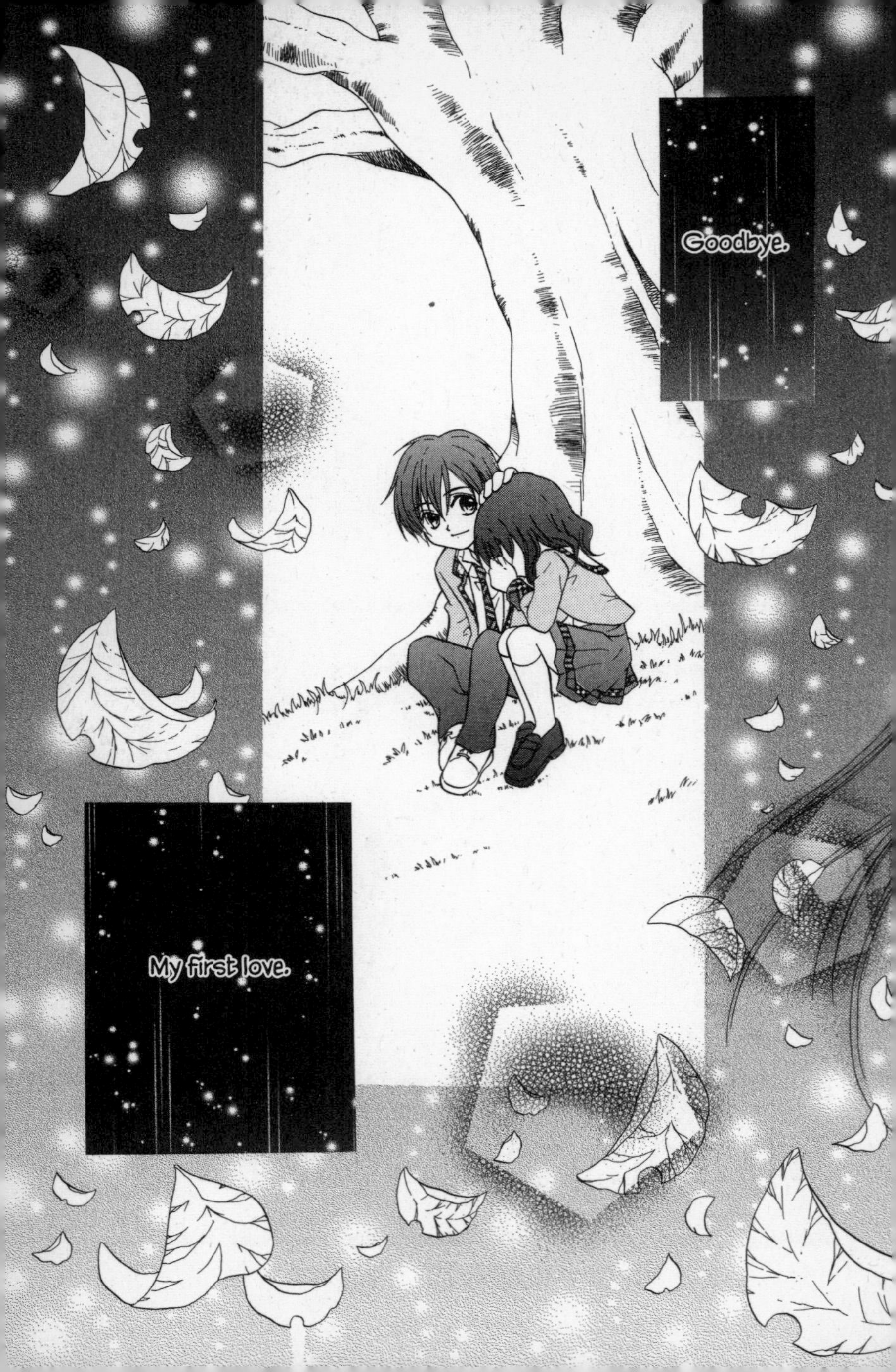
Goodbye.
My first love.

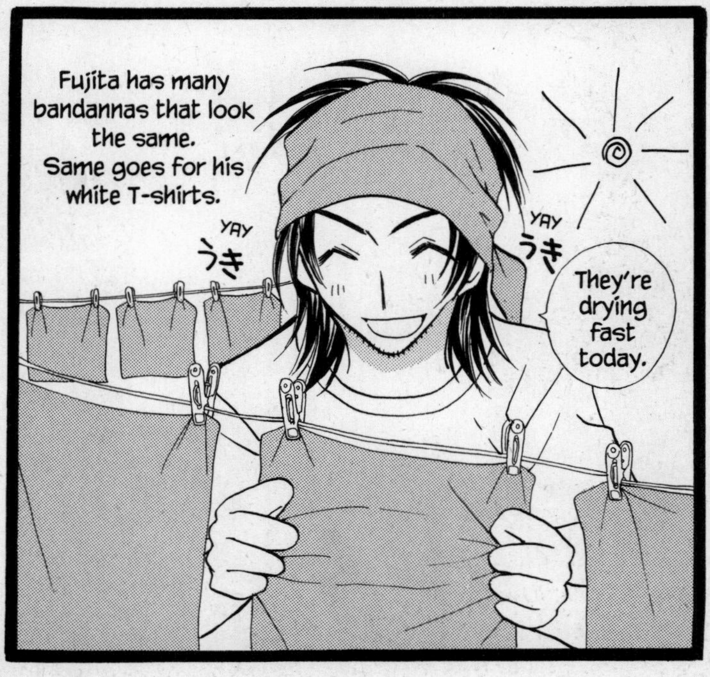
Fujita has many bandannas that look the same. Same goes for his white T-shirts.
YAY
うき
They're drying fast today.
YAY
うき

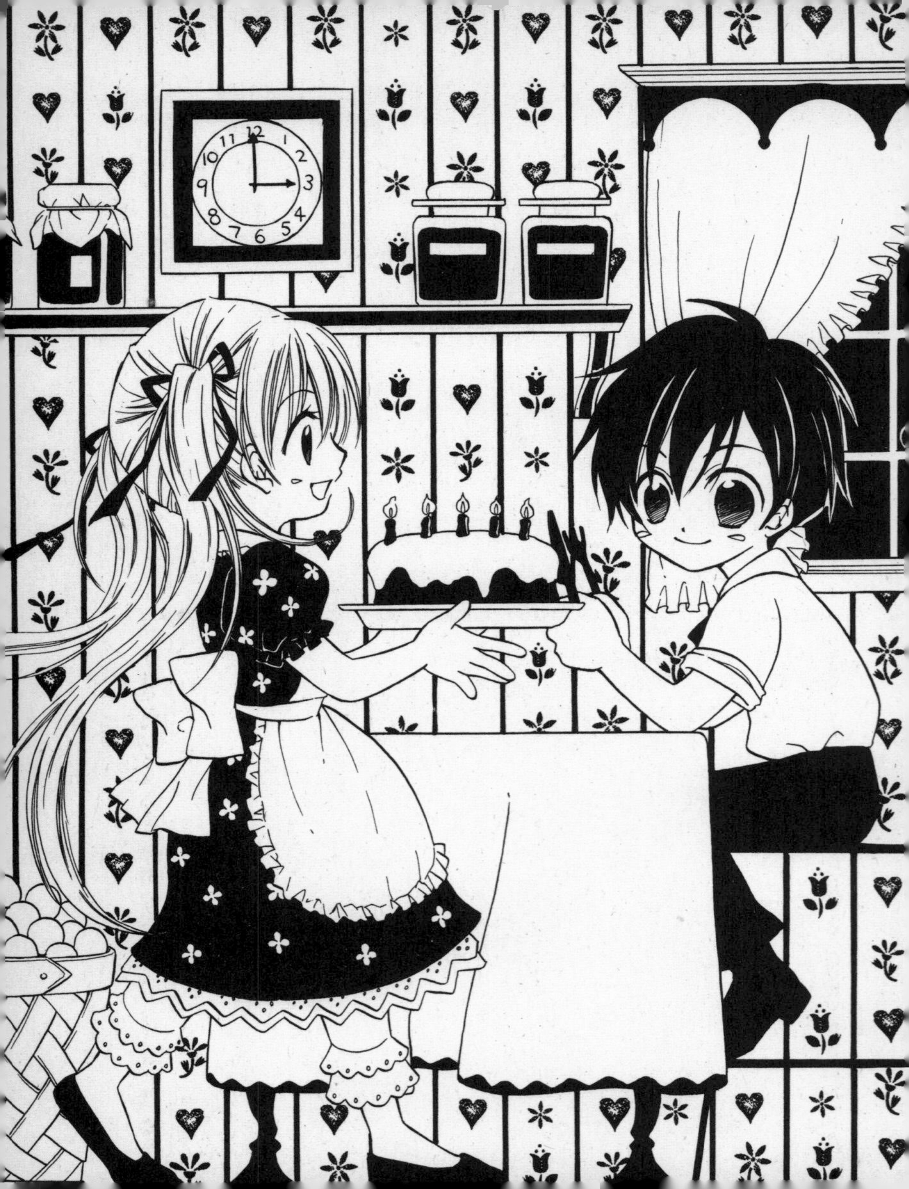

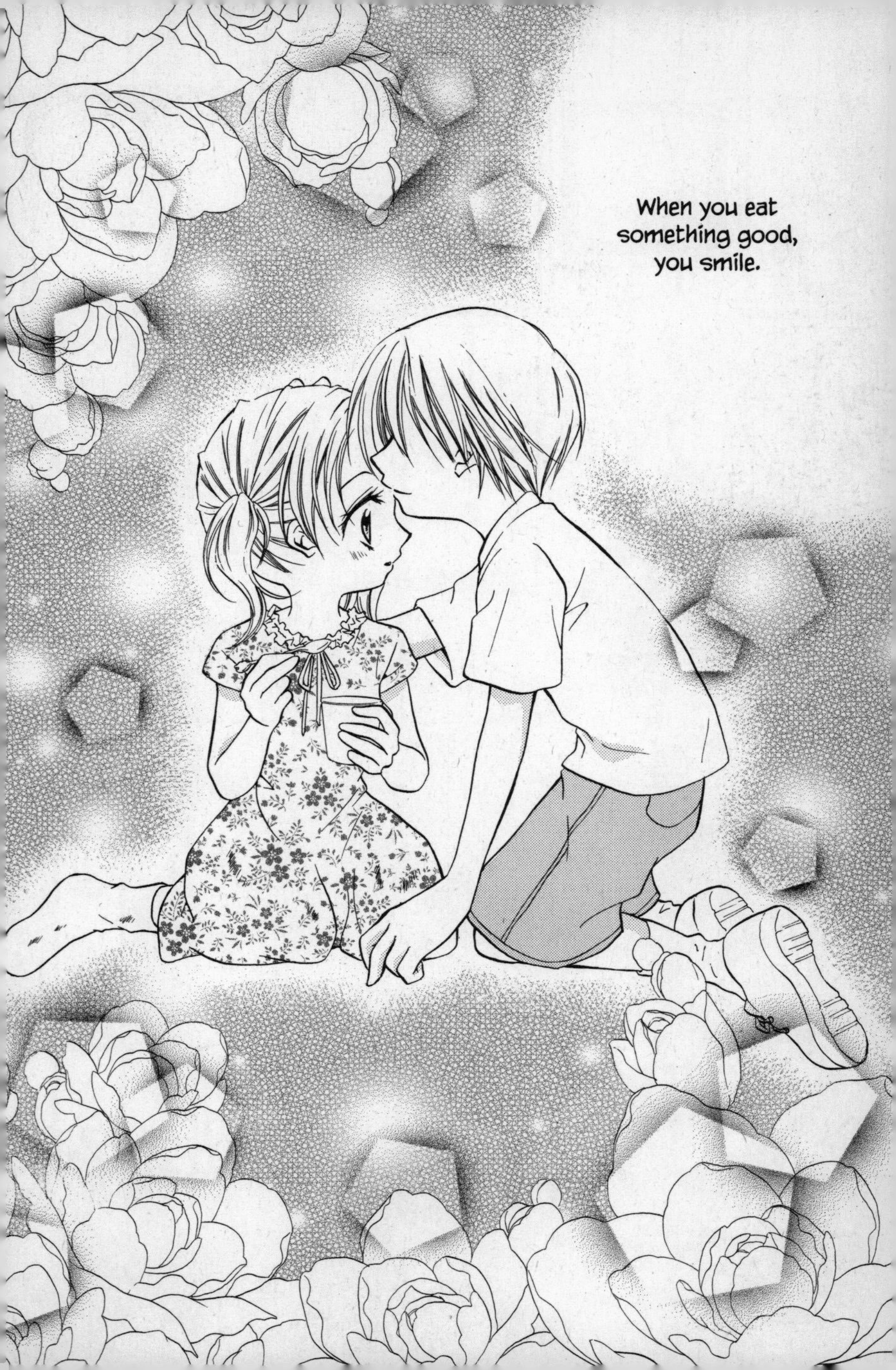
When you eat something good, you smile.

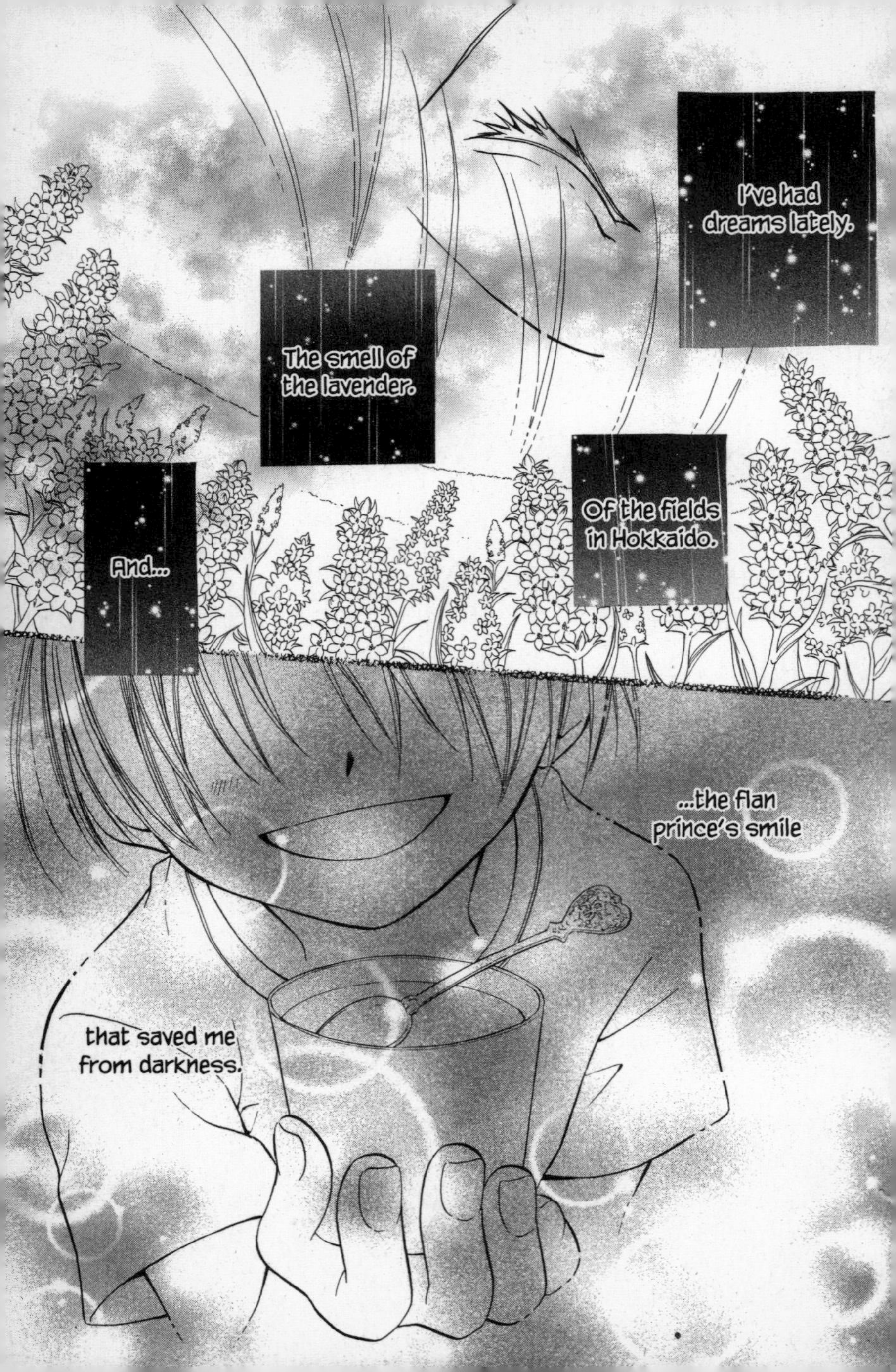
I've had dreams lately.
The smell of the lavender.
Of the fields in Hokkaido.
And...
...the flan prince's smile
that saved me from darkness.

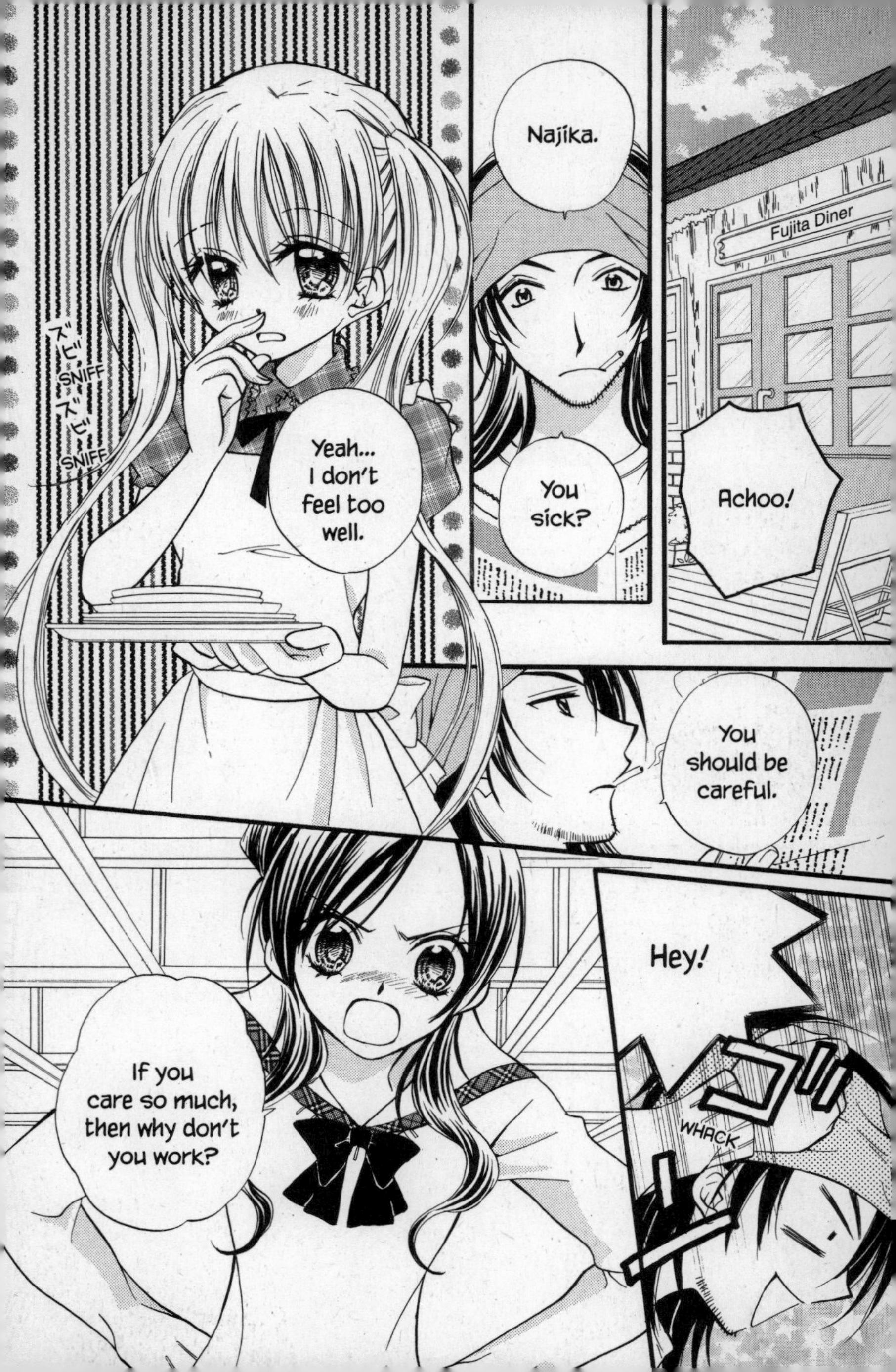
Fujita Diner
Achoo!
Najika.
You sick?
ズビ, SNIFF
ズビ SNIFF
Yeah... I don't feel too well.
You should be careful.
Hey!
WHACK
If you care so much, then why don't you work?

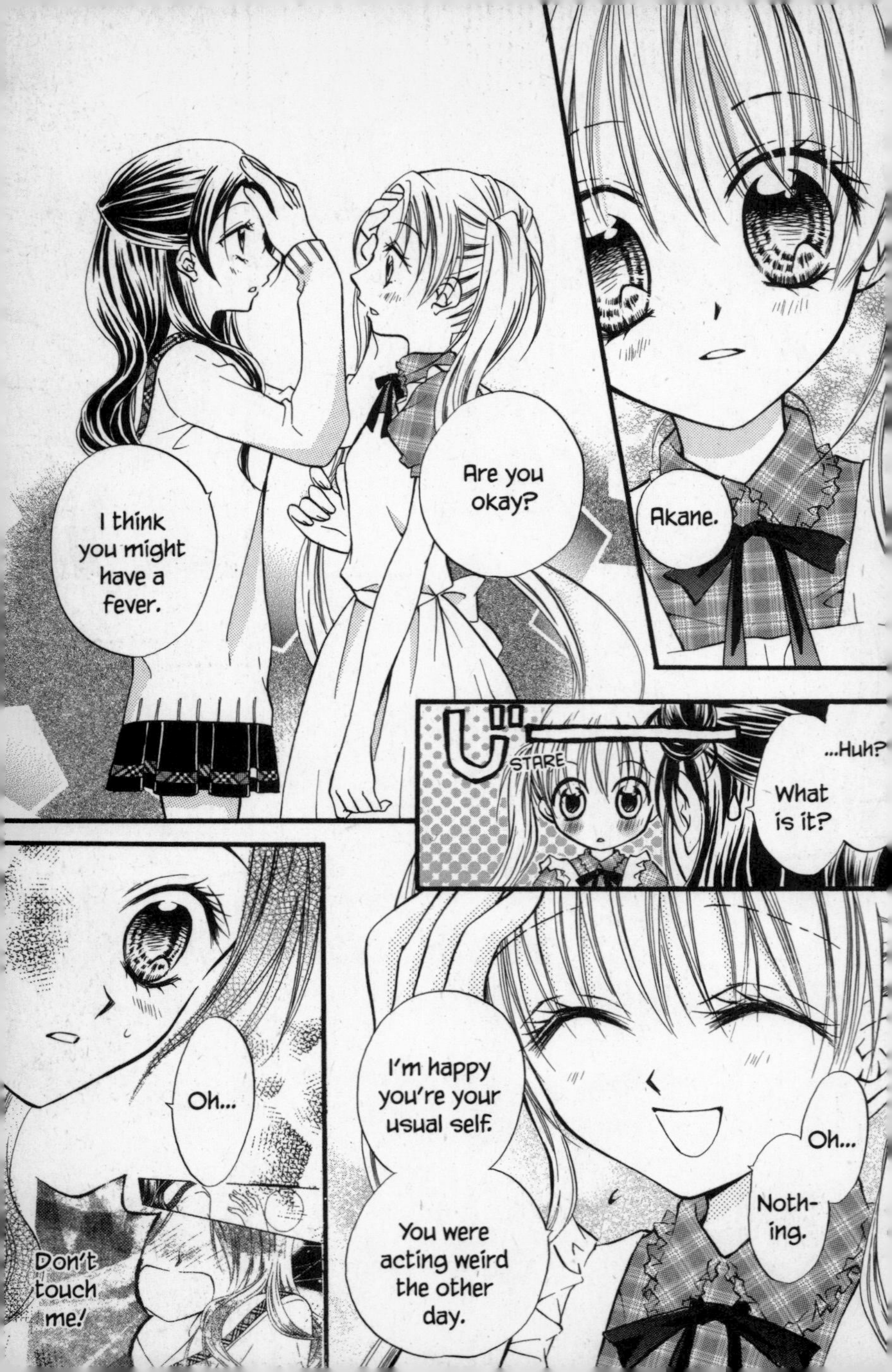
Akane.
STARE
...Huh?
What is it?
Are you okay?
I think you might have a fever.
I'm happy you're your usual self.
You were acting weird the other day.
Oh...
Noth-ing.
Oh...
Don't touch me!

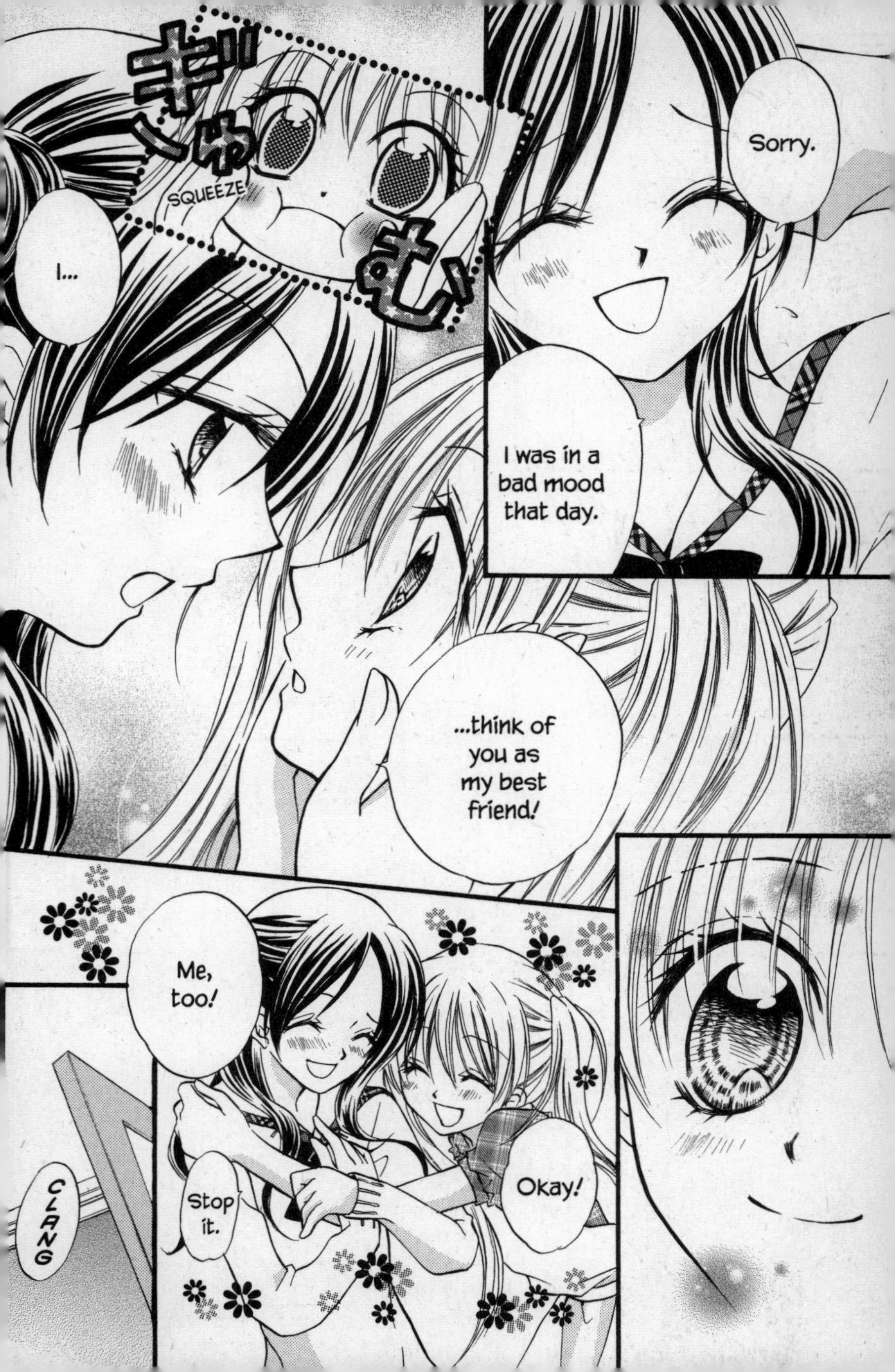
Sorry.
I was in a bad mood that day.
ぎゅむ
SQUEEZE
I...
...think of you as my best friend!
Me, too!
Stop it.
Okay!
CLANG

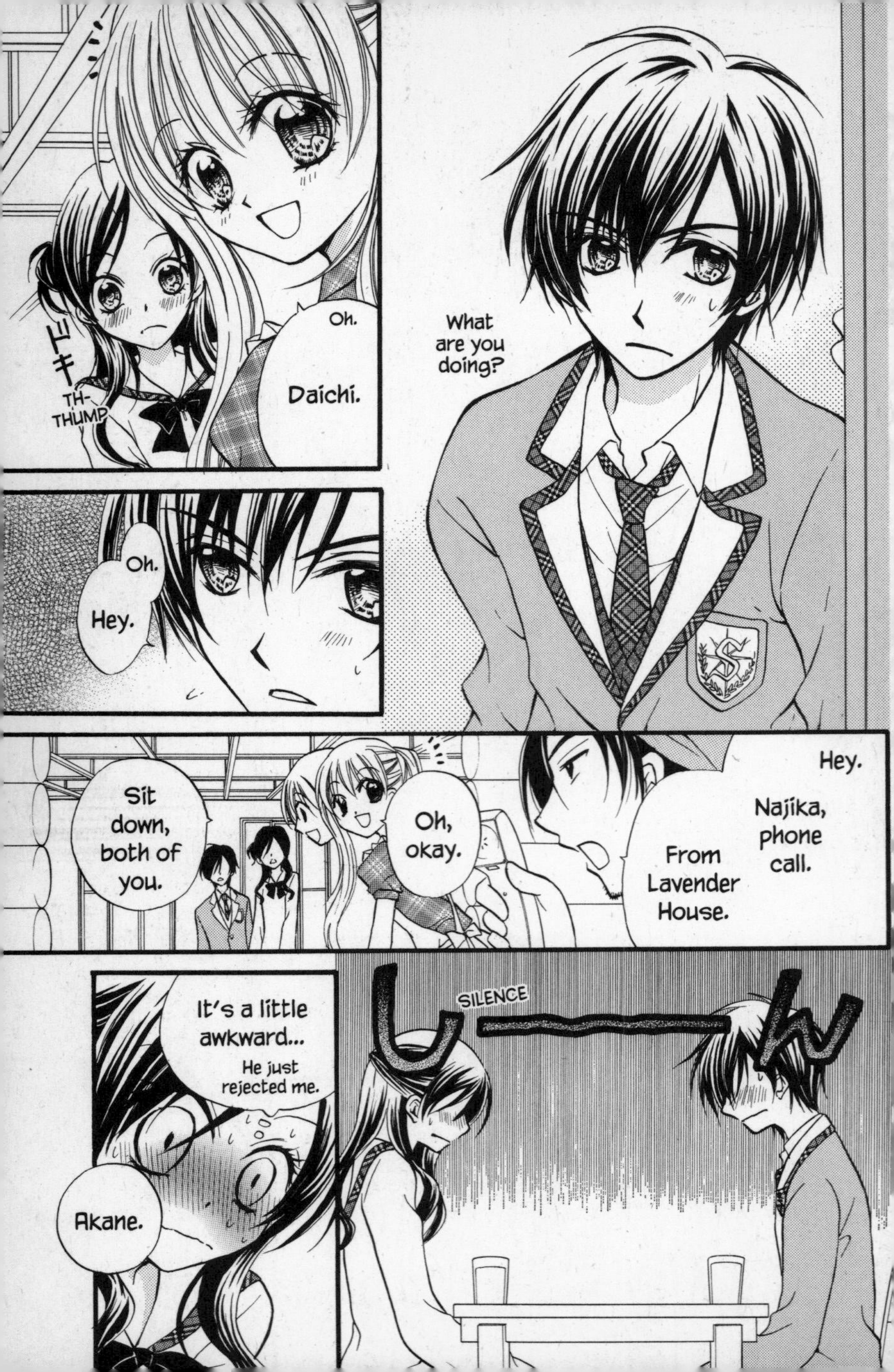
What are you doing?
Oh.
Daichi.
ドキ
TH-THUMP
Oh.
Hey.
Hey.
Najika, phone call.
From Lavender House.
Oh, okay.
Sit down, both of you.
SILENCE
It's a little awkward...
He just rejected me.
Akane.

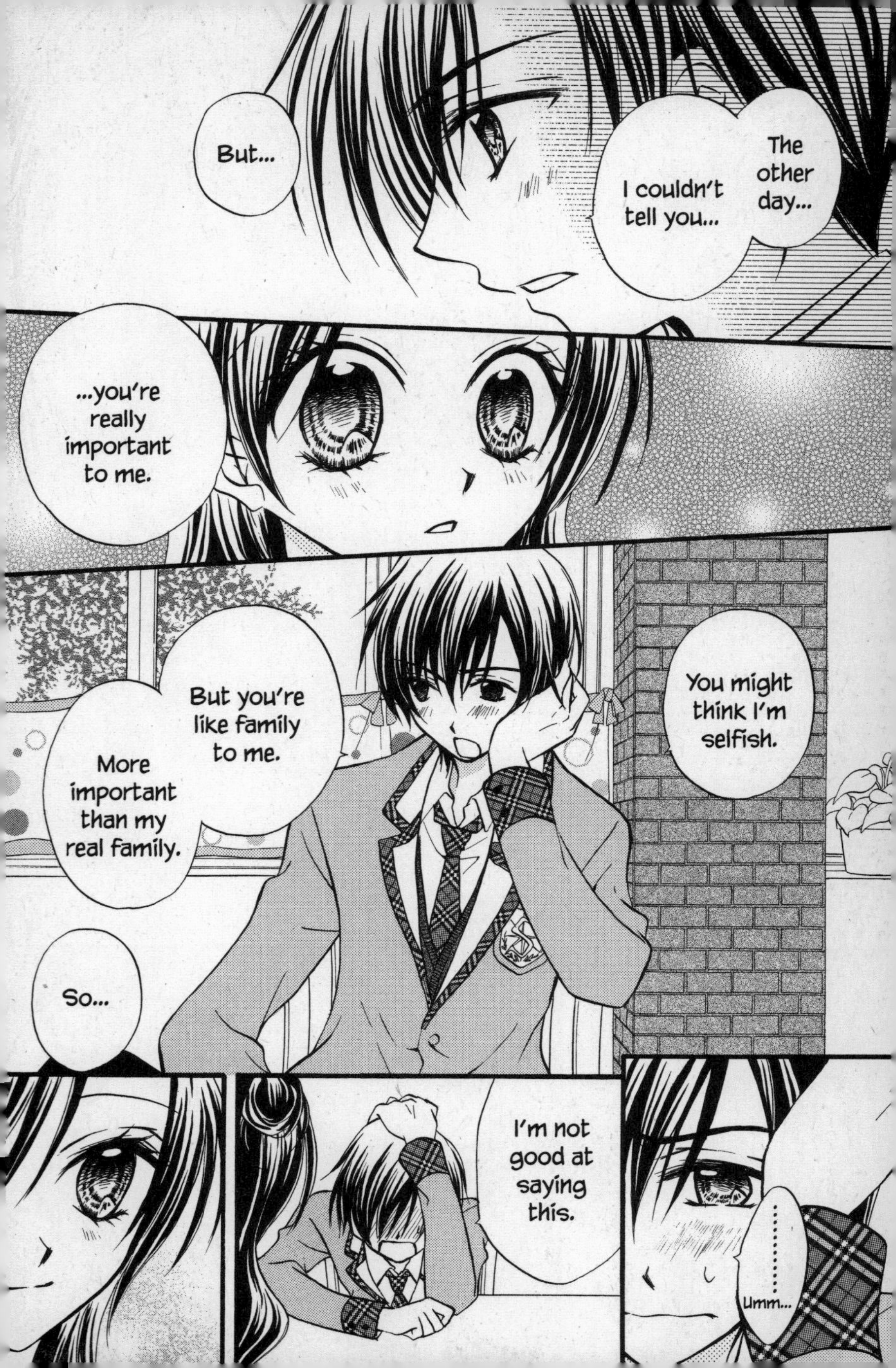
The other day...
I couldn't tell you...
But...
...you're really important to me.
You might think I'm selfish.
But you're like family to me.
More important than my real family.
So...
......
Umm...
I'm not good at saying this.

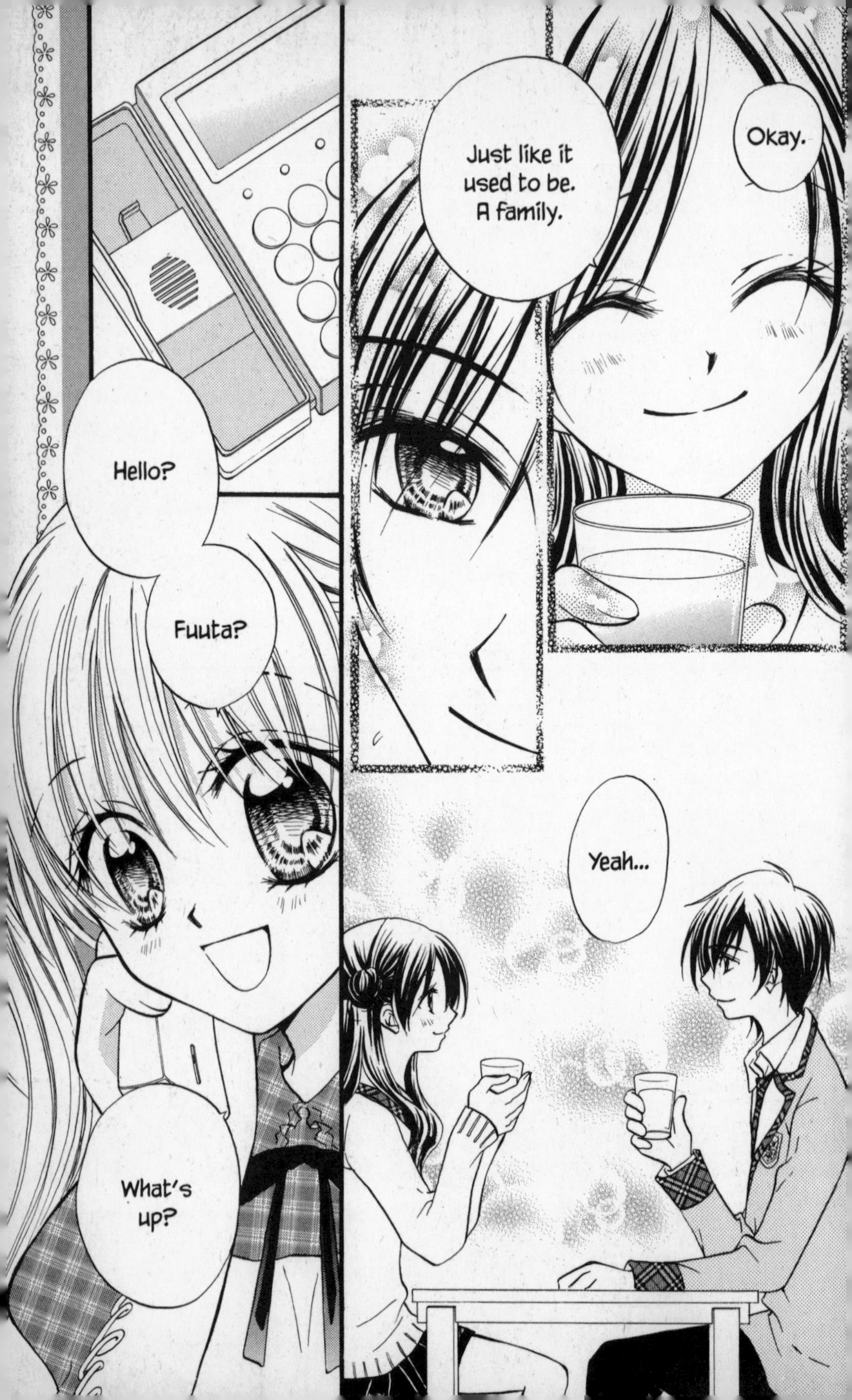
Okay.
Just like it used to be. A family.
Yeah...
Hello?
Fuuta?
What's up?

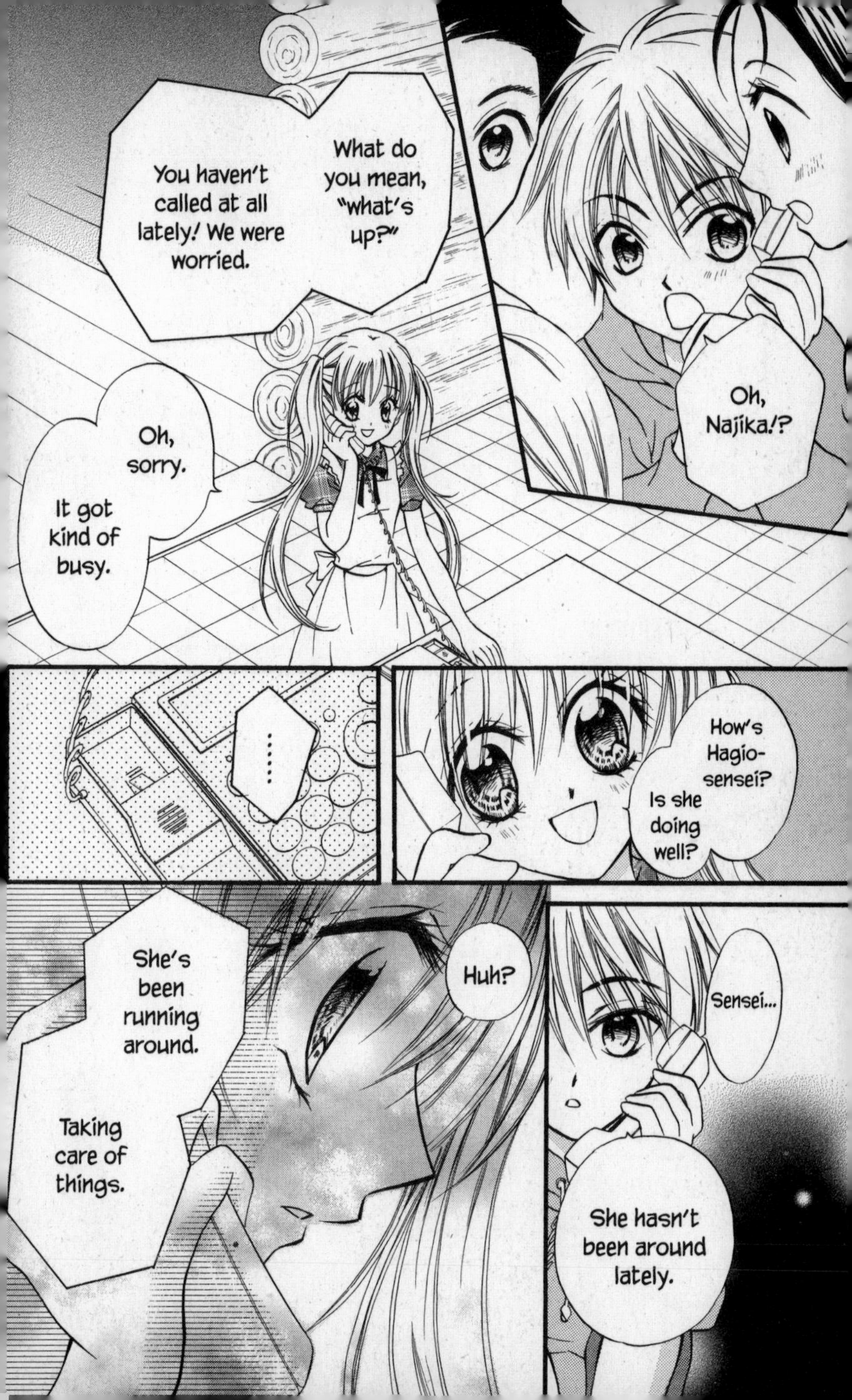
Oh, Najika!?
What do you mean, "what's up?"
You haven't called at all lately! We were worried.
Oh, sorry.
It got kind of busy.
How's Hagio-sensei?
Is she doing well?
......
Sensei...
She hasn't been around lately.
Huh?
She's been running around.
Taking care of things.

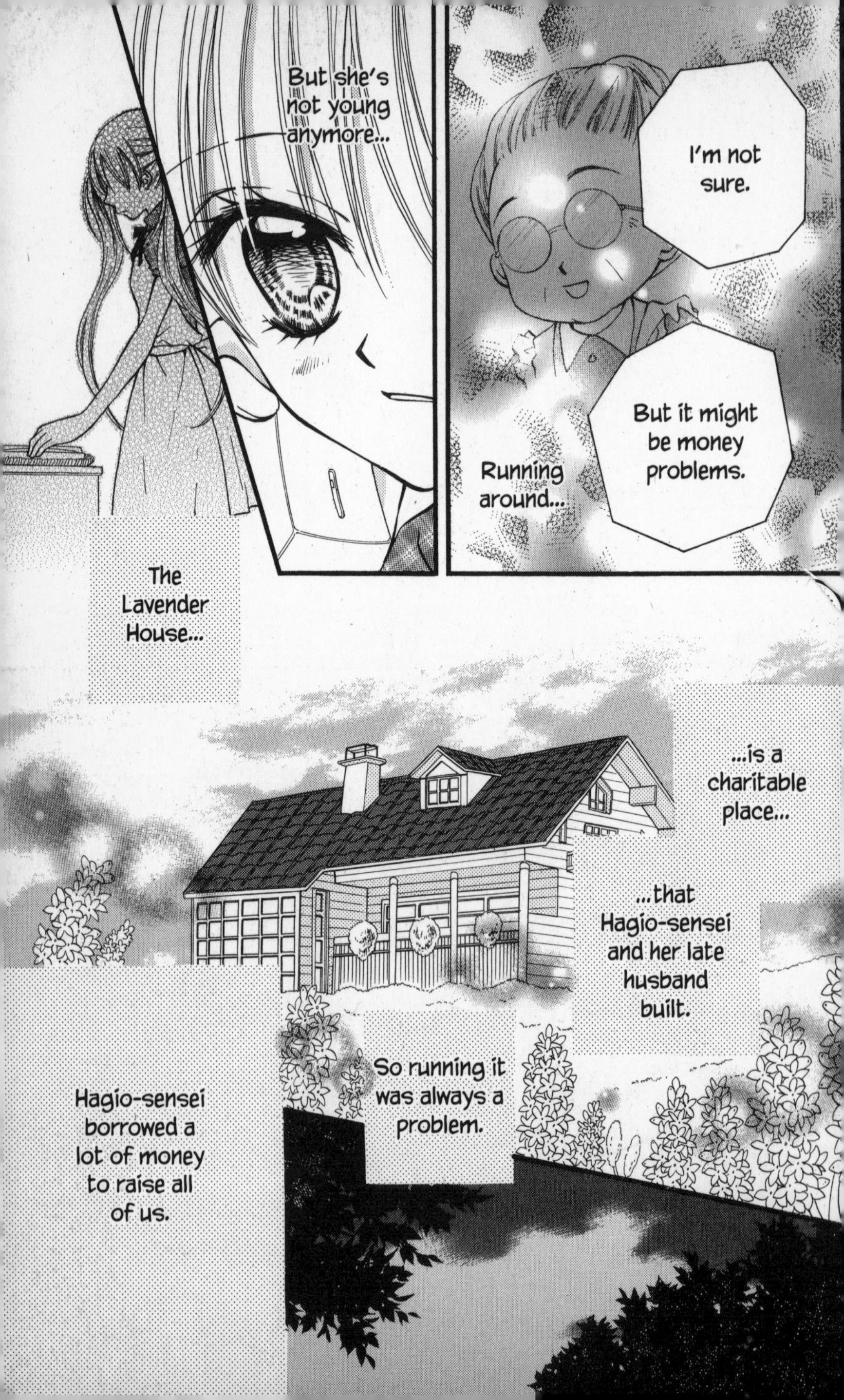
I'm not sure.
But it might be money problems.
Running around...
But she's not young anymore...
The Lavender House...
...is a charitable place...
...that Hagio-sensei and her late husband built.
So running it was always a problem.
Hagio-sensei borrowed a lot of money to raise all of us.

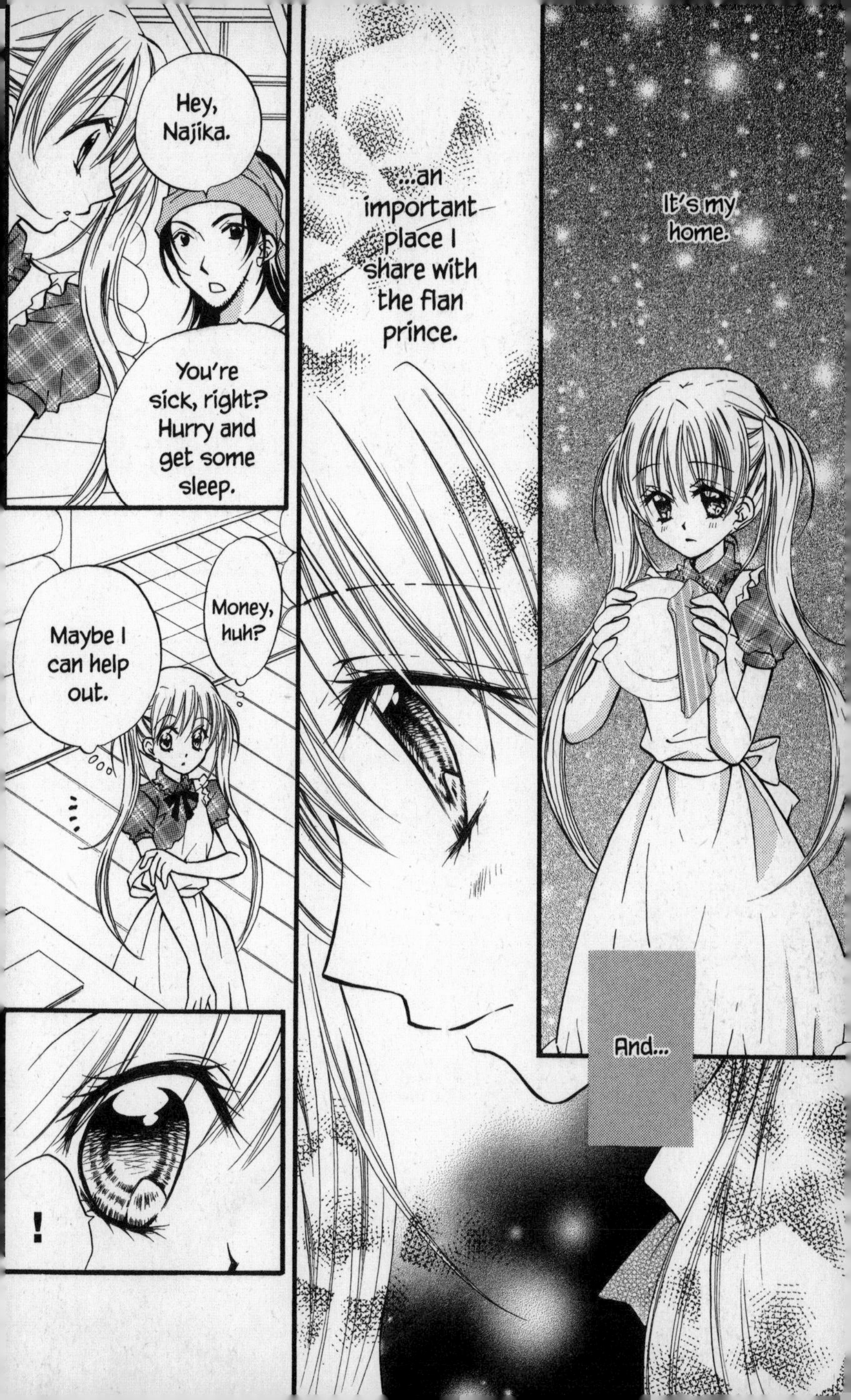
It's my home.
And...
...an important place I share with the flan prince.
Hey, Najika.
You're sick, right? Hurry and get some sleep.
Money, huh?
Maybe I can help out.
...
!

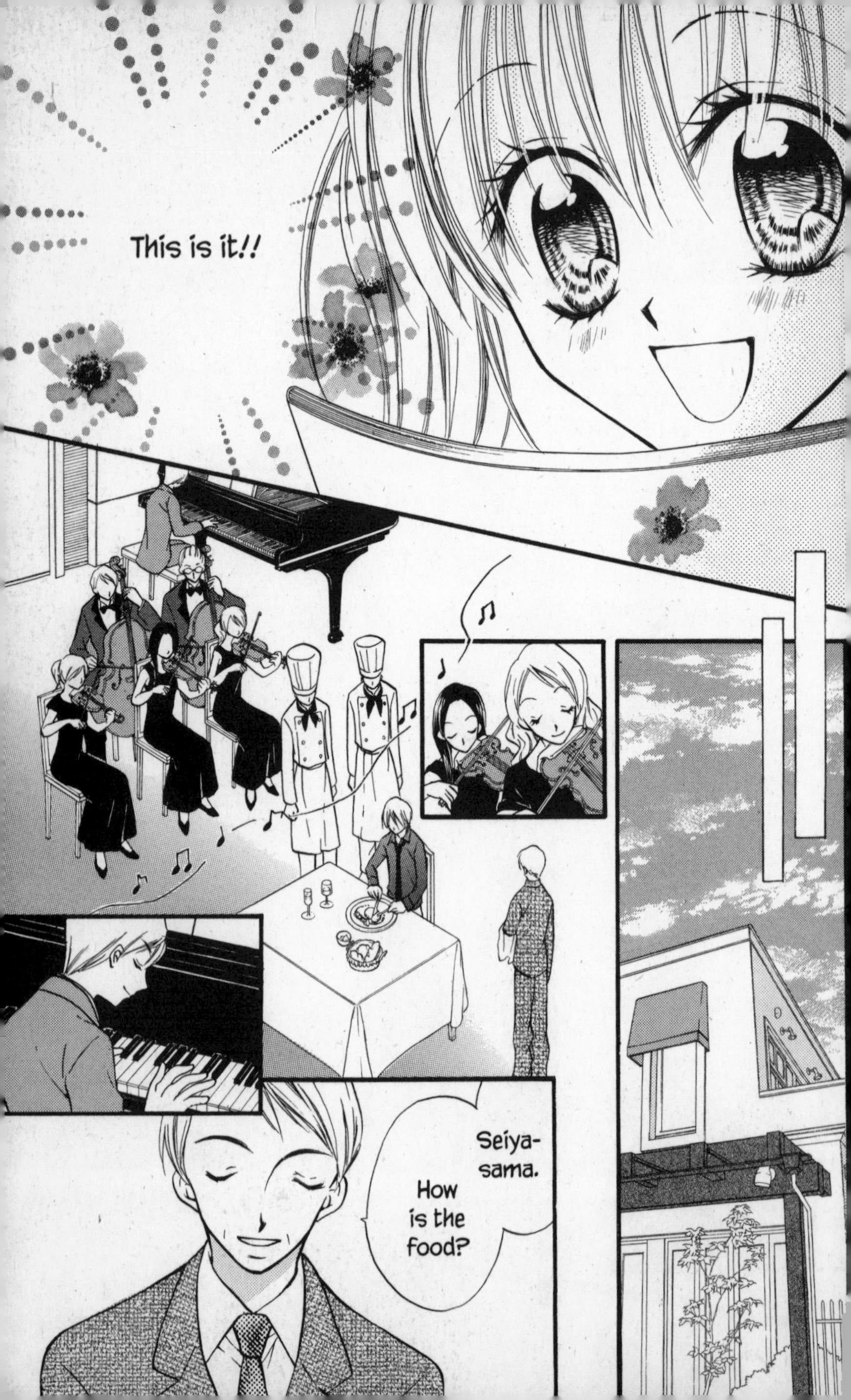
This is it!!
Seiya-sama.
How is the food?

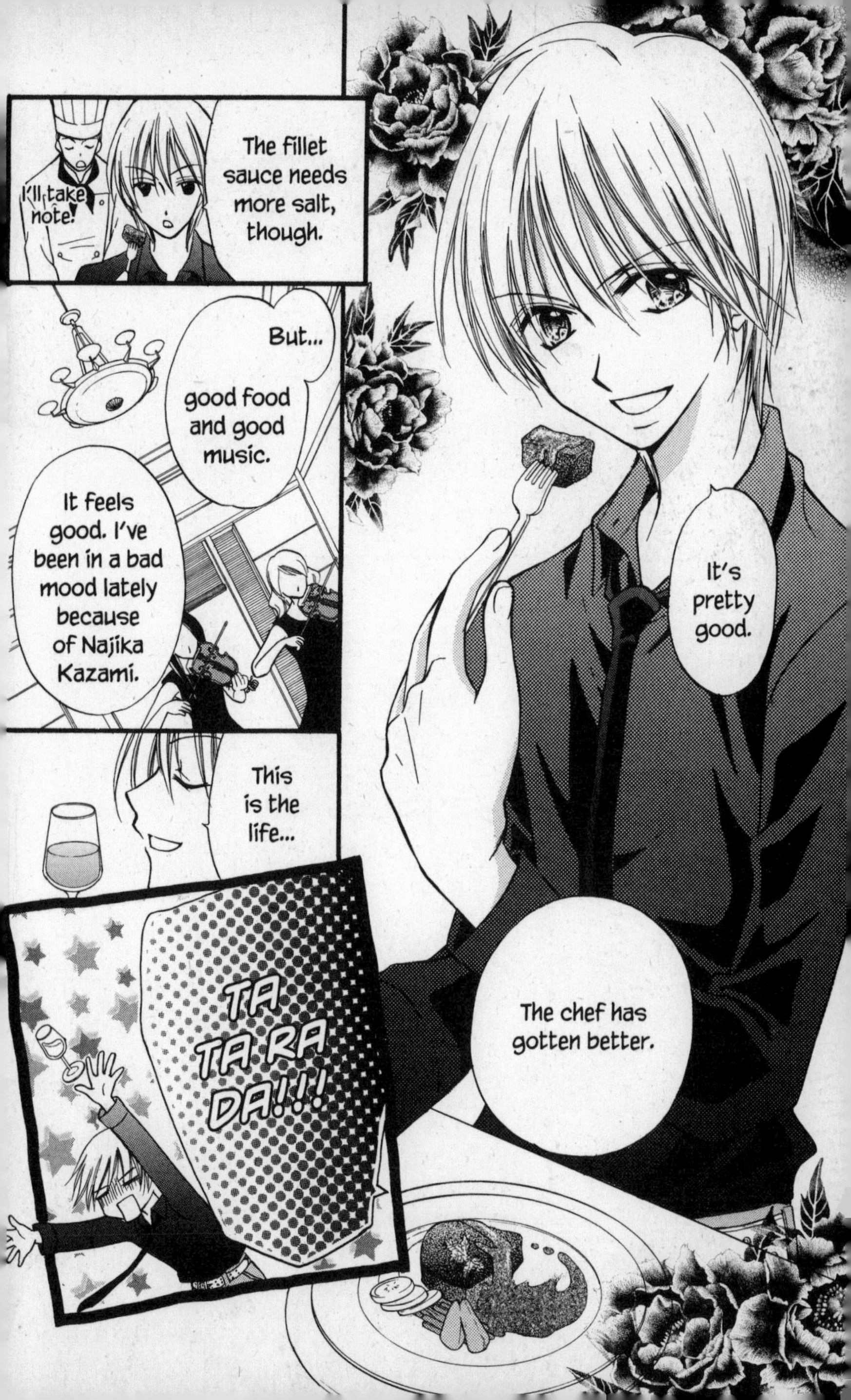
It's pretty good.
The chef has gotten better.
The fillet sauce needs more salt, though.
I'll take note!
But...
good food and good music.
It feels good. I've been in a bad mood lately because of Najika Kazami.
This is the life...
TA TA RA DA!!!

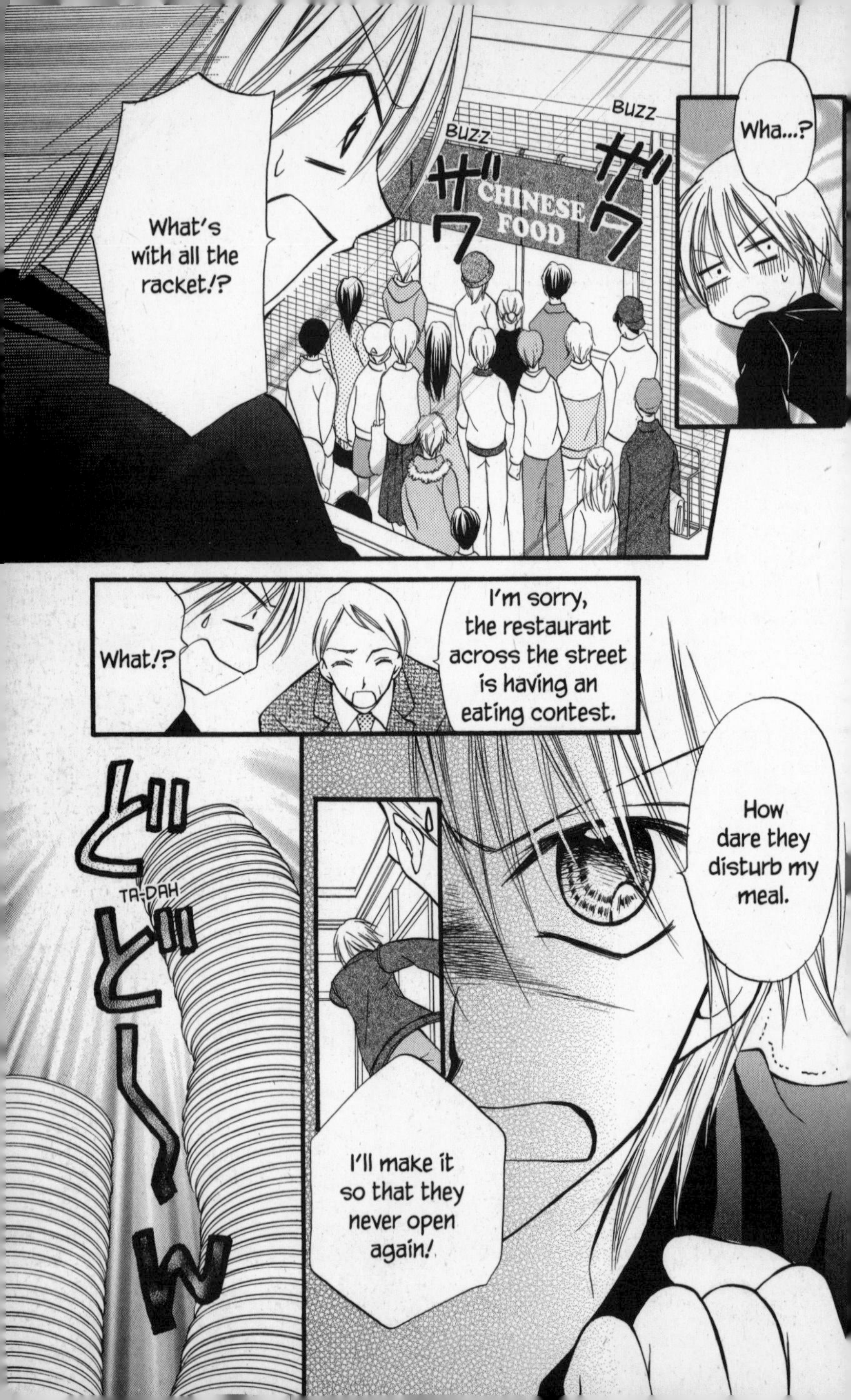
Wha...?
BUZZ
ザワ
BUZZ
ザワ
CHINESE FOOD
What's with all the racket!?
I'm sorry, the restaurant across the street is having an eating contest.
What!?
How dare they disturb my meal.
I'll make it so that they never open again!
TA-DAH

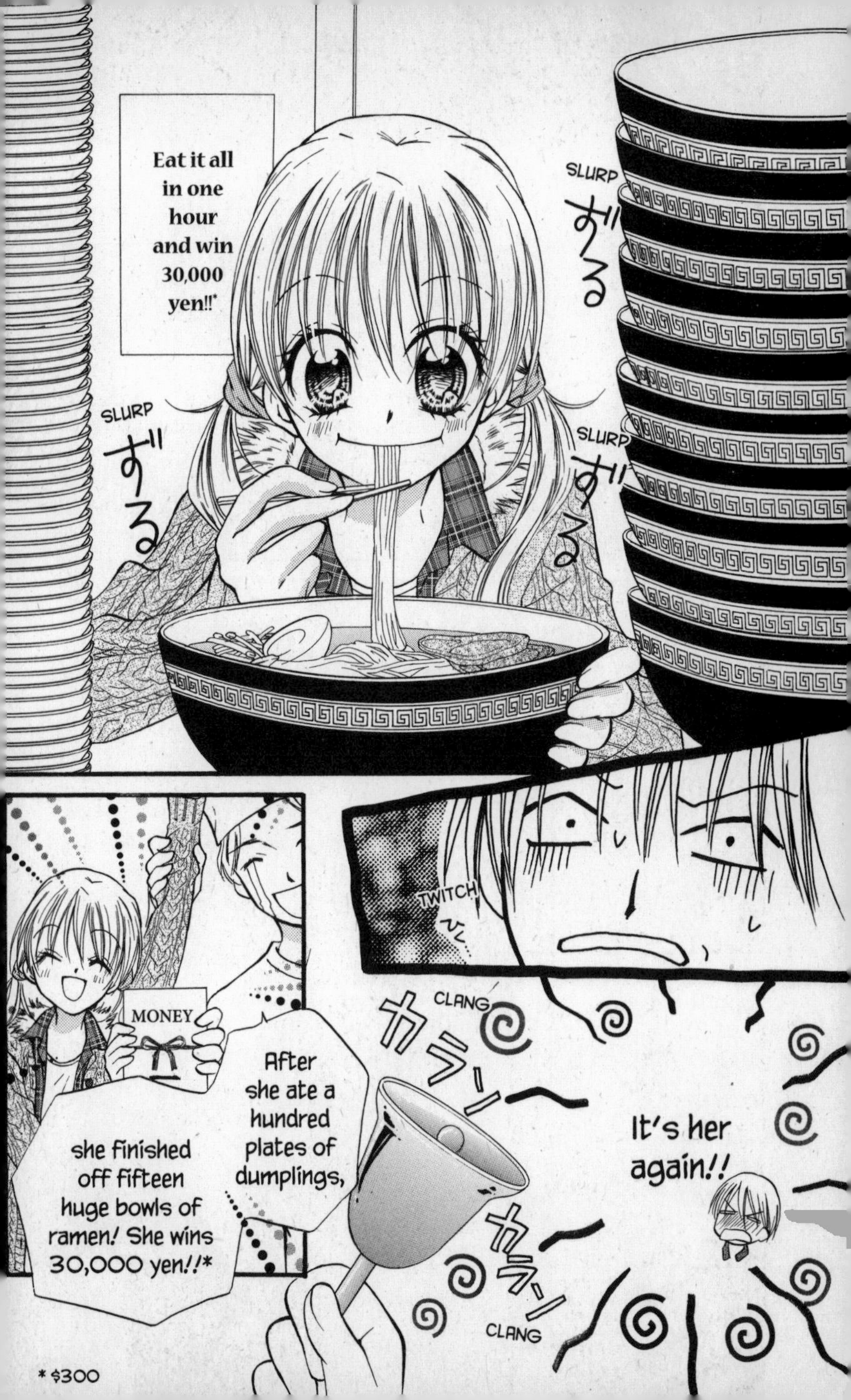
SLURP
ずる
Eat it all in one hour and win 30,000 yen!!*
SLURP
ずる
SLURP
ずる
TWITCH
ぴく
CLANG
カラ〜ン
It's her again!!
CLANG
カラ〜ン
After she ate a hundred plates of dumplings,
she finished off fifteen huge bowls of ramen! She wins 30,000 yen!!*
MONEY

* $300

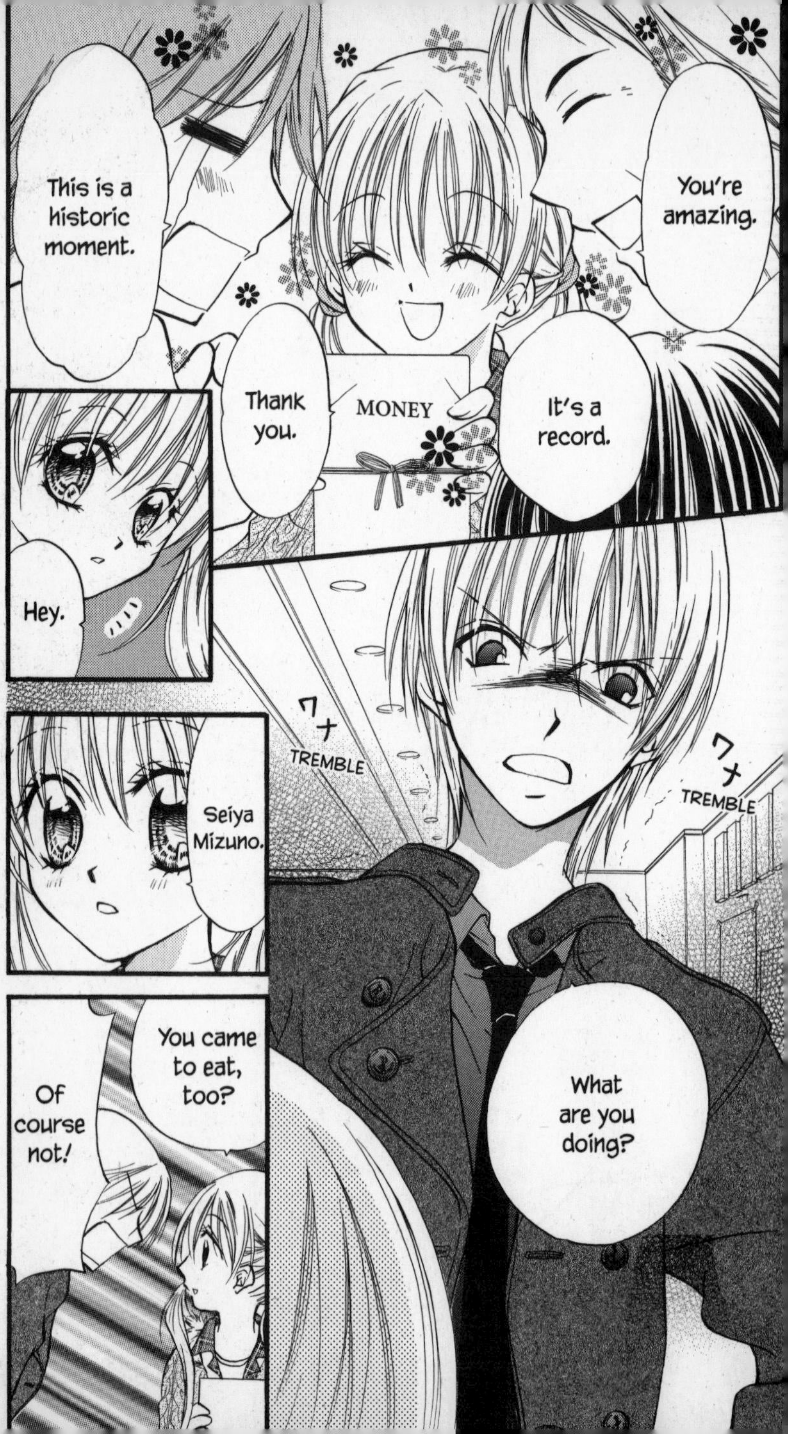
You're amazing.
This is a historic moment.
It's a record.
MONEY
Thank you.
ワナ
TREMBLE
ワナ
TREMBLE
What are you doing?
Hey.
Seiya Mizuno.
You came to eat, too?
Of course not!

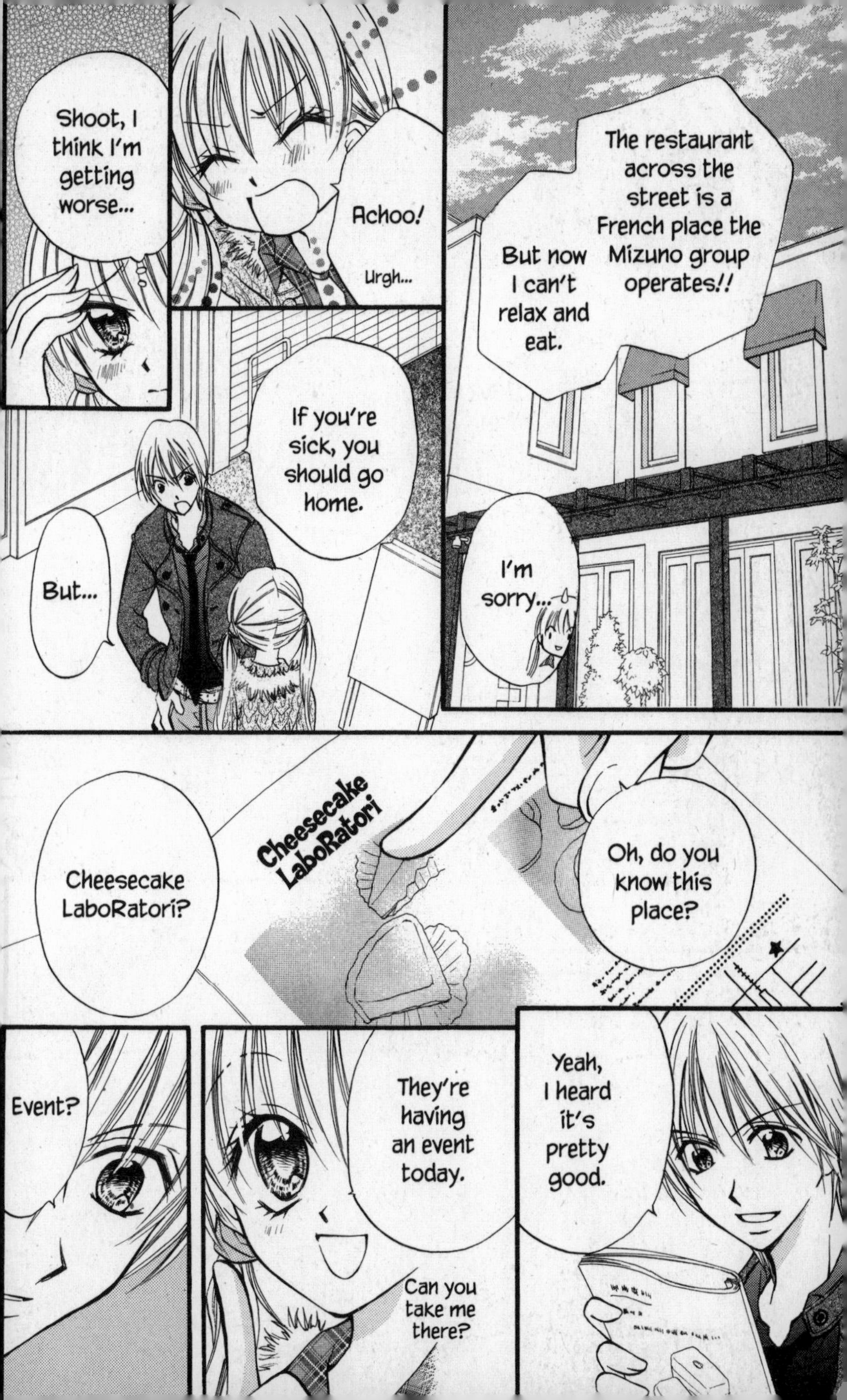
The restaurant across the street is a French place the Mizuno group operates!!
But now I can't relax and eat.
I'm sorry...
Achoo!
Urgh...
Shoot, I think I'm getting worse...
If you're sick, you should go home.
But...
Oh, do you know this place?
Cheesecake LaboRatori
Cheesecake LaboRatori?
Yeah, I heard it's pretty good.
They're having an event today.
Can you take me there?
Event?

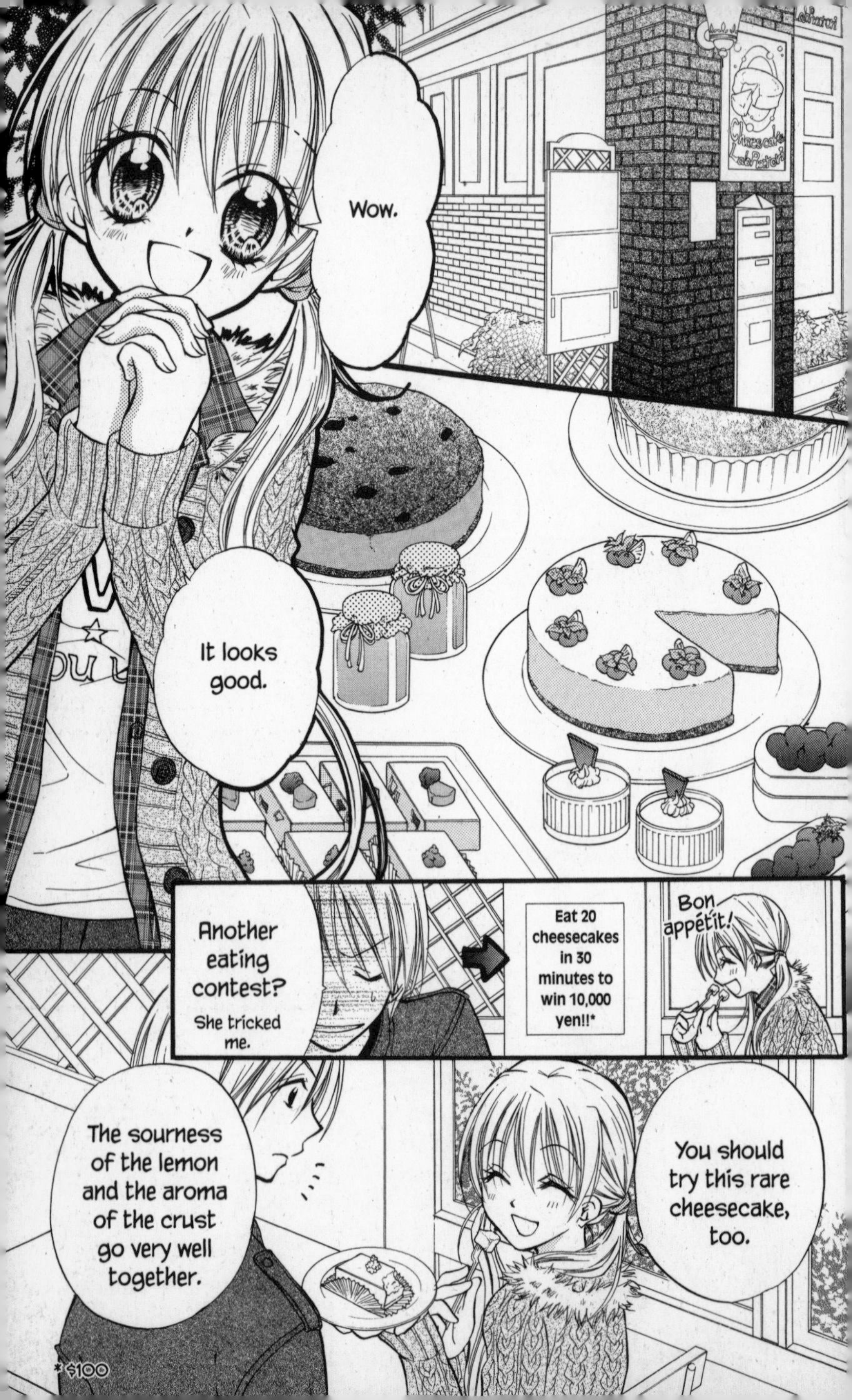
Wow.
It looks good.
Bon appétit!
Eat 20 cheesecakes in 30 minutes to win 10,000 yen!!*
Another eating contest?
She tricked me.
You should try this rare cheesecake, too.
The sourness of the lemon and the aroma of the crust go very well together.

* $100

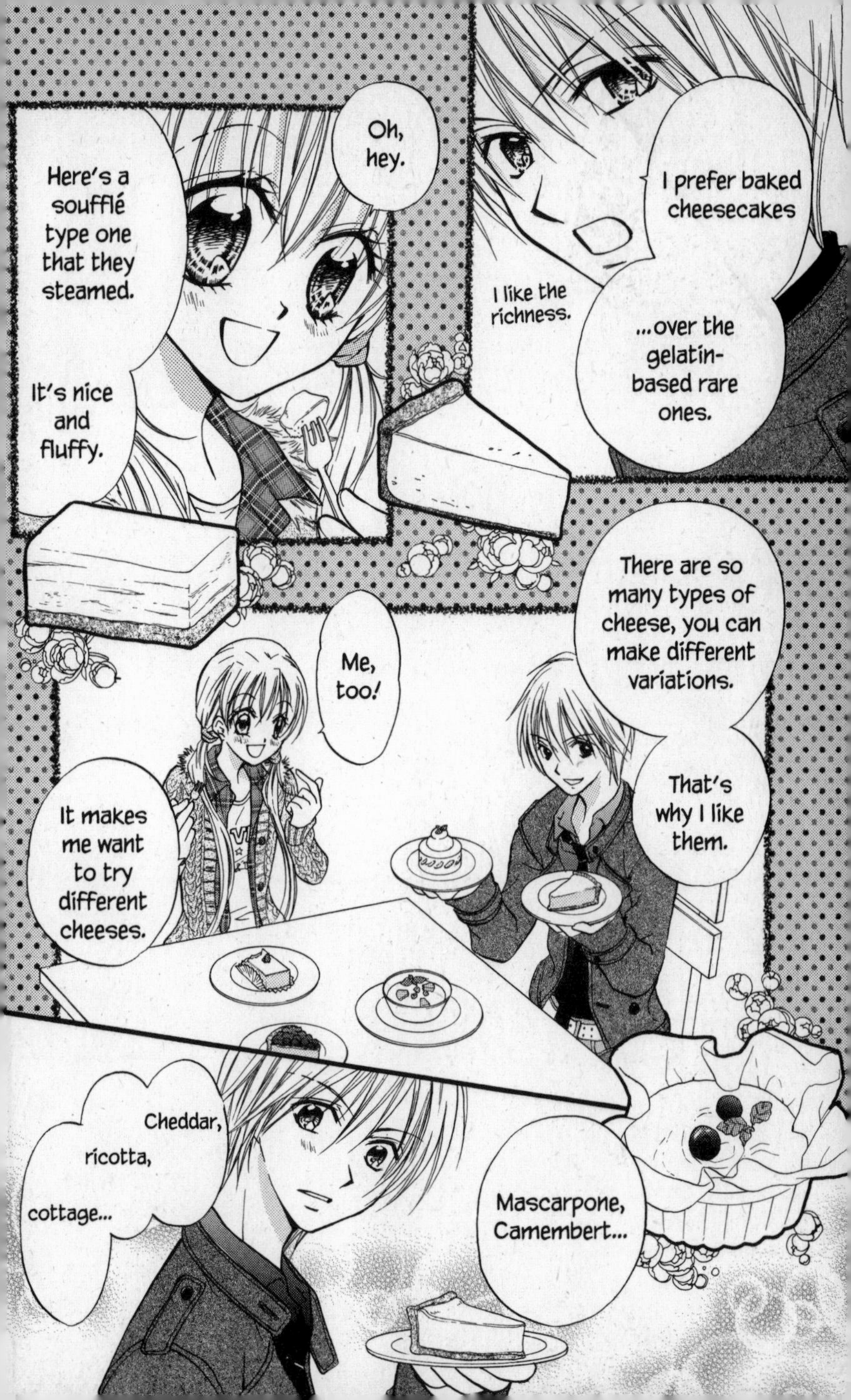
I prefer baked cheesecakes
...over the gelatin-based rare ones.
I like the richness.
Oh, hey.
Here's a soufflé type one that they steamed.
It's nice and fluffy.
There are so many types of cheese, you can make different variations.
That's why I like them.
Me, too!
It makes me want to try different cheeses.
Mascarpone, Camembert...
Cheddar,
ricotta,
cottage...

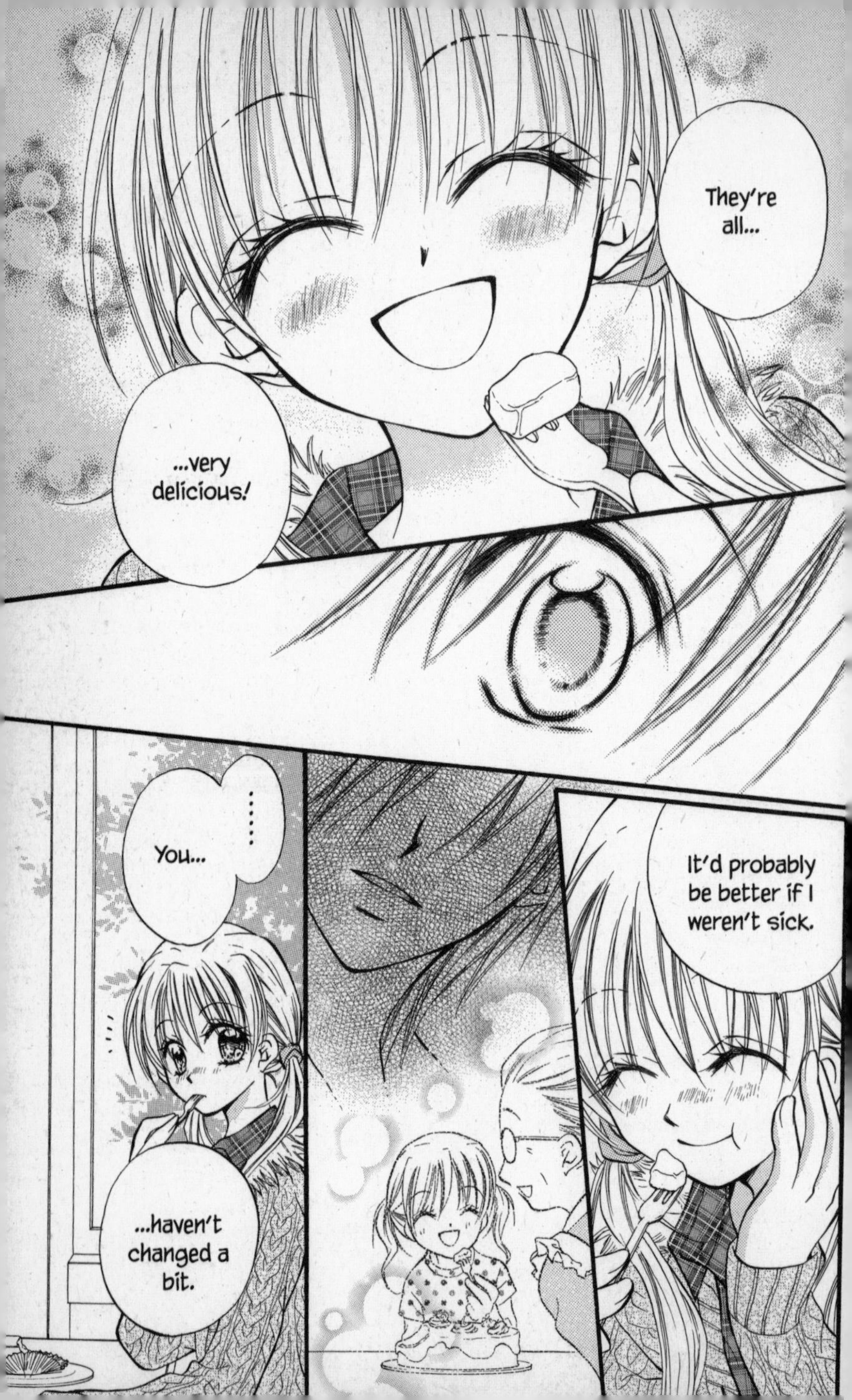
They're all...
...very delicious!
It'd probably be better if I weren't sick.
......
You...
...haven't changed a bit.

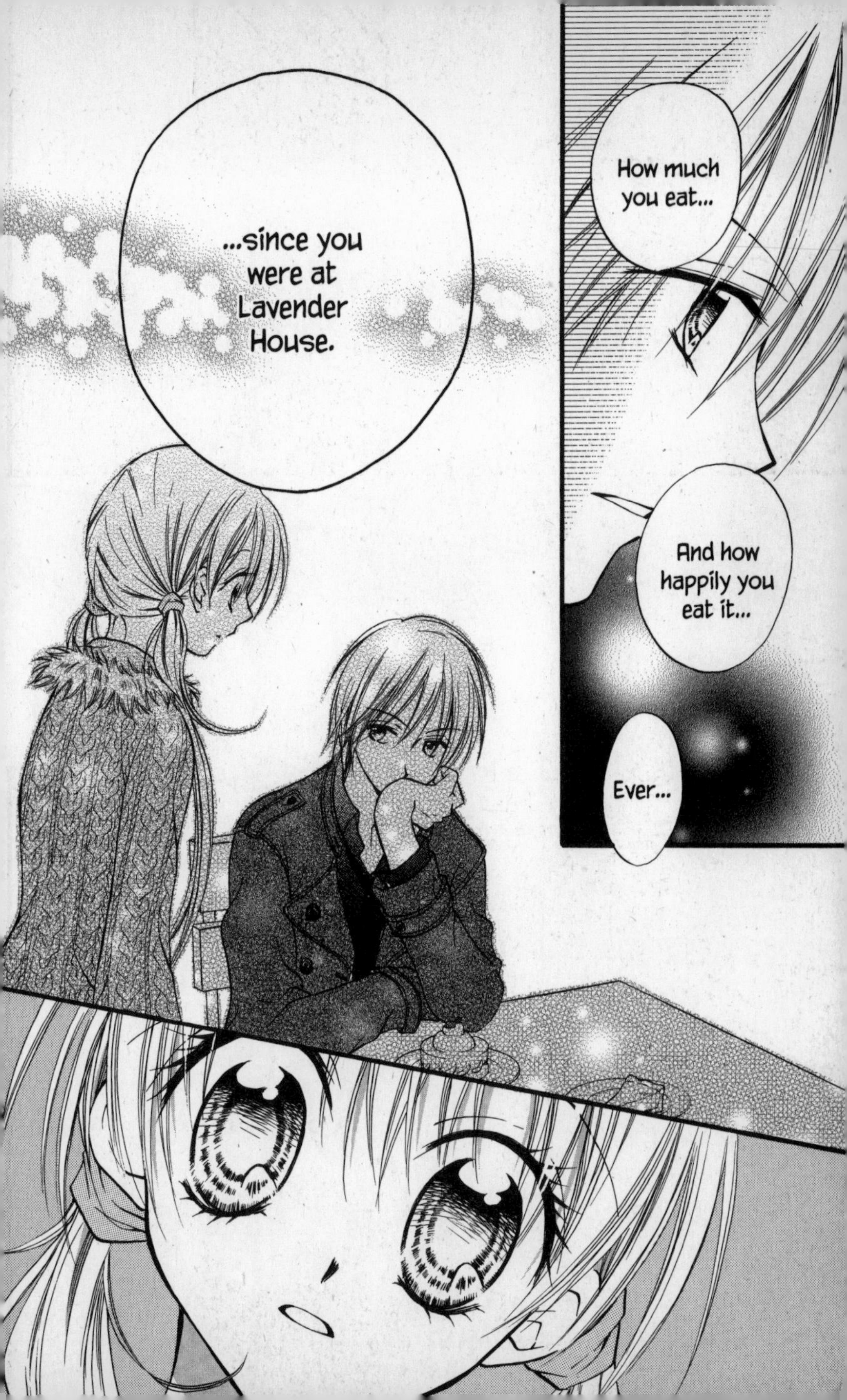
How much you eat...
And how happily you eat it...
Ever...
...since you were at Lavender House.

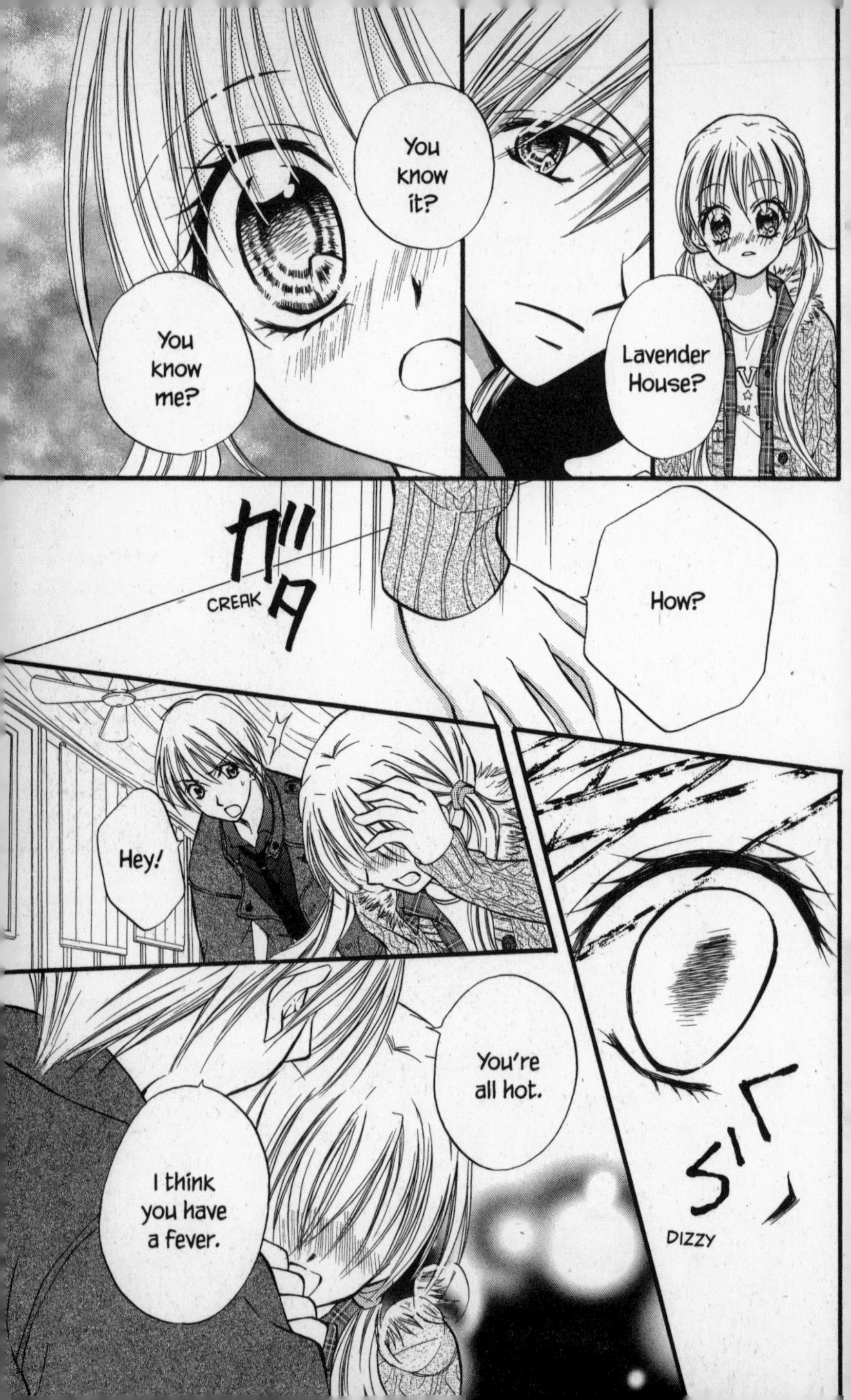

Lavender House?
You know it?
You know me?
How?
ガタ
CREAK
DIZZY
Hey!
You're all hot.
I think you have a fever.

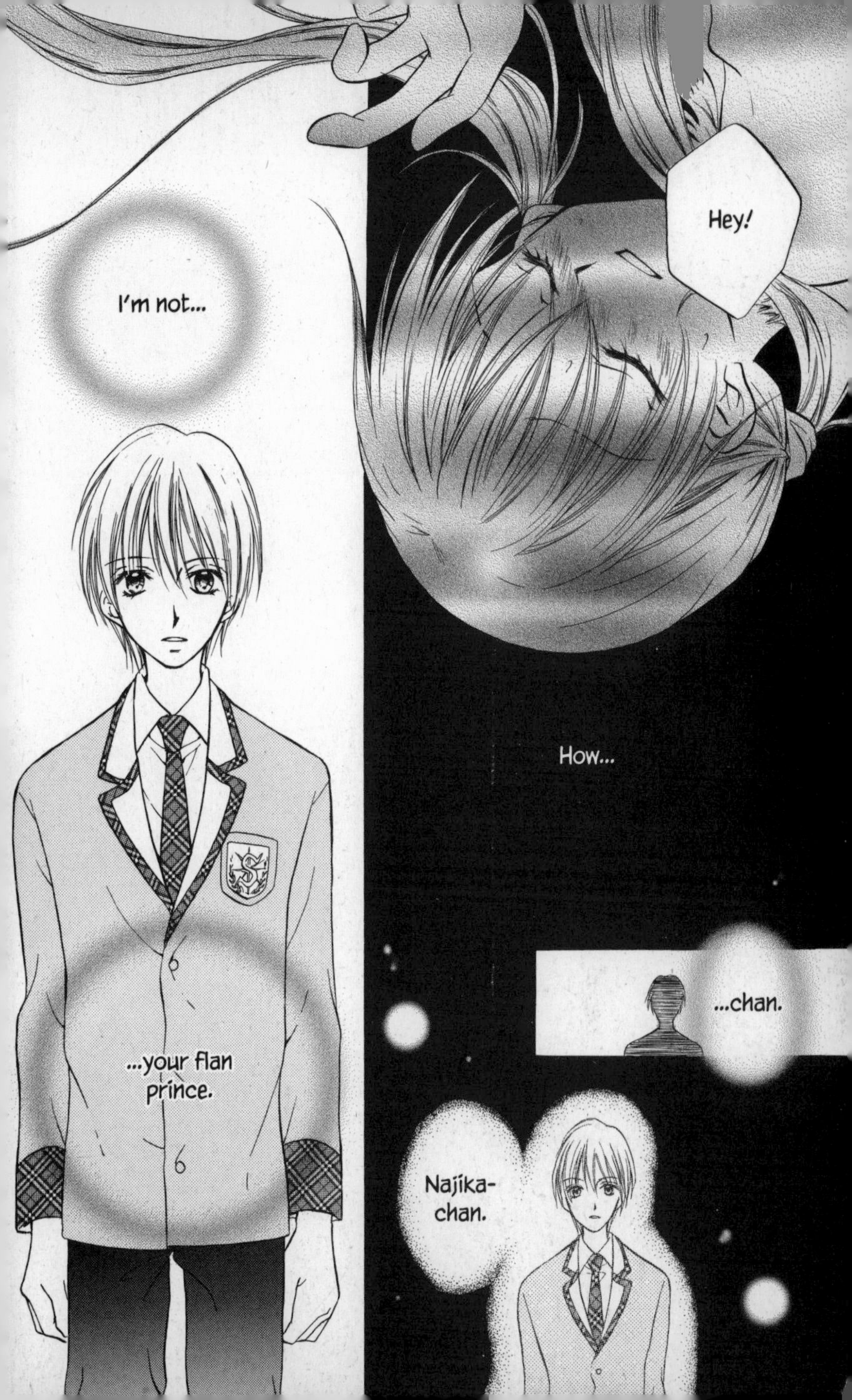
Hey!
How...
...chan.
Najika-
chan.
I'm not...
...your flan
prince.

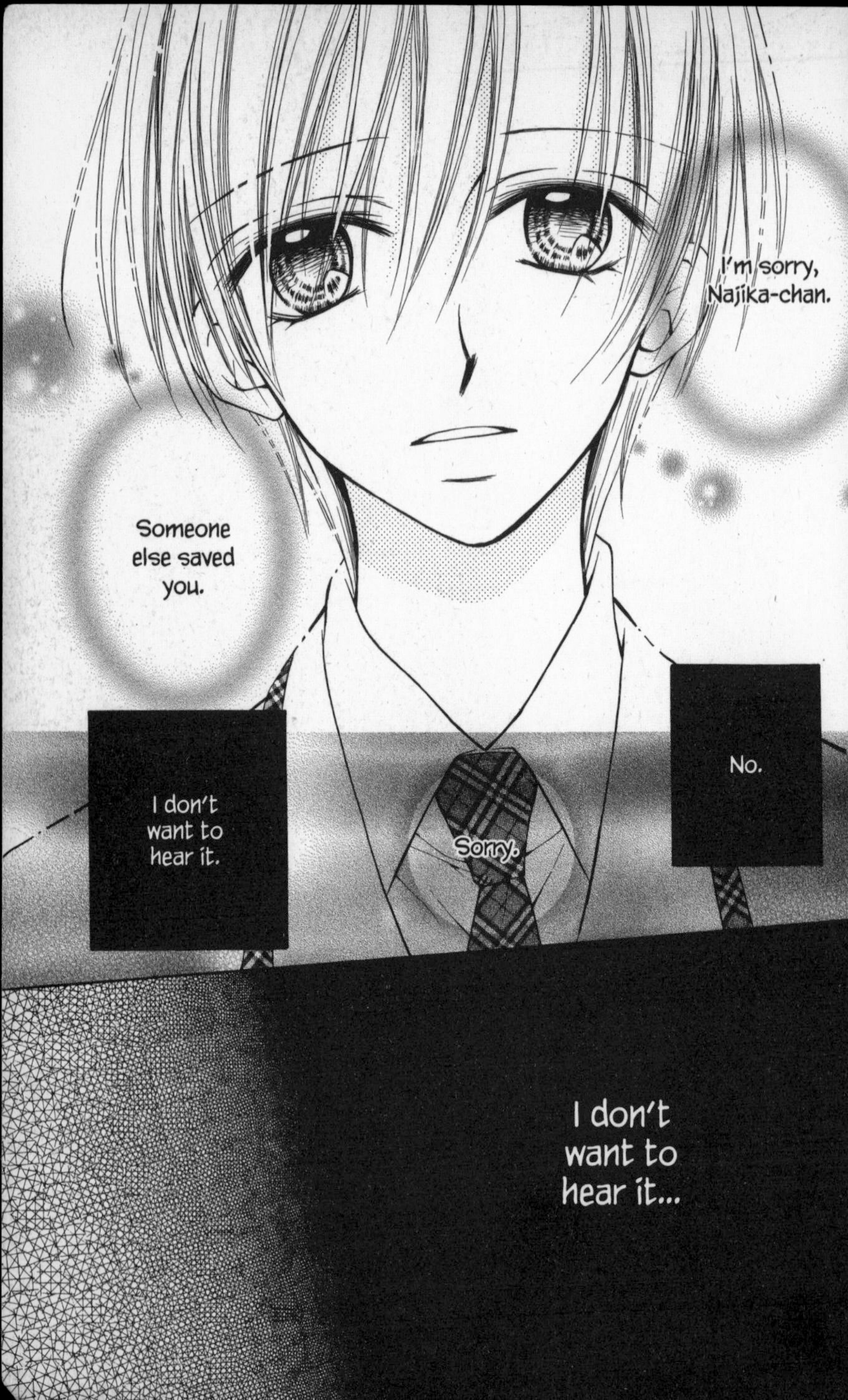
I'm sorry, Najika-chan.
Someone else saved you.
No.
Sorry.
I don't want to hear it.
I don't want to hear it...

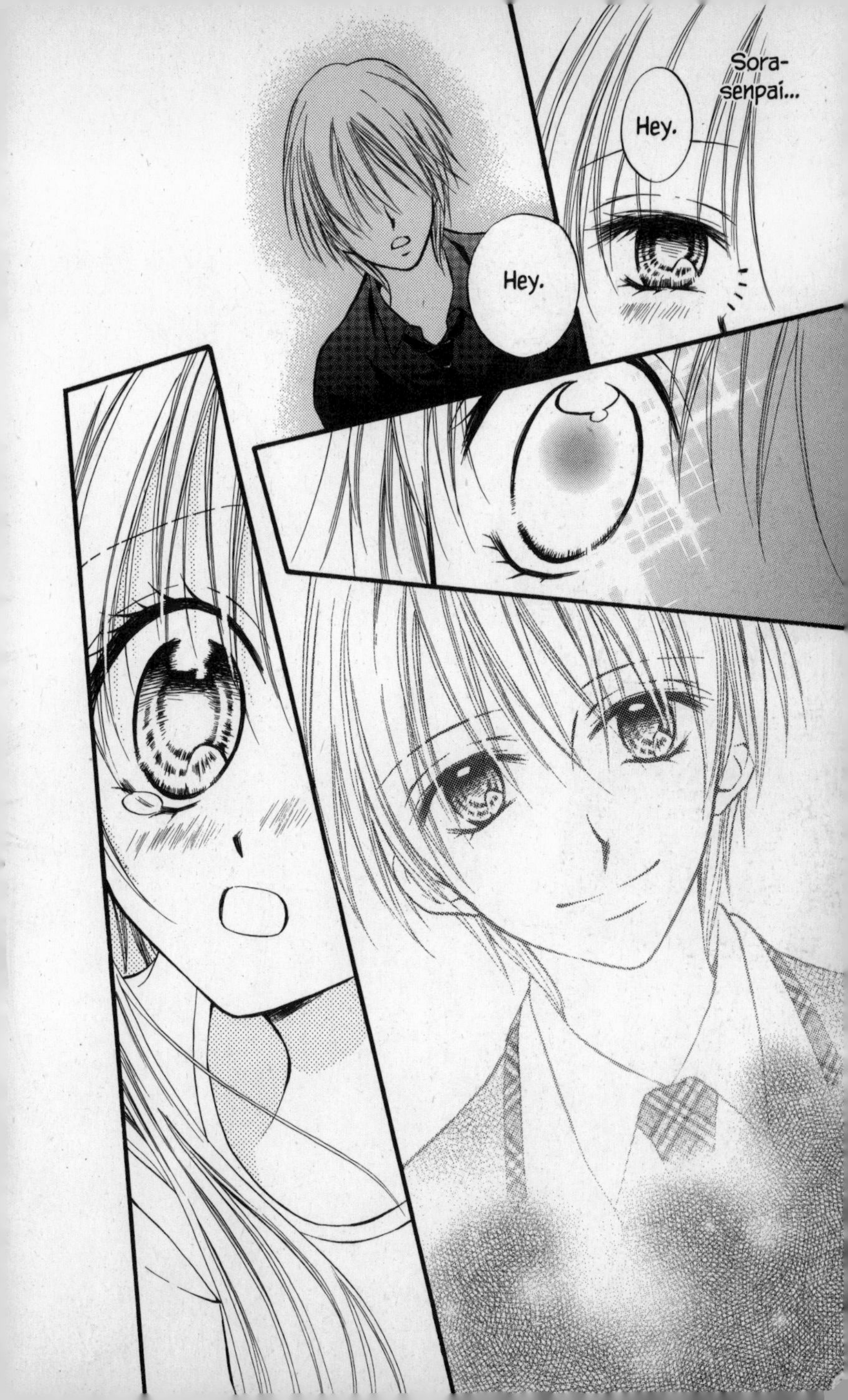

Sora-senpai...
Hey.
Hey.

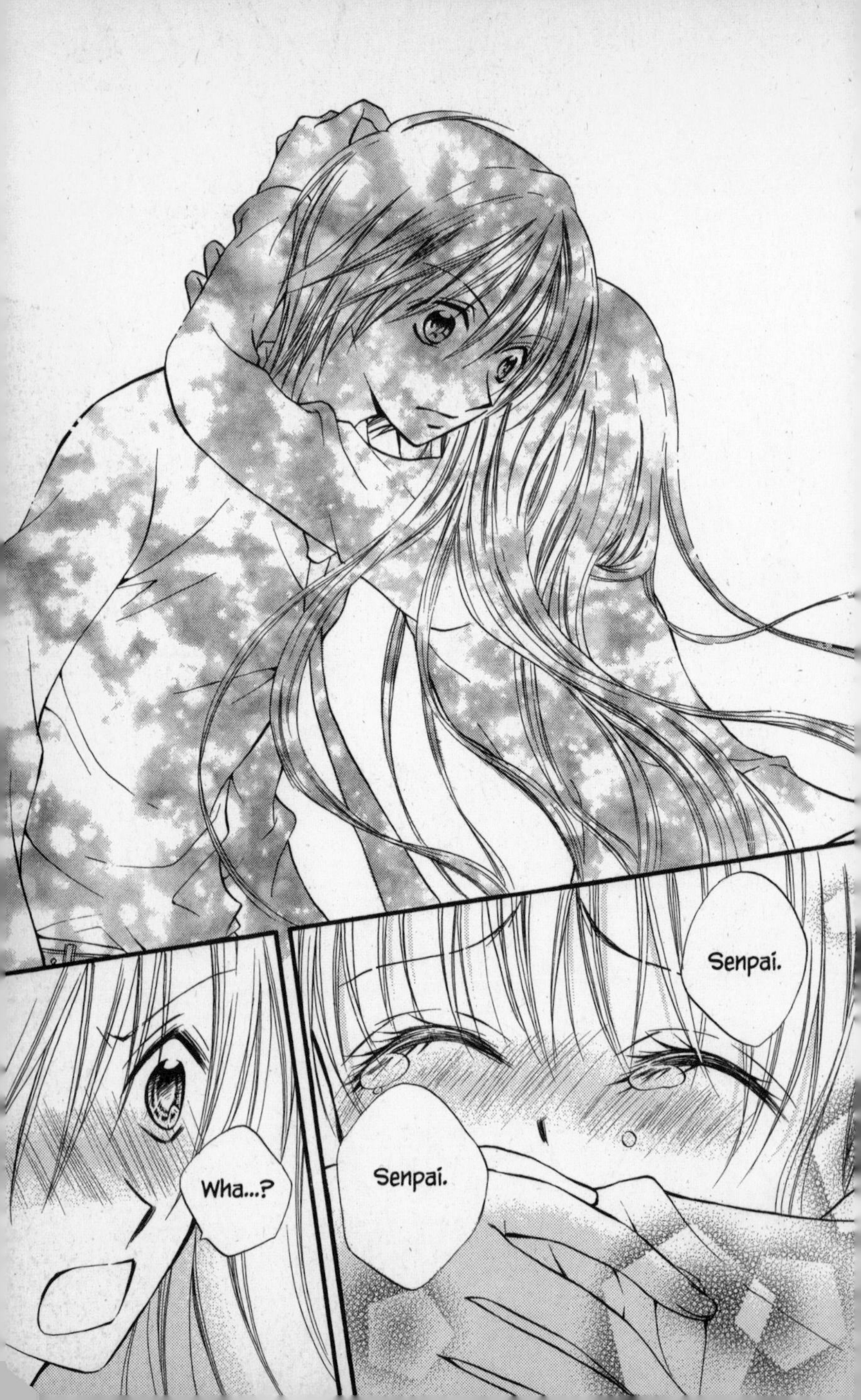
Senpai.
Senpai.
Wha...?

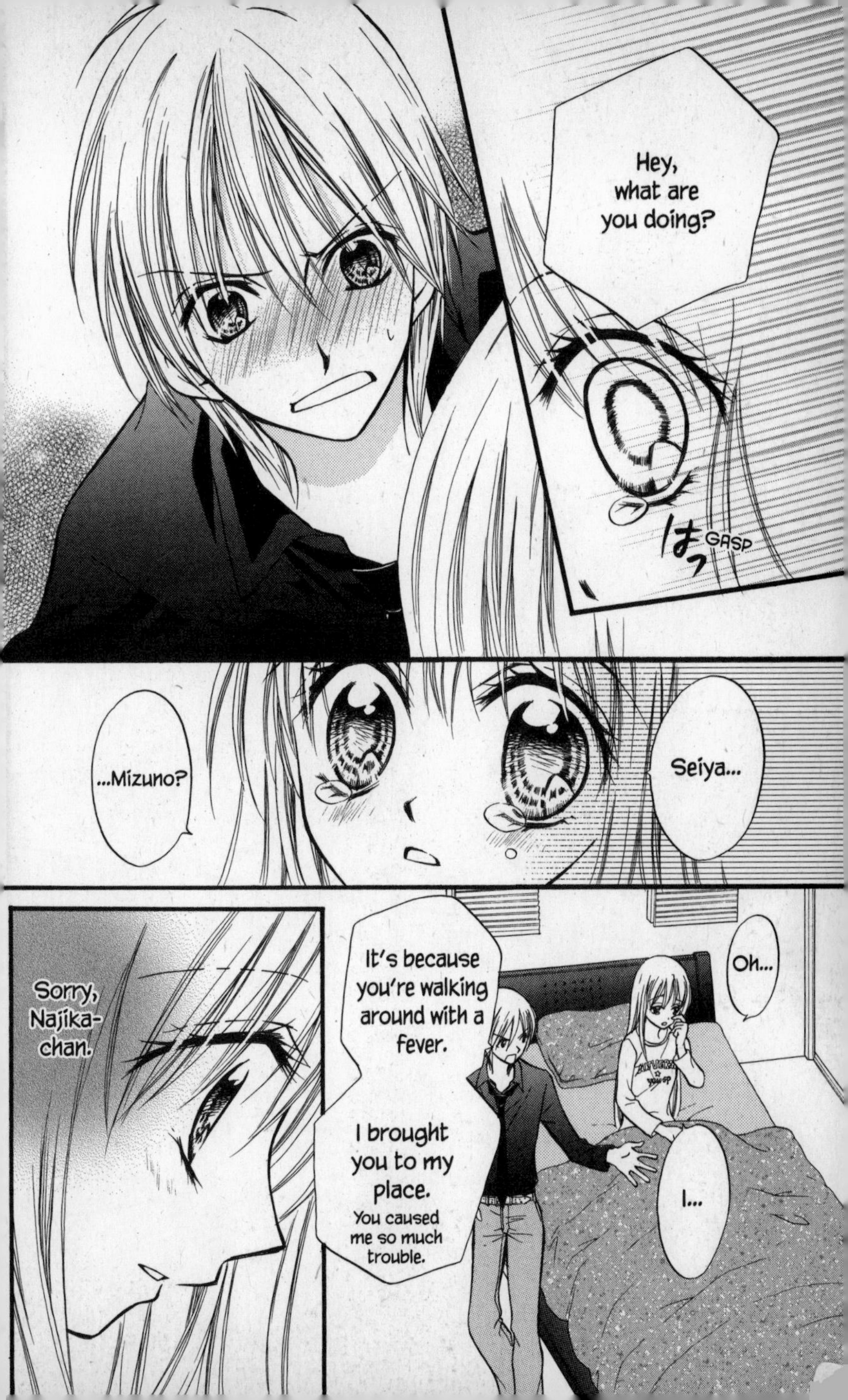
Hey, what are you doing?
はっ GASP
Seiya...
...Mizuno?
Oh...
It's because you're walking around with a fever.
I...
I brought you to my place.
You caused me so much trouble.
Sorry, Najika-chan.

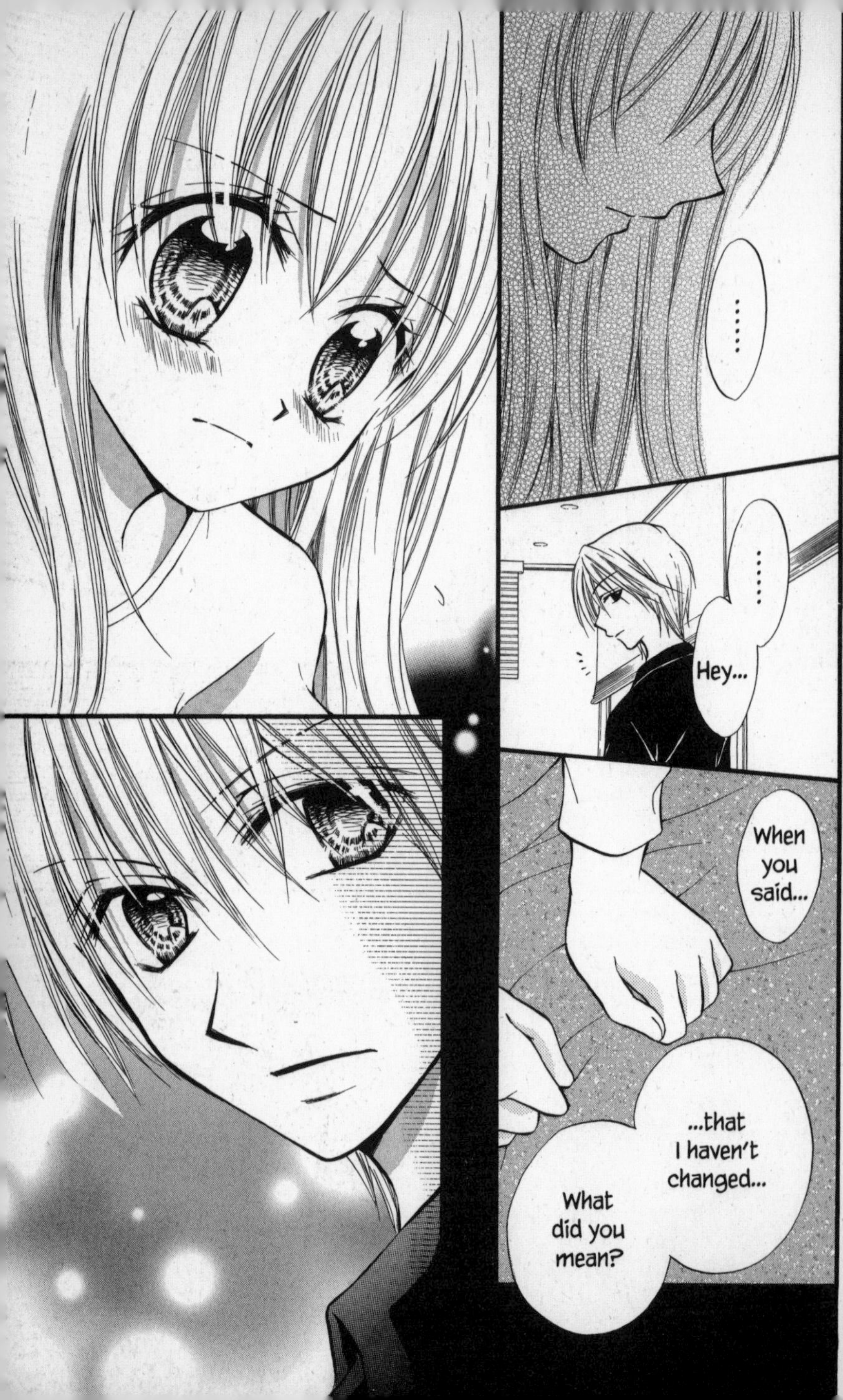
......
......
Hey...
When you said...
...that I haven't changed...
What did you mean?

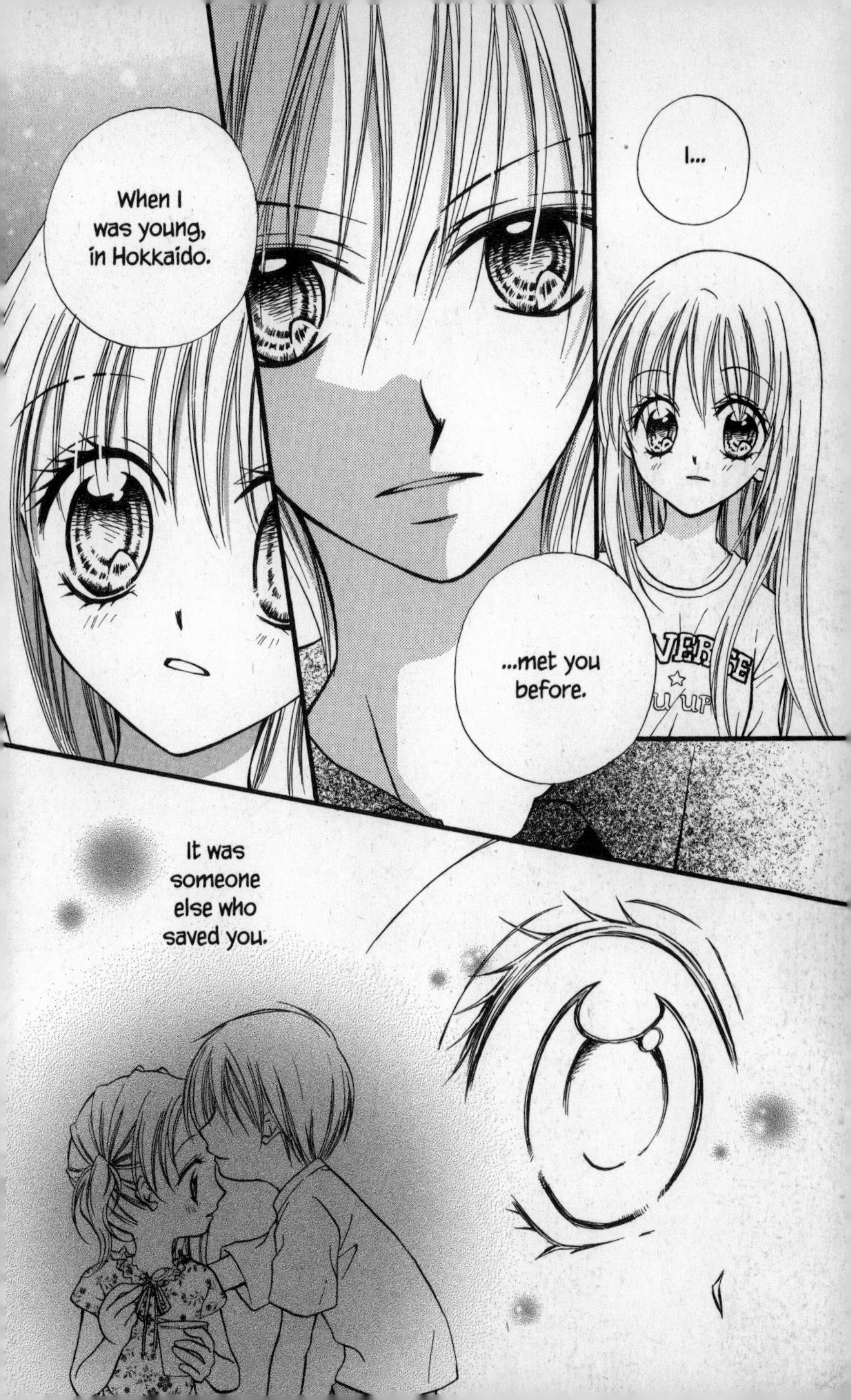
I...
...met you before.
When I was young, in Hokkaido.
It was someone else who saved you.

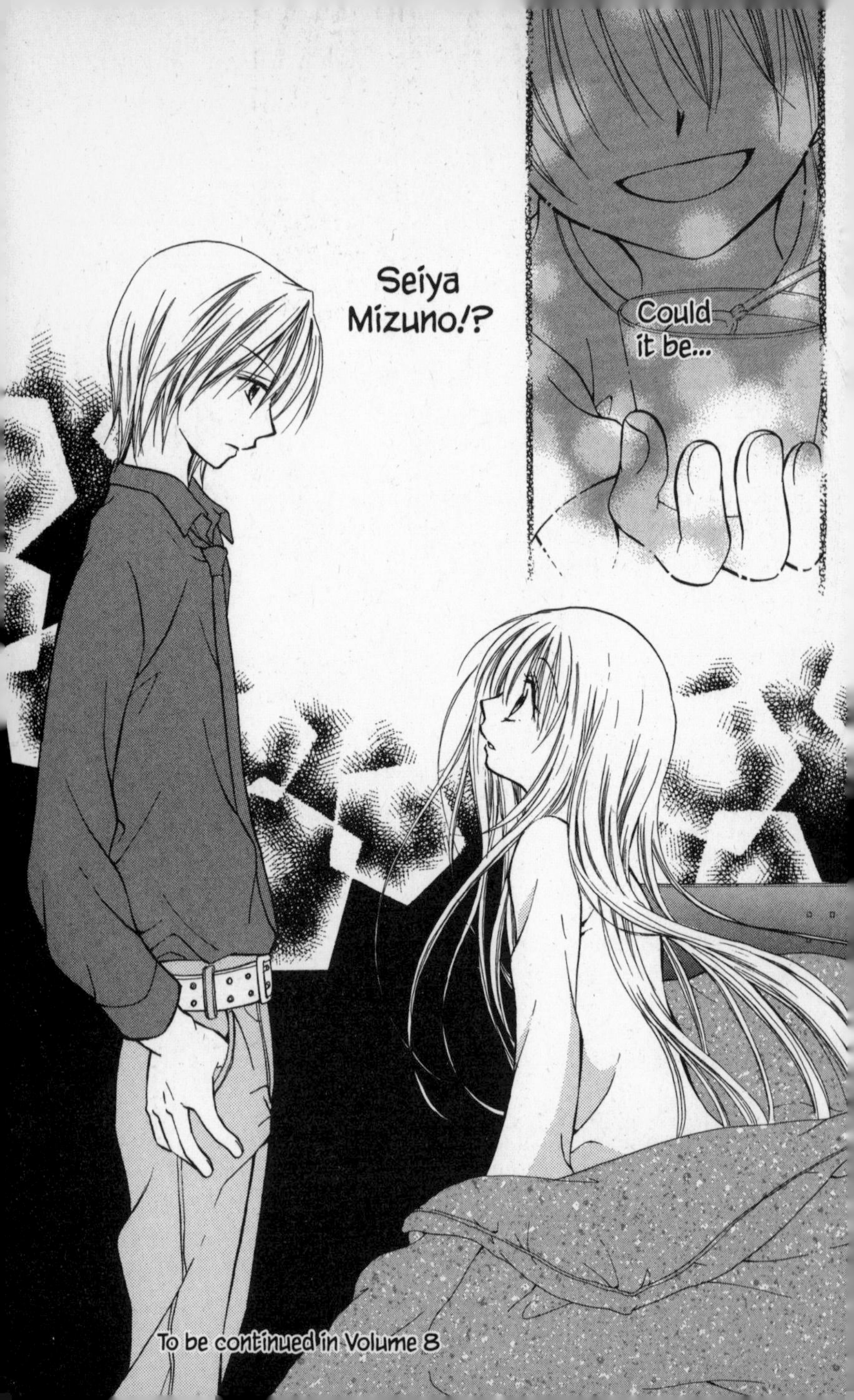
Could it be...
Seiya Mizuno!?
To be continued in Volume 8

Thank you very much!!

Sorry I didn't say hello till the end...
It's Volume 7! We have a new character, too!!
The story will continue (as will the love story), so I hope you enjoy it. I'm looking forward to drawing it as well.
But cooking is so hard to get good at...
I don't know how to measure seasonings to get a particular taste. ♠ I'm still just a beginner. ♠
I'm good with colors...I know what to mix to get a certain color, but how come I can't apply that to cooking?
I'll work hard so that I'll be better by the time the next volume comes out!!
I hope to see you in Volume 8. ♡

Natsumi Ando
Del Rey Manga
1745 Broadway
New York, NY 10019

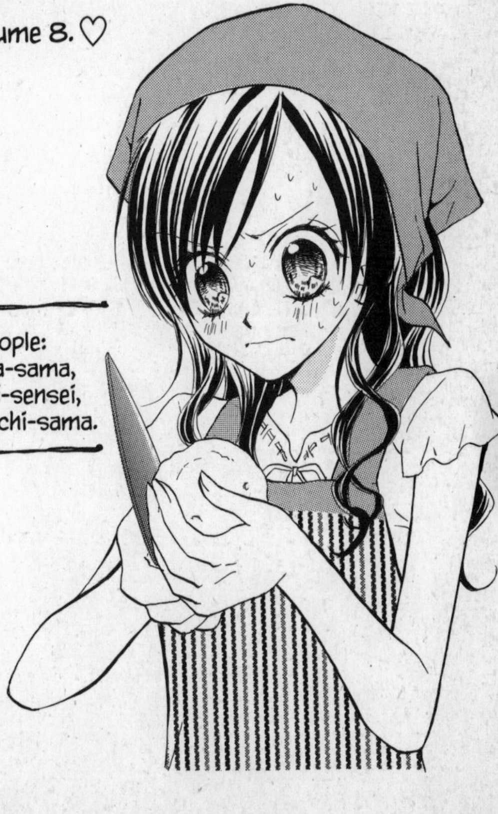

Thank you to these people:
Yamada-sama, Shirasawa-sama,
Shobayashi-sama, Miyuki-sensei,
Kishimoto-sama, and Miyachi-sama.

Akane is definitely bad at cooking.

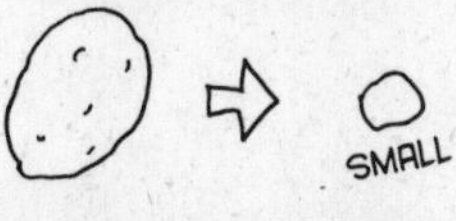
SMALL

When I peel potatoes, I run out of potato.

Kitchen Princess

From the Writer

Hello! I am the writer and the person in charge of the recipes, Miyuki Kobayashi.

Seiya Mizuno-kun, who looks exactly like Sora, appears in this volume. Yes, he is Najika's replacement.

Ando-sensei draws his selfishness so well. I always look forward to the storyboards when they come back from her.

Najika had lost her sense of taste, and Sora died, and it was a little gloomy until now, but Najika finally regains her cheerfulness in Volume 7. Yes, she makes sweets, she eats a lot, and is full of energy!

That is why writing this volume was really fun for me. (I felt sorry for Akane, but she should be fine.)

The madeleines that Najika and Seiya made are really easy to make. You don't need special ingredients. They're cute, and perfect for beginners who want to start cooking, so please try out the recipe. Looking for delicious bakeries is fun too, but making your own sweets is even more fun!

Finally, I would like to thank Natsumi Ando-sensei, my editor Kenji Kishimoto-san, and our editor in chief Matsumoto-san.

I'll see you in Volume 8!

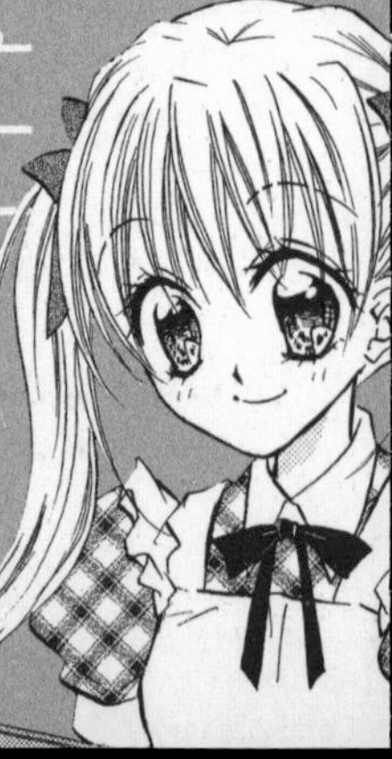

Kitchen Palace

Did you enjoy *Kitchen Princess*?
In this section, we'll give you the recipes
for the food that Najika made in the story.
Please try making them. ♥

Translation Notes

Japanese is a tricky language for most Westerners, and translation is often more art than science. For your edification and reading pleasure, here are notes on some of the places where we could have gone in a different direction in our translation of the work, or where a Japanese cultural reference is used.

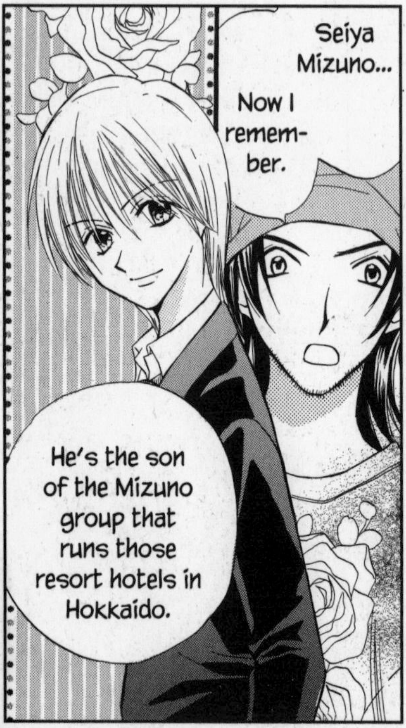
Seiya Mizuno...
Now I remem-ber.
He's the son of the Mizuno group that runs those resort hotels in Hokkaido.

Hokkaido, page 11

Hokkaido is located in the northern part of Japan. It is the second largest island and the biggest prefecture.

Screen tone, page 39

A *screen tone* is a patterned sticker sheet that manga artists use to decorate their art. There are hundreds of patterns with new ones coming out every so often.

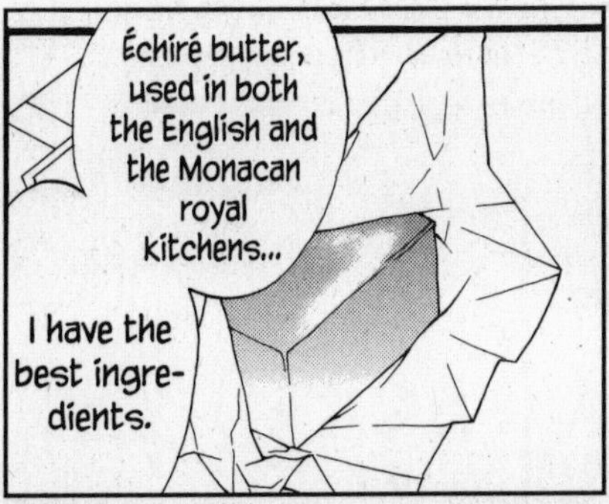
Échiré butter, used in both the English and the Monacan royal kitchens...
I have the best ingre-dients.

Échiré butter, page 50

Échiré butter is made in Échiré, a small village in western France. The village has gained an international reputation for its fine butters. The locals have reared cows since the village's beginning and the milk from these cows produces butter that is said to have a subtle and exquisite taste quite unlike anything else.

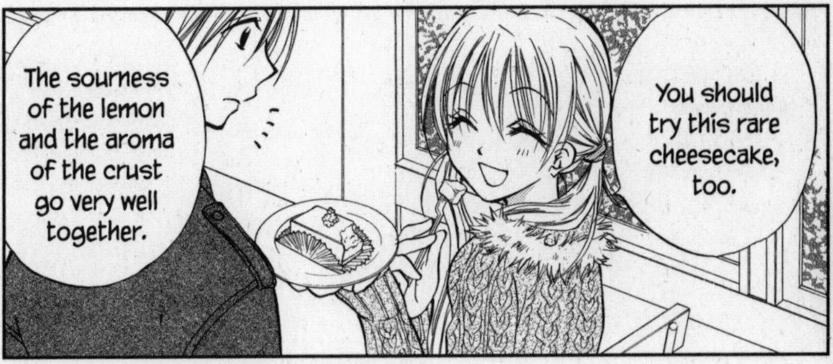
You should try this rare cheesecake, too.
The sourness of the lemon and the aroma of the crust go very well together.

Rare cheesecake, page 153

In Japan, cheesecakes that are not baked are called *rare cheesecakes*. These types of cheesecakes are gelatin based and do not require an oven. They are often served topped with fresh fruit or fruit sauces.

Preview of Volume 8

We are pleased to present you a preview from volume 8 of *Kitchen Princess*. Please check our website (www.delreymanga.com) to see when this volume will be available in English. For now you'll have to make do with Japanese!

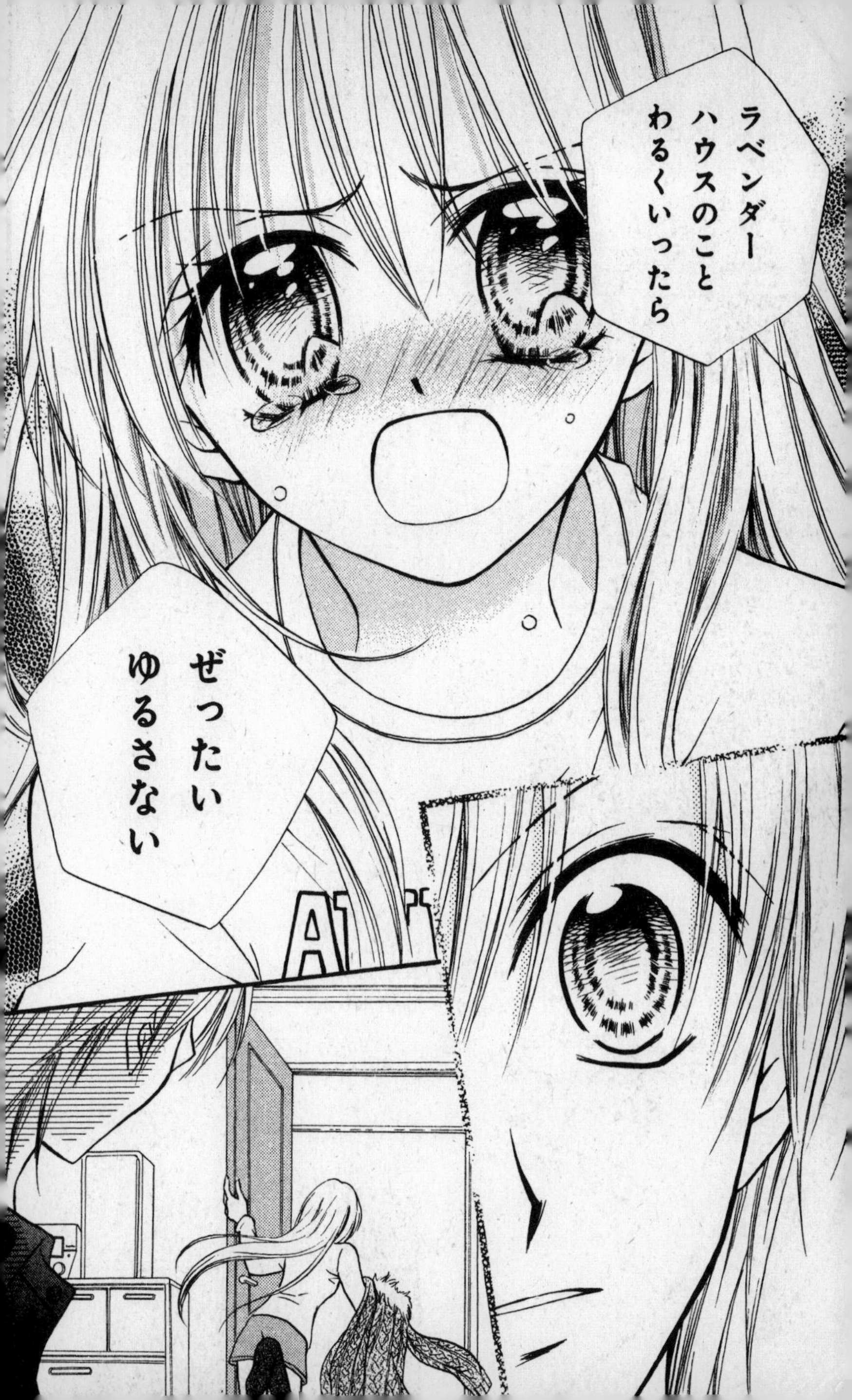
ラベンダーハウスのことわるくいったら
ぜったいゆるさない

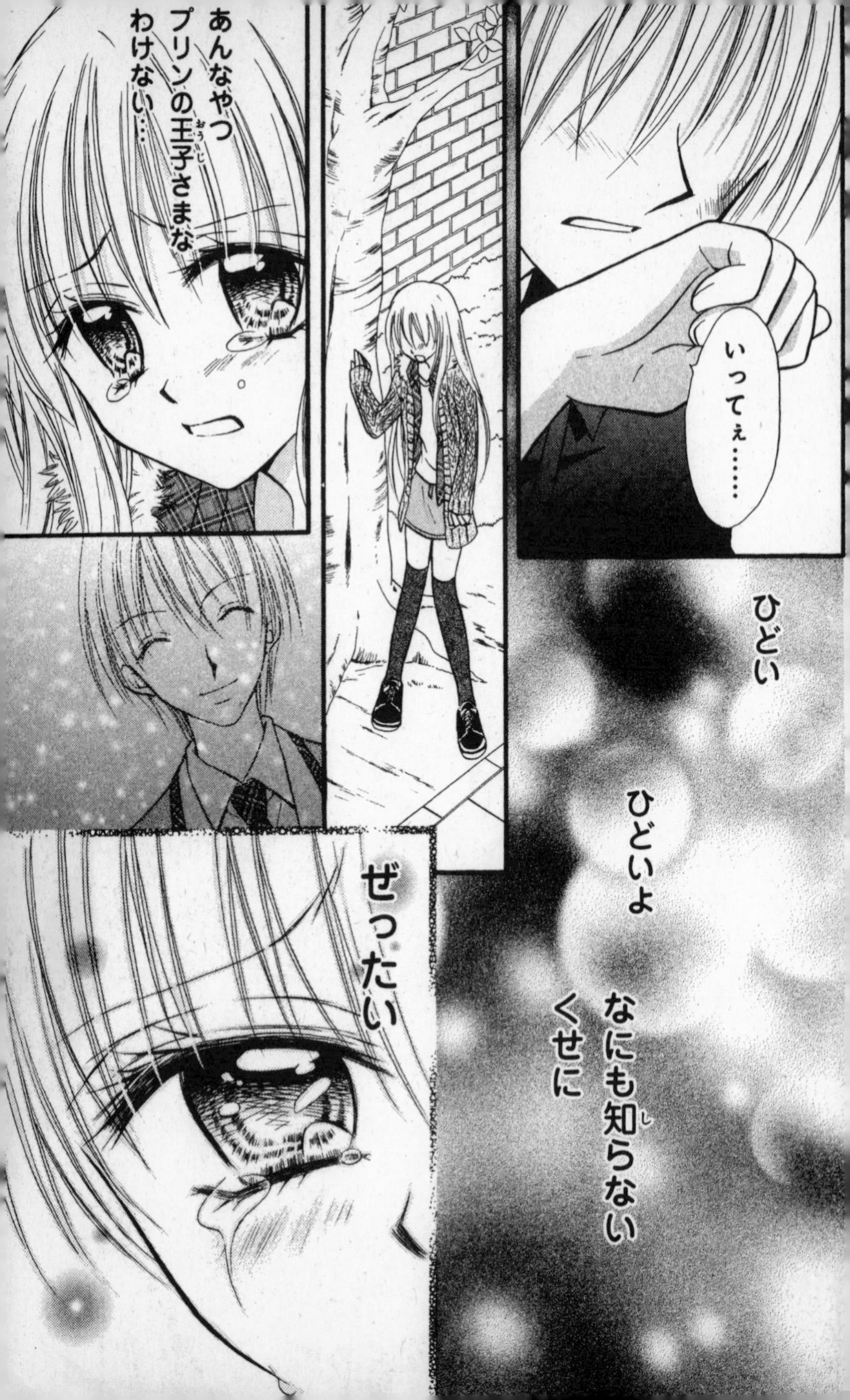
いってぇ……
あんなやつ プリンの王子さまな わけない……
ひどい
ひどいよ
なにも知らない くせに
ぜったい

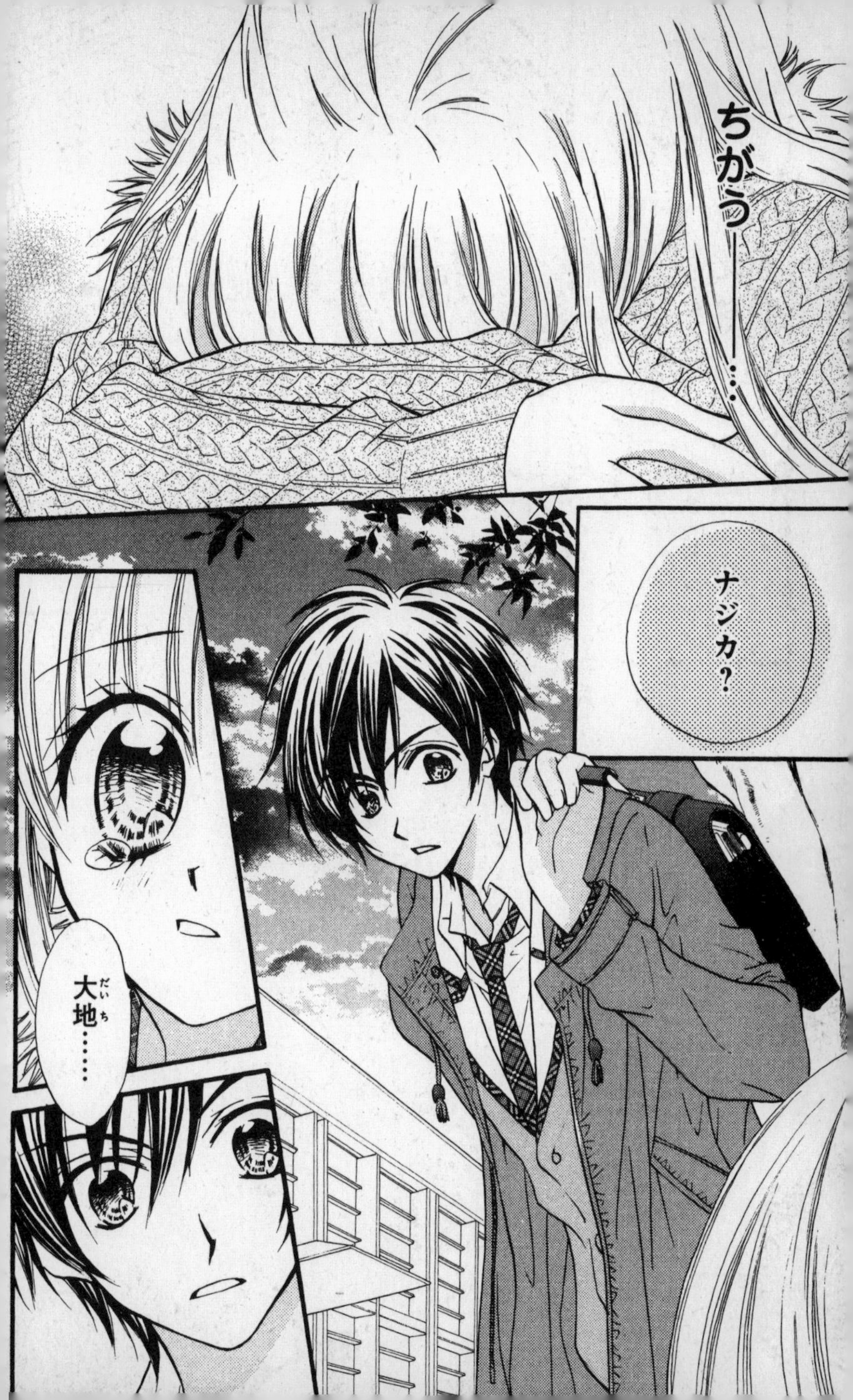
ちがう――……
ナジカ？
大地(だいち)……

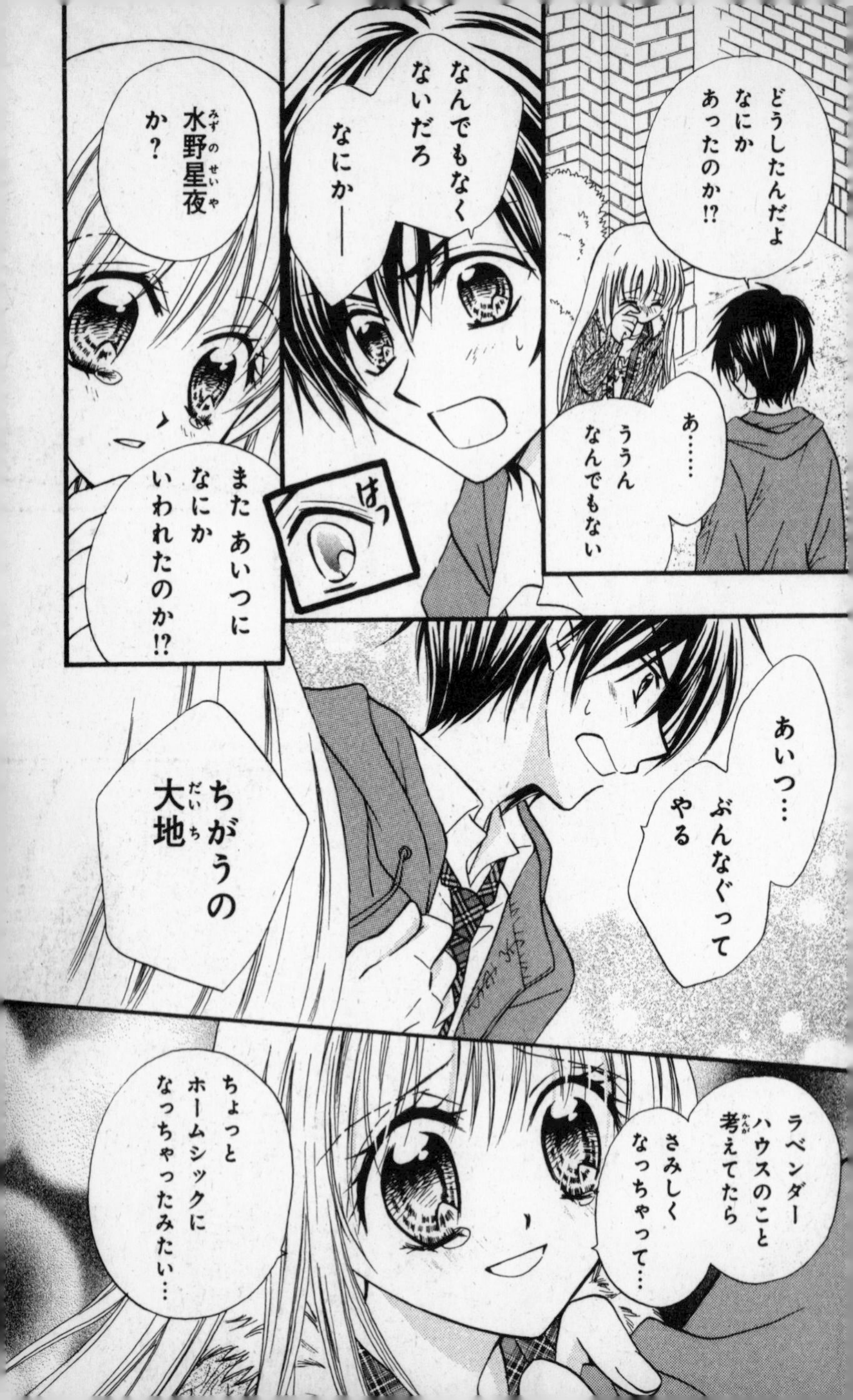

どうしたんだよ なにか あったのか!?
あ…… ううん なんでもない
なんでもなく ないだろ なにか——
はっ
水野星夜か？
また あいつに なにか いわれたのか!?
あいつ… ぶんなぐって やる
ちがうの 大地
ラベンダーハウスのこと 考えてたら さみしく なっちゃって…
ちょっと ホームシックに なっちゃったみたい…

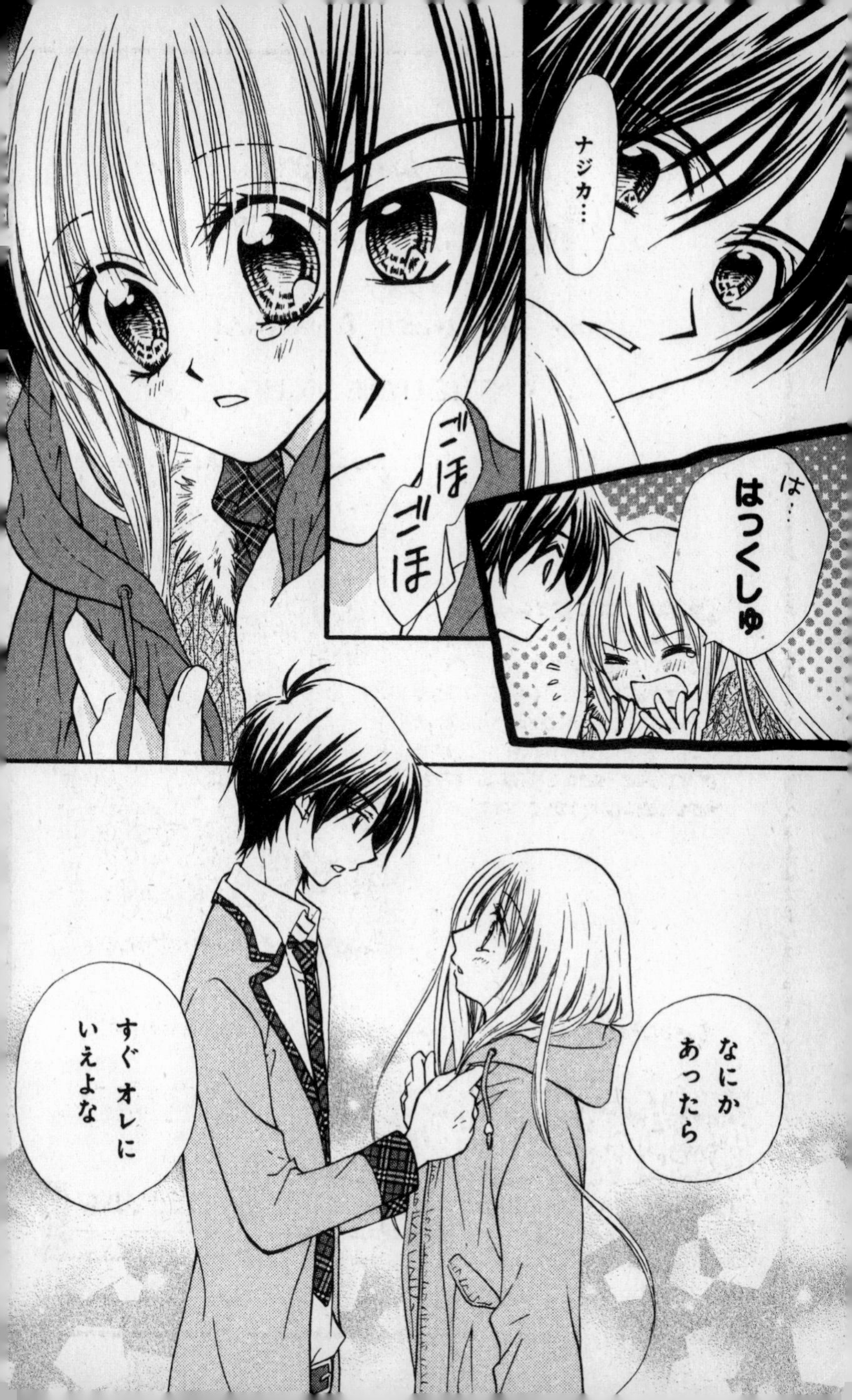
ナジカ…
ごほ ごほ
は…
はっくしゅ
なにかあったら
すぐオレにいえよな

BY MACHIKO SAKURAI

A LITTLE LIVING DOLL!

What would you do if your favorite toy came to life and became your best friend? Well, that's just what happens to Ame Oikawa, a shy schoolgirl. Nicori is a super-cute doll with a mind of its own—and a plan to make Ame's dreams come true!

Special extras in each volume! Read them all!

Kamichama Karin Chu

BY KOGE-DONBO

A GODDESS IN LOVE!

Karin is your lovable girl next door—if the girl next door also happens to be a goddess! Karin has a magic ring that gives her the power to do anything she'd like. Though what she'd like most is to live happily ever after with Kazune, the boy of her dreams. Magic brought Kazune to her, but it also has a way of complicating things. It's not easy to be a goddess and a girl in love!

- Sequel series to the fan-favorite *Kamichama Karin*

Kamichama
Karin Chu 1
Koge-Donbo

Special extras in each volume! Read them all!

VISIT WWW.DELREYMANGA.COM TO:
- Read sample pages
- View release date calendars for upcoming volumes
- Sign up for Del Rey's free manga e-newsletter
- Find out the latest about new Del Rey Manga series

RATING T AGES 13+

DEL REY MANGA デルレイ

The Otaku's Choice™

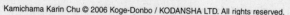

TOMARE!

[STOP!]

You're going the wrong way!

Manga is a completely different type of reading experience.

To start at the *beginning*, go to the *end*!

That's right! Authentic manga is read the traditional Japanese way—from right to left. Exactly the *opposite* of how American books are read. It's easy to follow: Just go to the other end of the book, and read each page—and each panel—from right side to left side, starting at the top right. Now you're experiencing manga as it was meant to be!